BEN-GURION
AND THE HOLOCAUST

BEN-GURION
AND THE HOLOCAUST

SHABTAI TEVETH

Harcourt Brace & Company

NEW YORK SAN DIEGO LONDON

Requests for permission to make copies
of any part of the work should be mailed to:
Permissions Department, Harcourt Brace & Company,
6277 Sea Harbor Drive, Orlando, Florida 32887-6777.

Library of Congress Cataloging-in-Publication Data
Teveth, Shabtai, 1925–
Ben-Gurion and the Holocaust/Shabtai Teveth.
p.   cm.
Includes bibliographical references and index.
ISBN 0-15-100237-1
1. Ben-Gurion, David, 1886–1973—Views on the Holocaust.
2. Holocaust, Jewish (1939–1945). 3. World War, 1939–1945—Jews—
Rescue. 4. Zionism—Palestine—History. I. Title.
DS125.3.B37T46   1996
940.53'18—dc20   96-5779

Designed by Trina Stahl
Printed in the United States of America
First edition
A B C D E

CONTENTS

GLOSSARY

Ahdut HaAvodah: Hebrew for United Labor, a party founded by Ben-Gurion and others in 1920, from which Mapai sprang in 1930. Revived as opposition party to Ben-Gurion in 1944.

AJDC: American Joint Jewish Distribution Committee (known also as the JDC and the Joint), founded in 1914 as the Joint Distribution Committee of American Funds for the relief of Jewish war sufferers, and developed into the largest nonpolitical international Jewish philanthropic organization strictly operating within the framework of U.S. laws.

Balfour Declaration: Statement by British foreign secretary Lord Balfour contained in a letter written and sent on Nov. 2, 1917, to Lord Rothschild, president of the English Zionist Federation, which read:

> I have much pleasure in conveying to you, on behalf of His Majesty's Government, the following declaration of sympathy with Jewish Zionist aspirations which has been submitted to, and approved by, the Cabinet:
> His Majesty's Government view with favour the establishment in Palestine of a national home for the Jewish People, and will use their best endeavours to facilitate the achievement of this object, it being clearly understood that nothing shall be done which may prejudice the civil and religious rights of existing non-Jewish communities in Palestine, or the rights and political status enjoyed by Jews in any other country.

British mandate in Palestine: In the wake of World War I, the League of Nations designated Palestine to be administered under a mandate that incorporated the Balfour Declaration. Pursuant to Article 22 of its Covenant, the League, on July 24, 1922, conferred this mandate on the British government. For twenty-six years (1922–48) Palestine was governed by the British mandatory regime. The mandate expired with the establishment of Israel on May 14, 1948, in line with UN General Assembly Resolution 181 [II] of Nov. 29, 1947, which called for the partition of Palestine into separate Jewish and Arab states.

Certificate: An official permit to enter Palestine issued by the mandatory government entitling a Jewish immigrant to claim Palestinian citizenship.

HaShomer HaTzair (The Young Guardian): An important Marxist Zionist kibbutz movement in strong opposition to Mapai.

High commissioner for Palestine: Article 1 of the mandate conferred on the British government "full powers of legislation and of administration" in Palestine. This charge was placed in the hands of the Colonial Office in London, which appointed a British high commissioner as nominal and executive head of the Palestine administration. The high commissioner's actions were governed by the orders-in-council issued by the Privy Council in London.

Histadrut (HaHistadrut HaKlalit shel HaOvdim HaIvrim BeEretz Israel): Hebrew for General Federation of [Trade Unions and] Jewish Labor in Palestine, an organization founded in December 1920 (after 1948 it became the General Federation of [Trade Unions and] Labor in Israel). The main and the strongest political, social, and economic entity in the Yishuv. Its daily organ, *Davar,* was, for all practical purposes, Mapai's and the JAE's official organ as well.

Illegal immigration: Jewish immigrants without proper certificates and Jewish tourists who unlawfully stayed on in Palestine were termed "illegals." If discovered, they were either deported or their number was deducted from the official "schedule."

Jewish Agency (JA): Articles IV and VI of the Palestine mandate called on the world's Jews to set up a Jewish Agency for Palestine that would cooperate with the (British) mandatory government "in the development of the country . . . to facilitate Jewish immigration and encourage close settlement by Jews on the land." Up to 1929, the World Zionist Organization and its Zionist Executive served in lieu of a Jewish Agency and a Jewish Agency Executive respectively. In 1929 the Jewish Agency and its governing body, the Jewish Agency Executive (JAE), were formed as supreme representation in Palestine of the entire Jewish people. The JAE was elected biannually by the Jewish Agency Council, which was composed of Zionists and non-Zionists. The Zionist half of the Council and the JAE was invariably made up of members of the Zionist Actions Committee and the Zionist Executive. There not being a worldwide all-Jewish organization, the non-Zionist half was composed of notables nominated and confirmed by the biannual Jewish Agency Council.

Jewish Agency Executive (JAE): Originally it was divided between Jerusalem—seat of its headquarters and administration, under the chairmanship of David Ben-Gurion—and London, seat of the branch under Chaim Weizmann, president of the World Zionist Organization. In 1943 a smaller branch began operation in New York under Nahum Goldmann.

Jewish immigration to mandatory Palestine: Initially the scope of Jewish immigration to Palestine was governed solely by an economic measure of "absorptive capacity." Based on its estimates of labor shortages, the JAE would submit semiannual demands for new Jewish hands—which would generally be met by the mandatory government's "schedules," i.e., semiannual quotas of certificates. Thus at the end of 1936 the Yishuv numbered 404,000 souls. To appease Arab opposition, manifested by the Arab Rebellion of 1936, the mandatory government introduced the "political" principle as the sole gauge for its "schedules," sharply curtailing Jewish immigration. This policy was exacerbated by the White Paper of May 1939, which restricted Jewish immigration to a mere 75,000 in the five-year period ending in April 1944. In these years—the Holocaust years—the Yishuv grew from

474,600 at the end of 1939 to 565,500 at the end of 1944, a growth of 90,900 including natural growth.

Mapai (Mifleget Poale Eretz Israel): Palestine Labor Party, founded in 1930 by the merger of Ahdut HaAvodah and HaPoel HaTzair (The Young Worker). It was by far the Histadrut's, as well as the Yishuv's, strongest party, known also as the ruling party.

Mossad LeAliya Bet: Hebrew for B [illegal] immigration, the JAE's undercover agency for promoting Jewish illegal immigration to mandatory Palestine. It was the foundation for Israel's Mossad.

National Assembly (Assefat HaNivharim): The mandate allowed the religious communities in Palestine to look after their own religious and cultural affairs. For these purposes the Yishuv elected every four years a National Assembly as its house of representatives.

National Council (Vaad Leumi): The Yishuv's ruling body, strictly in matters religious and cultural, elected by the National Assembly every four years.

Revisionist Party: Zionist rightist, anti-Histadrut party founded in 1925 by Ze'ev Jabotinsky, and in radical opposition to "compromising" official Zionist policy, as embodied by Weizmann and Ben-Gurion. In 1935 it seceded from the World Zionist Organization to found its own New World Zionist Organization.

War of Independence: Israel's term for the war in Palestine, first between Palestinian Jews and Palestinian Arabs (December 1947–May 14, 1948), and then between Israel and five Arab states (May 15, 1948–July 1949).

War Refugee Board (WRB): Board consisting of the Secretary of State, the Secretary of the Treasury, and the Secretary of War, set up on January 22, 1944 by President Franklin D. Roosevelt's Executive Order to take action for the immediate rescue of "as many as possible" civilian victims of Nazi and enemy savagery.

White Paper of May 1939: A statement of the British government's policy in Palestine, published on May 17, 1939, as Command Paper

6019. It can be seen as the last in a long chain of measures by which Britain withdrew from its commitment to establish in Palestine a national home for the Jewish people, and by which it whittled down the Balfour Declaration and the terms of the League of Nations mandate. The 1939 White Paper committed the British government to "the establishment within ten years of an Independent Palestine State." To ensure the Arab character of this state, Britain put an end to Jewish immigration to Palestine, allowing only 75,000 Jews to be admitted into Palestine during the five-year period commencing with 1939 and ending in April 1944, after which "no further immigration would be permitted unless the Arabs of Palestine are prepared to acquiesce in it."

World Zionist Organization: Worldwide confederation, founded in 1897, of national and regional Zionist parties and organizations, with the aim of promoting and abetting the return of the Jewish people to Eretz Israel (Palestine). The General Zionists led the World Zionist Organization until 1933. In the elections of that year the Labor party under Ben-Gurion turned the scales and assumed leadership.

Yishuv: Hebrew for either settlement or community, applied to the Jewish community in Palestine between 1882 and 1948, the majority of which was of Zionist persuasion.

Zionism: A multifaceted term formed on Zion as a biblical synonym for Eretz Israel (Land of Israel) and used to describe or denote (a) the love and the longing the Jewish people felt toward Eretz Israel throughout the ages; (b) the philosophy and doctrine that hold that the one and only viable solution of the "Jewish Question"—a wide blanket covering anti-Semitism, that is persecution of, discrimination against, or prejudice and hostility toward Jews—is their resettlement in a Jewish state in Palestine; (c) the worldwide political movement founded in 1897 by Dr. Theodor Herzl and whose first constituent congress of that year, in Basel, Switzerland, adopted the so-called Basel Program, whose professed aim was "to create a publicly secured, legally assured home for the Jewish people in Palestine."

Zionist Actions Committee: The Zionist parliament between the bi-annual World Zionist Congresses. During the war years, 1940–45, it was supplanted by a Smaller Actions Committee—mostly members of the Actions Committee resident in Palestine.

Zionist Executive: Ruling body of the World Zionist Organization elected by the biannual World Zionist Congress. Between congresses it reported and answered to the Zionist Actions Committee.

CHRONOLOGY

1925–26: Hitler publishes *Mein Kampf* (vol. 1 in July 1925, vol. 2 in May 1926)

Jan. 30, 1933: Hitler becomes chancellor of Germany. A cheap edition of *Mein Kampf* sells over 1 million copies in 1933.

Aug. 29, 1933: Ben-Gurion buys *Mein Kampf* at Munich's railway terminal, arguably the only Zionist leader to have done so. The book turns his somber premonition regarding the fate of Europe's Jews into bleak certainty.

Oct. 4, 1933: Ben-Gurion is elected to the JAE as head of its political department.

Jan. 13, 1934: At a Histadrut conference Ben-Gurion predicts: "Hitler's rule places the entire Jewish people in danger. Hitlerism is at war not only with the Jews of Germany but with Jews the world over. Hitler's rule cannot last for long without war, without a war of vengeance against France, Poland, Czechoslovakia and other neighboring countries . . . or against vast Soviet Russia . . . perhaps only four or five years (if not less) stand between us and that day of wrath."

Sept. 15, 1935: At a Nuremberg Nazi rally, some 250 anti-Jewish laws are made public, all aimed at degrading, isolating, and dispossessing Germany's Jews.

Nov. 11, 1935: Ben-Gurion is elected chairman of JAE.

Mar. 13, 1938: Nazi Germany invades Austria and later incorporates it in the German reich. Masses of Jewish refugees seek shelter.

July 8–15, 1938: The Evian Conference, an international conference called by President Franklin D. Roosevelt to solve the refugee (more accurately, the Jewish refugee) problem created by Hitler. The conference is utterly ineffectual: not a country in the world will open its gates to Jewish refugees, and Palestine's gates are being gradually shut.

Nov. 9, 1938: Kristallnacht (Night of Glass) pogrom. Ninety-one Jews are murdered in Nazi riots all over Germany, 267 synagogues are desecrated or burned, 815 Jewish shops and 29 department stores are broken into and robbed, 20,000 (some say 30,000) Jews are incarcerated in concentration camps, and an expulsion of all Jewish children and youths from schools comes into effect. The refugee problem aggravates.

Mar. 15, 1939: Hitler invades and occupies Czechoslovakia. More refugees seek shelter.

May 17, 1939: British government publishes a White Paper that closes Palestine's gates in the face of Jewish refugees.

Sept. 1, 1939: Hitler declares war on and invades Poland, provoking World War II. Masses of Jewish refugees try in vain to flee Nazi-occupied Europe.

June 10, 1940: Italy joins the war against the Allies.

June 8, 1941: Nazi threat to Palestine from the north is removed by Allied invasion of Syria and Lebanon, held hitherto by forces loyal to Vichy France.

June 22, 1941: Hitler invades Russia. Four *Einsatzgrüppen*—SS Special Action Groups—follow the German armies with orders to exterminate all Jews. Up to the beginning of the German withdrawal in the spring of 1943, 1.25 million Jews were murdered, besides hundreds of thousands of Soviet citizens and war prisoners.

October 1941: Auschwitz-Birkenau's capacity is greatly extended by Himmler's direct orders in preparation for mass killing, four months before the SS Wannsee Conference formalizes the Final Solution (systematic and industrial extermination of all Jews).

Dec. 8, 1941: The first methodical gassing of Jews in mobile gas chambers begins at Chelmno, the first extermination camp in history, set up in the woods forty miles northwest of Lodz, Poland.

Dec. 12, 1941: The United States joins the war against Germany and Italy.

March 1942: Transports of Jews from all over Europe begin to arrive at Auschwitz-Birkenau, 6–7,000 at a time, occasionally more than once a day. The new stationary gas chambers can accommodate 2,000 humans (as against 200 at Treblinka). A cautious estimate puts the number of human beings killed in Auschwitz-Birkenau at 1.5 million, mostly European Jews.

May 12, 1942: At the Biltmore Hotel in New York City, an all-Zionist conference accepts the Biltmore Program, which calls for free Jewish immigration to Palestine and the establishment there of a Jewish state. Shortly after, it would become the official Zionist line under the name of the Jerusalem program.

June 30, 1942: Nazi threat to Palestine from the south increases as Rommel's Afrika Korps defeats the British in the western desert and reaches El Alamein on Egypt's border.

July 21, 1942: High-water mark of Jewish American protest: mass meetings of protest and sorrow at the fate of the Jews in Europe are held in major American cities, the largest in Madison Square Garden, New York.

Aug. 8, 1942: Dr. Gerhardt Riegner, the World Jewish Congress representative in Geneva, cables Rabbi Stephen Wise in New York, using State Department facilities, communicating information received from German industrialist Eduard Schulte about the discussion of the Final Solution at the Wannsee Conference: Nazis prepare plans by which "three and a half to four millions [Jews] should after deportation and concentration in east be at one blow exterminated in order resolve once and for all Jewish question in Europe." A similar cable is sent to the Jerusalem JAE by Dr. Richard Lichtheim, its representative at Geneva. Both cables are met with suspicion and disbelief. The State Department delays delivery of the cable until Aug. 28. The JAE asks Lichtheim to verify the cable's information.

Sept. 3, 1942: First experiment with zyklon-B pellets is held successfully in Auschwitz, after which I. A. Topf & Sons, oven-builders of Erfurt, are contracted to construct and install large stationary gas chambers and corresponding crematoria furnaces for mass gassing.

Nov. 2, 1942: End of Nazi threat to Palestine as Montgomery's Eighth Army deals Rommel a crushing defeat at El Alamein.

Nov. 4, 1942: Polish government in exile minister of state resident in the Middle East, Professor Stanislaw Kot, arrives in Palestine and tells Yishuv leaders that "biological destruction of the Jews is taking place in Poland."

Nov. 18/19, 1942: Arrival in Palestine of sixty-nine Palestinian Jews from Europe, who provide the Yishuv leadership with first eyewitness reports of German atrocities.

Nov. 22, 1942: JAE publishes in Jerusalem an official announcement that systematic destruction of European Jewry is being carried out by the Germans. A similar announcement is made on Nov. 23 in the United States by Rabbi Stephen Wise, president of the World Jewish Congress.

Nov. 30, 1942: An emergency session of the National Assembly calls for a day of fasting, a general strike, and thirty days of mourning in reaction to the news of the destruction of European Jewry. In his keynote speech, Ben-Gurion appeals to the free world to prevent Europe becoming "one large Jewish cemetery."

Mar. 1, 1943: A second round of mass meetings is held in New York and other major American cities under the slogan "Stop Hitler Now."

Apr. 19–29, 1943: The Bermuda Conference, a U.S.–British attempt to solve the European (mostly Jewish) refugee problem. Like the Evian Conference, it produces no tangible results.

Mar. 19, 1944: The Germans invade and occupy Hungary.

Apr. 24, 1944: In Budapest, Eichmann charges Joel Brand with a mission to offer the SS Goods for Blood Plan to world Jewry—i.e., the exchange of 1 million Jews for 10,000 heavy-duty trucks and other goods.

Apr. 25, 1944: Alfred Wetzler and Rudolf Vrba submit their Auschwitz report, known as the Vrba-Wetzler Report, the first authoritative account on Auschwitz-Birkenau to reach the free world.

May 15, 1944: Joel Brand leaves Budapest for Vienna to meet JAE leaders on Goods for Blood Plan either in Istanbul or Jerusalem. On the same day Brand leaves Vienna, Eichmann begins the mass shipment of Hungary's Jews—12,000 a day—to Auschwitz's gas chambers.

May 22, 1944: Rabbi Michael Dov-Ber Weissmandel first proposes the bombing of Auschwitz-Birkenau.

June 2, 1944: Operation Frantic—a four-month-long shuttle-bombing system whereby U.S. bombers flying from either Britain or Italy could use the Soviet air base at Poltava, Ukraine, to extend their range—begins with the bombing of Hungarian marshaling yards at Debrecen. Bombing of the railroads from Hungary to Auschwitz is therefore possible.

June 7, 1944: Brand arrested by the British in Aleppo, Syria, en route to Jerusalem to meet Sharett.

June 8, 1944: Since this date Auschwitz-Birkenau is within range of Allied bombers based in Foggia, southern Italy, and in Great Britain.

June 26, 1944: The JAE endorses Weissmandel's proposal. Its offices in Jerusalem, London, and Geneva are instructed to seek the bombing of the death camps. The first demand is made by Dr. Richard Lichtheim, the JAE representative in Geneva, in a cable of June 26, 1944, to Douglas MacKillop at the British legation in Bern.

June 30, 1944: In London, Weizmann and Sharett present the JAE demand for bombing Auschwitz-Birkenau to U.S. Undersecretary of State for Foreign Affairs George Hall.

July 4, 1944: The War Department in Washington writes to the executive director of the War Refugee Board that the proposal to bomb "certain sections of railway lines between Hungary and Poland . . . to interrupt the transportation of Jews from Hungary" is "impracticable."

July 6, 1944: Eden receives Weizmann and Sharett and hears JAE's request to bomb Auschwitz-Birkenau.

July 8, 1944: The Farben plant at Monowitz is photographed from the air by the Allies for the fifth time. On April 4, a U.S. aerial reconnaissance plane had taken twenty exposures of Monowitz, on three of which Auschwitz itself appeared for the first time.

July 18, 1944: The Monowitz plant is designated for the first time as a bombing target.

August 6, 1944: U.S. Air Force heavy bombers, flying from England, strike targets in Poland, then land in the Ukraine. On Aug. 7 they attacked oil refineries at Trzebinia, thirteen miles from Auschwitz, while other U.S. planes, flying from Italy, raid Blechhammer, forty-seven miles from it.

Aug. 18, 1944: Joseph Linton, the JAE political secretary in London, is told in a letter from the Foreign Office that "technical difficulties" are causing the delay in bombing Auschwitz-Birkenau, and is asked whether the JAE still "wish it [the bombing] pursued."

Aug. 20, 1944: The first bombing of Monowitz: 127 Flying Fortresses of the U.S. Fifteenth Air Force drop a total of 1,336 bombs, causing damage to buildings and installations. Auschwitz inmates watch the raid.

Aug. 25, 1944: American reconnaissance planes take more aerial pictures of Monowitz. Once more the cameras record the industrial plant and nearby Auschwitz-Birkenau.

Aug.–Sept. 1944: 181 Royal Air Force heavy bombers and 110 B-17s and 150 Mustangs of the U.S. 18th Air Force fly over Warsaw and drop arms and supplies in support of the Polish uprising.

Sept. 1, 1944: British Minister of State Richard Law writes to Weizmann "that in view of the very great technical difficulties involved, we have no option but to refrain from pursuing the proposal [to bomb Auschwitz-Birkenau] in present circumstances."

Sept. 13, 1944: U.S. warplanes attack Monowitz again. This time a few bombs drop on Auschwitz-Birkenau by mistake.

Nov. 29, 1944: By Himmler's direct order, the Germans destroy the crematoria at Auschwitz and the industrial extermination there comes to an end.

Jan. 14, 1945: U.S. planes fly twelfth photographic reconnaissance flight over Monowitz. Once more Auschwitz-Birkenau appears in the photos.

Jan. 18, 1945: The SS evacuates Auschwitz's inmates, leaving the sick behind.

Jan. 20, 1945: The SS blows up the already largely dismantled remaining crematoria. On this day Monowitz is bombarded by the Allies for the last time.

Jan. 27, 1945: At three in the afternoon Soviet troops "liberate" Auschwitz-Birkenau.

May 8, 1945: VE-Day, war's end in Europe.

PREFACE

WHILE THE HOLOCAUST was still at its height, it was already being politicized. During and after the war years—and continuing to the present day—the Zionist leadership of the Yishuv (the Jewish community in Palestine) was accused not only of indifference to the fate of the European Jews but of actual responsibility for their deaths through collaboration with the Nazis.

This process of politicization resembles a drama in the style of Akira Kurosawa's film *Rashomon*: a horrific crime is witnessed and recounted by interested parties, each from a different perspective—so that the story is quite different in each version—and always with an ulterior motive and the intention of blaming another. What is more, the process is still going on today, and in fact has given rise to what can be called Jewish revisionism: Jews blaming Jews for not having rescued Europe's Jews from the Holocaust. Moreover, Jews are blaming Jews for helping the Nazis bring about the Holocaust.

Providing the different points of view in this drama of nonrescue is a wide range of critics on both left and right: rabbis, writers, and politicians, Jews and non-Jews. They offer two basic versions of the crime. In the first, the leaders of Zionism—and especially David Ben-Gurion, chairman of the Jewish Agency and the Zionist Executive and a leader of Mapai, the ruling Zionist Labor party—in their supposedly single-minded focus on the creation of a Jewish state in Palestine, were willing to sacrifice the non-Zionist Jews of Europe in furtherance of their goal.

In the second version, not only did these leaders cut deals with the Nazis that enabled selected Zionist Jews to escape to Palestine—leaving the rest to their fate—but they deliberately allowed the Diaspora Jews to go to their deaths in the extermination camps so that remorseful Christians would later be moved to grant a state to those Jews who remained. The critics claim that these acts were motivated by a long-standing disrespect and even contempt toward Diaspora Jews on the part of Ben-Gurion and the other Zionist leaders in Palestine.

Starting in 1968, eminent scholars bolstered the accusations made by political critics with the weight of their supposed academic impartiality, accusing Ben-Gurion of being "ashamed" of the legacy of the Diaspora and therefore failing to make the rescue of European Jewry a top priority. Because of this attitude, the scholars intimated, Ben-Gurion and other Yishuv leaders failed to save as many Jews as they could from occupied Europe, refusing to put money and effort into rescue attempts and devoting their attention instead to planning the future state.

This charge has been propagated most recently by the Israeli writer Tom Segev. In his best-selling book *The Seventh Million*,[1] which was translated into English and German, he lays out the full range of criticisms hurled at Ben-Gurion by left and right alike: Ben-Gurion and his colleagues in the Zionist leadership visited a catastrophe on two peoples—Palestinian Arabs as well as European Jews; Ben-Gurion and Hitler had common interests; Ben-Gurion did nothing to bring Hitler down; Ben-Gurion and his colleagues were "small people," full of contempt for Diaspora Jews and far from equal to the role History had assigned them; they gave preference to establishing a state over rescuing Europe's Jews and believed that to achieve this goal Jewish blood had to be spilled. Like his fellow critics, however, Segev has a certain agenda, which leads him to disregard plain truth.

Not until 1986, with the publication in Hebrew of Dina Porat's *The Blue and Yellow Stars of David*,[2] did defenders of Ben-Gurion and the Yishuv contribute a version of their own to this *Rashomon* story. Their tale casts all the circumstances in a very different light. For the fact is that no evidence—beyond a few sources whose spuriousness is revealed later in this work—supports the charges against Ben-Gurion, and the research that has been done has in fact disproved them. Indeed, my own research unequivocally refutes these charges and demonstrates beyond question that Ben-Gurion's thinking was quite the opposite of what his critics allege: If he could have rescued all the Jews of Europe by sacrificing the state, he would have done it. He would have done it if only for the simple reason that these Jews were needed to overcome the immigration restrictions imposed by the British and to create a state at some future time. Further, without these Jews, who constituted the largest reservoir of immigration and also of Judaic heritage, that state would never be secure, either militarily or culturally.

What is more, a wide range of documentation proves that Ben-Gurion's sense of history enabled him to foresee the imminent destruction (though not the industrial extermination) of the Jews of Europe as early as January 1934, and that the heart of his policy making and planning during the years preceding the war was an effort to promote the mass migration of both Zionist and non-Zionist Jews to Palestine, precisely in order to save them from the Nazi menace. This was his aim even though the influx of so many Jews not committed to Labor Zionism threatened to undermine the new Jewish workers' society that Ben-Gurion's party was committed to establishing.

The story of Ben-Gurion and the Holocaust, therefore, is in actuality a tale of his ceaseless efforts to save Europe's Jews—Zionist and non-Zionist alike. During the 1930s, while there was still time, he tried to bring them out of Europe—mostly to Palestine, since no other country was willing to receive them. Once the war began and he recognized the inability of the puny Yishuv to rescue large numbers of Jews from Europe, he turned his attention to preparing Palestine to receive the survivors and to laying the groundwork for the state, which would ensure that such destruction never happened again.

This work, then, is another pro–Ben-Gurion voice in the politicized debate on Jewish rescue efforts during the Holocaust. Its aim is to examine the charges of collaboration and murderous indifference and to document Ben-Gurion's efforts to rescue the Jewish people.

Ben-Gurion's Status

In looking back at the Holocaust years, it is hard to avoid seeing them through the prism created by the establishment of Israel in 1948 and the ensuing War of Independence. Neither of these events, in turn, can be visualized without Ben-Gurion. This is perhaps why it is so easy to assume that the status of Ben-Gurion, the Zionist movement, and the Yishuv as a whole was the same before 1948 as it was after 1948. In such a distorted view, it seems logical to expect that the powers and resources wielded by Prime Minister Ben-Gurion were also possessed by Jewish Agency Executive chairman Ben-Gurion. Such an assumption indeed underlies a good portion of the accusations. But it was hardly so.

A brief description of political institutions and relations in Palestine between the wars will provide the background against which the poisonous accusations against Ben-Gurion and his colleagues took shape. From 1920 through the war, Palestine was governed by the British under a mandate from the League of Nations. The British mandate over Palestine, which incorporated the 1917 Balfour Declaration's pledge of support in the establishment of a Jewish national home, had accorded the Jewish people a nearly equal part in building up Palestine. Articles IV and VI of the mandate called on them to set up an agency for Palestine—the Jewish Agency (JA)—that would cooperate with the British "in the development of the country. The primary duty imposed upon the [British] Administration of Palestine is to facilitate Jewish immigration and encourage close settlement by Jews on the land."[3]

The Yishuv was governed by two constitutional "institutions," as they were called. The first was the National Assembly, the Yishuv's house of representatives (forerunner of Israel's Knesset), elected every four years by universal suffrage. The National Assembly elected the National Council, the Yishuv's government, so to speak. The second institution was the Jewish Agency for Palestine, the supreme representative of the entire Jewish people. Its governing body was the Jewish Agency Executive (JAE), composed equally (at least in theory) of Zionists and non-Zionists. The JAE was elected every two years by the Jewish Agency Council, which usually convened right after the biannual World Zionist Congress. The Zionist half of the JAE consisted of the members of the Zionist Executive, which was elected by the World Zionist Congress. The non-Zionist half could not be elected since there was no worldwide non-Zionist Jewish organization; it was composed of representatives nominated and confirmed by the biannual Jewish Agency Council.

Serving as the Zionist parliament between congresses was the Zionist Actions Committee. The JAE had to report to it when the congress was not in session, as was the case between 1939 and 1946. Finally, the strongest political, social, and financial organization in the Yishuv was the Histadrut, the Federation of Jewish Workers in Palestine, and its Executive.

This array of organizations yielded a field quite favorable to inter-institutional and personal power struggles, which could easily have driven the Yishuv close to anarchy had not all the institutions submitted to the hegemony of Mapai and its leader, Ben-Gurion. Mapai and its coalition partners constituted the majority in the National Assembly, National Council, Histadrut Executive, Zionist Executive, Zionist Actions Committee, and, finally, the JAE. This is why Mapai was rightly called the Yishuv's ruling party. Its leader was Ben-Gurion. After he became chairman of the JAE in the summer of 1935, the JAE's political supremacy was recognized by a wide majority.

This being said, however, it must be remembered that the British, not Mapai, ruled Palestine. The mandatory government of Palestine was the government of the day—not the JAE, the National Council, or the Histadrut Executive. Moreover, the Yishuv was far smaller than the Jewish communities in the United States, Poland, the Soviet Union, Hungary, and Romania; and the Zionist movement itself comprised less than 10 percent of the Jewish people. The British-Palestine government, therefore, could always say that neither the Yishuv's institutions, the Zionist Executive, nor the JAE spoke for the entire Jewish people.

Although Ben-Gurion's status as leader of Mapai and the Yishuv facilitated his and the JAE's work, he paid a heavy price for it: All criticisms of the Yishuv, of the JAE, the other institutions, and Mapai were automatically aimed at him. Ben-Gurion had to answer for everything, to such an extent that even his critics and enemies, by seeing him as the source of all evil in the Yishuv, unwittingly contributed to his mythification, if not deification.

Ben-Gurion, who had arrived in Palestine from Plonsk, Poland, in 1906 at the age of twenty, was fifty-three in 1939, when the war broke out. A man of contrasts and contradictions, he came perhaps as close as a person can to being a pragmatist and a visionary at the same time. Moved by misery and suffering and capable of great compassion, but keeping this sentiment very private and always expressing it in collective terms, he remained, at least outwardly, utterly impersonal and unmoved. A strong leader who saw his path clearly (though he was capable of sharp about-faces), he was basically, as he said himself, a man of compromise, moving from one compromise to another to achieve his goal. A founder of Labor Zionism, he envisioned the Jewish state as a classless, welfare society. At the same time, he saw the Jewish state not as Zionism's ultimate goal, but as the means— "lever," in his jargon—of achieving that goal, the ingathering of the exiles in the Land of Israel. When all humankind became one family, undivided by nation-states, the Jewish state would expire as well. As a pragmatist, Ben-Gurion proved a politician second to none, never missing an opportunity to fortify his labor party, Mapai, leading it from strength to strength, and making it the ruling party from 1933 on.

Being number one in the Yishuv made Ben-Gurion number two in the World Zionist Organization, after Dr. Chaim Weizmann, who lived in London. The gap between them was, however, a wide one, for Weizmann was regarded as a world Jewish leader by Jews and non-Jews alike, while Ben-Gurion was hardly known to the non-Zionist Jewish masses. Weizmann, who had substantial support in Palestine and within Mapai as well as in the Diaspora, was Ben-Gurion's main rival. For a variety of reasons, Ben-Gurion sought to replace Weizmann as the leader of world Zionism, especially in Great Britain and the United States. Clearly, one reason for this was Ben-Gurion's own ambition to become number one in world Zionism. But equally important was his conviction that establishment of a Jewish state immediately after the war—as spelled out in a plan known as the Biltmore Program, adopted in May 1942—should be Zionism's next step. Weizmann, although coauthor with Ben-Gurion of the Biltmore Program, was not, in Ben-Gurion's opinion, sufficiently determined and vigorous in pursuing this end.

Another factor on the Yishuv political scene was Ben-Gurion's uncompromising Zionist political enemies, the Revisionists, who under the leadership of their founder, Ze'ev Jabotinsky, since 1925 had been calling for a revision of Zionist policy. By nature Ben-Gurion was a gradualist, an incremental Zionist, who subscribed to the concept "add an acre to an acre," or, as the saying was at the time, "add a goat to a goat." But the Revisionists were unwilling to wait for widespread colonization and a Jewish majority; instead, they sought a shortcut to a Jewish state. They had great faith in demonstrations and fiery slogans and very little respect for reality and historical development. Therefore their doctrine was that the only way to achieve the state was through arms—"iron," as Jabotinsky liked to say—both British and Jewish. Their disassociation from mainstream Zionism and its institutions afforded the Revisionists a unique position: they could criticize and offer superior solutions without taking responsibility for actions or being taken to task for failures. In the Holocaust years and afterward, they were able to assume a stance of "we told you so, you never listened" and level some of the most serious and wounding accusations against Ben-Gurion and his JAE.

The British, initially supporters of Zionism, began to experience a change of heart as the years passed. This shift first become noticeable after severe Arab riots in 1929, when Colonial Secretary Lord Passfield made the famous quip that there wasn't room in Palestine to swing a cat by its tail. Translated into the language of a White Paper in October 1930, this new sentiment read: "For the present and with the present methods of Arab cultivation there remains no margin of land available for [Jewish] agricultural settlements by new immigrants."[4] Jews would therefore be stringently restricted in the purchase of land, and without land to settle on, their immigration to Palestine would be sharply curtailed as well. Weizmann's greatest achievement—second only to obtaining the Balfour Declaration—was Prime Minister Ramsay MacDonald's repeal in 1932 of Passfield's White Paper. Palestine could then open its doors, as it did, to immigration from Poland and Germany.

The Arabs, however, put an end to large-scale immigration of Hitler's victims in 1936 by staging a general strike and launching a series of riots, known as the Arab Revolt, that subsided only in 1939 with the promulgation of a new White Paper. The prospect of a general European war had brought a radical shift in the British government's Palestine policy, embodied in this White Paper, which severely restricted both purchase of land by Jews and their immigration to Palestine.

Previously, there had been two ways Jews could immigrate to Palestine. First, anyone who possessed a certain amount of capital (originally 10,000 Palestinian pounds or $50,000, later 1,000 pounds or $5,000) could enter Palestine and settle there. The second way was by obtaining an immigration "certificate." The number of certificates issued each year was subject to what was called "the economic absorptive capacity." If the economy was booming, a larger "schedule" of certificates was announced; if unemployment reigned, the schedule was smaller. This rule of the economic absorptive capacity was very important to the Zionists, because by investment and development they could increase the schedule.

The White Paper of May 1939 abolished this rule and introduced a political factor that replaced the economic one. No matter how much the economy might be growing, or how large the demand for workers, the White Paper allowed a quota of only 75,000 new Jewish immigrants over the five-year period ending in May 1944. In other words, during the years of the Holocaust, Palestine was permitted to take in only 75,000 refugees—and in practice, as it turned out, many fewer.

Many Jews entered Palestine on tourist visas and remained in the country after their visas expired. Others entered on entry permits from Lebanon or Syria and also stayed to settle. These, plus the Jews who arrived in Palestine's ports without any papers at all, were termed illegal immigrants, or "illegals." The variety of immigrant categories allowed some elasticity in the application of the immigration regulations. However, once the May 1939 White Paper came into force, all illegals were deducted from the overall five-year quota of 75,000 certificates. Many refugees who were already in Palestine thus received certificates. But these became fewer and fewer as the mandatory government, on orders from London, turned away refugees who made it to Palestine's shores, expelling them to a variety of British possessions such as Ceylon, the island of Mauritius, and finally Cyprus, with the intention of shipping them back to their countries of origin after the war. Because of all these deductions, there remained in effect only 29,000 certificates available for the years 1942–44, when the gas chambers and crematoria were working at their highest capacity. Another vital factor was time. It took a very long time to obtain the certificates, and more than once those who were entitled to them died or were murdered before receiving them.

The British issued the White Paper with the intention of gaining the Arab world's friendship in the coming war. They never fully achieved this goal, but so ardent were they in the pursuit of their anti-Jewish policy that—as the following chapters will demonstrate—they became completely insensitive to the Jewish tragedy unfolding in Europe.

It was against these obstacles that Ben-Gurion struggled to rescue the European Jews, and his lack of success had nothing to do with Zionist ideology, his attitude toward Diaspora Jews, or his obsession with a Jewish state. At one point his own expectation of a general European war, together with the shift in British policy, played out against the background of Jewish misery in Europe, even drove him to entertain plans for armed revolt against the British. But Ben-Gurion could contemplate such an act only for a very clear and concrete cause. Such was his plan for an "immigration revolt" against the British ban on Jewish immigration to Palestine from Hitler's Germany and its neighboring states. But like all of Ben-Gurion's plans for rescue at a time when rescue was still possible, the revolt was precluded by the outbreak of the war.

During the war, as before it, a mass rescue of Jews was impossible. For one thing, no country other than Palestine would take Jewish immigrants. For another, the Allies refused to make the rescue of Jews from the Nazi death camps one of their war aims. And finally, Jewish leaders in the United States and Great Britain were afraid to demand this of the Allies. Each of these obstacles will be detailed in the pages that follow.

Shoah *and Holocaust*

Not even by the second year of the war could anyone have comprehended that a Western government would dedicate its great resources to inventing state-of-the-art methods—different from any means of destruction previously known to humankind—to accomplish genocide. This possibility simply lay beyond the boundary of human imagination.

The tragedy is, as will be seen, that the fact of genocide was not fully understood even when the death factories were already functioning at maximum capacity. Only after the war was the horror completely revealed—and not fully believed even then. Perhaps for this reason, it took a few years to find an appropriate word to denote the mass murder of the Jews in Nazi hands during the war years in Europe.

In English, the Greek "holocaust" originally meant "burnt sacrifice," then developed the more general sense of a large-scale sacrifice or destruction, especially by fire. Nothing illustrates this better—while at the same time demonstrating how the American press treated the story of the Nazi extermination of Europe's Jews—than two news stories in the *New York Times*. The first, on November 26, 1942, page 16, headed "Slain Polish Jews Put at a Million," is by the paper's London correspondent. He quotes Dr. Ignacy Schwarzbart, Jewish member of the Polish National Council in London, as saying that "nearly a third of Poland's Jewish population—1,000,000—has perished in the three years of German occupation." The story notes that plans outlined by Dr. Alfred Rosenberg, Germany's race theorist, "who says that 'the Jewish problem of Europe will be solved when no Jews are left,' are systematically carried out." The correspondent specifies "victims of executions by mass-murder and gassing."

Four days later, on November 30, the lead front-page headline reads "Boston Fire Death Toll 440; Night Club Holocaust Laid to Bus

Boy's Lighted Match." Under it are three separate reports from Boston of a fire that broke out in the Coconut Grove nightclub, describing Boston as "this stunned and grieving city" that had seen "the nation's worst fire disaster in almost four decades."[5] The story of the 1 million Jews slain in Poland was not accompanied by a statement that this was the human race's worst genocide ever.

Only in the 1950s, according to the *Oxford English Dictionary,* did historians begin to use "Holocaust" to refer to "the mass murder of the Jews by the Nazis in the war of 1939–1945." It was then that the word received its present common meaning.

The same evolution occurred in Hebrew. *Shoah,* the term that is today equivalent to "Holocaust," entered the Zionist lexicon in the wake of Hitler's ascendancy to power in 1933 as the equivalent of "catastrophe," "destruction," or "annihilation." In March 1934 Chaim Weizmann described Hitler's becoming chancellor to the Zionist Actions Committee as *"unvorhergesehene Katastrophe, etwa ein neuer Weltkrieg,"* which was translated into Hebrew as "unforeseen *shoah,* a new world war." Moshe Sharett spoke at the Mapai council in January 1937 of hard times for Jews in Germany as "the result of the Hitlerite *shoah"* and noted that *"shoah* has befallen the Jews of Germany." Addressing the Histadrut council of March 1937, Ben-Gurion evoked the approaching war in Europe "as a new world war *shoah* hanging over our heads." In 1938, Yitzhak Gruenbaum broke the news to the JAE that "European Jewry in Central and Eastern Europe is being destroyed from one day to the next" while "Romanian Jewry was saved from *shoah* only by pure chance."[6]

Only after a long, painful process of coming to understand the new reality and absorbing its full import did *shoah* acquire the meaning "Holocaust." Once the specialized meaning of "Holocaust" became established in English, Israelis began to restrict *shoah* to that same usage.

Since the Zionist reaction to the Holocaust is central to this work, I make a special effort to distinguish *shoah* meaning "catastrophe" from its later meaning of "Holocaust." The first sense will be denoted by the English "destruction" and its synonyms; the second by "Holocaust."

I make this distinction less for the sake of semantics than because it is essential for refuting the claim by revisionist anti-Zionist historians that Zionism not only prophesied the Holocaust, but actually looked forward to it. Their case rests mainly on misrepresenting the use of *shoah,* always translating it as "Holocaust," even in texts from the 1930s and early 1940s when it meant only "catastrophe." A case in point is Segev's *The Seventh Million.* He maintains that the "founding fathers of the Zionist movement . . . assumed that, in the long run, Jews would not survive as Jews in the Diaspora; they would disappear, sooner or later, in one way or another." To reinforce the validity of this assertion, Segev brings it up-to-date by quoting a comment made by Sharett in April 1943: "Zionism predicted the Holocaust [Sharett used *shoah* for "catastrophe"] decades ago."[7]

Zionism did predict that the Jews of Eastern and Central Europe would be visited by a catastrophe that brought destruction in its wake. However, those who made this prediction conceived of the catastrophe as involving economic destruction and spiritual decay, accompanied now and then by pogroms. Never did Zionism prophesy that those Jews would meet systematic, mass industrial death—in a word, Holocaust.

For Zionism's enemies, there was only one small step from asserting that the Zionists predicted the Holocaust to accusing them of collaborating with the Nazis to bring it about, either by silence or by active deception—and some have not hesitated to take that step.

INTRODUCTION

A FULL COMPREHENSION OF the egregious nature of the charge that Zionism and the Yishuv shared the blame for the Holocaust requires some background regarding Zionist ideology and its permutations, as well as the character and makeup of the Yishuv.

The Time Limit

To Ben-Gurion, Zionism was the only solution to the Jewish problem; and the major obstacle facing Zionism was shortage of time. It seemed to him that history, as if changing its mind after allowing Zionism to exist in the first place, had allotted only a narrow slot of time for Zionism to be realized—a one-time chance that was not likely to return. This recognition permeated Ben-Gurion's thinking and policy.

To explain the time limit, he cited a parable drawn from a Hebrew legend. Now and then, he said—you are never told when—heaven is torn apart and the foundations of the universe open themselves to your request, ready even to turn everything upside down for you. At this moment a new world order can be ushered in. All you need do to have your wish granted is seize the moment.

He would explain that amid the global play of powers there appears once in a while such a moment, and only then can a great historic upheaval take place. The unification of Italy, America's War of Independence, the October Revolution, the Balfour Declaration were all achieved at such moments. A political leader worthy of the name must therefore have the instinct to perceive the presence of the historic moment as well as the will and ability to act.

This notion of the time limit took root in Ben-Gurion's mind and directed all his political thinking. During the 1920s, it brought him into bitter conflict with his United Labor Party (Ahdut HaAvodah), which believed that its role and destiny was to transform the *"shtetl Jew"* into a "new Jew" in Palestine, no longer a shopkeeper or a broker, but a worker, a creator of material goods, preferably a pioneer, a farmer, and a socialist. This conflict can best be described in terms of two contradictory slogans he coined in the middle of the decade.

The first slogan, "From a Class to a Nation"—which conformed with Zionism's basic condemnation of the Diaspora—referred to the drive to make all Jews in Palestine producers instead of middlemen. This slogan naturally sat well with the party. But as the time limit took a stronger hold on Ben-Gurion's mind, he began to differ from his party with respect to how the realization of the Zionist dream must occur. United Labor, by nature more an educational than a political movement, maintained that the supreme goal of reforming the Jew would be achieved by founding a just, egalitarian, and peace-loving workers' society, something that required a long, painstaking process.

Ben-Gurion, however, insisted that in order to realize its goal the party had to take control of the world Zionist movement. This position gave birth to his second slogan, "The Conquest of Zionism," which meant opening the party to all sectors of society—that is, professionals, businesspeople, and all other nonworkers—with the purpose of winning a majority in the biannual elections to the World Zionist Congress (held in nearly every country in Europe and the Americas, in Australia, and in the Middle East), unseating the General Zionists led by Weizmann, and staffing in their stead Zionism's ruling bodies, the Zionist Executive and the Jewish Agency Executive (JAE). Ben-Gurion proposed to use the power that would come with electoral victory to speed up the implementation of Zionism labor's way.

Feeling, however, that there was plenty of time, most members of his party rejected the second slogan. Nevertheless, Ben-Gurion's sense that time was running out grew ever more acute. Britain's growing coolness toward Zionism and the colonial administration's prejudice in favor of the Arabs; the increasing strength of some of the Arab states as they approached independence; the growing misery of Poland's Jews; the ban on immigration from Europe to America—all these factors prd Ben-Gurion in the 1920s to look for new, fast ways to realize Zionism.

Two events seemed to confirm Ben-Gurion's fateful vision that if Zionism was not realized quickly, it never would be. On August 23, 1929, the Arabs unleashed bloody riots all over Palestine and raided Jewish settlements. This uprising entirely changed the reality of Palestine and the direction of the Zionist movement there, for the earlier hope that there could be peaceful coexistence between Jews and Arabs dwindled. Second, for the first time a British tendency to withdraw from the commitments to the Jewish people laid out in the Balfour Declaration and the mandate became evident.

This tendency was manifest in Colonial Secretary Lord Passfield's White Paper, published in October 1930, curtailing Jewish immigration to Palestine because of the lack of arable land. At that time there were in Palestine about 165,000 Jews and 960,000 Arabs. Yet the Passfield White Paper reinterpreted the Balfour Declaration to emphasize its promise not to prejudice the rights of the country's non-Jewish inhabitants. The view that the commitment to the Jewish national home took precedence was rejected as erroneous. Declaring the development of the country, immigration, and unemployment to be related problems, the White Paper rejected the Zionist idea that Palestine could be divided into two separate economies and made the economic absorptive capacity of the entire country the sole determinant of the scale of Jewish immigration.

These events were accompanied by an internal threat: the rapid growth of the Revisionist movement, sworn enemies of Labor and the Histadrut. In the 1931 elections to the World Zionist Congress, the Revisionists received 21 percent of the votes, compared to 29 percent for Mapai, making them the third-largest faction in the Congress. Potentially they could join with the second-largest faction—the General Zionists B—and the religious faction (HaMizrakhi, the fourth largest) to outvote Mapai.

All these developments formed the background for Ben-Gurion's first public, unambiguous demand that Mapai prepare itself to become the majority party in the Zionist organization. In a speech on July 2, 1932, at the Mapai council, he told his comrades of a feeling he had that the ground was burning under the feet of the Jewish people and that the sword of Damocles hung over them. Only in Palestine, he argued, could "the masses of Israel," whose "existence is being steadily destroyed, and over whom hangs the threat of physical and spiritual annihilation, decay and destruction," find the remedy they required. Therefore, "it is our duty to take over the Zionist organization" to ensure that this remedy would be effective.

But again his arguments met unreceptive ears, and the conflict between the aspiration for a just, pioneering workers' society and Ben-Gurion's sense of the burning ground was left unresolved. Even his own supporters, out of clear concern for the movement's values, opposed "taking Zionism into our hands." With both sides equally unrelenting, Ben-Gurion had, in the end, to foist the conquest of Zionism on the party as a whole.

In the 1933 Zionist Congress elections, Ben-Gurion faced off against Ze'ev Jabotinsky, founder and leader of the Revisionist Zionist Party, ten years older than the forty-seven-year-old Ben-Gurion and recognized as the Zionists' most formidable public speaker. Labor won 44 percent of the vote worldwide, making it the largest faction in the Congress. This resounding victory catapulted Ben-Gurion as well as Mapai—virtually against its will—to the head of the Zionist organization and of the Yishuv, and eventually brought about the establishment of the state of Israel.

Ben-Gurion's sense of the burning ground and his belief that he himself was endowed with the ability to discern when a historic moment had arrived had now the chance to prove themselves as both the engine and the compass of Zionism's political thinking and action. It is ironic that there were, later, those who described him as a leader perennially on the watch for his chance, ready to spring at the historic moment and seize it—and who asserted that this moment was the Holocaust.

Foreseeing Destruction

During his campaign to assume control of the Zionist movement—
first within his own party and then in the 1933 elections—Ben-
Gurion's eyes were opened to the Nazi menace. In April 1933, he was
campaigning in Poland, Lithuania, and Latvia amid news of Hitler's
earliest infringements on the freedom of Jews and the first rumors of
concentration camps. At an election meeting in Memel he thought
aloud about the "repression, trampling on freedom and dictatorship
in Germany" that might bring about a world war in which "Jews will
be butchered" and "the Jewish people will prove to be the war's primary victims"—an incredible prophecy. On August 29, 1933, waiting
for a train in the Munich station, he bought *Mein Kampf* (he is arguably the only Zionist leader to have done so at this stage). He read
the book studiously, and his somber premonition regarding the fate of
the Jewish people in Nazi hands turned into bleak certainty. His
awareness of a time limit now became the conviction that he was in
a desperate race; and the burning ground now seemed a conflagration
that would drive him to wield all his power to rescue Hitler's would-
be victims while there was still time, before Hitler set out on his de-
monic course.

From now on, the major—even the only—meaning of Zionism for
Ben-Gurion became the rescue of the Jewish people. This understanding was influenced by his notion of the conquest of Zionism. Originally, this conquest meant the opening of United Labor, and later
Mapai, to all Zionists, regardless of their social position or occupation.
By the same logic, rescue operations run by the JAE should certainly
encompass all Jews, Zionists and non-Zionists alike.

Elected in October 1933 to the Jewish Agency and charged with
conducting its policy, Ben-Gurion was aware that he bore a national
responsibility. His speech at the Histadrut conference of January 1934
contained another astonishing prediction: "Hitler's rule places the entire Jewish people in danger. Hitlerism is at war not only with the
Jews of Germany but with Jews the world over. Hitler's rule cannot
last for long without war, without a war of vengeance against France,

Poland, Czechoslovakia and other neighboring countries . . . or against vast Soviet Russia. . . . [P]erhaps only four or five years (if not less) stand between us and that day of wrath." Ben-Gurion had, therefore, realized that Hitler intended to annihilate the Jewish people and even prophesied how Hitler would do it: by starting a general war in Europe, then taking Poland and vast areas of the Soviet Union—the two countries that contained the largest numbers of Jews. Without conquering those two countries, there could be no Holocaust, since there were not enough Jews in the other European countries. Then, under cover of war, Hitler would commit his crime. He could never have accomplished real genocide in peacetime.

In October 1934, Ben-Gurion publicly redefined the realization of Zionism. This, he asserted, was "the mission of our generation." And to carry it out, the Jewish Agency should take as its central task the "creation of a powerful Jewish presence in Palestine." In November of that year, he told a party meeting: "A war may happen . . . and those who were in leadership positions and did not make use of all the possibilities, and did not try to use this opportune moment, will have betrayed their trust." In 1936 he warned the Zionist Actions Committee, "We don't have time to spare. The question of massive immigration is now a question of life and death for the Jewish people and for Jewish Palestine." After the abandonment of Czechoslovakia in September 1938, Ben-Gurion confided to his diary, "I'm afraid it's now our turn. We the Jews will not be among the last victims of this Nazi triumph . . . all the Jews of Europe and Asia, and maybe America too, will feel the victory of evil." For no one would come to the aid of the Jews, not even North America or the League of Nations.

The *Kristallnacht* riots on the night of November 9, 1938, seemed to him the confirmation of all his past fears and a sign of things to come. "Millions of our people face destruction," he wrote British Colonial Secretary Malcolm MacDonald.

The nearer world war loomed, the closer Ben-Gurion clung to his vision. In June 1939 he told the Zionist Actions Committee, "There may be a war which will visit upon us catastrophe [*shoah*]. . . . We have Hitler, and we can rely upon him for this. . . . If there is a world war . . . he will do this thing, destroying first of all the Jews of Europe." In August 1939 he told the Labor delegates to the Zionist World Congress, "Zionism's future is more than looking after the handful of Jews who have arrived in Palestine."[1]

To Ben-Gurion's political eye, Hitler's rule, world war, the conquest of Poland and parts of the Soviet Union, and the destruction of the Jewish people were part and parcel of the same historical development. Hitler would be able to destroy the Jews of Europe only in time of war, when Eastern Europe was in his hands. This perception proved complete and precise.

Ben-Gurion's foresight was not confined to speeches and statements. It underlay the political line that guided his policies and actions. His reading of the future anticipated several developments: (1) The Arab countries would grow stronger, support Hitler, and try to use his military support to destroy the Yishuv. (2) The British government would adopt a policy of conciliation toward the Arabs and would close the gates of Palestine to Hitler's fleeing victims. (3) No other country would be ready to receive the tens or hundreds of thousands of Jewish refugees. (4) Hitler's atrocities would strengthen anti-Semitism elsewhere in the world and possibly pave the way for further destruction of Jews. (5) The Jews' only salvation would be a Jewish state in Palestine. All these predictions proved true, except the last one: for the Holocaust preceded Israel.

The plans Ben-Gurion made, based on his foresight, varied with the changing circumstances, but the goal of all was to minimize the catastrophe by increasing immigration while there was still time. An early plan was a scheme to open Palestine between 1932 and 1938 to Jewish immigration that would double the Yishuv. Another was a proposal for a "federal Palestine," which Ben-Gurion brought in September 1934 to aides of the Mufti of Jerusalem, the main leader of the Palestinian Arabs. It involved establishing an Arab federation, of which a Jewish Palestine would be a member state that could accept 6–8 million Jews. A third plan, developed after the Nazis passed the anti-Jewish Nuremberg Laws of 1935, envisioned the transfer of a million Jews and their settlement in Palestine. Still another plan was based on the report of the Peel Commission in 1937, which proposed a partition of Palestine between Jews and Arabs, with the establishment of a Jewish state in part of Palestine. Following the Munich Pact of 1938, Ben-Gurion proposed an "immigration revolt." Masses of illegal immigrants would arrive by ship and fight to land in Palestine; ultimately Haifa and its environs would be conquered and declared a Jewish state, and the port would be opened to mass immigration.[2]

Except for the fact that the repeal of the 1930 White Paper did allow the Yishuv to double between 1932 and 1939, none of these plans came to fruition. Ben-Gurion struggled fiercely to induce his Zionist allies and opponents to accept them, only to see the plans defeated by the Arabs, the British, and, above all, by the outbreak of the war, which checked his bold and imaginative leadership. It has never been sufficiently appreciated that in order to save the Jews while there was time, Ben-Gurion was ready to pay in sacred Zionist principles: compromising complete Jewish sovereignty (in the federation plan he put before the Mufti), giving up the principle of the indivisibility of the Land of Israel (in his embracing of partition).

In the event, all the Jewish people got from the British government was the White Paper of May 1939, under which only 75,000 Jews would be allowed to enter Palestine during the years of war and Holocaust. On this trick of fate Ben-Gurion mused in 1944 at his party's conference: "Had we had a Jewish state seven years ago, we would have brought to it millions . . . and they would be here with us. But we shall not bring them . . . because those Jews are no more."[3]

Confronting the War

Soon after his return from the 1939 Zionist Congress on Saturday night, September 2—the day after Germany invaded Poland—Ben-Gurion came to believe that Britain "will not be able to decisively defeat Hitler," who had made a pact with Stalin. In the first days of the war he told the National Council (elected by the National Assembly, the Yishuv's parliament, as its executive body) that he saw "harbingers of catastrophe [shoah]." "Tens and hundreds of thousands in Poland are doomed to slaughter," he declared, and "there is no guarantee that the angel of death will not visit the neighboring countries." Ben-Gurion compared the two world wars from a Zionist point of view: In the Great War, "the most important limb of the body of the Jewish people, Russian Jewry, was torn away for a long period." Now the second war had begun with the tearing away "of the only other important member remaining to us, Polish Jewry." From this analogy he derived a decision to direct his efforts to three objectives: continuation of his efforts to accelerate immigration from Europe; defense of the Yishuv; and the participation of the Jewish people, as a nation, in the war against Hitler.

Ben-Gurion's proposed "immigration revolt" was intended to achieve his first objective. His plan to achieve the second two objectives involved establishing within the British army two units. The first would be an army of Jewish volunteers from Palestine and the free world, plus refugees from occupied Europe; it would help combat Hitler on the same terms as the Free French army and the Polish army. The second would be a military force raised in Palestine to defend it against invasion and destruction. He envisioned these two armies together making it possible for the Jewish people to create the Jewish state in Palestine after the war.[4]

Achieving these three objectives depended in part on British consent, and to obtain this Ben-Gurion made three long trips to England and America between November 1939 and October 1941. During his absences, he received newspapers in Hebrew and other languages, news agency dispatches, reports from the JAE offices in Europe and the United States, reports from the Polish underground and the Polish government in exile in London, letters from *landsmanshaften* (associations of people who had immigrated to Palestine from the same country) and from political organizations, and intelligence gathered by the Haganah [the Jewish paramilitary underground] and the Organization for Illegal Immigration (Mossad). He also garnered much information in his many meetings with military officers, secret service agents, and British and American statesmen and diplomats—a varied and comprehensive pool of information, occasionally augmented by correspondence arriving directly from occupied Europe. In this manner he learned from letters sent from Poland at the end of 1939 that "about 30,000 lives were lost" in the wake of the occupation "and tens of thousands were injured in Warsaw. . . . [T]he situation is going from bad to worse, and if it continues we shall face the loss of a million and a half Jews." They were being expelled to newly created ghettos, their means of livelihood were being destroyed, and famine was spreading among them. A great many were being kidnapped into forced labor, and "women are victims of great suffering."[5] Of Eichmann's particular role, Ben-Gurion first learned in November 1939. It was reported to him that "a Gestapo officer in charge of Jewish affairs" in Prague had begun on October 12 "to organize Jewish migration from Czechoslovakia." This was one of the first experiments in what was later known as the Final Solution. It involved transport by train of 6000 Jews—lasting two days "in closed cars without water" —to a *Reservat* in the Lublin region. To a plea that the JAE help those Jews, Ben-Gurion responded: "The Executive should do all it can, as if we ourselves were inside this inferno."

A 1940 report to the Jewish Agency, later published in the press, pointed to the conclusion that the Jews of Poland "are being destroyed without pity, with naked brutality." The report indicated that behind these persecutions lay a systematic, overriding purpose. Ben-Gurion, therefore, had in his possession the evidence that his 1934 vision was becoming fact.

It seems, then, that Ben-Gurion was outwardly well prepared to meet the exigencies of the war and of Nazi occupation. Yet there was a wide, almost unbridgeable gulf between what the ears heard, the eyes read, and even what the brain understood and the conviction that what was taking place in occupied Europe was real. Not only did people's minds revolt against such atrocities and peremptorily discount them, but the memory of the *"greuel"* or gruesome propaganda of the Great War—the famous untrue charge that the Germans had used human fat to make soap—was still very much alive. In November 1942, when far worse cruelties were recounted and believed, Eliahu Dobkin, of the JAE, told a Histadrut meeting that Ben-Gurion had already heard these stories in America, adding, "but they took them to be another sort of 'greuel propaganda' and discounted them."[6]

The mind has its own obscure ways of directing behavior and thought, and although we might have expected Ben-Gurion to recognize that—according to his own accurate prophecy—within a short time there would be no Jews left in Europe, in fact he had to struggle to comprehend and internalize the full scope and reality of what was happening. He issued warnings to others, but he himself could not come to terms with the enormity of the events about to occur. And perhaps this was impossible—beyond the capacity of truly human imagination, his own included. What was more, like many another, before and after, in times of crisis—in this case, unprecedented crisis— he had only his old tools available to work with. Devices for dealing with the horrors that Nazi Germany had in store had not been—and could not have been—invented in advance.

This must have been one reason why, in the first years of the war, Ben-Gurion and the Yishuv leadership continued as before to de- mand—nearly exclusively—immigration, defense of Palestine, and the Jewish people's participation, as a warring nation, in the battle against Hitler. And it must also have been why Ben-Gurion went on using his familiar trustworthy and efficient tools to achieve Zionism's political goals.

Disaster Is Power

One of these old tools was a third slogan he had coined: "Disaster Is Power." There had developed in his mind a recognition that Jewish misery could be made into a source of strength, and that the role of a leader was to turn Jewish disaster to the overall advantage of the Jewish people by using it to help ensure their future survival.

It is critical to bear in mind that this concept never implied that a disaster should be created in order to glean an advantage from it. Rather, the concept reflected Ben-Gurion's conclusion that, since the Jews were unable to prevent the disaster from befalling them, they should at least employ it as best they could in their defense. Disasters had befallen the Jews since time immemorial, but no one before Ben- Gurion had ever dreamed of using them as weapons—as "leverage," in his word—or viewed them as sources of strength. In this he was absolutely unique in the Zionist movement.

The idea that disaster could be transformed into political power had taken root in his mind after the 1929 riots. Whereas others—true to tradition during pogroms—bemoaned the suffering and called for help, Ben-Gurion's reaction was utterly different: "The blood we shed cries out not for pity and help but for doubling of our strength and of the Zionist enterprise." Thus did Ben-Gurion, the Histadrut secretary, cable to the Zionist Executive from the ship that brought him back from the 1929 Congress. In the manifesto he offered in the name of the two Labor parties that by their merger created Mapai, he wrote: "The Jewish people will redeem the spilled blood of their children, by increasing the Yishuv by thousands and tens of thousands of new builders and defenders. This should be our one and only revenge."

Ben-Gurion used the word "exploit" for the first time in a meeting of the Histadrut secretariat on September 5, 1929, saying: "The present mood in the Jewish world should be exploited to maximize settlement in Palestine." Just after the riots, a worldwide "Voluntary Fund" appeal had been launched, especially in Europe and the United States, to raise 5 million Palestinian pounds ($25 million at the time or $750 million in today's dollars) to be distributed among the victims. But Ben-Gurion suggested that this enormous sum should go "entirely to new construction, defense, and expansion," as well as to the immigration of at least 50,000 young people within less than a year.[7]

It seems, then, that in 1929 he was already seeing Jewish disaster as a kind of steam power that could be harnessed for political and military purposes. On January 19, 1933, he told the Mapai council, "From an abstract Zionist perspective . . . there is no need at the moment to make propaganda for Palestine. Jewish life in the Diaspora provides the strongest propaganda, and this propaganda is produced by the destruction . . . of all possibility for existence for great masses of Jews . . . Jews by the thousands are charging at Palestine's gates." He asked the council: "Is it not perhaps possible to turn Jewish destruction into creative energy?"[8]

He was not the only one to have this idea. The same concept moved Dr. Chaim Arlosoroff, the head of the political department of the JAE, to dedicate his last months, before he was murdered in June 1933, to establishing a public company named Transfer whose sole business was to transfer the property of German Jews from Germany to Palestine, with the hope that the owners would be able to follow it. This arrangement lasted from 1934 to 1938. The company, a non-Jewish firm directed and managed by two respected English businessmen, would buy Jewish property, which the Jews themselves could sell only at a fraction of its worth, and barter it for German goods exported to Palestine, where the proceeds of their sale were reimbursed to the German Jews who had immigrated there. This was the only way German Jews could save part of their possessions. The interim financing was handled by a special JAE budget.

However, Ben-Gurion himself envisaged a political Zionist "exploitation" of German Jewry on a much larger scale: a massive flow of immigrants and capital. A large settlement project in the context of rescuing German Jewry "must certainly be implemented now."[9] And indeed, the emergency immigration between 1933 and 1936 did more than double the Yishuv.

In 1936, against the background of a new outbreak of riots combined with the continuing British tendency to curtail their Balfour Declaration commitments, Ben-Gurion resolved "to begin the policy of the Jewish state." He told his party's political committee in 1936, "An action must be launched to turn Palestine into a shelter for Jewish masses, an action that should make Palestine a Jewish land. The purpose of our political action now is: to bring a million Jews out of Europe . . . and direct them toward Palestine. . . . For this need is not only a matter of theory, but an imperative of reality that speaks the language the entire world hears and understands—and in this I see the lever for our political action."

A brilliant example of Ben-Gurion's tactic of exploiting disaster was his response to the 1936 "Disturbances" (in the British term) or "Arab Revolt" (the Arab term), which erupted in April and nearly paralyzed the country for three years. Ben-Gurion, who in the fall of 1935 had become the JAE chairman in Jerusalem, the recognized leader of the Yishuv, produced against Arab terror the "weapon of restraint." He decreed that counterterror "will only bring political advantage to the Arabs and will cause us damage." Therefore the Yishuv must restrict itself to self-defense and punishment only of the perpetrators. In May 1936 he explained to the JAE that restraint would strengthen the Haganah. And in fact, during the riot years the mandatory government enlarged the Jewish settlement auxiliary police, the public arm of the Haganah, and issued weapons to Jewish settlements for self-defense. This strengthening of the legal arm of the Haganah benefited its clandestine arm as well.

Along with the economic damage caused by the riots, the general strike and total boycott called by the Arabs could have irreparably harmed the Yishuv economy. Fear that the Yishuv would collapse completely was widespread—but did not affect Ben-Gurion. "The principal and primary lesson that these riots must teach us," he told the National Council three weeks after they began, "is that we must rid ourselves of all economic dependence upon the Arabs." He worked, therefore, to make an imposed temporary condition into a desired, permanent one: in other words, to bolster the Yishuv as a separate, self-sufficient national economic unit.

The events of 1936 made Ben-Gurion reconceptualize the sequence of events commonly considered necessary to achieve Zionism, which went as follows: by promoting immigration (1) the Jews would become a majority (2), which would solve the Arab question (3), and lead to the establishment of a state (4). The Jewish state would open its gates to all Jews, and with the ingathering of the exiles Zionism would achieve its purpose (5). But Ben-Gurion feared that Hitler's persecution of the Jews in Europe, along with the likelihood that under Arab pressure the British government would pursue a "new course," would thwart the Zionist enterprise. He concluded that an immediate, accelerated increase in immigration such as only a state would be capable of was called for.

Thus the need to save Jews dictated a new sequence of events, according to which the early establishment of a state (1) would make possible massive immigration (2) that would create a decisive Jewish majority (3), solving the Arab question (4). Finally there would be the ingathering of the exiles, and Zionism would be achieved (5).

The months following the riots were among the most important in Ben-Gurion's political life. It was then that, in both thought and action, he laid the foundations of his "policy of the Jewish state," which was, essentially, the exploitation of the Jewish disasters in Europe and in Palestine. For it was the terrible Jewish plight in Europe which drove

Jews to Palestine, and it was Arab violence that pressured the British to shut Palestine's gates in their faces. The disaster that had befallen the Yishuv and the disaster that had befallen the Jews of Germany had become interlocked.[10]

From the outset it was clear that, far from being able to support the Yishuv, the Jews of Europe needed support themselves. But to extend such support, the Yishuv needed more immigrants. This dilemma could be resolved only by an impossible feat of turning disaster into strength. Jews kept crowding through the doors of the Palestine visa offices throughout Europe, and Central and Eastern Europe seemed more than ever like an unvented boiler in which steam was building up.

If Ben-Gurion was in quest of "creative energy," there was certainly no lack of hardship available to draw upon. In this sense, Jewish disaster was an inexhaustible natural resource that Ben-Gurion skillfully transformed into Zionist momentum. The harsher the Jews' plight became, the more resolute he grew. In May 1936, he told Mapai, "It's in our interest that Hitler should be wiped out, but as long as he remains we are interested in exploiting his presence for the building up of Palestine." It was this type of thinking that, in the beginning of 1937, led him to embrace the report of the Palestine Royal Commission (the Peel partition scheme), in which he perceived a way of exploiting "the Hitler disaster [shoah]" so as to carve out a shortcut to the establishment of a state.

This approach achieved its full expression after war had broken out, when Jewish suffering and despair reached new depths. In June 1941 Ben-Gurion told a Mapai conference, "We have no choice . . . but this also is a source of strength, perhaps our major source of strength."[11] This was the mark of great leadership: that in a time of darkness, total despair, and utter impotence, Ben-Gurion told his people that from their very helplessness they could draw strength.

In February 1941, against the backdrop of the war and the atrocities of the German army, Ben-Gurion returned with renewed vigor to his concept of the state as the only way to rescue the Jews of Germany. He was working out a plan for the quick transfer of millions of Jews to Palestine when the war was over. "After England's victory," he told

Mapai, "there will be five or eight million displaced and ruined Jews in Europe. . . . It's necessary to establish a Jewish state in Palestine because this is now the only way to transfer millions of Jews from a destroyed Europe and settle them in Palestine."[12] In London that October, in preparation for a trip to the United States, he wrote some notes to himself in which he said: "The magnitude of the Jewish problem, the magnitude of future Jewish immigration, the suffering and injustice inflicted upon the Jews, the need for a New Deal after the war, the vast changes that will occur in the postwar world, the vast, sparsely populated Arab countries that are due to win independence after the war, the smallness of Palestine, and the fact that Palestine is the only place in the world where the Jews have a national home—all these prove that the establishment of a Jewish state in Palestine is both essential and feasible."[13]

On his return from the United States to Palestine in October 1942, Ben-Gurion did not yet have confirmed information about the death camps. This must be borne in mind in reading what he told the Zionist Actions Committee on October 15: "Disaster is power if we know how to channel it in a productive direction; the whole 'trick' of Zionism is its ability to turn our disaster not into depression and helplessness, as has happened more than once in the Diaspora, but into a fountain of productivity and exhilaration."[14]

Did he still think this way when it became absolutely clear that the Germans were carrying out systematic, full-scale genocide? Did he ever ask himself if history had not played on him a cruel jest, as if to test the steadfastness of his resolve? The fact is that the more he became aware of the scale of the destruction, and the more his early vision was borne out by events, the less he repeated his "Disaster Is Power" slogan, speaking instead of "the power inherent in suffering." Certainly it seemed at the time—and still does to many people today—that Ben-Gurion was no match for Hitler, and that total destruction would make a solution of the Jewish problem—and by the same token creation of a Jewish state—unnecessary.

For a while Ben-Gurion, like everyone else in the Jewish world, was in a state of deep confusion. In December 1943 he told Mapai that "the Zionist enterprise relies not only on the facts on the ground

that we have already created but also on the fact of the Jewish disaster. . . . [T]his must be brought home to the Gentiles."[15] For the first
time, that is, he had to admit that the Jews by themselves could not
achieve Zionism without support from the Gentiles. Ben-Gurion's
achievement was that despite his confusion—why should the British
assist the Zionist enterprise while combative Zionists were fighting
them?—he could nevertheless instill hope in the hearts of Jews not
only in Palestine but in Nazi Europe as well.

Only at the last stages of the Holocaust, desperately hoping that a
sizable remnant of European Jewry would be left—only then did Ben-
Gurion return to his formula that disaster was power. By that time he
must have felt some glimmer of hope that, in the standoff with Hitler,
the Jewish people would not be the vanquished ones. As will be seen
in Chapter 16, it was then that he began to construct detailed economic and developmental blueprints for building a Jewish state.

A New Zionist Approach to Rescue

As the scale of the destruction and the way it was being carried out
became clear, and as the word "catastrophe" (shoah) began to acquire
its dreadful significance, the word "rescue" also underwent a change
of meaning in the Zionist lexicon. There was no more ardent believer
than Ben-Gurion in the Zionist concept that the ingathering of exiles
in Palestine was the only solution to the Jewish problem. Individuals
and parties, Jews and non-Jews, were still flying the banners of other
solutions—such as settling Jews in other countries—but Ben-Gurion
regarded these as "voodoo" solutions, mere sleight of hand. In his
opinion, these "solutions" would only make the plight of the Jewish
people more permanent and prompt further attacks on their existence.
He therefore considered immigration to Palestine the only true means
of rescue; and this was also the official position of the Zionist Congress. It was why Zionists referred to rescue in the form of immigration to Palestine as "redemption."

As the Congress's executive, the JAE was required to distinguish
between people applying for "redemption"—settlement in Palestine—
and those who wanted to go there only briefly for "rescue," then move

on to settle elsewhere. By its mandate, the JAE was responsible for the immigrants, while the welfare, shelter, and support of the refugees was the charge of philanthropic organizations (such as the Hebrew Immigrant Aid Society and the Joint Distribution Committee) and Jewish communities in every country the world over.

Ben-Gurion referred to the considerations behind these two categories of assistance as the "Jewish agenda" and the "Zionist agenda." He used these terms to express the difference between concern for the physical safety and civic equality of the individual or local community and concern for a radical, collective change in the status of the nation that only independence in Palestine could guarantee.

Some of his colleagues felt that such a distinction would be taken out of context and used as a weapon by Ben-Gurion's opponents. However, the JAE was bound by Zionist Organization regulations and could not disregard them without the Congress's authorization. All the members of the JAE were aware of this, but they wanted Ben-Gurion to soft-pedal the fact instead of emphasizing it.

Yet already in the first stages of the war, Ben-Gurion had come to recognize that the distinction between immigrants and refugees was no longer valid. As early as November 1941 Leon Simon, head of the British Zionists, criticized him for arguing that "the supremely important thing now is salvage, and nation-building is incidental. . . ." Simon argued that "the fundamental object of Zionism . . . is nation-building, not salvage."[16]

By 1943 Ben-Gurion found it necessary to dwell on this internal "debate" in a Mapai seminar. "What is Zionism?" he demanded. "Is it the solution to the refugee problem, referred to in political jargon as 'rescue,' or is it the solution of a historic problem, called 'redemption'? Some argue that . . . the refugee problem has nothing to do with Zionism . . . and that we are under no obligation to solve the refugee problem. But can anyone really imagine that there is any justification for the Zionist movement . . . if this movement does not look after the burning needs of millions of Jews?"

In his thinking, therefore, the Zionist agenda and the Jewish agenda had become one. The reality of events made it plain that the refugees had no place else to go. The Zionists would have supported wholeheartedly refugees finding rescue in any other country; but none was available. As early as April 1936, describing the worsening plight of Poland's Jews, Ben-Gurion had told the high commissioner, General Sir Arthur Wauchope: "Our weightiest concern is the 'no-exit' situation of our people . . . the Jewish situation that was never good has now become desperate. . . . Had there been the possibility of bringing Poland's Jews to the United States or Argentina, we would have done so regardless of our Zionist beliefs. But the world was closed to us. And had there also not been room for us in Palestine, our people would have had only one way out: to commit suicide."[17]

Conclusive proof that no country in the entire world was open to the Jews was provided in 1938 by the Evian conference, which was supposed to find countries to receive immigrants but came up with not a single one. An initiative of President Roosevelt, the conference turned out to be not "much more," as *Time* magazine correctly predicted, "than a grandiose gesture." Roosevelt himself admitted as much in private. Four months later *Kristallnacht* shook public opinion in the United States, but Roosevelt's only reaction was to call home Ambassador Robert Wilson from Berlin. The immigration quota remained.[18]

The fact that by the early years of the war Ben-Gurion had ceased to make a distinction between immigrants and refugees is manifest in comments urging that Jews be brought from Europe to Palestine regardless of their orientation toward Zionism. In December 1942 he expressed regret for a statement he had made two months before at his party's conference: "I said then to bring over two million Jews as soon as the war was over—now I say: Bring them here now. This is a must. . . . All the Jews that it is possible to bring to Palestine immediately—this is the only rescue."

Unlike others, he did not recoil from the prospect of "a flood of Jews" entering Palestine. "Would there be a catastrophe in Palestine if masses of Jews came?" he asked, as if challenging those who advocated gradual, orderly absorption, for the immigrants' own good. He answered, "And would those Jews fare any better in Poland?" To Rabbi Yehuda Leib Maimon of the JAE, who feared that the immigration of a million Jews would turn out to be a catastrophe, leaving them homeless or starving, Ben-Gurion said, "You have not lived the new Zionism if you fear such difficulties, which are in fact far worse than you can imagine. If we recoil before such difficulties, Zionism will not win."[19]

A Hope Deferred

For a long time, Ben-Gurion's discussions of the destruction were accompanied by the hope that his conviction that Hitler was intent on destroying all the Jews of Europe would prove wrong. According to his calculations, there were in 1937 about 16.5 million Jews in the world, of whom 9.846 million were in Europe; of those, about 6.3 million were in Poland and the Soviet Union. The remainder comprised 5.2 million in South and North America and about 1.5 million in Asia, Africa, and Australia. At a JAE meeting in February 1941, when there was still hope that the war would be over soon, he argued that the war "will end with a Jewish disaster," because after the victory "there will remain in Europe five or eight million displaced Jews." For this reason, "Zionism now is one, and only one, thing: the concern for the rescue of five million Jews."

After Germany invaded the Soviet Union he estimated a lower number of survivors. In May 1942, at the Biltmore Conference—an all-Zionist conference held at the Biltmore Hotel in New York, which proposed the Biltmore Program for establishing a Jewish state in Palestine—he said that there would remain between 3 million and 5 million survivors "who will have to emigrate" to Palestine, which, he added, was capable of absorbing them. It was here that he first conceived a plan to transfer 2 million Jews at one time to Palestine.[20]

In November 1942 the Yishuv received definitive, confirmed information that systematic destruction was going on. The result was a radical change in the public's concept of the extent of the catastrophe. In place of the skepticism and disbelief with which the Jews had greeted initial accounts of atrocities, there was now a foreboding sense of utter catastrophe that proved entirely accurate. On January 4, 1943, the headlines of the Hebrew papers announced that 75 percent of the Jews of occupied Europe had already been exterminated. In an eight-column banner on its front page, *Davar* declared, "REALITY SURPASSES IN HORROR THE DARKEST PROPHECIES." Since the number of Jews under Nazi occupation was put at 8 million, the number of victims was fixed at 6 million. This correct total was, therefore, arrived at at least a year and a half before it was a fact.

In a particularly bitter comment to a kibbutz conference in mid-January 1944, Ben-Gurion said, "There was a time when the argument in Zionism was about whether, if all the Jewish people came to Palestine, there would still be a Diaspora. There were those who condemned the Diaspora, and those who saw positive qualities in it. But this was all only theoretical. Today, the possibility that all Jews will be in Palestine can come to pass in an entirely different way: simply because all the others were exterminated."

At this conference Ben-Gurion himself first used the number 6 million, but added in the same breath: "I do not know how many millions have been destroyed. Nobody knows." Even he, who had correctly divined Hitler's intention, still felt doubt and hope. A week later, having internalized the number 6 million, he made this historic statement: "The Jewish people is no more, there is something else now." He meant that because the destroyed one-third had been to a large measure the bearer of Jewish tradition and values, the remaining two-thirds—of which one large segment was assimilating in America, and another being dejudaized in the Soviet Union—constituted a totally different Jewish people, less rooted in the past.

This notion must have been in his mind for some time before he expressed it publicly. In any case, as will be seen, from now on the defense and perpetuation of this "something else" became the focus of his efforts, with the hope that what Hitler had stolen from the Jewish people would eventually be restored. In this last bout between Ben-Gurion and Hitler, Ben-Gurion was not the vanquished one.

Would Ben-Gurion have sacrificed Zionism and the state of Israel for the 6 million Jews? This question has never been raised, for it did not matter either to Hitler or to the Allies. But it is this author's strong opinion that, had such a bargain been offered Ben-Gurion, he would not for a moment have hesitated to accept it.

When Rescue Is Not Possible

Nothing did more damage to Ben-Gurion's reputation than his decisive recognition, once the real war started in Europe, that very little could be done to rescue the Jews there from the fate Hitler had designed for them. Endorsement of this view came, unknown to him, from the highest authority—from Zivia Lubetkin and Yitzhak (Antek) Zuckerman, leaders of the Jewish resistance in Warsaw, who wrote in November 1943 to Yitzhak Tabenkin, Meir Ya'ari, and Eliahu Dobkin in Palestine: "We know you would have done everything in your power to rescue us, but we realize all too well that you do not have the means. It is easier for us to die in the knowledge that a free world will arise and the belief that Palestine will become the homeland of the Jewish people."[21]

Yet a case can be made that in focusing his energy on preparing for the postwar revival of the Jewish people in Palestine, Ben-Gurion showed unprecedented courage and determination. Where others resorted to tears and wailing, he took up the tools of the mason to rebuild the ruins. In this story, all Ben-Gurion's strengths and weaknesses became manifest. In evaluating his actions, it is well to remember that history had never before put anyone to such a test.

Ben-Gurion returned from the United States on Friday, October 2, 1942, after an absence of over a year, resolved to push through the Biltmore Program, which he and Weizmann were sponsoring amid news of mass murder in Nazi Europe. Seeing in it a way to prevent a new destruction after the present one, Ben-Gurion began working to build a consensus for it in both Palestine and the free world.

He turned his immediate attention to preparing the ground for his party to endorse the Biltmore Program and adopt it as its political platform, which it did at a conference that same October. To achieve this, he was even ready to split the party in two; and a split indeed occurred, after two years of intense struggle with Tabenkin and his camp. Later, those two years drew the wrath of Ben-Gurion's critics, who claimed that while the destruction in Europe was claiming millions of Jewish lives, he was locked in petty party maneuvers. At the time, to those who doubted that the remaking of the party was more important than anything else, he explained that the defense of Palestine—which in 1941 and 1942 was being threatened by a Vichy French army in Syria and a German army in the western desert—and the preparations to rescue the Jewish people in Europe after the war, should any be left, were the main concerns and must be the focus of all efforts. But in order to do this, he said, there must be a clear policy and goal around which to unite the collective effort. As long as the party was in perpetual disagreement, no national effort was possible. He saw, therefore, that unless the party was remade with a clear structure of authority and political program, nothing could be achieved.

The criticism of Ben-Gurion evoked by the infighting over the Biltmore Program was considerably amplified by the fact that he spent much time and effort on economic affairs, preferring the JAE's planning committee to its rescue committee. At the center of this criticism lies the assumption that if Ben-Gurion had seen rescue as his primary field of action, it would have been possible to rescue more Jews. This was and is fallacious. It attributes to Ben-Gurion capabilities that he did not have at the time. There is no doubt that had even the narrowest opening for a rescue existed, no matter how improbable, Ben-Gurion and with him the entire JAE would have devoted themselves wholeheartedly to such a mission. The tragic fact is—and about this there is a consensus among the first rank of Holocaust historians, as well as among many of the survivors—that no matter how much effort Zionism and the Yishuv might have invested in the attempt, only very few more Jews could have been rescued.

The planning committee and rescue committee, both successors of other bodies that had dissolved without accomplishing their missions, were set up in the first months of 1943. Ben-Gurion's decision to head the planning committee, not the rescue committee, reflected not only his recognition that very little rescue could be achieved while a fierce war was raging but also his long-standing practice of channeling his efforts into areas where he could have the greatest effect—what can be called his "efficacy rule." He intended the planning committee to prepare the economic and administrative infrastructure that the state would need when the time came to increase immigration. It was this stance that gave rise to the accusations that he saw rescue as secondary to the establishment of the state. Research and better understanding of Ben-Gurion's motives, however, demonstrate that this claim is mistaken.

The rescue committee established in 1943 was the result of demands by other parties and public organizations in the Yishuv for a committee that would represent the entire Yishuv, arouse public opinion worldwide, and be far more active than its predecessor. After tedious bargaining, in January 1943 the Jewish Agency for Palestine Committee for the Rescue of European Jewry, known as the rescue committee, was born. To satisfy the many claimants who wanted a share, it had an elaborate, top-heavy, cumbersome structure that invited pressure from all sides, rendering the committee ineffective. There is, therefore, some truth to the argument that the JAE regarded it as unimportant, a mere lightning rod to attract public anger.

Indeed, in practice all rescue operations, whether operational or in the planning stage, were directed by the senior JAE leadership—Ben-Gurion, Sharett, and Eliezer Kaplan—not by the rescue committee.[22] And in fact the rescue committee did not rescue, and could not have rescued. For Hitler had made the annihilation of the Jews his supreme goal, and his armies had been putting his plan into execution meticulously, undisturbed, while the Allies lifted not a finger to rescue Jews, and did not allow the Yishuv to do so.

Ben-Gurion drew the conclusion that he must devote his efforts to making a radical change in his people's situation. The war years must be used to pave the way for a postwar new global order, while also making sure that the peace conference that decided the fates of peoples and countries was persuaded that the solution to the Jewish problem was Palestine. Then, he hoped, his great dream could come true: bringing over the last remnants; bringing about the ingathering of the exiles; and setting up an independent state. In this plan—the Biltmore program—he saw the great and true rescue of the Jewish people. Only a Jewish state would render impossible another devastation in the future.

The Fear of Destruction after the Destruction

Fear of another, future destruction of the Jews was very much alive in Ben-Gurion's mind in 1942 and 1943. This fear derived to a large extent from his perception of anti-Semitism as a universal phenomenon that would worsen as long as the Jewish people were dispersed among the nations. Furthermore, in destroying the Jews in Europe, Hitler was setting an example of how it could be done and inviting others to follow suit. In November this concept was central to a lecture he gave at a Mapai seminar: "The Jews bring anti-Semitism with them. Where there are Jews, there is anti-Semitism." And because of Hitler's example, people who "do not want this affliction named anti-Semitism . . . will rid themselves of it by getting rid of the Jews."

"There are now many in the world who are neither Hitler nor Nazi nor German," he announced in January 1944, "who think that the best way is as follows: 'it's really a shame, the way we treat those Jews, those kikes'—however they choose to call them—'the really important thing is to wipe them out.' Such ideas abound in every nation now"—and, naturally, among the Arabs as well. Therefore in Palestine, too, "our existence is not assured. This time we were saved. A miracle has happened. Rommel has made it as far as Al Alamein . . . and Rommel will be wiped out. . . . But Nuri al-Sa'id [Iraq's prime minister] is still around, and so is the Mufti."

In Ben-Gurion's view, the virus of anti-Semitism attached itself even to the most enlightened of nations, and even in the New World, America. "There is a general rule," said Ben-Gurion to the Zionist Actions Committee, "that if the number of Jews goes over a certain percentage, then the majority does not tolerate them." In the West, he said at a mass meeting in Haifa in August 1944, "where the Jews seem secure, as in America, anti-Semitism is stronger than ever." Those who opposed America's involvement in the war "tend to blame 'Roosevelt the Jew' who got America into the war against the enemy of the Jewish people"; what was more, "unemployment in America may heighten the hatred of the Jews."[23]

As the news from Europe proved increasingly reliable, Ben-Gurion's concern grew for the Jews of Islamic countries—800,000 strong by his count—half of whom were in great danger, especially those in Yemen, Iraq, and Syria. After the war, he told the JAE in March 1943, "these Jews may be the first to be destroyed. . . . [I]n Iraq there is a tradition of massacring minorities [referring to the massacre of the Assyrians or Nestorian Christians after World War I, which the Iraqis had repeated in August 1943], and the very fact that Jews are being destroyed in Germany will facilitate the Iraqis massacring them in their own country."

In July of that year he called for bringing the Jews of Iraq to Palestine in order "to liquidate the Iraqi exile . . . lest they are liquidated Hitler's way." If this occurred, the JAE, which was responsible for rescue, "will not be able to say that we did not know it was bound to happen."[24] He seems to have been applying the lesson that the devastation in Europe had taught him: to undertake first of all a rescue that could still rescue, and preferably by immigration. In the event, the Palmach, the Haganah's striking units, did bring Jews illegally from Syria, on foot.

Ben-Gurion's campaign to establish a state did not arise, therefore, from an obsession or from personal ambition. Simply, the state was to him the one and only rescue. It was a tragedy that none of his plans to set it up before the war and the Holocaust succeeded. Nevertheless, he did not lose heart. On the contrary, in the face of the Holocaust, his resolve only grew stronger to establish the state for the sake of preventing a destruction after the destruction—a specter that occupied an equal place in his mind to the one that was ongoing.

Ben-Gurion Devotes Himself to Rescue

Although Ben-Gurion did argue that only an Allied victory could prevent Hitler from destroying completely those Jews under Nazi occupation, it would be a great error to imagine that he washed his hands of rescue. Not only later scholars have made this mistake; his contemporaries, and even members of his party, made it too. Suffice it to quote Anselm Reiss, a leader of the Association of Polish Jews, who said later, "He did not believe in rescue."[25]

The fact is that even when all courses of action initiated by the JAE proved futile, Ben-Gurion continued working for rescue. He could do so at full steam, however, only after Palestine itself was no longer in danger of Nazi invasion.

In 1942 Rommel's army reached the Egyptian border, and the threat that the entire Middle East would fall into his hands was very real. Yet even during this period, Ben-Gurion repeatedly criticized the Yishuv for being concerned only with its own fate. "There is in me no special feeling for the Jews of Palestine as compared to those in Poland," he said in December 1940. In April 1941 he repeated that the Yishuv was no more important than any other Jewish community, and that its members were not more "privileged" than the Jews of any town in Poland. "Concern for the Yishuv alone is an anti-Zionist attitude," he said. The Yishuv was special only in being "a very large and a very precious deposit of the Jewish people's aspirations." Its importance lay in its role as "the leader of the effort to realize the people's hope for renewed resurrection." If it was destroyed, the people's last hope to return to their land would be lost forever.

Therefore, the accusation that Ben-Gurion preferred the Yishuv over the Jews of Europe has no foundation either in fact or in logic, and directly contradicts his concepts and policy. But it was only after the threat to the Yishuv's existence had faded that the JAE could give all its attention to rescuing Jews from Europe, and it was Ben-Gurion who demanded a study of "any proposal that offers even the slightest hope for rescuing Jews from the Nazi inferno."[26]

Ben-Gurion also continued trying to rally world public opinion and demanding that the Allies take action to rescue Jews. But he had no great hopes in these areas, and he was not the only one to feel that way. In a meeting devoted to this subject, Dobkin said: "All our efforts to rouse public opinion will be useless if they are not followed by actual rescue operations. With respect to this, we have not yet been able to shock anyone into action." Rescue, he explained, meant first of all getting people out of occupied Europe, then obtaining a "transit permit, and ultimately entry to another country," and these things "we are unable to bring off by ourselves."[27]

All the members of the JAE knew that massive rescue could occur only if the Allies made it one of their war aims—just as Hitler did with the destruction. But they were also aware that it was not in their power, nor in that of the Jewish people, to force this agenda on the Allies. Even so, the JAE made the rallying of public opinion in the free world its principal objective. On November 30, 1942, an emergency session of the National Assembly called for a day of fasting, a general strike, and thirty days of mourning, meant not only as an expression of the Yishuv's reaction to the news of the destruction in Europe but as a tactic to achieve the objective of rallying world opinion. Ben-Gurion stood at the forefront of the rescue efforts, doing his utmost; had there been any chance at all to achieve concrete results, he would have made it his only concern.

His keynote speech to the emergency session of the National Assembly was an appeal to the conscience of the free world. He asked it to work to prevent the destruction so that "when the victory of democracy, liberty and justice" arrived, Europe would not be "one large Jewish cemetery." Directly addressing the "three greats"—Churchill, Roosevelt, and Stalin—he asked them "to stand in the breach, with everything you have, and not permit the destruction" of the Jewish people. It was clear to him that only they could stop it. He entreated them to exchange German nationals in their own countries for Jews held in Europe and to warn Germany's leaders and military commanders that they would be held personally responsible for the "Jewish blood" and, on the day of victory, prosecuted on criminal charges.

He saw a particular chance of rescuing the Jews of the countries "not under direct Nazi rule," believing that a strong warning by the U.S. government to the governments of Hungary, Romania, and Bulgaria, containing a threat that whoever assisted in the destruction of Jews would be considered a war criminal and judged accordingly, might have some effect. The responsibility for the destruction, he added, "should be also on the heads of all those who are able to rescue but do not do so, all those who are able to prevent the destruction and will not, and all those who are able to save and will not do so."

Even as Ben-Gurion called for Jews to be rescued to countries outside Palestine, however, he remained convinced that the only real rescue was immigration to Palestine. Thus he demanded that the British government "Cancel the infamous order . . . that Jews from enemy countries are not allowed to return to their homeland. As long as this shameful order is in force, as long as the gates of our country are shut to Jewish refugees—your hands too are red with the Jewish blood that is shed in the Nazi hell."

Unfortunately, this warning could do little. First of all, the most moving, sensational passages of Ben-Gurion's speech were censored by the mandatory government. Second, the press in Britain, the United States, and other countries did not print the speech, which meant that Ben-Gurion's chances of influencing world public opinion were next to nothing.[28]

In early December 1942, Ben-Gurion cabled Felix Frankfurter, as part of his plan to arouse Jewish public opinion, especially in the United States and Britain, in order to spur the Allied governments into rescue action. Ben-Gurion entreated Frankfurter to arouse Jewish public opinion to demand that Roosevelt press the British government "to allow the entry into Palestine of all the children that can be rescued from those countries." He ordered Goldmann in New York, Berl Locker (a member of the JAE) in London, and Sharett in Jerusalem to assist in this action.[29]

Early in December, Ben-Gurion met in Jerusalem with Minister Stanislaw Kot, a representative of Poland's government in exile, and—as will be seen later—asked for help in sending secret agents of the Yishuv into occupied Poland. He also entreated Kot to exhort his people not to assist in the destruction and to request the Vatican to work for the rescue of Poland's Jews.[30]

On December 17, in response to a request from the Polish government in exile, Anthony Eden, the British foreign secretary, in the name of his government and of the governments of the Allies, condemned Nazi atrocities, promising retribution. But this proclamation contained no "firm demand to stop the massacre . . . and nothing in relation to rescue."[31] Indeed, it turned out that the United States and Britain intended to do nothing in the way of rescue. They argued that the destruction would end with their victory, and toward that goal all efforts must be directed. Advocating that the Nazis be punished for crimes against the Jews in particular would not only provoke the Soviet Union, which did not recognize "national" distinctions, but would also confirm the impression in Britain and America that the war in Poland was a Jewish war, thereby harming the war effort. Certainly a great majority of Jews in America, Great Britain, and South Africa were afraid that a forceful demand to make rescue a war aim would intensify anti-Semitism. Weizmann, whom these Jews saw as their leader, was equally intent on softening the Jewish protest and diverting it into secret diplomatic channels, fearful that too vigorous a protest might do more harm than good.

In accordance with Ben-Gurion's general directive that "It is our duty to do everything. By no means should we say in advance that there is no possibility for rescue," such possibilities were discussed at three consecutive JAE meetings during the end of November and first half of December 1942. Following his rule of efficacy, Ben-Gurion suggested "concentrating on two major issues that can be put forward as the demands of the entire Jewish people and receive the endorsement of the enlightened world. These are: (a) stopping the massacre and rescuing children; (b) enabling the Jewish people to make war as a Jewish nation."

He entrusted the main job of rescue to the JAE's secret agencies, certain that it was they and not the clumsy public, partisan committee headed by Gruenbaum that should carry out operations such as the sending of the secret agents (referred to as "commandos" or, later, "paratroopers"), which required skill, speed, and secrecy.[32] Such an operation, however, could be carried out only with the help of the British, and they did not agree to do so until 1943. In 1943 and 1944 the "paratroopers"—thirty-seven Yishuv volunteers—were dropped into occupied Europe by the RAF, with the double mission of freeing British pilots from prison and organizing Jews to carry out rescue operations.

Rescuing Children

The expectation that the rescue of children would be an exception to the Allied indifference toward rescuing Jews rested on several assumptions. The Germans would be glad to be rid of them, since "they are not a work force, yet they eat," as Gruenbaum put it,[33] while the Arabs did not regard them as an immediate threat to the balance of power in Palestine. Finally, the British government would not be able to object, as it usually did, that there were "undercover agents" and "Nazi agents" among them, and therefore would find it difficult to resist a public demand that they be allowed entry into Palestine on humanitarian grounds.

On December 7, 1942, a seeming miracle occurred: the mandatory government notified the JAE, not for publication, that "it allows the entry of 4000 children, to be accompanied by 500 women from Bulgaria, into Palestine." This news set Ben-Gurion's imagination aflame. "This is only the beginning," he told his party's activists on December 8. In his mind's eye he saw in living color all those children flocking from the crumbling Diaspora into liberated Palestine, to become, when they grew up, "the generation of state-builders."

On the ninth a report from Dobkin gave the JAE good reason to believe that it might be possible to bring in 5000 children who already had their certificates. What was more, within a day or two the JAE seemed to be getting clear signals from the mandatory government that the immigration of children might be doubled or even trebled.

Overnight Ben-Gurion's vision became a war plan, and the JAE subcommittee was given the responsibility for "the absorption of the children and for their welfare"—Ben-Gurion, Kaplan, Gruenbaum, Dobkin, Moshe Shapira, and Dov Joseph—met on December 14[34] and discussed the immigration of children from the Balkan countries, the plan for absorbing them, and the necessary financing. It also discussed the "Teheran children," about 1000 Jewish children, mostly orphans, belonging to families who had escaped from Poland into the Soviet Union after the German invasion. They and some 800 adults accompanying the Polish army of General Anders had arrived between April and August 1942 in Iran.[35]

These hopes arose because the British announcement had led Ben-Gurion and the other JAE members to believe—mistakenly, as it turned out—that the number of immigration certificates for children would be dependent on the JAE's capacity for bringing them over and absorbing them, and that the British government would help the JAE in doing this. They also allowed themselves to believe that the British would not consider the children as part of the White Paper quota of 29,000. Thus toward the end of 1942 a kind of general, undefined plan for an immigration of children, known as the "Twenty-nine Thousand Plan," was born. It was, unhappily, only an illusion.

On February 3, 1943, Colonial Secretary Oliver Stanley stated in Parliament that "Some weeks ago the Government of Palestine agreed to admit from Bulgaria 4,000 Jewish children, with 500 adults to accompany them on the journey. . . . Steps are being taken immediately to organize the necessary transport, but I must point out that the practical difficulties involved are likely to be considerable"—as though the British government itself had not had a hand in creating them. Stanley went on to say that the government would admit into Palestine "Jewish children, with a proportion of adults," up to the "29,000 still available under the White Paper."

Asked "Is there any necessity still to preserve the numerical limit laid down in the White Paper?" Stanley answered: "It is essential, from the point of view of stability in the Middle East at the present time, that that arrangement should be strictly adhered to."

On February 7, the JAE published its reaction, drafted by Ben-Gurion, expressing both gratitude and protest: gratitude for the certificates, protest against the arbitrary White Paper. But the mandatory censorship struck out the protest, and only the gratitude was published in the press in Palestine.[36]

Sharett, then in London, was quick to discern the British government's deception: the colonial secretary's statement had not announced a new immigration policy, but only made public a previous secret announcement. Furthermore, since the children's immigration would be deducted from the White Paper quota, there was no call for a dramatic statement in the Commons, except to mislead public opinion. And finally, the government had given the false impression that it was responding to the JAE's appeal to rescue "especially children, and first of all children." But in practice, Sharett predicted, this apparently magnanimous gesture would have the effect not only of preventing the immigration of adults but of subjecting the immigration of children to so many delays that even that would never actually occur. And so it was. Due to a series of bureaucratic obstacles, no certificates were ever used, and the entire plan for the children's immigration came to nothing.

The hope that children would be a "special case" had thus been dashed, and with it a second hope—that a children's immigration would prompt a more general rescue. Yet, even though this outcome seemed to put an end to any further rescue efforts, Ben-Gurion and his colleagues at the JAE worked as hard as they could to bring off four further rescue attempts: the "Transnistria plan," the "Slovakia plan," the "Europa plan," and "goods for blood."

These plans were ransom programs involving attempts to bribe various Nazi officials to allow Jews in Central Europe to emigrate. They were based on the belief that corrupt SS and Gestapo officers would be ready to trade Jewish lives for money. This belief, however, did not take into account the fact that "the Final Solution" was as important to Hitler as winning the war, and—in its last stages—even more important.

The result of all the JAE efforts is best summed up by Professor Yehuda Bauer: "Did the [JAE] leaders do their utmost for rescue? Could they have done more? It seems the answer to both questions is Yes. It is clear today that the leadership, and especially the leading trio—Ben-Gurion, Kaplan, and Sharett—did indeed make very great efforts as soon as they learned of the systematic destruction. . . . Did the Yishuv leadership leap to respond? The answer is Yes. What more could they have done? They could have raised more funds." That is, there was no chance at all for mass rescue, but if more funds had been raised—especially in America, for financing Joint operations in Europe—more individuals and small groups could have been saved. This evaluation is supported by other leading Holocaust historians.[37]

In summation it can be said that Zionist rescue efforts were constrained first by the smallness of the Yishuv. At the outbreak of World War II, September 1939, the Yishuv was 474,600 strong. It grew to 565,500 at the end of 1944. It had no army, no navy, and no air force.

British policies and restrictions on Jewish immigration to Palestine further constrained rescue efforts. The only effective rescue open to Zionism and the Yishuv was to bring Jews out of Nazi Europe into Palestine, where they could care for them. However, the White Paper of May 1939 restricted Jewish immigration to a mere 75,000 in the five-year period ending in April 1944. At the end of 1942—when Hitler's death machinery moved into high gear—there was left in Palestine room for only 29,000 more "legal" Jewish immigrants, i.e., refugees, of all ages. This quota spelled the scope of Zionist rescue.

Finally, Allied war aims and policies ruled out any massive rescue plans. The Allies banned on contact with the enemy or transferring funds to them, and insisted that the only real rescue would be an Allied victory; therefore every resource was to be devoted to this supreme objective. In practice this meant the relegation of Jewish rescue, by either direct or indirect Allied action, to low, and even very low priority.

In the race between VE-Day and Auschwitz, the latter prevailed, and the JAE and the Yishuv could do nothing about it.

CHAPTER ONE

THE CHARGE SHEET

AMONG THE PLAGUES Hitler inflicted on the Jewish people should be counted the fratricidal self-hatred that eats at them like a malignancy: an ever-growing search for the guilty within their own ranks. This teaches us that all Hitler's victories were temporary, except what he did to the Jewish people.

Although Ben-Gurion was blessed with amazing foresight, it is hard to imagine that he could ever have foreseen the accusations leveled against him today. Even when only the Jewish Agency Executive (JAE) or the Zionist movement is mentioned, it is clear that the finger is being pointed at him, for it was he, as chairman of the Jewish Agency and the Zionist Executive in Jerusalem and as a leader of Mapai, who stood at the head of the Yishuv and was nominally responsible for its failings during the Holocaust years. Even some who acknowledge his greatness and unique contribution to the Jewish people's survival argue that the Holocaust is a "black blot" in his biography.

If we look at the debate over Ben-Gurion and the Holocaust as a public trial, the prosecution represents a wall-to-wall coalition of both right and left: ultra-Orthodox, traditional religionists, laypeople, Zionists, anti-Zionists, post-Zionists, ordinary citizens, academics, Jews, and non-Jews; flaming heretics, Western leftist intellectuals including fanatic partisans of the Soviet Union, a Hasidic rabbi, a leftist British playwright, a German historian, and many others—all with their own motives.

Despite their diversity, the accusers all make similar charges, which can be grouped into two main counts: (a) collaboration, active or passive, with the Nazis; (b) indifference, lack of empathy, and even arrogance and contempt toward Diaspora Jews—the destined Holocaust victims—and consequent failure to try to rescue them. These sentiments are said to have derived from Zionism's classic attitude of "condemnation of the Diaspora," the foundation of Zionist doctrine.

Regardless of their political coloration, the different charges stem from one central accusation, made by ultra-Orthodox rabbis, which appears over and over as proof of Ben-Gurion and the JAE's guilt. It is best, then, to begin with this charge, which was articulated forcefully by Rabbi Michael Dov-Ber Weissmandel, the principal figure in what was known as the "working group" of Slovakia.*

Born in 1903 in Debrecen, Hungary, Weissmandel was sent by his father, the town's *shohet* (sacramental slaughterer) to the yeshiva in Sered, and then on to Rabbi Shmuel David Unger's yeshiva in Nitra, both in Slovakia. His outstanding talents attracted Rabbi Unger's immediate love and attention: He made Weissmandel his principal assistant, traveled with him in 1935 to Palestine, and in January 1937 married him to his daughter Bracha Rachel. Weissmandel traveled frequently to visit with the great rabbis of Poland and Lithuania; his special interest in medieval Hebrew manuscripts drew him three times to the Bodleian at Oxford. The yeshiva at Nitra was his home.

The Nazi rail transport of Slovakia's Jews to Auschwitz began on March 26, 1942, with a shipment of girls aged sixteen and up. As the shipments continued and rumors concerning the true function of Auschwitz abounded, Weissmandel, somewhat belatedly, joined the working group (euphemism for rescue committee), about ten Jewish activists who had come together as a cell within the "Jewish Center" (generally known by its German name *Judenrat*) imposed by the Nazis on the Jews. Although self-appointed, this group can be considered the true Jewish leadership in Slovakia. When necessary, it intervened directly with the SS officers in charge of "Jewish affairs." Composed of

---

* Under Nazi pressure, an independent Slovakia was established on Mar. 14, 1939, by Slovak nationalists.

religious and lay Jews, Zionists and non-Zionists, the working group was united in its dedication to the cause of rescue. The ultra-Orthodox Weissmandel's decision to join this predominantly Zionist group can be attributed to the group's guiding spirit, the heroic Gisi Fleischmann—a devout Zionist, but also Rabbi Unger's cousin and thus Weissmandel's relative. Together they soon became the group's joint leadership.

The working group's rescue strategy focused mainly on bribes, bringing them into close contact with the SS officers and their Slovak henchmen. This strategy eminently suited Weissmandel, for no one believed more strongly that bribery and ransom were the Jews' safest defense and the only way of saving themselves. In joining the group, he brought to this strategy vastly enhanced imagination and momentum.

Thus in July 1942 Weissmandel conceived a rescue plan that came to be known as the Slovakia Plan (or, in Palestine, the Rabbis' Plan): In return for $50,000 in bribes paid to SS officer Count Dieter Wisliceny, then in charge of Jewish affairs in Slovakia, and through him to his SS superiors, transports of Slovak Jews to Auschwitz would come to a stop. And in fact in October 1942, after 60,000 of Slovakia's Jews had been shipped to Auschwitz, the transports did stop. It seemed that Weissmandel and the group could give themselves credit for the rescue of the rest, generally put at 25–30,000.

Emboldened by this assumed success, Weissmandel went a quantum step further, incorporating the Slovakia Plan in the far bolder Europa Plan: In return for more bribes, to be paid to the same Wisliceny, all transports, to all death camps, would come to a halt. Not losing a moment, the working group started negotiations with Wisliceny that same November. By March 1943, according to Weissmandel, an agreement was reached: in return for $2–3 million, negotiations would be held on stopping the entire mass murder of the Jews, thus saving about 2.5 million from cruel and certain death. Wisliceny's one condition for putting this program into action was a down payment of $200,000 cash, in U.S. dollars, to be paid to him by that August.[1]

In Weissmandel's book *Min Hametzar*[2] (From the Straits), published posthumously in 1960 by disciples and admirers in New York, he lays out a detailed charge that his Europa Plan was deliberately shot down by the Zionists. This charge was taken up by anti-Zionist and post-Zionist historians as the ultimate proof of Zionist-Nazi common interests. They asserted that the rescue of Europe's Jews was possible, but that the JAE and its agencies failed to implement it for ideological reasons.

There are three protagonists in Weissmandel's tale: the good guy—himself—dedicated entirely to the work of rescue; and two bad guys—Saly Mayer, former conservative president of the Union of Swiss Jewish Communities and, at the time of the Europa Plan, the Swiss representative of the American Joint Distribution Committee (the great American Jewish philanthropic organization, known as JDC or the Joint), and Nathan Schwalb (Dror), the delegate of the Zionist Pioneer Movement to Geneva. According to Weissmandel, Schwalb put pressure on the Joint, the World Jewish Congress, and the JAE not to send the down-payment money to the working group and thereby destroyed the plan.

In his book, Weissmandel supports this factitious accusation by quoting from a letter he claims Schwalb wrote that came to his notice. He admits that he quotes this letter from memory, in New York after the war: "The letter was written to Schwalb's cronies in Pressburg [Bratislava in German] . . . and it stands before my eyes as if I had read it over a hundred and one times." It had the following to say: Using the opportunity of a messenger, Schwalb writes to his Zionist crowd that they "must bear in mind at all times *the most vital and essential,* what must always be our beacon, that in the end the Allies are bound to win the war. They will establish a new world order, as they did after the first world war." No price was too great to pay, Schwalb supposedly wrote, in order that "The Land of Israel [Palestine] should turn into the State of Israel . . . and if we don't make sacrifices, by what right shall we sit at the table [of the postwar peace conference]? If this is so, it is folly, even arrogance, on our part to ask the Gentiles [the Allies] who spill their blood [in the war against Hitler] to allow the bringing in . . . of money to the country of their enemies *to protect our blood,* because we shall have the country [Palestine] only thanks to blood. As for you, my *pals, atem tajlu,* for which purpose I provide you, by means of this same messenger, with black [smuggled] money."

Weissmandel confesses that the meaning of the Hebrew *atem tay-elu** (you take a walk) escaped him, and it was "days and weeks" before its true meaning dawned on him: "For the Zionists a 'walk' means rescue; in other words, you, the [Zionist] crowd, fifteen or twenty strong, take a walk outside Slovakia and save your souls; as for the rest, their blood—the blood of all the women, all the old and all the babies feeding on their mothers' breasts—*will buy us our land* [i.e., state]. Therefore, to save the people's lives it is a crime to bring money into enemy territory, but to save you, beloved and friends, here I am, providing you with black money."[3] In short, Europe's Jewry "is the blood, the sacrifice, that will make Palestine the patrimony of Zionism."†

In quoting the letter Weissmandel thus makes two other grave charges: (1) The argument that no money can be transferred into Nazi-occupied territory because of the Allied ban is only a Zionist pretext. (2) The Jewish Agency is virtually conducting a "selection" of its own: the young Zionists to live, all others to die as sacrifices for the state.

Weissmandel's book ran into many editions, becoming a standard anti-Zionism, anti-Israel work in the ultra-Orthodox canon. From there his charges reverberated through the Jewish world, making their way, by translation and quotation, into anti-Zionist libraries. This repetition of Weissmandel's accusation, comments Holocaust scholar Yehuda Bauer, is "explicable only in psychological terms."[4]

Similar accusations were made by other Orthodox rabbis. The gist of the ultra-Orthodox arguments was that the nationalists (that is, the Zionists) had abandoned the old way of God's will, which was that throughout the generations Jews had saved themselves from the

---

* "Tayelu" in phonetic spelling in English.
† This accusation provided the ultra-Orthodox Rabbi Scheinfeld with the opportunity for a pun about the Goods for Blood Plan (see Ch. 12): Eichmann proposed "Goods for Blood," the Zionist leaders answered with "Blood for State."

boundless hatred of the Gentiles by means of humility. Zionists, they asserted, had not tried to rescue the Jews of Europe because they had determined that they needed the spilled blood of the Jewish masses of Europe to awaken remorse in the Gentiles that would engender support for a Jewish state. Because of their contempt for Diaspora Jews, instead of spending money on the ransom plans, the Zionists in the JAE and the Yishuv spent it on land and settlements in Palestine (this charge was later taken up by academics and leftists). Finally, the ultra-Orthodox charged that the Zionists in the rescue committee in Hungary, in return for their own safety, had deliberately deceived the Jews of Hungary into believing that the transports were heading to labor camps, thus delivering them instead to the death camps.

Among the ultra-Orthodox accusers, the most fanatical was the Satmar Hasidic rabbi Joel Teitelbaum, who from his residence in Williamsburg, Brooklyn, pontificated to his followers in America, Israel, and Europe. Teitelbaum—who had been saved from Auschwitz by Dr. Rudolf Kastner, the Zionist leader of Hungarian Jewry during the Holocaust—wrote: "For their [the Zionists'] hands are stained with blood, and they are the reason for the terrible disaster of the killing of six million Jews." His son, Rabbi Moshe Teitelbaum, writes of the "Zionist emissaries" of "the other side" (meaning that of Satan), "the impure who defile the entire world." It was these "impure" who, on Satan's errand, in exchange for "the false, deceptive redemption," had "snatched" away the chance for true redemption that had appeared "after our brethren, the children of Israel, had suffered terrible troubles inflicted upon them by the German despot." He means, writes Holocaust historian Dr. Dina Porat, "that the suffering caused by Hitler signified, in fact, the birth pangs of the Messiah, the beginning of the redemption, whose coming was delayed by Satan with the help of his Zionist emissaries. Thus secular Zionism is identified with the devil in open defiance of the Creator."[5]

Another ultra-Orthodox rabbi went a step further and likened Ben-Gurion—the staunchest champion of the Jewish state—to Hitler. Just as Ben-Gurion (so he claimed) was "driven by hatred of Judaism . . . an irrational urge with him, . . . Hitler, too, according to many historians, was motivated by irrational hatred of Jewry."[6]

In fact, however, the Schwalb letter is entirely a figment of Weissmandel's imagination. Schwalb's letters from this period in Geneva are extant. They demonstrate that, despite his doubts about the practicability of Weissmandel's rescue plans, he presented them to the JAE, exhibiting the utmost trust and confidence in Weissmandel. As early as December 4, 1942, in a letter to the JAE, he recommended Weissmandel's Europa Plan in the following terms: "There is a possibility of rendering void, annulling or . . . minimizing the persecutory expulsion in all of [occupied] Europe . . . [from] Poland to France and to Greece" through Wisliceny, "who has already shown his competence" in Slovakia. Weissmandel and his colleagues "inform [us] he is due to be promoted" to be in charge "of all [transports from] southern-eastern Europe" to Auschwitz, and "will be in very close contact with the chief officer [Himmler]." Weissmandel and his colleagues "also add" that Wisliceny "was as good as his word [in the past], fulfilling his commitments down to the last iota."

If Schwalb had initially doubted "whether to open negotiations" with the SS, "and whether there was reason to believe [the SS's] promises, etc.," he wrote the JAE, all these doubts were now dispelled. In presenting the Europa Plan, he emphasized "that the deal in Slovakia proved" that Wisliceny and his superiors "are nonetheless trustworthy." Schwalb ended his letter by urging Jerusalem to state its position, concluding, "needless to tell you with what anxiety I await your opinion."

In March 1943 Weissmandel broke the news of his "arrangement" with Wisliceny to Schwalb in a letter that Schwalb described as "hysterical, written half in rabbinical Hebrew, half in Yiddish." Informing him of Wisliceny's stipulation that without a down payment of $200,000 by August, he would renew the transports and the Europa Plan would be canceled, the Bratislava group beseeched the JAE, the American Jewish Congress, and the Joint to rush them the ransom money, particularly the down payment.

On March 10 Schwalb wrote the JAE in Jerusalem: "Had we been then [December 1942] able" to pay the money demanded, "perhaps we would have been able to lessen the catastrophe" in Poland as well as in other countries. "We must therefore concentrate on the major issue [Europa Plan] and do our utmost on its behalf, for if it comes through we will save so many lives, and if, Heaven forbid, it fails, primarily because of lack of means, then we will lose all. . . . I have the utmost faith that the Yishuv, its ruling bodies, and American Jewry (despite all) will, at least now, after three years of silence, turn to action. This is the main thing."

Schwalb says that he also sent Weissmandel's March letter "as an SOS to Moshe Sharett." A week later Sharett phoned Schwalb in Geneva to ask: "Nathan, did you understand his [Weissmandel's] Hebrew? I have to say I didn't. However, I can say that I well understood its contents and I well understood his use of horrible words, for horrible it is going to be if we don't promptly come to his help.'"[7]

Quite contrary to Weissmandel's accusations, then, Schwalb had become Weissmandel's and Fleischmann's enthusiastic champion.[8] He was in fact trying to get the bribe money, and he was tireless and unrelenting both in carrying out aid and rescue work himself and in prompting others to do it, including Saly Mayer, whom he pressured to send the bribe money to Bratislava.[9]

Today we know for a fact that the discontinuance of transports from Slovakia was due to a change in the Nazi timetable—Auschwitz-bound shipments of Greek Jews were given a higher priority—and that Wisliceny had in fact set the condition for the negotiations entirely on his own. In August 1943 he was ordered by his superiors to break off all contacts with the working group. What is more, research and documents prove[10] that, despite being skeptical of the plan's legitimacy, by August 9 the JAE had sent at least $85,000 and probably even $132,000 of the required $200,000, on Schwalb's recommendation. Initially, it had been agreed that the Jewish Agency's share of this total would be $50,000 to $100,000—this remains unclear—and the balance would be paid by the Joint. But in fact the Joint paid out only $53,000, through Saly Mayer—whom Weissmandel attacks ferociously—while the JAE paid $132,000, through its rescue mission in Istanbul, which it had established between November 1942 and January 1943.[11]

The reason Mayer gave so little was that he was out of money. The JDC had allotted him a total of $235,000 for 1942, of which $105,295 was preempted by the Swiss government's demand for money to support Jewish refugees sheltering in Switzerland. The balance, $129,705, was all he had to offer, in this first year of industrial mass murder, to Jews in Romania, Hungary, Slovakia, Croatia, Italy, and France. According to Bauer, Mayer "had to bear the burden of this knowledge virtually alone. He could not admit how inadequate his funds were, even to Schwalb."[12] In fact, Mayer paid his share of the Slovakia plan bribe money not out of charitable dollars from the Joint, but in Swiss francs that he had raised from Swiss Jews.

Weissmandel's invention of the letter can be understood on religious grounds: A pious believer like him is unable to shake his fist at heaven but finds it easy to blame heretic Jews, his long-standing enemies. But there is perhaps a psychological explanation as well. Weissmandel must have carried to his grave a measure of mental torment and feelings of guilt, for he himself had been rescued from a train to Auschwitz, leaving his wife and five children to meet their deaths in the gas chambers.

On September 5, 1944, Weissmandel and his wife and five children—four girls and a boy—were captured in a roundup in Nitra and taken to Sered labor camp, which was also an assembly area for transports to Auschwitz. On the pretext that Weissmandel was an irreplaceable member of its economic committee, however, the remainder of the working group was able to arrange a "leave" for him, and he left for Bratislava. But this reprieve was short. On September 28, he and another member of the working group were summoned by telephone to the office of SS *Hauptsturmführer* Alois Brunner, who was now in charge of all Jewish affairs in Slovakia, to discuss social work at the Sered camp. Although they smelled a rat, the two decided to report on time. On arrival they were put under arrest, and that night the Nazis and their Slovak collaborators arrested 1800 Jews, including the members of the working group.

The next day, September 29, the whole lot were shipped to Sered. On the 30th, a shipment of 1860 Jews of all ages was on its way to Auschwitz. It was the first of eleven shipments totaling 12,306 Jews, of whom 7936 were destined for Auschwitz, 2732 for Sachsenhausen, and 1638 for Theresienstadt.

Still in Sered, Weissmandel made his last attempt to persuade Brunner that negotiations—clearly a euphemism for ransom or bribes—were the best resolution for all concerned. This, at least, is the story as told by Dr. Abraham Fuchs of Jerusalem, Weissmandel's admirer, interpreter, and biographer. According to his *Karati veEin Oneh* (The Unheeded Cry), Weissmandel told Brunner that since the war was about to end in a crushing Nazi defeat, Brunner would be wise to prepare for himself a solid defense, by hindering the expulsion of Slovakia's Jews. Weissmandel also promised him a fat sum of money in a Swiss bank. Incredible as it may seem, this last talk lasted for two hours. At one moment, in the heat of argument, Weissmandel, for emphasis, struck Brunner's desk with his fist. In the end, before putting him on a train to Auschwitz, Brunner had Weissmandel photographed from twenty-two different angles, to ensure his capture in case he escaped.

Before getting on the train to Auschwitz, Fuchs's version continues, Weissmandel passed around metal files that he had hidden in a loaf of bread, advising those close to him to saw off the locks of the boxcar doors. After "hard soul-searching," Weissmandel himself sawed the handle off the door, jumped out of the moving train, and under cover of darkness made good his escape, leaving behind his wife and five children.

It is not at all clear from Fuchs's story how Weissmandel and others could have sawed off the outside door locks. Surely, the Germans did not lock the doors from within. Indeed, during the 1950s Professor Yeshayahu Jelinek of Ben-Gurion University in Beersheba, himself a Slovak and a survivor of the Holocaust, interviewed some of the other participants in Weissmandel's escape. Jelinek offers an altogether different, and in certain respects more plausible, version: that the files were prepared by young Jews employed in the locksmith's shop of the Sered labor camp. They hid the blades in loaves of bread, one of which they gave to Weissmandel, who arrived in Sered only a short time before being put on the cattle train. They knew that the boxcars were made of wood, and their escape plan was to saw a hole in the wooden floor, through which it was safe to drop to the ground when the train, climbing the mountains, slowed down on the numerous steep uphill curves. According to Jelinek, the young organizers of the escape agreed with the elders remaining on the train that Weissmandel's escape was vital so that his rescue efforts could continue; his escape could mean the salvation of many. Weissmandel made them promise that they would drop his youngest child through the hole after him, a promise they did not keep, in order to ensure the success of his escape. He made his way to a "bunker" in Bratislava, a hospice for escaping Jews, and was saved.[13]

From his bunker Weissmandel established contact with Kastner in Budapest. Much has been made of "Kastner's rescue train," which in August 1944 carried 1685 Jews, among them Joel Teitelbaum (the Satmar rabbi) and his family, from Hungary to Bergen-Belsen, instead of Auschwitz, and from there to Switzerland. But little is known of "Kastner's rescue truck," which also gathered handpicked Jews—one of whom was Weissmandel—in Slovakia and Austria, and brought them to Switzerland on April 1, 1945, four days before the capture of Bratislava by the Red Army. In both instances Kastner and Schwalb cooperated by telephone (see Chapter 9).

In Switzerland, Weissmandel was stricken by a heart attack and spent a long time in the hospital. In 1946 he emigrated to the United States, where he reestablished the Nitra Yeshiva in Mount Kisco, New York. It was there—that is, after the Holocaust, as Jelinek notes—that his hatred of Zionism intensified. He died from his heart condition on November 29, 1957.

Whether or not he was the initiator of the escape, Weissmandel could not have jumped off the train with his entire family. But the fact that he survived and his wife and children went up in smoke was to haunt him for the rest of his not very long life. It is conceivable that putting the blame for the circumstances of his survival on his heretical adversaries gave him some relief. This explanation is supported by the fact that, before the loss of his family, Weissmandel, who was a latecomer to the working group, had not hesitated to cooperate with the Zionists in it[14]—not even after he supposedly saw the fictitious Schwalb letter, which he says occurred at a time when the group was at the height of its activity.

Clearly the strongest tie between Weissmandel and the group, to which he was a latecomer, was Gisi Fleischmann, regarded by many as its real heroine. Weissmandel refers to her in *Min Hametzar* as "the important Mrs. Fleischmann." Arguably, he would not have joined this group, with its Zionist preponderance, had Fleischmann, herself a Zionist, not been a leading member. However, Fleischmann was caught by a Gestapo agent while writing a letter, probably to Schwalb or Mayer, and also taken to Sered, on October 15. The Nazis said they would let her stay there if she revealed names and addresses of Jews hiding in Bratislava. She refused and on October 17 was deported to Auschwitz, never to return.[15] Once she was gone, Weissmandel's last (if not only) connection with Zionism was gone too, and there was nothing left to restrain him from attacking it as bitterly as he could.

But why, of all Zionists, did he make Schwalb the target of his hatred of Zionism? A simple answer could be that he had no other firsthand acquaintance with an important Zionist functionary. He had met Schwalb before the war, at a conference in Bratislava called by the Orthodox Agudat Israel Party that discussed the situation in Europe and the scarcity of entry permits to Palestine, and Schwalb was the only Zionist official he had ever directly cooperated with. In short, Schwalb was in the forefront of his memory, so to speak, handy and within reach.

Another answer might be that, after he jumped from the train, Weissmandel could have been led to think that if Schwalb had furnished the down payment to Wisliceny in time, his family would be safe and alive. Some hints in Fuchs's biography suggest such a hypothesis.

Fuchs claims it was impossible, even for a religious Jew like himself, to penetrate the wall of secrecy that enveloped Weissmandel's private life. Perhaps this is why Fuchs is so vague and tight-lipped in regard to both Weissmandel's escape and his new family in Mount Kisco, New York. Fuchs only hints that Weissmandel, having left his wife and children on the Auschwitz-bound train, "experienced excruciating pangs of conscience," and that "the war's horrors and his despair . . . which gnawed at his mental and physical health" were responsible for his heart condition.[16] Thus Fuchs enfolds these aspects of Weissmandel's life in mystery and contradiction.

It is, however, precisely because Fuchs does not reveal the ages of Weissmandel's children that one is readily led to imagine a close connection between their ages, the incessant self-torture inflicted by Weissmandel's pangs of conscience, the secrecy that enshrouded his new family in Mount Kisco, and his blaming Zionism for the Holocaust.

On October 3 or 10, 1944, when he boarded the Auschwitz train, Weissmandel had been married for seven years and eight months. His eldest daughter could not have been more than seven, the second oldest six, and the rest mere toddlers; his only son must have been a baby. His last sight of the mother embracing her babies could never have disappeared from his mind's eye—particularly when he was looking at his new children, the oldest of whom could not have been more than nine when Weissmandel died in 1957.

His friends wrote in their preface to *Min Hametzar* that Weissmandel had written "this book of his in blood and tears, each line he filled with tears . . . mourning in his agony toddlers and babies feeding on their mothers' breasts, fathers and mothers," and all others slain and cremated. Weissmandel himself was far more explicit. On his deathbed he wrote that since his escape he had been praying, "Now, O Lord, take away my life, for it is better for me to die than to live" (Jonah 4:3). So resolute were he and God both in this respect that a virtual standoff, or perhaps tug of war, occurred. The good Lord, on one side, "doing his part, gave me a second life and brought me all the way hither, I [on the other side] clung to the serious heart ailment that beset me." His friends, as they indicate in the preface, believed that at his death heaven showed him compassion: "Providence took away his pen from his hand on the sad day [on which he died] to relieve his soul from its agony."[17]

Perhaps the ever-present image of the mother and children on the Auschwitz-bound train, all the more vivid against the background of the new mother and babies in Mount Kisco, amplified and deepened the guilt and pain that settled in his heart, while also bolstering his belief that, had it not been for the Zionists, his Europa Plan would have paid off and his wife and children would be alive. It stands to reason, therefore, that it was Weissmandel's need to vindicate himself that dictated to him the imaginary letter he ascribed to Schwalb, which "proves" that the Zionists were after a state at any price, even that of "the blood of all the men, women, the old and babies feeding on their mothers' breasts." This image of suckling babies recurs frequently.

It must be said, finally, that Weissmandel did not concoct his slander against Schwalb and Zionism out of wickedness or malice. He wrote *Min Hametzar* after the establishment of the state of Israel in May 1948. There was no doubt in his mind that this was an act of blatant defiance of God's will. Looking back at the Holocaust and its aftermath, and fully aware of the argument that the UN resolution that called for the establishment of a Jewish state in Palestine was an expression of Christian guilt as well as a wish to expiate past persecutions of Jews by Christendom, he saw what he believed to be a logical chain of cause and effect: The Zionists shed Jewish blood to deepen Christian remorse, in order to achieve the state as compensation. In this he was not unlike a historian who reviews the past from the point of view of his beliefs and values. With one difference: Weissmandel did write his history with the blood of his heart.

Be that as it may, Schwalb's "letter" became the symbol of the selfless, unrelenting representative of tormented Jewry putting his life on the line to rescue the Jews of Europe, while being forced to contend with a Labor Zionism that preferred a state over rescue. Apparently, Weissmandel put in Schwalb's mouth words that, in his mind, he heard Ben-Gurion saying. Porat says that the presumed Zionist attitude expressed in this letter as quoted by Weissmandel reflects the outlook of ultra-Orthodox circles that consolidated after the war. They believed that "secularism, the mother of all sins, leads to nationalism [i.e., Zionism], [and] the striving to attain national statehood leads, in turn, to the spilling of the blood of the Jews who are not needed to attain this goal."[18] In short, Zionism abandoned the Jews of Europe for the sake of a state; and Weissmandel's false accusation served as an eternal source of "proof" of Zionist-Nazi collaboration. Subsequently, this accusation found many supporters on the anti-Zionist left, who shared with the ultra-Orthodox a penchant for blaming Ben-Gurion.

The entire process of politicizing the Holocaust began in 1942, with the accusation that the JAE and the Yishuv were not doing enough to rescue the Jews of Europe. It was voiced in Mapai, in the Yishuv's rescue mission in Istanbul, in parties of the Zionist coalition, and among the opposition. This accusation, however, essentially represented the call to do more than is normal in any constituency; it reflected the characteristic conflict between field and headquarters.

On the Zionist left, Meir Ya'ari, head of the Marxist HaShomer HaTzair movement, in a January 1943 article titled "Facing the Disaster," criticized the JAE for not making public before November 23, 1942—the date this news was first officially published in Palestine—the information that Europe's Jews were subject to systematic destruction. Ya'ari claimed the JAE had obtained this information prior to that date, apparently referring to a cable from Dr. Gerhardt Riegner, the Jewish World Congress representative in Geneva, to Rabbi Stephen Wise in New York. Riegner informed Wise that in Hitler's headquarters a plan had been discussed according to which "three and a half to four millions should after deportation and concentration in east be at one blow exterminated in order resolve once and for all Jewish question in Europe." This was the first indication that the Final Solution had been discussed at the Wannsee Conference in January 1942. The wire was sent on August 8, 1942, but its delivery to Wise was delayed by the Department of State until August 28. A copy sent to the JAE in Jerusalem by Dr. Richard Lichtheim, its representative at Geneva, was met with disbelief, and Lichtheim was asked to confirm his information.

This accusation that the JAE had concealed the news of the death camps retained its currency in later years. But this secrecy had a purpose. At first there was uncertainty as to whether the information about systematic destruction was reliable and a desire to avoid unnecessary or unjustified panic. Second, the rescue plans that the JAE was developing required total secrecy (which in fact was demanded by the JAE's rescue emissaries in Istanbul) in order not to provoke the Arabs.

Publicizing a plan to bring into Palestine 29,000 children, for example, would have caused an uproar, if not an uprising, for even young children would grow up to bear arms in the struggle over Palestine.

As for the JAE's chairman, Ya'ari went on: "In the meantime, Ben-Gurion settled in Washington to deal with the Jewish army and the Biltmore plan. . . . What has happened to the Zionist movement? Have we lost all morals and conscience?"[19]

And on the Zionist right, amid news of the destruction of the Jews of Hungary, the Revisionist Party's organ published these words: "What will the Yishuv in Palestine do at this final hour for Hungarian Jewry, watching the remnants of these people struggling against the ferocious waves pulling them into the abyss? We have grown tired of calling and demanding time and again, morning and evening, for days and years, to a bumbling leadership interested in obscuring our struggle and distracting public opinion with false rumors of miscellaneous rescue plans. With these tactics the leadership is helping lead our Hungarian brethren to destruction. Will the Yishuv, even at this very late hour, when death stares from the eyes of the last of our brethren, be fooled by this anesthetizing tactic of the official leadership?"[20]

The rightists' charge that the "bumbling leadership" aided the destruction of Hungarian Jewry became more vociferous over the years. In 1953 Malkiel Gruenwald, a survivor from Hungary living in Jerusalem, published pamphlets in which he accused Dr. Rudolf Kastner of collaborating with the Nazis and called for his execution. Kastner—a lawyer, journalist, and activist in the Ichud movement, Mapai's international organization—had served as head of the rescue committee in Hungary. His crowning achievements had been sending 18,000 Hungarian Jews to labor camps in Austria, which eventually saved their lives, and getting a train carrying 1685 Jews sent to Bergen-Belsen and then to Switzerland in August 1944. Taking up the charges made by the ultra-Orthodox, Gruenwald, a religious man himself, asserted that in order to retain their privileged position—as members of the Hungarian rescue committee they were allowed a certain freedom of movement, were immune from "regular" arrests and being seized for shipment to Auschwitz, had more to eat, and so forth—Kastner and his colleagues lulled Hungarian Jewry into believing that they were being transported to labor camps. In other words, they knowingly delivered their brethren to Eichmann and the death camps. Had they been alerted to the truth, the accusation went, the Hungarian Jews would have resisted, rebelled, and made a smoothly operating destruction impossible.

With the consent of Kastner, then a senior official in the Trade and Industry Ministry, the attorney general of Israel pressed charges of criminal libel against Gruenwald. In the subsequent trial at the district court in Jerusalem, Gruenwald was defended by Shmuel Tamir, a young lawyer striving to achieve prominence in Herut, the rightist party founded by Menahem Begin late in 1948 as successor to the Revisionist Party (which had broken away in 1935 from the World Zionist Organization), in preparation for Israel's first Knesset elections in February 1949.

Gruenwald won. The judge, Dr. Benjamin Halevi, cleared him of the more serious charges, thereby finding Kastner guilty of collaboration with the Nazis, indirectly responsible for the mass murder of Hungary's Jews by preparing the ground for their extermination. Halevi stated that Kastner had "sold his soul to Satan." He found Gruenwald guilty of some minor offenses and sentenced him to pay symbolic damages of one Israeli lira ($1.80). Kastner appealed, and in January 1958 the supreme court reversed Halevi's judgment, finding that Kastner's hands were clean, and that he had in fact done the most he could under the horrendous circumstances under which he worked. But Gruenwald's symbolic fine remained unchanged. Although Kastner was ultimately victorious, the effect of Halevi's sentence—even though he later publicly regretted his phrase "sold his soul to Satan"—left an indelible impression on public opinion.

At the district court, Tamir played a double role. In defending his client, he presented Kastner as a traitor and collaborator. At the same time, he wrote unsigned editorials about the trial for the antiestablishment weekly *HaOlam HaZeh* in which he not only praised himself fulsomely to advance his own political career (he later ran for the Knesset on the ticket of the New Regime, a party he founded with Judge Halevi, who was number two on the list; ultimately Tamir became minister of justice in Begin's first government) but pilloried

Kastner as a representative of Mapai and the Zionist Executive, which he claimed had suppressed news of the destruction in Europe.

Indirectly, Tamir made the same charge against the JAE as he did against Kastner. Both the JAE and the rescue committee in Hungary, Tamir intimated, were staffed by self-serving cowards who betrayed their people for personal gain. Just as Mapai had betrayed the Jews of Hungary to the Germans in the person of Kastner, its leaders in the Yishuv collaborated with the British in order to preserve their own privileged status and maintain Mapai as a ruling party. Here Tamir was referring to the fact that Mapai, which objected to the terrorist activities of the Irgun and Lehi (Freedom Fighters of Israel), handed their operatives over to the British police, at Ben-Gurion's incentive. Had it not been for Kastner's deception, Tamir claimed, Hungary's 800,000 Jews would have rebelled against the Nazis. Similarly, if not for the JAE, the Jews of Palestine would have rebelled against the British.

Tamir conducted his defense of Gruenwald in a way that enabled the press to quote sensational "sound bites," and in his role as reporter he made sure that the public understood his implications. In making his case—especially with respect to the Goods for Blood Plan for rescuing Hungarian Jewry—Tamir painted a picture of the JAE that pointed directly to the conclusion that Moshe Sharett, head of the JAE's political department, and Ben-Gurion's close aides Ehud Avriel and Teddy Kollek were traitors. While Kastner in Hungary was collaborating with the Nazis and the JAE leaders in Palestine were licking the boots of the British, Tamir claimed, they let go by a chance to save nearly a million Jews through the rescue plans.

Uri Avneri, owner and editor of the newsweekly *HaOlam HaZeh* and at the time Tamir's ally, later admitted that Tamir had used the court for his own political purposes, seeing his actions as "part of the campaign to overthrow Mapai's rule." According to Avneri, Tamir, motivated by "bottomless hatred" of Ben-Gurion, taught the Herut Party that "liberating the government compound from the hands of Ben-Gurion precedes liberating the Temple Mount."

Avneri also told the Knesset that "all that was said by Tamir at the Kastner trial has been used ever since by the Soviet Union in its most venomous propaganda, to make the monstrous argument that the Zionist Executive collaborated with the Nazis." The most egregious part of this propaganda was a series of articles headlined "The Zionists Are Responsible for the Destruction of the Jews of Europe, 1941–1945," published in the Soviet Union on the fortieth anniversary of the "liberation" of Auschwitz.[21]

Kastner did not live to celebrate his victory before the supreme court. In March 1957 he was assassinated by a nationalist fanatic who believed Tamir's accusations. This assassination marked the high point of the politicization of the Holocaust. In commemorating Kastner, the poet Nathan Alterman wrote in his weekly column in *Davar* that, figuratively speaking, the bullets that killed Kastner had been aimed at Ben-Gurion.[22]

The truth of Alterman's interpretation is evident from Herut's manifesto, published on June 27, 1955, before the July general elections. Attacking Mapai's defense of Kastner (before the reversal of Halevi's judgment by the supreme court), it charged, "This identification with a man who was found morally guilty by the district court for capital crimes against the Jewish people can be accounted for by two assumptions: (a) Mapai and its supporters, who collaborated with the British rule during the war of liberation and who betrayed the Hebrew freedom fighters [that is, the Irgun terrorists], justify on principle collaboration with any conqueror, including the German Nazi conqueror; (b) in the hands of the Mapai member Dr. Kastner, there was material which, if published, may harm those who were and still are his superiors."[23]

Thus adopting Tamir's accusations that Mapai leaders had collaborated with the Nazis, Herut asserted that it was they who had plotted Kastner's assassination, fearful lest the secret would be revealed and their treachery exposed. The analogy between the betrayal of the Irgun fighters to the British police and the alleged collaboration with the Nazis left no room for doubt that the charge was aimed at Ben-Gurion.

In the ensuing years, the accusations made by Tamir united ultra-religious anti-Zionist Jews, ultra-Zionist rightists, and non-Jewish anti-Zionist leftists. A member of the last group, British playwright Jim Allen, based his play *Perdition* entirely on the Kastner trial,[24] except that it takes place in a royal court of justice in London. Allen quotes freely from the Jerusalem district court's record to support Gruenwald and Tamir's accusations against Kastner and the JAE. He claims that Kastner "informed the Jewish Agency almost daily about the pace of the extermination program"—a thing that in reality is quite inconceivable—and thus the JAE became his accomplice. Allen is certainly acquainted with some translations of *Srufei Hakivshanim Maashimim* (The Victims of the Ovens Accuse) by the ultra-Orthodox Rabbi Moshe Scheinfeld, published by members of the important anti-Zionist worldwide Orthodox Agudat Israel.[25] In this oft-printed publication, Scheinfeld affirms, "That which the heads of Zionism inflicted on European Jewry during World War II cannot be described as other than killing in the proper sense of the word." These Zionist leaders "were the criminals of the Holocaust who contributed their part to the destruction." He also asserts that the hands of the Zionist leaders were "stained with blood, and the foundations of the walls [of the State] are laid [with bodies of] the children of Israel destroyed in the Exile."[26] This accusation was later repeated, in an altogether different fashion, by the poet Harshav, better known as Professor of Comparative Literature Benjamin Hrushovski.[27]

But what receives pride of place in Allen's play is Weissmandel's fabrication. Schwalb's letter that never was is read in full in the royal court in London. In Allen's not too accurate translation from Weissmandel's rabbinical Hebrew, Schwalb writes to his friend in Bratislava: "Since we have the opportunity of this courier, we are writing to the group that they must always remember that matter which is most important; which is the main issue that must always be before our eyes. After all, the Allies will be victorious. After the victory, they will once again divide up the world between the nations as they did at the end of the first [world] war. As for the cry that comes from your country [Slovakia], we must be aware that all nations of the Allies are spilling much blood, and if we do not bring sacrifices, with what will we achieve the right to sit at the table when they make the distribution of nations and territories after the war? And so it would be foolish and impertinent on our side to ask the nations whose blood is being spilled for permission to send money into the land of their enemies in order to protect our own blood. Because only through blood will the land [Palestine] be ours. . . . As to yourselves, members of the group, you will get out, and for this purpose we are providing you with funds by this courier."

Weissmandel's accusation that the Zionists' contempt for Diaspora Jews led them to spend money on land and settlement rather than rescue was also taken up by academics and by Segev. During the 1960s, two events opened previously locked valves, releasing hitherto pent-up inhibitions and emotions. The first was the 1961 trial of Adolf Eichmann in Jerusalem. Many of the prosecution witnesses were Holocaust survivors, who for the first time gave vent in public to their pain and wrath. The result was a change in the behavior of both the surviving remnant and the general public in Israel, allowing freer discussion of the Holocaust. The second event was Israel's flash victory in the Six-Day War of 1967, which generated a widespread feeling of security, as well as waves of immigration and economic development. Israel felt secure enough to discuss the past and conduct a much wider and deeper soul-searching than ever before. Beginning in 1968, a spirit of criticism of Ben-Gurion's and the Yishuv leadership's supposed attitude of "condemnation of the Diaspora" became the prevailing atmosphere among Holocaust scholars. The accepted notion was that this attitude was responsible for the Yishuv leadership's indifference to the misery and destruction of Europe's Jews.

This critical spirit was exemplified by Professor Israel Gutman, of the Hebrew University in Jerusalem, who offered as proof his discovery that at the height of the Holocaust, when Poland's Jews were being gassed en masse, Ben-Gurion and his colleagues were spending their time discussing with the Polish government in exile the irrelevant subject of whether Jews in postwar Poland would receive equal rights. As will be seen, however, Gutman's perception was distorted, to say the least.

It must be remembered that when Israel acquired its new sense of security, Levi Eshkol was its prime minister and Moshe Dayan its minister of defense. Israel was no longer dependent on Ben-Gurion, and the younger generations saw him very much as grown-up, secure, well-to-do children regard their parents—feeling free to discuss, and at times even invent, his shortcomings as well as abuse him. Israel's occupation of Gaza and the West Bank and its role as a military oppressor of the Palestinians strengthened this inclination to find fault with the founding fathers. In the process an unjustified link was created between the Holocaust years and the post-1967 era, engendering a confusion that helped unite, for the first time ever, left and right, lay and religious, ultra-Zionist and equally impassioned anti-Zionist, in a circle of blame centered on Ben-Gurion.

Amid these accusations and recriminations, which the following work will examine, Ben-Gurion appears alternately as hero and villain of a *Rashomon*-like account of the Holocaust—his role depending on a given narrator's approach and point of view. Among the various perspectives to be represented will be found—incredible as it may seem—what may be called "Jewish revisionism," that is, Jews who do not deny the Holocaust but blame other Jews for its having taken place in the manner that it did. Nothing more fully epitomizes the tragedy of Jewish fratricidal self-hatred, undiminished even by that harrowing time, than this latest addition to the company of Holocaust narrators.

CHAPTER TWO

THE ATMOSPHERE OF THE ACADEMY

O NE CAN UNDERSTAND the motives of the ultra-Orthodox:
They could not shake their fists at God. One can also understand the motives of the politicians: They wanted to topple Mapai in
order to take over the government, and there was no one to set limits
on their behavior other than the voters. Academics, on the other hand,
are supposed to be detached, not swayed in their quest for the truth
by ambition or other motives. Like the other two groups, however,
most academics, including those who contributed their points of view
to this *Rashomon* drama, are not entirely free of personal prejudice.

The most notable prejudice common to the academics to be discussed here was that, as survivors of the Holocaust, they could not rid
themselves of a resentment against the Yishuv and its leaders, a feeling
rooted in the deepest recesses of their hearts: While the survivors
and their kin in occupied Europe were the victims of cruelty hitherto
unknown to humanity, the Yishuv led a normal—at times even
happy—life. In a sentence: While we were being led into the gas chambers, you, in Palestine, were celebrating Hanukkah and Purim.

Thus Professor Benjamin Harshav, formerly of Tel Aviv University,
now at Yale—an outstanding literary scholar and poet, truly a category unto himself—was apparently quick to latch on to a whole host
of lies propagated by Matti Meged, a writer who could not always
differentiate between reality and fantasy. Meged's story was that in
1948 Ben-Gurion issued an order for the deployment of young
Holocaust survivors, upon their arrival in Palestine, in special units

that were thrown without proper training into the battle of Latrun, where many—hundreds, a thousand?—became cannon fodder. But others tell a story quite different from Meged's.[1]

On May 14, 1948, Ben-Gurion declared the establishment of the state of Israel. On the 15th, the neighboring Arab states invaded western Palestine, and on the 17th Jordan's Arab Legion, under British command, took Latrun, a stronghold commanding the coastal road to Jerusalem. The city, with its large Jewish population, was now under complete siege—running short of water, food, fuel, electricity, ammunition, and reinforcements, utterly at the mercy of Jordan's constant sniping and artillery bombardments. Its military and civilian leaders cabled Ben-Gurion that the city could hold out no longer than two weeks. Ben-Gurion, in his capacity of minister of defense, ordered GHQ to open the Jerusalem road at all costs. GHQ assigned the task to the Seventh Brigade, its only available reserve. During the night of May 24 and on May 25, the Seventh attacked the Arab Legion at Latrun.

The Seventh, which consisted of one armored and two infantry battalions, had been put together hurriedly. While its field-grade officers were veterans of the British army who had seen action in Europe, and its subalterns and noncommissioned officers were trained Haganah instructors, its ranks were made up of 500 green recruits, brought directly from the recruiting centers, and of soldiers transferred from other units. Of the "greens," 140 were survivors of the Holocaust who had arrived from Europe by boat on May 14. Along with other greens, they were assigned to Aleph Company and Bet Company of the Seventy-second Infantry Battalion, where their brief training included target practice on a rifle range, "not altogether a trifling thing in those chaotic days," in the words of a scholar who studied the battle of Latrun.

Aware of the Seventh's deficiencies, GHQ attached to it a fourth battalion, the Thirty-second, from another brigade, consisting of four companies (about 360 men) who were experienced veterans, nearly all Israeli-born. Still, the Seventh was not ready for battle. The men were not outfitted, the artillery was unranged, the machine guns still lay greased in their packing cases. Only about a quarter of the men of the Thirty-second Battalion had water canteens, while those of the Seventy-second had very few among them; and it was a hot May. The Seventh hardly had the time to consolidate and create a regimental esprit de corps. Its chances against the fully equipped, professionally trained regular soldiers of Jordan's Arab Legion, under their British officers, were nil.

The offensive was a total failure, and a legend grew up that the Seventh lost hundreds of its men—a thousand, according to one rumor—nearly all newly arrived survivors of the Holocaust. Thorough studies show, however, that this was not true. The veteran Thirty-second's casualties were 48 (52, according to another version) dead and 46 wounded, while the Seventy-second's were 23 (20 in the other version) dead and 47 wounded. Of the 71 (or 72) killed, 8 were Holocaust survivors, all from Bet Company of the Seventy-second Battalion. There were five more assaults on Latrun, in which 96 more men were killed, none survivors of the Holocaust.[2]

Although the lies about Latrun were publicly exposed and the facts made known,[3] this accusation nevertheless appears to have inspired Harshav's poem "Peter the Great."[4] In a striking analogy, Harshav compares the czar's indifference to human life in building his capital, St. Petersburg, on—as is commonly said—the bodies of millions of serf laborers who died of hunger and cold to that of Ben-Gurion in committing the young survivors just arrived in Palestine—also a kind of serf, whose lives did not matter—to secure the capital of the new Jewish state. Gabi Daniel, the poet's alter ego, declares that "David Ben-Gurion paved the way to Jerusalem . . . with the bones of Holocaust boys," as if many Yishuv boys did not also fall at this bloody battle. Inflammatory and easy to remember, this parallel was convincing because Harshav was above politics and party bickering. A great many who did not understand the poem, let alone read the whole thing, were taken by this sensational comparison.

Harshav, a Diaspora boy who saw service with the Palmach, seems to have combined the accusations leveled at Ben-Gurion from outside with those leveled against him from within the labor movement. For even among academics who belong to the labor movement, one finds those who swallow undiscriminatingly such accusations and conclude that the leader of the Yishuv and founder of the state participated in the "scandal" of the Holocaust. Dr. Idith Zertal, for example, states that Ben-Gurion and his colleagues "failed the test" of the Holocaust, "and did not rise to [its] demands." Their "behavior . . . when confronted with the Holocaust," and their "reaction to the devastation, were marked by failure in almost every possible respect, apart from malice." Furthermore, their "enslavement to ideologies, and predetermined concepts . . . precluded a correct response to an unprecedented situation such as the Holocaust"[5]—as if such response were available. Once the limits of logic are shattered, anyone can believe that the Diaspora was the citadel of the Jewish people, and that it was Zionism and its striving for ingathering into a state that brought the catastrophe upon them.

Other important historians of the Holocaust held a similar opinion. They radiated, while lecturing to their students, an aura of criticism of the leadership of the Yishuv, and Ben-Gurion in particular, arguing that the rescue of the Jews was not the leadership's main concern. Some explained the leadership's failure as originating in the "condemnation of the Diaspora." Despite the fact that to this day no research has ever been done to prove that the "condemnation of the Diaspora" produced a contemptuous attitude, or even that the Zionist leaders had such an attitude, many students accepted this attitude as axiomatic. The assumption of the "condemnation of the Diaspora" as the original sin serves as the point of departure and basis of criticism of the leadership in these students' own work.

One who shared this critical attitude was Saul Friedlander, professor of history at both Tel Aviv University and the University of California at Los Angeles, who in 1968 said in an interview that made a substantial impression on other scholars: "I have not researched in detail this aspect of the problem [whether everything possible had been done to rescue Jews], and accordingly my opinion is not supported scientifically, but my impression is that there is indeed room for self-criticism. It seems to me that there was here a profound lapse on the part of the Yishuv. . . . I argue that the Yishuv's leadership and the Yishuv in general did not put their minds to this sufficiently. In the order of priorities of the Jewish leadership in Palestine (and here

I aim mainly at Ben-Gurion's attitude), the rescue of Europe's Jews did not occupy first place. For the leadership the important thing was the struggle for the establishment of the state in Palestine. It was this matter that preoccupied them during the war years. . . . It seems to me that Ben-Gurion, and many others like him, 'are ashamed' at the historic legacy of the diaspora Jewry."[6]

It is a great misfortune that Friedlander was unaware of a letter Ben-Gurion wrote in 1955, during the Kastner trial, to A. S. Stein of the newspaper *Davar,* a letter that throws light on his attitude toward the Jews of occupied Europe. First of all, writes Ben-Gurion, "I would not have taken it upon myself to judge any Jew who lived there while I lived here," in Palestine. Second, he had "no fear that the 'Judenrats' [the Jewish councils organized by the Nazis, which many in Israel felt should be condemned as treacherous collaborators to ensure that no one followed their example; he makes it clear that he does not use this term pejoratively] . . . will influence our children" in Palestine. He added, "There is reason to fear that they [the children] will distance themselves from the positive things that did exist in the Diaspora, but there is no fear that they will acquire the bad things that existed in the ghetto, and least of all [for example] begging on your knees, which diminishes the dignity of a human being."[7]

It is clear therefore that Ben-Gurion was not "ashamed" of the Diaspora legacy and did not summarily and indiscriminately judge the Judenrats.

Dr. Dina Porat described the atmosphere that reigned in the academy during the 1970s and '80s as "a search for vermin." She recollected that on January 22, 1974, during her student days, Gershom Schocken, editor in chief of *Ha'aretz,* Israel's most important morning paper, gave a lecture to her class on the Hebrew press and the Holocaust, in which he said that the Hebrew press had become aware of the systematic destruction of Europe's Jews only in November 1942, when sixty-nine Jewish Palestinians exchanged for German prisoners (to be described later) arrived from Europe with firsthand news of the ongoing destruction.

Porat was the first to react, accurately reflecting the then-prevailing academic atmosphere. She drew his attention to the fact that five months earlier, on June 30, 1942, *Ha'aretz* itself had published a report by Samuel Artur Zygelbojm of the National Council of Poland in exile in London in which he told of the systematic destruction and named a few death camps. She then intimated that this report had gone unnoticed—and even slipped from Schocken's memory—because "the prevailing attitude" then was one of "ignoring" Europe's Jews.

In a letter the next day Schocken admitted to having forgotten about Zygelbojm's report, and wondered himself why it had not been accompanied by an editorial. He found an explanation in an article by the Hebrew poet Avraham Shlonsky, a member of the paper's editorial board, published in the same issue. Shlonsky, protesting the "Yishuv's indifference" to the events in Europe, made a plea for more attention on the part of the Yishuv. Schocken explained this indifference in the context of Rommel's army getting nearer and nearer to Palestine, which at that moment was the Yishuv's prime concern. "Add to that," he wrote, "the feeling of our helplessness and inability to affect the horrible developments in Europe, which must also have influenced us."[8]

As Porat worked on her dissertation, which she submitted in 1983, she occasionally ran into scholars who, having heard her subject, "The Yishuv in the Face of the Holocaust, 1942–45," would exclaim, " 'Aha!' as if I were about to uncover horrendous cockroaches." She admitted that "at first it had a strong effect." But as she went on with her work, her attitude changed—"for I did not find the roaches." When her work was published[9] in Hebrew in 1986 and later by Harvard University Press (as *The Blue and Yellow Stars of David*), it broke new ground, for it presented a picture very different from the acid, one-sided criticism that prevailed—and, in some quarters, still prevails.

Dr. Yechiam Weitz damned this critical atmosphere as "the fashion." His doctoral thesis, written between 1982 and 1987 and published in 1994 under the title *Aware but Helpless: Mapai and the Holocaust, 1943–45,* strengthens Porat's thesis that the Yishuv and its leaders did the best they could to rescue Europe's Jews. But even he is not absolutely free of "the fashion." He does not ascribe the importance Mapai attributed to the "upbuilding of Zion" to "Palestinocentrism," to ignoring the Holocaust, or to insensibility; he writes that Mapai was moved by "a strong identification with the Diaspora and its plight." But he adds that this was "accompanied by condescension," "arrogance," and "deep contempt toward the Diaspora." He supports this assertion by quoting Avraham Givelver, a kibbutz activist, who spoke at a kibbutz conference in January 1944 of the Diaspora as "crying out for compassion, crying out for rescue," saying that "if we want to rescue [the remnants], we must also redeem them." Weitz dwells on this quotation: "We witness, therefore, an additional link between deep empathy for the Diaspora, its remnants and survivors, and a contemptuous attitude, often a righteous attitude." It appears to be that same fashion that led Weitz to give such weight to Givelver's use of the term "redeem." In fact, however, Givelver himself had immigrated to Palestine only in January 1941, and it is quite impossible that any whiff of Palestinian contempt toward the Diaspora could have emanated from him. Indeed, his use of the terms "rescue" and "redeem" was only normal Zionist discourse.[10]

Silence: Mapai and the Holocaust, 1939–1942, the dissertation of Dr. Hava Eshkoli (Wagman), published in 1994, also supports Porat. Although in previous works Eshkoli had followed the fashion, as a result of her quest for the truth she wrote, "I did not hesitate to change my evaluation as my research progressed." She explained: "As for the Zionist leadership's [so-called] abstention from proper rescue efforts, we should examine the degree of Zionist capability under the circumstances of those days . . . it seems, therefore, that even if human factors, like confusion or ideological concepts, did in fact affect the scope of the rescue efforts, they were not the dominant factor. The central factor in this matter was the limits of the Yishuv's capability. On one hand there was the small, poor Yishuv, less than half a million strong . . . under British mandatory rule; and on the other hand, a world divided between destroyers of the Jewish people and those collaborating and indifferent to the fate of the Jews, and only the few lending a hand."[11]

Even Professor Anita Shapira of the Institute for Zionist Research at Tel Aviv University seems to have fallen victim to the prevailing atmosphere. In *Berl*, her 1980 biography of Berl Katznelson, she thanks "Mrs. Dina Porat for having given me advice and information in all that concerns the Holocaust"—during the time when Porat, still doing her research, was under the powerful influence of the "atmosphere."[12] Porat gave Shapira a paragraph from Joel Palgi's *With a Great Wind*,[13] describing the Yishuv leaders' farewell to the "paratroopers" before they set out on their mission to Europe in 1944. They asked the leaders what their main task should be. Palgi makes it abundantly clear why the paratroopers needed such clarification: Their mission was a double one. They were representatives of the Yishuv, going to encourage and rescue the Jews, and at the same time soldiers of the Royal Air Force, which had trained them and would drop them in Europe with the mission of helping captured pilots escape from German prisons. Their question to the leaders and the leaders' answers must be understood in the context of this double mission. But Shapira made the mistake of assuming that the double mission was contradictory—that is, it consisted of a "Jewish" mission to save all Jews, Zionist and otherwise, and a "Zionist" mission to save only Jews who were Zionists or ready to become so—and from the answers of the leaders she drew an erroneous deduction regarding their attitudes toward rescue.

She quotes the leaders' answers from Palgi's book: " 'to teach Jews to fight,' said Eliahu Golomb, the Haganah chief. 'That Jews should know that Palestine is their home and castle,' said Ben-Gurion. 'Save the Jews,' said Berl, 'all the rest will follow later. If no Jews remain, Palestine and the Zionist venture will vanish as well.' "[14]

Here three prototypes of Jewish leaders are represented: Golomb, the warrior; Ben-Gurion, the statesman dedicated to a state; and Katznelson, the Jew with the warm heart, the only one whose heart went out to the Diaspora suffering under a catastrophe. The reader is led therefore to the conclusion that, unlike Ben-Gurion and Golomb, only Katznelson saw rescue as his main concern. This is a major error, and it is reasonable to assume that Shapira would not have made it had she not been under the influence of the "atmosphere." For the simple logic behind Ben-Gurion's and Golomb's answers is that if the Jews were not rescued, they could not be taught to fight or to understand the meaning of Palestine. The need to rescue the Jews first and foremost is plain in the quotes of all three leaders, and the proof of this lies in Katznelson's own words when he summed up the statements of the other two in saying "All the rest will follow later," and adding that if no Jews remained, Palestine would vanish. There can be no doubt therefore that the three leaders were giving the paratroopers the same instructions, each in his own way, but all took for granted that rescue was the first priority. In 1986 Porat, no longer affected by the "atmosphere," herself argued that the double mission was not a Jewish one and a Zionist one. In her book she joined the quotation from Palgi with another quote from *Operation Amsterdam,* the story of Chaim Chermesh, a paratrooper who was present at the farewell. According to Chermesh, as quoted by Porat, after Ben-Gurion said "that the Jews should know that Palestine is their home and castle," he added, "and that they should storm the closed gates of Palestine and open them right after V-day."[15]

But Shapira, affected by the atmosphere, on the strength of this one quotation claims that only Katznelson gave thought to the rescue of the Jews and even leaps to the conclusion that he was "exceptional in the intensity with which he lived the experience of the Holocaust." She adds that Katznelson was "unlike his colleagues, whose road to Zionism was easier and lit by shining hopes. The colleagues found it difficult to digest what was taking place in Europe, they repressed these things, even when the news hit them in the face. The escape from the Holocaust, the ignoring of it, hiding their heads in the sand to avoid the terrible truth—all these characterized leaders and rank and file."[16]

As Katznelson's biographer, Shapira is entitled, of course, to describe his attitude toward the Holocaust and explain it in any way she sees fit. But when she asserts that his attitude was "exceptional," and that Katznelson was "unlike his colleagues," she has to prove it. Furthermore, it seems that only in that atmosphere could Shapira so cavalierly tarnish an entire movement—leaders and rank and file alike—reproaching them for repressing, escaping from, and closing their eyes to the Holocaust.

What is more, it seems that only in such an "atmosphere" could Shapira deduce Katznelson's special attitude from a negative.

"Katznelson," she writes, "did not dwell much on this matter" of the Holocaust, and she concludes, "it seems this matter was too painful to be talked about in worn-out clichés." But she does not draw the same conclusion when she deals with the silence of his colleagues; in fact, she draws the opposite conclusion. If Katznelson really was exceptional in living the Holocaust, is it not strange that he failed to open his colleagues' eyes to the extremity of the catastrophe? Is it conceivable that Katznelson, "the teacher of a generation," as he was called, could see his colleagues utterly indifferent before the Holocaust and not rebuke them for the stoniness of their hearts? It is more probable that his silence was not a proof of his being exceptional, but rather a proof that he was just as lost in the face of the Holocaust as were his colleagues, and like them could not find the right words to speak. Indeed, the phenomenon the scholars refer to as being "struck dumb" also affected poets and writers of the Yishuv, and the explanation of this phenomenon still awaits a scholar to attempt it.

One manifestation of Professor Friedlander's influence appears in Tom Segev's *The Seventh Million.* In April 1968, Segev and two friends interviewed the eighty-two-year-old Ben-Gurion in his desert retreat of Sdeh Boker for *Nitsots* (Spark), a student-union paper. Reading Ben-Gurion excerpts from Friedlander's interview quoted above, they asked him "whether it is true" that he was " 'ashamed' of the legacy of the Diaspora Jews." According to Segev, Ben-Gurion was unwilling to discuss this and preferred to talk about a subject close to his heart: the people of Israel as *am sgulah* ("treasured possession," in the Bible) or "a light unto nations" ("exemplary people," according to Ben-Gurion[17]). But the *Nitsots* interviewers returned to their question again and again. Finally, writes Segev, they challenged Ben-Gurion: "Friedlander maintains that you have not understood correctly the meaning [of the Holocaust]." Ben-Gurion then "settled into a long silence; only the buzz of a single desert fly could be heard in the room. Suddenly he raised his eyes and said: 'What is there to understand? They died and that's it.' "[18]

Thus did Segev—in 1968!—find one more proof of Ben-Gurion's indifference toward the Diaspora Jews and the Holocaust. I was unable to obtain the tape of this interview from Mr. Segev to verify his quotations. However, by comparing the response Segev reports with Ben-Gurion's answers to similar questions, we get a different impression of his feelings. In a meeting in Jerusalem in September 1943 he said he found it hard to talk "about the disaster" because "I don't have the words, I think the language for it has not been created yet."[19] In his already quoted letter to Stein, Ben-Gurion opined that "the matter of the Judenrats (and perhaps the matter of Kastner) must be left to the judgment of history in a future generation." In the same letter he said that "the Jews who lived securely in Hitler's day should not take it upon themselves to judge their brethren who were butchered and incinerated or those few who survived." On visiting the displaced persons' (DP) camps in Europe after the war he had heard, he wrote, "some terrible things" that the survivors had perpetrated and he also saw "among them some very ugly behavior." But "I did not see myself entitled to be their judge and instructor since I know what they went through."

The end of this letter is extremely relevant to the quote "They died and that's it," in Segev's interview. Segev inserts this part of the letter in his book in quite a different, remote context, describing it as "a rare expression of emotion" by Ben-Gurion: "The tragedy is deeper than the abyss,* and the members of our generation who did not taste that hell would do best (in my modest opinion) to remain sorrowfully and humbly silent. My niece, her husband, and her two children were burned alive. Can such things be talked about?"[20] Segev foolishly imagines that anybody, himself included, could come to Ben-Gurion at any time in his life, and expect the old man to pour his heart out as though he were an opera singer on a stage. When Ben-Gurion declined to do so, Segev jumped to the instant conclusion that his heart was made of stone.

In fact, Ben-Gurion generally kept his feelings to himself in his public appearances, making an effort to keep his expressions and language businesslike and detached. Thus to some extent the criticism of him was justified; at a time of national crisis and suffering, people expect

---

* A better translation is "the tragedy is deeper than any deep," as the King James Bible renders the word Ben-Gurion took from Genesis 1:2.

their leader to say something that expresses their horror and sorrow. Ben-Gurion, however, appeared collected and unruffled. In a rare moment of self-exposure he told students in 1961 that he knew well that Golda Meir "lives inside her the Holocaust," adding "the Holocaust is alive no less within me, but I am given more to the future than she, and I am not so susceptible to psychological complexes. It is my way to weigh my words, and at times I feel it is my duty to uproot all feelings from my heart." Ben-Gurion seemed to be saying that his role as leader required him to look toward the future and not allow himself emotional outbursts that led nowhere.[21]

CHAPTER THREE

BEN-GURION AND KOT

PROFESSOR ISRAEL GUTMAN, a leading Holocaust scholar, was an important narrator in the unfolding tale of *Rashomon*. The critical spirit of the academy permeated his classroom criticism of Ben-Gurion. Gutman tended to blame Ben-Gurion and the Yishuv leadership for an inappropriate "attitude" toward the Diaspora Jews, from which, he claimed, grew their attitude toward the Holocaust. The history of Gutman's contribution to the "atmosphere" is told by Porat:

> *Toward the end of 1942, Professor Stanislaw Kot, the Polish government in exile minister of state resident in the Middle East, visited Palestine and met in Jerusalem with members of the JAE and a group representing the association of Poland's Jews, who were known as the* reprezentacja (representation). *In the early 1980s, a noted historian found in an archive in Jerusalem the report written in Palestine in 1942 of this meeting, and he learned that the participants discussed a variety of subjects. Among them—in a conspicuous place—the situation and civil rights of Poland's Jews after the war. "I ask you," said the historian indignantly to some of his colleagues, "is this what they had on their minds—the civil rights of the Jews after the war?! Didn't they understand what was going on?! Even Ben-Gurion?!"*

Here we see this authoritative scholar portraying Ben-Gurion as a senile old man who talked about the future of Poland's Jews even when it was known that no Jew would be left alive in Poland by then. Gutman is ready to present Ben-Gurion to his colleagues and students at the Hebrew University in Jerusalem as someone to whom the concentration of Jews in the ghettos and their systematic destruction, which at that time had been going on for six months, was not of prime concern. Porat continues:

> After a while the historian came back from research at the London archives of the Polish government in exile, and he told his interlocutors that he had found the report Kot sent his government about the visit to Palestine. Kot, he said, wrote that after the meeting Ben-Gurion took him out on a nocturnal stroll and said to him more or less as follows: "What was said at the banquet in your honor is one thing. What I'm going to say to you now is another matter, and this is the important thing: I do not sleep nights out of fear for the fate of Poland's Jews. You must help the Polish Jews who are being killed! This is the most burning issue at the moment, and we will never forget it if you do not come to their assistance!"[1]

Here again Ben-Gurion is represented as an ineffectual leader who spends his time at a banquet discussing trivial matters, and only under cover of darkness, as if sharing a personal secret with Kot, confides that he does not sleep nights—not discussing during these precious moments practical strategies to help the Jews, but only feebly shaking his finger at Kot, vowing never to forget, as if this were a potent threat.

Gutman has identified himself as the famous historian whom Porat referred to and has confirmed her quotation of his remarks. The most conspicuous feature of the conversation between Ben-Gurion and Kot as he reports it is that, even at this period (the banquet was held on January 19, 1943), Ben-Gurion refers only to "killing," not to the fact that a systematic destruction of Polish Jews was going on, as if the JAE were unaware of it and it had never been mentioned during the discussions with Kot.

Research in Jewish and Polish archives in Israel, England, and the United States, however, reveals a radically different story. As will be seen, the talks Kot held in Palestine centered on the systematic annihilation of Poland's Jews and the means to save them; they were far from mere lamentations or sharing of anecdotes. It is a chapter worth telling from the beginning.

In August 1942 Eliahu Dobkin, the head of the JAE immigration department, had visited Teheran, where he met Minister Kot, a close associate and confidant of Wladyslaw Sikorsky, the head of the Polish government in exile (PGE), which Kot had served previously as minister of the interior and ambassador to the USSR. The JAE detected a possibility of bringing to Palestine many of the 400,000 Jews who had been driven by the Soviets in 1939 from the Soviet-occupied zone in Poland to the heartland of the Soviet Union, along with millions of Poles. Many of them were serving in the Free Poland Army. Dobkin had come to Teheran, among other things, to discuss this possibility of a "grand rescue,"[2] as well as the chances of bringing over the "Teheran children," with Kot.

Early in November Kot came to Haifa for a rest and stayed at the Carmel Pension. Sharett, having read about Kot's arrival in the press, wrote him "that I would be happy to make your personal acquaintance." Eliahu Elath of the JAE political department was about to visit the British ambassador to Iraq, who was also staying at the Carmel Pension, and Sharett authorized Elath to make contact with Kot. In a discussion on November 7, Kot proposed a Polish-Jewish collaboration that would be beneficial to both parties, in return for American Jewish support for the Polish government's plan to establish after the war a federation of Eastern and Central Europe. Elath, who was willing to do whatever was necessary to get the 400,000 Jews out of Russia, confirmed Kot's "conviction that American Jews had a great deal of influence in the highest circles in their country," but refrained from making a commitment with respect to the federation plan. Kot gave Elath a letter to Sharett, promising to get in touch with him at the earliest opportunity. At their meeting, which took place a week later, Sharett raised the question of the Teheran children and discussed with Kot transporting them by sea, since Iraq would not allow them to cross its borders.

Before his return to London at the end of January 1943, Kot held a dozen meetings with leaders, public figures, and newspapermen of the Yishuv.[3] During the first of these meetings, with Dr. Moshe Sneh and Dr. Avraham Stupp, members of the *reprezentacja* of the Polish Jewish Association,[4] it became immediately clear that the PGE had more complete and up-to-date information from sources in occupied Poland about the destruction of Jews than did the JAE.

The JAE's information was secondhand. That which did not derive from neutral countries or from the press came only from Jewish sources in Poland. It was sent out of the country through the Polish underground to Jewish leaders in London, New York, and Geneva and did not always reach Jerusalem. At that meeting, therefore, Kot had superior information, except for news from one source: On November 18–19, a few days before the meeting, the "exchangees" had arrived in Palestine. This was a group of sixty-nine Palestinian Jews who had gotten stuck in Europe and were exchanged for German residents of Palestine. They provided the first eyewitness reports of the atrocities to reach Palestine, and their accounts of life in the ghettos and the mass murders made a horrific impression. But even they did not have reliable information about the industrial destruction—the vast death camps, the gas chambers and crematoria. They had heard only rumors: For example, a locomotive engineer returning from Russia had told how the Jews "are being forced to enter special buildings and being destroyed by gas."[5]

This was the most disturbing information that the JAE had received. A report to the Polish government in London by Dr. Henryk Rosmarin, the Polish consul general (this is not the report Gutman reported reading in London), notes that Dr. Stupp opened the meeting with Kot by saying that "somewhere in the environs of Treblinka and Malkin, as well as in Belsen, there are installations specially built [for cremating] the Jews in the places where they are being murdered en masse."

Kot interrupted angrily: "Why are you telling me this? Do you imagine that I don't know it? These facts have been known to us for some time. The Polish government has written and spoken about them frequently. But so far we have not seen any reaction from the Jews. I must say that in this war Jewry has not been active . . . neither here in Palestine, nor in America. There is no need to convince us to do anything. We began quite some time ago to bring pressure to bear on the Allies to put an end to these acts of murder. I assure you, gentlemen, I will show you the material received by us from inside Poland."

This criticism of "Jewry" for not being active on Poland's behalf was, as became evident, Kot's chief reason for visiting Palestine. The Poles believed, like all anti-Semites, that the Jews had vast but well hidden influence in business, the media, and government, which they were not using to support Poland in its territorial dispute with the USSR. Kot felt that as Polish patriots they ought to do more for their "motherland."

Dr. Stupp responded: "We have not heard about those things. Neither the government in London nor its consulate here has reported to us any of these things. Until a few weeks ago, Dr. Schwarzbart was corresponding with us about aid parcels to Poland. We have sent parcels to thousands of addresses which it seems are no longer valid. Recently we received an answer from Minister [of Foreign Affairs, Count Edward] Raczynski saying that this news [about the destruction] has not been confirmed and that the Polish government in exile is doing its best to obtain confirmed information."

Kot: "But these things are well known. They have appeared in the press. They have been discussed in many press conferences."

Sneh: "This information has only just reached us, and in relation to it we have a number of requests which we would like to address to the Polish government through you. These are our requests," and Sneh detailed four requests that he was submitting by authority of the JAE:

(1) That the government and national council of Poland proclaim that all who take part in the persecution and murder of Polish Jews will be held responsible for their acts. (2) That the Polish government should try to exert influence on the Allies to take all necessary measures against the Germans; and that the Polish government should bring pressure to bear on the neutral countries to admit all those Jews who are able to escape German occupation and on the Germans to let them go. And perhaps the Polish government could do something through urging the Vatican to intervene. (3) That in its broadcasts to Poland the Polish government should instruct the Polish people not to be influenced by the anti-Jewish provocations and to resist the barbarous acts of the Germans. Reports arriving in Palestine from Poland make it clear that such educational work is needed. (4) That the Polish

government should persuade the Polish clergy that it must raise its voice in protest against what is going on exactly as was done by the clergy in France.

The rest of the conversation focused on the demand to help Poland's Jews and to stop the destruction on Polish land.[6] But its first part, quoted above, is sufficient to show that the Yishuv lacked information—due to the circumstances of war, not, as Professor Shapira says, because of escapist ignoring of the Holocaust, or because the JAE was hiding its head in the sand.[7]

Sneh reported the discussion with Kot to Ben-Gurion, who put the information to immediate use. On December 8, in an attempt to rally American Jewry, he wrote Felix Frankfurter, informing him that "Hitler's decision to destroy all Jews in Poland is apparently his first step to destroy all Jews in occupied Europe," and that "absolute confirmation of unimaginable acts of atrocity" had been obtained "a week ago," as well as from Minister Kot.[8]

Ben-Gurion had also decided that, in his own meeting with Kot, he would discuss "sending our agents to Poland and the rescue of Polish Jews in Russia," as well as "the intervention of the Polish government with the Vatican and the bringing over of Polish Jews from Teheran."

On December 3 Ben-Gurion received Kot in his office at the JAE in Jerusalem. Brief minutes of their conversation, written by the Polish consul general, R.P. Korsaka, are kept at Yad VaShem.[9] Ben-Gurion began by asking whether the Polish government could send to Poland through its own channels a number of "secret agents" of the JAE and enable them to transmit to Jerusalem accurate information about the situation of the Jews. Ben-Gurion had already discussed this idea of sending "commandos" to Poland at a JAE meeting in November.[10]

In his response, Kot elaborated on the difficulties and emphasized that these agents "will have no way of returning." He also noted that the Polish government had complete, authoritative, and accurate information about what was happening in Poland, most recently updated in October by a report by Jan Karski, a Polish underground delegate who had arrived in London on November 15, 1942. This was a partly eyewitness report that confirmed beyond doubt that systematic destruction was taking place. At the end of 1942 it was estimated that the number of Jews murdered by the Nazis was 2 million. "Perhaps the numbers are not accurate," Kot commented.[11] Nevertheless Kot promised he would communicate the request to his government.

The second item Ben-Gurion brought up was the 400,000 Polish Jews in the USSR. He noted that, according to a recent statement by its embassy in Washington, which had quoted a proclamation of August 19, 1942, by Marshal Georgy Zhukov, the Soviet Union did not object to their leaving its borders. It considered their departure entirely a decision for the PGE. Kot responded that, to the contrary, the Soviets regarded those Jews as Soviet citizens, which meant that they were forbidden to leave, and the PGE was powerless to change their status. Finally Ben-Gurion inquired whether the PGE would be able to help the Teheran children slip through Iraq with teenagers and adults outfitted in the uniform of the Free Poland Army, so as to evade the Iraqi government's refusal to allow them passage. Kot responded that it could not.

Ben-Gurion's report to the JAE states that they discussed in detail the extermination taking place in Poland. "Kot told him that according to the PGE's information, there is no 'destruction committee' at work in Poland but a 'purification committee' "—that is, a committee focused not on "mere" destruction but on total extermination. As for the sending in of secret agents, Ben-Gurion reported, "Kot at first said this was impossible, 'since experience had shown that all who went there [to occupied Poland] never came back' and also that it was very difficult to provide information from there." Nevertheless, Ben-Gurion "insisted, claiming that our people were ready to risk their lives, and after consulting with the Polish consul . . . Kot gave his consent." Therefore, "following PGE's authorization, the agents will have to go to London to train before setting out on their mission . . . again Kot repeated his apprehensions that the agents would be unable to survive there for long." The remainder of Ben-Gurion's account tallies with the Polish consul's minutes. He and Kot agreed to meet again at 2:00 p.m. on December 7 to work out details. But that meeting never took place.

To jump ahead, Kot kept his word and put the request for secret agents on his government's agenda. PGE discussed it several times until it was rejected in June 1943 and finally taken off the agenda by Stanislaw Mikolajcik, the deputy prime minister.[12]

The account Ben-Gurion gave Mapai's activists of the JAE's plans and of his own requests to Kot indicates that his trust in PGE and its readiness to be of help was quite limited; otherwise he would not have turned to British friends who were in positions of far less influence. "We have asked our friends in England," Ben-Gurion told his listeners,

> to demand that PGE drop leaflets from RAF planes addressed espe-
> cially to Poland's Jews, and that the RAF, in cooperation with PGE,
> drop leaflets addressed to the Polish populace in general, to come to
> the Jews' defense, to defend them and rescue as best they can all who
> can be rescued; and that PGE should make it known, by leaflets, that
> the Jewish people in Palestine, in England and the United States are
> doing all they can for their rescue. We have further proposed that our
> English friends demand that His Majesty's Government scatter leaflets
> all over Germany, addressed to the German people, telling them about
> the massacre and atrocities committed by their government, for we
> have reason to believe that these are hidden from the German people
> (from what we have heard from our people in Poland as well as from
> PGE, the massacre is conducted so as to conceal it from both the army
> and the people of Germany), and to ask the people to stay the
> murderers' hand. We have also asked them to demand that the English
> government address an appeal to the governments of Bulgaria, Ro-
> mania, and Hungary . . . charging them with the responsibility if they
> allow the Nazis to conduct in their lands the massacre they are con-
> ducting in Poland.[13]

On December 5, at 4:00 p.m., Kot met at Gat Rimon Hotel in Tel Aviv with Anselm Reiss, Sneh, and Stupp of the *reprezentacja*, then held a lengthy press conference, after which he convened with rabbis from Poland. In all these encounters Kot's interlocutors complained about the anti-Semitism prevailing in occupied Poland and in PGE, both in London and in its offices and army in the USSR. In response Kot accused Poland's Jews of "speculation [black market activity] and smuggling" and especially of disloyalty "to the Polish homeland," lack of readiness to come to its aid, and even collaboration with its Soviet enemies. He struck back at his listeners with the charge that "We don't see any action on the part of the [Jewish] leadership, the various organizations and the press" on behalf of Lvov and Vilna.

From these frank exchanges, the purpose of PGE and its emissary Kot emerged clearly: to persuade the Palestinian Jews to mobilize U.S. and British Jews to influence their governments to support, at the eventual peace conference, Poland's claim to the territories annexed by the USSR at the beginning of the war. The issue of postwar civic equality for the Jews—as a reward for this contribution they would thereby be making to the new Poland—was discussed in this context. This issue could also have come up in another context: Neutral countries had consented to allow the entry of limited numbers of Jewish refugees, but on the condition that PGE guarantee that at the war's end these refugees would return to Poland. Securing equal civil rights was seen as a litmus test for PGE's attitude toward the Jews and as a proof of its willingness to allow Jewish survivors to return to Poland after the war. Such proof was demanded by Meir Ya'ari of HaShomer HaTzair in the Zionist Actions Committee in November 1942.[14]

More significant for our purpose are, first, Kot's announcement that—as he put it at his meetings with members of the *reprezentacja* and with Ben-Gurion—"In Poland biological destruction of the Jews is taking place" and, second, the fact that a JAE demand immediately arose that PGE should act to rescue them. Also crucial is the fact that the talks focused on rescue, aid, escape routes, dispatch of "secret agents," and the like. Gutman's reproof "I ask you, is this what they had on their minds . . . ?"[15] has therefore no basis in fact. What Ben-Gurion and his colleagues had on their minds was above all the "biological destruction" of Poland's Jewry and the means of rescue. Postwar equality for Poland's Jews was to them an entirely marginal issue that they were forced to discuss in response to Kot's criticism.

On December 6 Kot hosted the "Yishuv leadership"—including Chief Rabbi Isaac Halevi Herzog, members of the JAE, and representatives of other institutions and organizations—at a reception in Jerusalem. At the beginning of his remarks, Kot declared that "the war is first and primarily a war against the Jews and against Poland," because side by side with "the biological destruction of the Jews on a scale unprecedented and beyond the comprehension of civilized nations, . . . destruction of Poles" was also taking place, and "a Judeo-Polish alliance to win" was absolutely necessary. The two peoples must insist that "the Allies give the appropriate answer to the murderous acts against the Jews and the Poles."

Ben-Gurion took the floor next. After some civilities, acknowledging "the tragic shared fate of Jews and Poles," he noted that "to our disappointment we are not in a situation in which we can do something for our brethren anywhere in Europe, but perhaps there are things PGE is able to do." First, it could bring to bear its influence on the Vatican to act for the Jews' rescue. "Our second request is that PGE facilitate the dispatching of our people [the secret agents] to occupied Poland." His third request was that PGE beseech the Poles to come to the Jews' aid. And the fourth was that PGE help establish a Jewish army, on the lines of the Free Poland Army—for "our situation is far worse than others' . . . we have no country of our own and no government of our own." Ben-Gurion ended by saying: "I do not know how the Jews could be of help to Poland, but there is no other people in the entire world as ready to help the Polish people in its struggle as the Jewish people."[16]

In his meetings with Ben-Gurion and the Yishuv's representatives Kot had said repeatedly that PGE "would like to see you do something in regard to the Russian matter." He even warned that if the Jews did not support PGE on the question of the eastern border, this would "add fuel to the Polish-Jewish bonfire." This was a clear threat—that PGE's helping the Jews hinged on their supporting PGE's territorial claim. From Kot's point of view, however, it was a simple quid pro quo, and he was apparently disappointed in Ben-Gurion and the other Yishuv representatives, concluding that their great interest in Russia's Jews prevented them from fully backing PGE.[17]

Ben-Gurion's last meeting with Kot took place on January 19, 1943, at the Tel Aviv San Remo Hotel, at a farewell reception given by the *reprezentacja* in Kot's honor. Designed to smooth over the discord that had arisen between Kot and the Yishuv leaders, this was very likely the "banquet" Professor Gutman referred to. But if so, his version of the episode is inaccurate on at least two points. One, his account makes sense only if this was Kot's first or second meeting with Jewish leaders in Palestine, not the second to last (the last being on January 25, at the King David Hotel in Jerusalem, with *reprezentacja* members only). Two, the banquet took place not in Jerusalem, but in Tel Aviv, where Ben-Gurion lived at the time and could have taken Kot on a nocturnal stroll.

Finally, Gutman is correct in saying that the issue of equal rights for Jews in postwar Poland was raised at a reception. But the reception was not in Jerusalem and did not occur at the start of Kot's talks. Nor, according to the annual comprehensive report of the *reprezentacja,* was equal rights the main issue raised; in fact the mention of it ran counter to the farewell reception's smoothing-over purpose. Reiss, the first speaker, referred in a single, short sentence to "full equality of rights in the new Poland." He was followed by Chief Rabbi Herzog, JAE chairman Ben-Gurion, National Council chairman Yitzhak Ben-Zvi, Agudat Israel president Rabbi Yitzhak Meir Levin, Tel Aviv mayor Israel Rokach—who also referred indirectly to the equal rights issue—and Professor Martin Buber of the Hebrew University. The one who diverged the most from the harmonious tone of these valedictory addresses was Rabbi Levin, who said: "You [Kot] happen to be in the Holy Land when harrowing news reaches us about our brethren in Poland and in Europe . . . we think of nothing but the waste of our dying people, not even of the future, for what kind of future is in store for us when a threat of annihilation is hovering over the Jewish people? We, Orthodox Jews, believe that these times we live in are a trial for one and all . . . the responsibility for what takes place in occupied Europe does not fall on the Germans alone. It is also the responsibility of all those who shut their ears to our people's plea for succor and who shut their countries' gates in the face of potential survivors . . . I appreciate PGE's initiatives, and I ask that it continue its efforts and wish that a free, strong Poland shall rise soon."

Kot responded in a long speech, reiterating that "biological destruction" of the Jews and ruthless brutality toward the Poles were occurring in Poland and that "the common suffering" was "a means toward fellowship." He expressed the hope that "there would be other times" after the war when "the venom and the noxious gases which Hitlerism has spread and inflamed, to ignite universal anti-Semitism, will vanish." He then pledged: "We have no doubt that in the Poland of the future . . . there will prevail the principle of 'equal rights and equal duties for all citizens,' as succinctly put by our prime minister [Sikorsky]."[18]

If this indeed was Gutman's "banquet," it must be noted that only three of the speakers referred to Jewish equal rights in postwar Poland, and Ben-Gurion was not one of them. Furthermore, given the outspoken way in which Kot had imparted his information about the occurrences in Poland in previous meetings, it is inconceivable that Ben-Gurion would dismiss "what was said at the banquet" and raise the question of the bitter plight of Poland's Jews for the first time on a walk afterward, as if he had not heard Kot speak of their "biological destruction" and had not himself made a number of demands and brought up various ideas for rescue during their talks.

Given these facts, it is deplorable that Gutman did not present Ben-Gurion's comments to Kot—that PGE must "help the Polish Jews who are being killed," that this was "the most burning issue at the moment," and that "we will never forget it if you don't come to their assistance"—in an accurate context.

CHAPTER FOUR

BEN-GURION VS. BEN-GURION

B EN-GURION PLAYED his own role in this *Rashomon* story.
Strange as it may seem, he himself helped considerably to provide his critics, the other narrators, with ammunition. Quite often
he ignored (to use his own terminology) the individual's agenda when
at work on the nation's agenda. He frequently employed stark, bold
language, which as time passed was used by his foes to "prove" the
disgracefulness (to use a subdued term) of his behavior during the
Holocaust years. In particular, his habit of arguing a political conviction by means of reductio ad absurdum eventually was turned
against him.

A case in point is a remark he made to his party's central committee
in December 1938, in reaction to the British government's decision, in
the wake of the *Kristallnacht* riots, not to allow 10,000 Austrian and
German Jewish children whose parents had been either killed or expelled to enter Palestine, but to offer them instead asylum in Britain.
Ben-Gurion said: "Were I to know that all German Jewish children
could be rescued by transferring them to England and only half by
transfer to Palestine, I would opt for the latter, because our concern
is not only the personal interest of these children, but the historic
interest of the Jewish people."[1]

Foes from both inside and outside the party pounced upon this
unfortunate remark as if it were Ben-Gurion's standard, bearing the
essence of his dehumanized Zionism. They willfully ignored the fact
that he made this comment nine months before the war broke out,

before "rescue" and its antonym received their fateful meanings as life and death. Thus they used against him this weapon of his own manufacture, to make him seem a man with an idée fixe, a mad "Palestinocentrist" obsessed with Palestine, and with Palestine only.

But no reasonable person can believe that Ben-Gurion was willing to sacrifice half the Jewish children in Germany on the Zionist altar. It is certain that those children's lives were dearer to him than Zionist theory—if only because Zionism was expressly created for their sake, and because only Jewish children could become its practitioners.

What is more, if Ben-Gurion's listeners at the time had interpreted his remark the way his critics do today, there would have been an uproar, not only within Mapai, but throughout the Yishuv. The fact is—as the stenographic record demonstrates—that none of the central committee members objected. They all understood the remark in the spirit in which it was said. Ben-Gurion's good friend Yitzhak Ben-Zvi, known for his sensibilities, was even moved to clarify the remark by putting it in context: "ten thousand children are a small part of Germany's [Jewish] children. . . . They [the British] don't intend to save Germany's Jews, and certainly not all of them. The moment the Jewish State Plan [the Peel plan] was shelved, the possibility of complete rescue of Germany's Jews was shelved with it."

Undoubtedly, Ben-Gurion's harshness was a reaction to Britain's refusal to allow the children into Palestine. The British pretext was that the Arabs would boycott the talks on Palestine's future that were due to open in January 1939 at St. James's Palace in London. Ben-Gurion argued that this was not the only reason for the refusal. Weizmann, too, regarded it as a harbinger of a change in British policy, a first step toward introducing restrictions on Jewish immigration to Palestine, and sternly warned Malcolm MacDonald, the colonial secretary, against this "tendency," which indeed found its full expression in the May 1939 White Paper.

Ben-Gurion also spoke against appeasement of the Arabs: "even immigration of children is subject to the good graces of the Arabs, and not only of Palestine's Arabs, but of the Arabs in neighboring countries."[2] He argued further that the refusal was congruent with propositions aired in Whitehall suggesting that the entire Jewish problem could be solved in Angola, British Guiana, and other lands. But Ben-Gurion was convinced that sending the children to countries other than Palestine would not prove beneficial for them. In all other countries, he predicted, they would face an evil fate. And history proved him right: For even if the European countries had opened their gates to masses of Jewish children, they would shortly have fallen into Hitler's hands and been massacred; while what awaited them in the neutral countries was the unhappy life of defenseless refugees, without national status.

Ben-Gurion's unfortunate, brutal remark might also have been a reaction to the Evian Conference of July 1938, in which the free world's indifference to Jewish suffering became evident. In any case, it was uttered with the intention of forcefully implanting in the public's mind the axiom that the only true rescue of the children, and of the entire Jewish people, could be in Jewish Palestine.

In the end, Ben-Gurion's remark withstood the test of events. After extensive deliberations, many of the 10,000 children were admitted into Britain between December 1938 and September 1939. But with the outbreak of the war the British government imposed an absolute ban on all immigration from Germany and its occupied territories into all parts of the British Empire. This ban was not lifted until the war ended, so that only 10,000 more Jews were fortunate enough to find shelter in Britain throughout the war years. In March 1943 Viscount Cranborne, lord privy seal and member of the war cabinet, acknowledged in the House of Lords that the United Kingdom was "admitting over 800 refugees [of all creeds] a month"—most of whom intended to join the armed forces—which was the limit "beyond which, in this country, we cannot, and will not go."[3] Had the government admitted half the Jewish children in Nazi-occupied Europe into Palestine—as Ben-Gurion's remark postulated—they would have been rescued and alive. What did happen was that more than a million Jewish children found their harrowing deaths in the Holocaust.

A second remark that appeared to demonstrate a certain callousness—and also became a cannon turned against Ben-Gurion that used his own ammunition—was made on February 1, 1945, at a meeting of the Sixth Histadrut Conference dedicated to "Diaspora and

Palestine," which heard soldiers just returned from Europe. The floor was also given to Rozka Korczak, a member of HaShomer HaTzair and a hero of the Vilna ghetto and the partisans. Korczak, who had arrived in Palestine on December 12, 1944, was prompted to take the floor by her HaShomer HaTzair friends. Since the conference was conducted in Hebrew, a language she did not know, she understood nothing of the proceedings. Suddenly, as she later recalled, Aharon Zisling, the chairman, announced her name and introduced her. She found her way to the podium and recounted in Yiddish—"out of the heart, not out of notes"—everything that had happened to her and to her comrades-in-arms in the ghetto and in the woods. Years later she said and wrote, "Ben-Gurion took the floor after me and began by saying, 'Although the speaker before me used a foreign language that grates on the ear . . .' and did not continue, because they would not let him continue. An uproar broke out in the hall, yelling, heckling, total pandemonium, with everybody taking part."[4]

In various versions, this account later served repeatedly as proof of Ben-Gurion's "condemnation of the Diaspora" and of the derision and contempt he felt for Holocaust survivors.

But what really happened at the conference? This has been the subject of a long debate.

There are two records of the conference proceedings: the original stenographic pads and the typed transcript of them, which Ben-Gurion kept in his own archives, and the official, edited record, published six months later. According to the official record, Ben-Gurion did not immediately follow Korczak on the podium. He was the ninth speaker to follow her, being preceded by the remarks of the returned soldiers (which may have been in the form of letters read from the podium and therefore not taken down by the stenographers).

Ben-Gurion began by saying that unity was a must in the face of the approaching struggle, which required one and all "to brace for the morrow." He then castigated the squabbles and quarrels within the labor movement and among its parties and factions, which, he said, made for separatism and ill will. "In the labor movement there is a breakdown in faith in the collective and in the will to belong to it;

only the parties seem worthy of their members' loyalty." Therefore, "what we need is a constant, resolute effort, patience and tolerance— here, a moment ago, you all listened attentively and alertly to a refugee friend," and in all probability he meant to say that Korczak's message also called for more unity, but was unable to refrain from noting, "although she used a language that is foreign to many [of us]. . . ." At this point there were "heckling and disturbances on the part of Poale Zion Left," a small Marxist faction.

The chairman, Zisling—a leader of Ahdut HaAvodah, which had broken away from Ben-Gurion's Mapai and run its own ticket in the 1944 elections, and a fierce opponent of Ben-Gurion and Mapai— quickly rebuked the hecklers and quieted them down. Addressing the Poale Zion Left delegates, he said: "You're so excited that you get all worked up over nothing. Only a few moments ago I told those delegates who asked that Korczak's address be translated, that translation is out of the question." Clearly, there were some conference delegates who did not understand Yiddish and demanded translation. But the Histadrut had always had a policy of using Hebrew only. Otherwise, the need to translate from Hebrew to languages brought from all over the globe and back again would have made the proceedings intolerably long.

Zisling continued: "I have listened to Ben-Gurion speak, and if it had not been for the interruption no one would have taken his words as offensive—I, as chairman, am authorized to interpret and put things in their true light."[5]

After this, Ben-Gurion went on with his speech, encountering no further interruptions.

This official record shows, therefore, that the entire conference did not jump at Ben-Gurion's throat, and that it was not "condemnation of the Diaspora" or "derision toward Holocaust survivors" on his part that triggered the disturbance. The ruckus was the exclusive doing of Poale Zion Left, exponents of "klassen Kampf" (class war) and defenders of Yiddish as the language of the Jewish proletariat. This episode therefore was taken as just another round in the old "war of the languages" that had had its heyday in 1906–20, in the long-defunct

Poale Zion, Ben-Gurion's former party. As a Hebrew fanatic, he had refused, in 1907, to take part in writing and editing Poale Zion's first paper in Palestine, the Yiddish *Der Anfang* (The Beginning).

Ben-Gurion's attitude toward Yiddish was tied perhaps to his mother's death when he was eleven years old, an event that caused some peculiarities in his adult behavior: He could not remember his mother's face, the color and shape of her hair, or her family name and relations. Perhaps he did not want to use the language that was exclusive to the two of them, for from a tender age he spoke Hebrew with his grandfather and father. He may not have liked Yiddish because it was so symbolic of the European Diaspora, from which he made up his mind to flee when he was fourteen. And he may have disliked it because it was a mixture of primary tongues—German, Hebrew, Polish, and Russian; perhaps he felt Yiddish defiled Hebrew. This we shall never know.

Despite his harsh judgment on Yiddish, he used it all his life for counting and calculating. He campaigned in it during all his party and Zionist work in Europe through the 1930s and the 1940s. Much of his correspondence with his wife, Paula, before and after he married her, was in Yiddish. He corresponded exclusively in Yiddish with Marc Jarblum of Poale Zion in France, and used it as his *lingua franca* during all his visits to the DP camps after the war. In 1945 at Bergen-Belsen he copied out the Jewish partisans' song "Never Say This Way Is My Last" (Sog Nisht Kein Mal Ost Du Geist Dem Lezten Weg) as well as other Yiddish poems. In sum, it seems that insensitivity and a complete lack of tact led to his remarks at the Histadrut conference, rather than derision or disdain for the Diaspora.

After some reflection Korczak also concluded "that Ben-Gurion's remark was aimed against the language, not the person or the Diaspora . . . personally I was not offended." She added, however: "in that situation, in the mood that prevailed in the hall after my address, it was remarkable lack of tact and consideration on Ben-Gurion's part, and even lack of good taste."[6]

The Hebrew press was divided as well. Since *Davar* was the Histadrut's official organ (and the semiofficial organ of Mapai), it was this paper's minutes of the conference that were later published as the official record, so *Davar*'s version is identical to that record.[7]

Mishmar, the organ of Korczak's own party, HaShomer HaTzair, reported that Ben-Gurion said that Korczak spoke "a foreign, grating language," at which point hecklers from the Poale Zion Left benches called out, "Take back your words." When Chairman Zisling gave his interpretation and explained that the speaker did not mean to offend Yiddish, but only to note that there were deputies in the hall to whom Yiddish is a strange language, the storm died down.[8]

The independent *Ha'aretz,* under the headline "Linguistic Incident," also quoted Ben-Gurion as having said "foreign, grating" language. But this paper too attributed the uproar to Poale Zion Left.[9]

Neuewelt, Poale Zion Left's weekly, headlined the incident "Uproar Against Ben-Gurion for Having Insulted Yiddish." Its account is very close to Korczak's version, stating that "as if in passing" Ben-Gurion "rudely offended the Yiddish language," using an "unjustified, inhuman and uncivilized expression," an expression that "truly electrified the entire hall," and Poale Zion Left would not let him go on "unless he retracted 'foreign and grating' and apologized." Only after the chairman "exerted maximal effort" and interpreted Ben-Gurion's "meaning," and because Ben-Gurion "swallowed" without a word the chairman's interpretation, did "the storm die down." However, the weekly went on, the incident became the talk of the conference, and it was unanimously agreed that Poale Zion Left had honored the conference by their behavior.[10]

A comparison between the typed transcript and the official record explains the difference between *Davar*'s version and that of the other papers. The stenographer records Ben-Gurion as saying: "You have all listened thirstily and attentively when you were spoken to in a language which is grating and foreign, but which is the language of those who died [heckling and disturbances on the part of Poale Zion Left]." Whereas *Davar* and the official record have him say: "You have just listened alertly and attentively to a refugee friend, although for many her language was foreign [heckling and disturbances on the part of Poale Zion Left]."[11]

It is clear therefore that *Davar* and the official record omitted "grating" and "the language of those who died." On the other hand, they added "refugee friend." They also modified "you have all listened" to "you have just listened," most probably to take account of Zisling's explanation that not all the conference delegates understood Yiddish.

The stenographer's rendition of Zisling's intervention is also slightly different from that of *Davar* and the official record. This is because the speakers were given the opportunity to edit their remarks for publication. It is obvious that Zisling made liberal use of this privilege. Not only did he improve the grammar and syntax of his remarks, he also omitted three phrases. The first, "None of us here need special authority to stand up and defend the Yiddish language," could have been a barb at Poale Zion Left's posturing as the language's only defenders in the labor movement. The second was apparently meant to exculpate Ben-Gurion and further reprimand Poale Zion Left: "There is no one among us who does not feel his [or her] ties with it [Yiddish] and its roots; it is the language Jewish people used, for years and generations, to create and to struggle, and which the Jewish people loved and exalted. There was no call, at this juncture in our lives, to cause this uproar." His third omission was: "I am certain this was only a slip of the tongue by Ben-Gurion. We don't have today, in Palestine, a war of languages." This, as explained below, can be interpreted as an apology on the part of Ben-Gurion, because right after it the stenographer notes, "Disruption on the part of Poale Zion Left continues." Then the stenographer goes on with Ben-Gurion's remarks as if nothing had happened. Some off-the-record exchange, therefore, must have taken place between the chairman and the hecklers, on one hand, and between the chairman and Ben-Gurion, on the other, until a compromise was reached.

I believe that while Ben-Gurion stood on the podium, facing the heckling and disruption from the Poale Zion Left benches, he and Zisling reached a compromise that was the basis for the latter's intervention. Otherwise Ben-Gurion would have brought down on himself the wrath of the entire conference—Mapai delegates included—and the protest would not have been confined to Poale Zion Left. Yiddish-loving Mapai leaders would have risen as one to demand an apology, and until it was given, the conference would not have returned to its business. Furthermore, Zisling himself would have insisted on an apology—as can be gathered from the stenographer's transcript—and only after Ben-Gurion consented to his utterance being described as a slip of the tongue did the chairman stand by him and the conference proceed. In any event, had there not been a compromise, Poale Zion Left would have dwelled on the remark in the debate that ended the day's proceedings.

This impression is strengthened by the *Neuewelt*'s boast that Poale Zion Left did not let Ben-Gurion continue "until he retracted 'foreign and grating' and apologized" and that only after the chairman "exerted maximal effort" and interpreted Ben-Gurion's "meaning"—and because Ben-Gurion "swallowed" without a word the chairman's interpretation—did "the storm die down."

Did Ben-Gurion also edit his remarks for publication? The records show that he did, but only for grammar and style. Was it he who omitted in the official version that Yiddish was "grating" and "the language of those who died"? This of course is possible. But it is far more probable that it was done for him by others, with his consent. In any event, he kept in his private archive a copy of the original stenographer's typescript, unchanged. This suggests two things: that Ben-Gurion did not tamper with records and documents, and that he was utterly unaware of his notorious tactlessness.

One puzzle remains: Why was Ben-Gurion's phrase about Yiddish being "the language of those who died" also struck from the published record? Obviously, his strongest defense would have been that he meant to say that regardless of its being "foreign" and unpleasant to the ear, it must be respected as the language of many who were murdered by the Nazis. Indeed, in the calm after the storm he clarified his meaning: Just as "tolerance and patience are needed in understanding the past [when Yiddish reigned as a Jewish language]," he said, there was need for "stubborn perseverance and tenacious struggle in entrenching the new values" created in Jewish Palestine. Therefore modern, everyday Hebrew must also be taught to all, "without flinching from difficulties" and "without estrangement and disrespect for the Diaspora heritage, its customs and languages." This passage, taken from the official record, differs only grammatically and stylistically from the stenographer's transcript, not in substance.

IF BEN-GURION, LIKE all the other speakers who followed him, had alluded only to Korczak's address, he would have avoided significant trouble. For it became accepted dogma that he had labeled Yiddish a "foreign language, grating to the ear" of Jews in Palestine. Rumor gave this notion much currency in the Yiddish papers in America, where Yiddish writers got to the point of calling a boycott of Ben-Gurion. However, when he was in New York in July 1945, he met with some of the most notable ones—including Leo Halpern (H. Leivick), Avraham Reisin, Menahem Boreyshe, Kadia Moldowsky, and Benyamin Bialostotzky—and managed, according to his diary, to pacify them. Nevertheless, the reverberations reached as far as the Soviet Union, where Ben-Gurion's words made, as Korczak put it, "a grave impression" on the great Yiddish poet Avraham Sutzkever, who also found them offensive.[12]

CHAPTER FIVE

BEN-GURION'S "FRIEND"

THROUGHOUT HIS LIFE, Ben-Gurion used to say he had four
lifelong friends. He generally named the same ones: Shlomo
Lavi, from his Plonsk childhood; Yitzhak Ben-Zvi, his political partner
before and during World War I; Shmuel Yavneli, with whom he shared
his first experience as a farm hand in the Galilee in 1907 and 1908;
Berl Katznelson, with whom he had founded Ahdut HaAvodah and
Mapai; and Yitzhak Tabenkin, his main rival in the labor movement.
To keep the number at four, he would leave out one or another of
these names. But whatever the composition of the quartet, it never
included anyone born in the twentieth century.

This way Ben-Gurion avoided offending the many people he
worked with during his sixty-odd years in politics. No matter how
enchanted he was with his younger aides—Moshe Dayan, Teddy
Kollek, and Shimon Peres—they never made it into his quartet.

This circumspection on Ben-Gurion's part, however, did not prevent some individuals from claiming friendship and closeness with
him—even, if necessary, by ruse and fabrication. One such character,
who thrust herself forcibly into the *Rashomon* tale, was Ruth Aliav
(Klueger), who caused Ben-Gurion almost irretrievable harm. Considered an effective organizer of illegal immigration to Palestine during
and after World War II, and close to members of the JAE, she achieved
some fame when she published her memoirs.[1] She was also found
worthy of a long taping session by the Ben-Gurion Heritage Institute's
Oral Documentation Department. The fictitious, highly imaginative

57

story she told them, widely believed to be reliable and authoritative, served as another proof of Ben-Gurion's supposed callousness toward the Holocaust and its victims.

In her oral account, Aliav described herself as Ben-Gurion's only traveling companion and bodyguard on his visit to the DP camps in Germany—the first such visit by a Zionist leader—in October 1945. Having been given a rank equivalent to that of full colonel in the U.S. Army, she was entitled, she claimed, to accommodations on a train and an army jeep with a soldier driver. She added that she and Ben-Gurion were the only occupants of the sleeper car on the night train from Paris to Frankfurt.

According to her story, she took Ben-Gurion in the jeep to his appointments in Frankfurt and on a tour of the ruined city. They became fast friends, to the degree that she allowed herself to call him by his initials, "Bee Gee," thus inventing, she said, his most popular nickname.

It seems, however, that she discovered that her Bee Gee was more interested in rare books than in his fellow Jews. This notion of course caught on quickly and found its way into books, Hebrew and English.

In *The Seventh Million*, Segev uses Aliav's oral interview to emphasize Ben-Gurion's "compulsive passion for collecting books," bordering on bibliomania. Aliav, Segev writes, "recalled with a shudder how he made her drive him through the ruins of Frankfurt, evading American military police barriers, to see if any books remained there." She protested, she said in her oral account, saying no books were left, and feeling very angry at him for not being moved by the total extermination of Frankfurt's Jewish community. But he persevered, and the following dialogue ensued:

Bee Gee: "I am sure that in the Jewish Quarter, where Rabbi Carlebach's synagogue used to stand, I can still find something."

Aliav: "It's all in ruins."

Bee Gee: "Let's search, maybe something is left."

Aliav: "We cannot get there, it's all ravaged and collapsing, can't you see that?"

But Bee Gee did not give in and she, against her will, and in disobedience of army orders, took him there, despite heaps of rubble.

And then, while the driver negotiated around chunks of iron and huge blocks of concrete that had been parts of buildings, "somehow we found a street more or less whole with a few stores with lit candles in their shop windows."

Bee Gee: "Stop the jeep!"

"It was right at the entrance to the Jewish Quarter, near the synagogue . . . ," Aliav told her interviewers. "There he found 'treasures, treasures!': ancient Haggadahs, a 19th-century Bible, a copy of *Kuzari* by the 12th-century Hebrew poet Judah Halevi, and loose pages from old books. He dug through them with an expert hand, saying 'this yes, that no,' loading what he found on the jeep."

The shopkeeper, a goy, "perhaps a Nazi," added Aliav, "was glad to be rid of—" But she was interrupted before she finished her sentence. Did she mean the goy was glad to have the rare books taken off his hands? We shall never know, for the rattled interviewers asked in disbelief: "He collected all these?"

Aliav: "Collected, carried, I carried, the driver carried, we all carried together . . . we came out loaded with a heap I didn't know what to do with." Yet Bee Gee apparently did not have enough and intended to go back to collect more, for Aliav continued: "[Till] I said: 'Well, Ben-Gurion, now we must meet with the Jews.' "

Bee Gee: "OK. But in the afternoon we shall go book-hunting again."[2]

Had Aliav been the only source to describe Ben-Gurion's first visit to the camps, her picture of him as an acquisitive, insensitive, greedy man would be hard to contest. Fortunately, other sources, more reliable, portray him quite differently.

It is puzzling that an experienced writer like Segev relied on Aliav's account without wondering how a personage of Ben-Gurion's political status could have traveled through a military zone only five months after the war's end, then gone wandering through Frankfurt's ruined streets, accompanied only by "Colonel" Aliav as guide and guard. Did he not ask himself why the goy bookseller ("perhaps a Nazi," in Aliav's account) should be so glad to be rid of very expensive rare books, nor how Ben-Gurion paid for them—did he happen to be carrying fat wads of dollar bills? But more important, if the bookseller was a Nazi, his rare books must have been loot plundered from their Jewish owners, or from the nearby synagogue. Did Ben-Gurion's bibliomania drive him to be an accomplice to Nazi criminals?

What is more, the mere fact that there never was a Rabbi Carlebach's synagogue in Frankfurt—the Carlebach rabbis served in north and central Germany (Bremen, Lübeck, Altona, Hamburg, Berlin, Cologne, Leipzig, etc.)—should have put Aliav's listeners and readers on their guard. And finally, an avid collector of books, as Ben-Gurion certainly was, normally keeps a record of his acquisitions.

Indeed, keeping such records, in the minutest detail, was a happy pastime for Ben-Gurion. On October 23, 1945, on his arrival in Heidelberg, in the American zone, he noted in his diary: "This is the first time that I have in Germany a spacious room with a private bath, and what's more amazing, with bath towels. So far I have been told that there are no books in [old] Greek to be found. Sold out." This must be why he acquired so little. For on November 24, 1945, after his return to Jerusalem, he summed up in his diary all the books he had bought in his travels that year: "I have received the package of books from Paris (my first visit May 12, 1945) . . . I have still to receive from London 96 books, from Paris 150, from Heidelberg 21, from the States 669—in toto 936." And from Frankfurt?—none. Ben-Gurion was not ashamed to buy books in Germany, as is evidenced by his Heidelberg entry, and there is a strong likelihood that had he acquired in Frankfurt ancient Haggadahs and a *Kuzari,* he would have noted that in his diary.

Further investigation reveals that Aliav willingly helped him, from afar, to acquire books. In May 1945, five months before his visit to Frankfurt, Ben-Gurion wrote to Zvi Maimon, his secretary, that Aliav had sent from Paris "a few books to Cairo, to be delivered to me from there to Palestine," and that she still had "a few more books (Greek and French) which she is about to post" to him via Cairo.[3]

At this point, a pro-Ben-Gurion character enters the *Rashomon* drama, coming to his defense by wholly refuting Aliav's testimony: the American rabbi Judah Nadich.

On this first postwar visit to Germany, in October 1945, Ben-Gurion was the official guest of the U.S. Army and its commander,

Gen. Dwight D. Eisenhower, whose SHAEF (Supreme Headquarters, Allied Expeditionary Force) was in Frankfurt. Eisenhower's chief of staff, Lt. Gen. Walter Bedell Smith, put army chaplain Rabbi Judah Nadich at Ben-Gurion's disposal as an aide-de-camp. On October 17 Ben-Gurion noted in his diary, "Had supper with the American rabbi [Judah Efraim Nadich] . . . we set out the itinerary and the program of the visit to Germany." The next day Ben-Gurion noted, "at 2 pm Nadich came . . . at 6 in the evening I set out to Frankfurt with the Army Chaplain, Rabbi Judah Nadich."

Indeed, it was Rabbi Nadich, whose rank was equivalent to that of a major, who reserved for Ben-Gurion a berth in the sleeper of the American army shuttle train, "the only train as yet linking Paris and Frankfurt," as Nadich wrote in his book *Eisenhower and the Jews*.[4] It was he who reserved their two-bed compartment, a privilege of field-grade officers only. "In the train car there were only the two of us," Nadich recalled in an interview, "not a sign of Aliav."

Nadich, who was acquainted with Aliav, expressed his opinion of her chivalrously: "Ruth is a very capable woman, but also a highly romantic person, seeing herself in episodes in a way that is close to the truth, but not the entire truth." Ehud Avriel, an illegal-immigration activist at the time, and later a close aide to Ben-Gurion, and Teddy Kollek, who worked with her and knew her well, made similar evaluations of her character.[5]

Ben-Gurion and Nadich stayed up till 2:00 a.m. talking. In interviews and in his book, Nadich spoke of the "rare opportunity" of a "private and uninterrupted" conversation "with this extraordinary man who was soon destined to lead the Jewish people into a new and happier chapter of its history." Jews from outside Europe had just "discovered" the Holocaust. They wondered what amount of damage it had inflicted on the survivors and asked many questions. Would they be welfare cases to the end of their lives, or could they be rehabilitated? And if so, how long would it take to restore them to normal life?

These same questions worried Ben-Gurion. He, too, wanted to know what scars years of persecution had left on these Jews. Were they broken? Would they have to be hospitalized, and if so for how long? But he also wanted to know where they would want to go from their DP camps—to Palestine or to other countries? Nadich responded that 80 percent would opt for Palestine. Ben-Gurion then asked what kind of human material they were. His key concern was whether they were "good material"—Nadich's phrase—for the Yishuv, and whether it would be possible to make the survivors citizens of the Yishuv—how long would that take?

The purpose of Ben-Gurion's visit was to discover if it would be possible to rally the DPs behind the Zionist campaign for free Jewish immigration to Palestine. When in May 1944 the White Paper's quota of 75,000 certificates had expired, the British did not announce a new quota nor did they annul the White Paper. Public opinion in both Britain and the United States was calling for Jewish immigration to Palestine. Ben-Gurion's and the JAE's tactic was to insist on "free immigration" and the annulment of the White Paper. In a letter to Dr. Nahum Goldmann in New York, he wrote: "I intend to explain to them why we refused, and continue to refuse, to receive [immigration] certificates [from the mandatory government] as long as the White Paper is in force, and how they can be of help to the Zionist struggle." In the DP camps he told his audience, as reported by the DP Yiddish newspaper *Unzer Weg*, "In the coming struggle yours will be an important role. I know what you went through, and it is not easy to demand this from you. Nevertheless I must, because you constitute a strong factor. You are not only the ones in need but a political force. Looking at you I can see that there are not only massacred Jews but Jewish warriors as well." On his return to Palestine he told the Mapai secretariat that he had gone to the DP camps to see if it was possible to organize in Europe a Zionist *Résistance* (he used the French term), "for I knew that there was in Europe one community that would have special significance for or against our struggle, and that community is *Sherit HaPleta* [the remnants] in Germany. We have been told that if we do not grant them certificates, they will either die, be lost for Zionism [out of resentment at the JAE's hard-line policy of refusing certificates], go back to Poland, or assimilate, and that will be that. I had to face the question: are these Jews a hindrance to Zionism or a source of strength?"[6]

In speaking to the DPs, Ben-Gurion did not try to comfort them or salve mental or spiritual wounds. There was nothing maternal or even avuncular in his appearance. There were those who expected the Yishuv's leader, and the upcoming leader of the Zionist movement, to mourn the 6 million dead, to promise vengeance, to shake a fist at the world, to weep with his listeners. There were others who thought it would have been fitting, not to mention in good taste, for his sole interest to be the welfare of the survivors and how best to look after them, without imposing upon them political tasks and ideological commitments. For some, Ben-Gurion's failure to demonstrate compassion and human interest proved that he lacked interest in the survivors as human beings, regarding them as no more than pawns in Zionism's political struggle. Certainly, Ben-Gurion was no Mother Teresa.

But he was an unusual man, and it is also true that the survivors were an unusual audience. At any rate, their encounter produced a kind of magic, one that generated a great light and no shadows. To judge by *Unzer Weg,* at least, the DPs derived great satisfaction from Ben-Gurion's pragmatic, businesslike approach. His reception on this trip by the groups of survivors, described below, can be accounted for in several ways. Perhaps the last thing a survivor of the inferno needs is a wet nurse and a shoulder to cry on. Perhaps the shock of being turned from a weak, needy recipient into a potentially strong person who can give and do for others brought about a transformation. Perhaps they understood—as Ben-Gurion must have wanted them to —that in making demands upon them, he, not UNRRA and the welfare people, was giving them new life. For what is new life to the half dead, if not a goal and a struggle to achieve it?

Then, finally, what was the alternative? To be repatriated to Poland, where everybody still hated them as Jews, as if there had been no war and no Holocaust, or remain in hateful Germany? It must be remembered that the doors of America, England, and many other coveted lands in the West were firmly shut. In those circumstances, Jewish Palestine was a very good choice.

Finally, there must have been the issue of pride. Only Ben-Gurion and the struggle for a free Jewish state in Palestine, land of the Patriarchs and forefathers, could offer them real pride and a feeling that their sacrifice had not been entirely in vain. In this respect the downtrodden, the half dead in body and spirit, are like the blind. Just as the blind prefer the return of the light of their eyes over anything else, so the meek in DP camps preferred pride above all. Ben-Gurion offered them the most fantastic gift of all—the pride of soldiering for their own free land.

Ben-Gurion must have been aware of the resuscitation he produced in the half dead, and he was as proud as they. On his return to Palestine he described to his party how he had told them of his policy—either free immigration and the annulment of the White Paper, or no certificates at all—and how they responded: "Maybe they [the British] will throw us a bone [a limited number of certificates], but the White Paper will remain in force. Would you rather have us give in only so you would be able to go to Palestine, or not [meaning we should go on fighting]? They said: 'We will wait, after everything we went through, we are ready for that too, if this is Zionism's call."[7] The scene brings to mind Ezekiel's vision (chapter 37) of the dry bones in the dark valley coming to life.

In *Eisenhower and the Jews,* Nadich summed it up: "Like all great men who are forever identified with the cause to which they have consecrated their lives, Ben-Gurion was consumed with only one burning passion—Palestine and the coming free Jewish State. The Jewish DPs in the camps . . . were his wards and he was their guardian and protector, because they were the future citizens of the Jewish State to be."

These, then, were his concerns, and he wanted to carry out his tour in a way that would answer his questions. It was a kind of bargain: He would see the DPs and hear them, and in return he would infuse them with Zionism. Indeed, he made good on his word. "He spoke with the vigor of a young man [he was fifty-nine] and the strength of a zealot," Nadich wrote after the tour. "He could have only pity for those Jews who were complacent and self-satisfied and who did not eagerly seize the privilege of participating personally in the great historic Jewish achievement of our times—the building of a free Jewish commonwealth."[8]

They arrived in Frankfurt at 9:00 Friday morning, October 19. A car and driver awaited them at the railroad station. Next, Nadich noted in his wartime diary, he took Ben-Gurion "to Billeting Officer" for accommodation, meal tickets, etc., "to Finance Officer" to get American army scrip for the PX, and then "to Hotel Excelsior," where the army put up its guests. Then they lunched in the officers' mess at the casino at the Carlton Hotel (Rabbi Nadich was "shocked and upset" to see Ben-Gurion order and eat pork).

After lunch Nadich took Ben-Gurion in his car to the first DP camp that he would visit, at Zeilsheim, half an hour's drive from Frankfurt. Nadich parked a little distance beyond the gates, asking Ben-Gurion to stay put until he made the necessary arrangements. On his way back to the car he saw a small group gathering around it, and one of the Jews peering inside. Recognizing Ben-Gurion he suddenly screamed "in an unearthly voice," "Ben-Gurion! Ben-Gurion!"

To a man, wrote Nadich, the entire group turned toward the car and began shrieking, shouting the name of the man whom all accepted as their own political leader. "But he was far more than that to them. He was the personal embodiment of all their hopes for the future. . . . That hope had given them that last ounce of strength which they had needed to be counted among the handful of survivors at the end. Palestine! Palestine! Now, after all these many years, here was Palestine right in the midst of their DP camp on German soil. For who better than Ben-Gurion personified Eretz Israel and its fight for freedom and independence?"

The shrieks and cries multiplied, and the crowd quickly grew larger and larger, till Nadich became frightened, he wrote, of a possible riot. He promised that they would all have the chance to see and hear Ben-Gurion if they followed his instructions and gathered at the camp auditorium. The word flashed throughout the camp, and in a few minutes Nadich led Ben-Gurion into the large hall, all the seats occupied, all the aisles filled, every inch of space packed, many crowding near the doors or leaning over the windowsills. As he brought Ben-Gurion in, the refugees burst into "the Zionist hymn 'Hatikva' [The Hope]." As Ben-Gurion stood on the platform they broke into cheers, into song, and finally into weeping. "At last," wrote Nadich, "he began to speak, his voice choked up, his eyes filled. He had to stop as he broke down for a moment. In the sudden quiet one could hear the muffled sobbing" of his audience. "Very few eyes were dry. For the incredible had happened. Ben-Gurion was in their midst and they had lived despite Hitler . . . [despite] all the diabolical instruments of destruction . . . they had lived . . . to this day when they could welcome Ben-Gurion!"

Ben-Gurion spoke to them, in Yiddish, words of comfort and consolation. He brought them "the message of good tidings" from their brethren in Palestine, "who anxiously were awaiting their coming." He assured them they would be welcomed with open arms. He promised that the Jews of Palestine would brave every obstacle in order to transport them to Palestine as quickly as possible.

The visit to Zeilsheim had to be rushed, because Ben-Gurion had a meeting with Eisenhower at five o'clock that afternoon and the general's chief of staff, Bedell Smith, wished to see him first. So Ben-Gurion had to shorten his speech in order to inspect the camp with the head of the UNRRA team that managed it. Large crowds accompanied them wherever they went, and finally to Nadich's car.

Ben-Gurion's meeting with Smith lengthened, because Eisenhower could not return in time from an inspection tour. In his diary Ben-Gurion mentioned only his interview with General Smith and his meeting at six in the evening with the local Jewish committee (a group of DP leaders representing the Jews in the nearby camps and those of Frankfurt and neighboring areas), noting in minute detail the information he gathered from the members. He did not mention his visit to Zeilsheim at all, not even noting the time or name. The reason can perhaps be found in his report to the Mapai secretariat on his return to Palestine: "The first meeting [with the DPs] took place at Zeilsheim, near Frankfurt. The gate's name is in Hebrew, the streets are named after Bialik [the Zionist national Hebrew poet], Jerusalem and Tel Aviv. Although I was a little disappointed [in some of the camp's people] after the great impression of my first visit there, in general, there is no way to describe what such a meeting means to every Jew. I did not find there much knowledge of Hebrew, but not a little Zionism. Of course I could not inquire about what really interested me there [the Zionist potential of the refugees], but the essence of the experience [the Holocaust experience and what it has done to the refugees] I won't talk about."

Ben-Gurion's "disappointment" can be explained by his comment to his party that "to my astonishment I found there [in the camp] cases of corruption [black marketeering], but less than can be expected under the circumstances. [But] I found the people [generally] healthy, first of all in body, but in spirit as well. The great majority are dear Jews, dear Zionists."[9]

Levi Shalit, a survivor who took part in Ben-Gurion's meeting with the Jewish committee, recalled that he "began by asking questions about ourselves, who we were, where we came from. He followed with more personal questions but avoided inquiring about our experiences in the ghetto, in the [death] camps."[10]

This near obsession with minute details of personal practical matters, along with an utter inability or unwillingness to express his feelings on the Holocaust, recurred time and again. The Holocaust was one case where Ben-Gurion was simply out of words. In this he was not the only one—Palestine's, and later Israel's, greatest poets were struck with the same silence.

October 19 ended with supper with Nadich at the officers' mess in the Carlton Hotel.

ON THE FOLLOWING five days, Nadich had to accompany Judge Simon Rifkind, Eisenhower's adviser on Jewish affairs, and Ben-Gurion went on his tour of the major DP camps in an army car in the company of a Major Penny, who was appointed his ADC.

Aliav arrived in Frankfurt on the 22nd, Nadich's war diary notes. Ben-Gurion returned to Frankfurt on the afternoon of the 24th in time for a 4:30 meeting with General Smith that lasted till 5:30. "Busy with him all day," Nadich noted in his diary, meaning that Nadich and Rifkind, who participated in the meeting with General Smith, went on to discuss Jewish matters. Following that, Nadich recalled "a long meeting" in which Ben-Gurion "told me his views [on the DP camps]. He then gave me notes and told me to prepare a report to submit to Eisenhower and Smith."[11]

On the 25th Ben-Gurion began a tour of the DP camps in the

British Occupied Zone, without the permission or knowledge of the British authorities there. For accommodation and food, he had to rely on Jewish Palestinian soldiers serving with the British army.

At 10:30 in the morning he was driven in an American army car via Kassel to Hanover, where he arrived at 8:00 in the evening. The next two days and nights he spent at an army camp near Bergen-Belsen. He visited this labor camp, whose graveyard contained 30,000 of its inmates, and the nearby DP camp. In Bergen-Belsen he met with men and women who had served with the partisans, and so impressed was he with their hymn that he copied it in Yiddish into his diary. In an auditorium full to capacity, he spoke, as he noted in his diary, "on the catastrophe, on [the prevention of] its recurrence, and on Palestine as a Jewish center that does not entrust its security to others, but puts its trust in its own strength, will and independence."[12]

He returned to Frankfurt at 4:30 on the afternoon of October 28. In his diary for that day he noted that in Frankfurt he had met Zerah Warhaftig of the Labor Zionist religious party, and there he saw Ruth Aliav, "who reported that fifty [Jewish] children are being sent to Palestine and that they are about to send two thousand children from Lemberg (Lvov) to a place in the West." That evening he met with Joseph Schwartz, the American Joint Distribution Committee (AJDC) chief in Europe, and Ayala Fleg (later Mrs. Sachs-Abramov) "to discuss modes of operation."[13]

By this point he had met individually with hundreds of Jewish DPs and scores of Jewish soldiers and immigration activists, and addressed thousands of DPs in the camps at Zeilsheim, St. Ottilien, Landsberg, Feldafing, Dachau, and Föhrnwald, and in the cities of Frankfurt, Munich, Stuttgart, and Hanover.

In St. Ottilien, a monastery turned into a hospital for survivors, the 800 patients greeted him with a blue-and-white flag wrapped in black, and orphans presented him with flowers and greeted him in Hebrew. At Landsberg, the largest camp in Bavaria, he appeared in the sports stadium. In the British Zone he spoke at the Bergen-Belsen cemetery, near the common grave where many thousands of Jews were buried. In all the camps he was greeted in the same way as he had been in Zeilsheim.

In St. Ottilien his inability or unwillingness to speak about the atrocities the Jews had undergone manifested itself publicly. "The tears in his eyes," reported *Unzer Weg,* "testified to his feelings at the sight of the orphans" who sang in a choir in his honor. "I will not try to express the feelings within me," he told his audience. "Such a thing is impossible."[14]

On the morning of October 29 Ben-Gurion met the philanthropist Edward Warburg, and toward noon he was driven in Eisenhower's car to meet the general at his headquarters. They had a long discussion; Eisenhower, according to Nadich, thought well of Ben-Gurion's suggestions and accepted most of them. Eisenhower later told Smith that he was very much taken by the Jewish leader, who impressed him as a top-notch statesman and a man of brilliant intellect.[15]

At 4:00 p.m., Nadich noted in his diary, he "confer[red] with Ben-Gurion & Ruth Aliav." At 5:00 they were "joined by Rifkind." At 6:00 Nadich met Schwartz, the AJDC chief for Europe, who offered him a "job as JDC director for Germany." Nadich had dinner with Jack Trobe of the AJDC, after which he met with Ben-Gurion to ask his opinion of the AJDC job offer.

This is confirmed by Ben-Gurion's diary for the 29th: "Nadich came in the evening. Schwartz offers him directorship of Joint in Germany after his demobilization in a month's time. Asked for my opinion. I said his experience of the situation in Europe and his American contacts could enable him to do important work in the States, but at present the work among the refugees in Europe is of greater importance, for this Jewry now plays a decisive role in the political destiny of Zionism, and a Zionist like him who knows the country and is close to the refugees is needed as a teacher. He is inclined to accept the offer but would still like to think it over."[16]

Next day, the 30th, Ben-Gurion left for the airport at seven in the morning and flew back to Paris in an American air force plane. All told, he spent in Frankfurt only parts of three days—the 19th, 24th, and 28th—and the whole day of the 29th. He could not have spent the entire morning of any of these days in the company of Aliav, hunting for rare books, completely oblivious to the Jewish survivors, as she describes him.

Mordechai Surkis, a sergeant in the Jewish Brigade Group with the British army who was present during Ben-Gurion's third visit, in October 1946, to the DP camps in the British Zone of occupation, saw a completely different Ben-Gurion. He told the Oral Documentation Department of the Ben-Gurion Heritage Institute that, encountering the "horrid conditions [that] prevailed . . . dilapidated barracks . . . people sleeping on three-tier berths . . . Ben-Gurion took in the entire picture with tearful eyes."[17]

When Ben-Gurion returned to Paris, he was met by Aliav's colleague Ehud Avriel, who reported that Ben-Gurion looked like "a broken man, as if suddenly aged by years . . . completely grey, as if he had lost the lust for life. He would not touch any food."[18] Avriel's account makes it clear that the Ben-Gurion he saw was a devastated man, visibly shaken by his experience in the camps.

Nadich remained associated in his mind with that experience. In 1947 Ben-Gurion wrote him in New York, where he had become the rabbi of the Park Avenue Synagogue: "I received your letter—it touched my heart. Especially your remembrance of the camp people in Germany. Like you I shall never forget this experience—the powerful combination of boundless suffering with unflinching, undaunted hope."[19]

CHAPTER SIX

DANGERS OF THE HUMAN CONSCIENCE

T OM SEGEV, LIKE Shakespeare's Bottom, is not content with playing only one role in this drama. His *The Seventh Million*, subtitled "The Israelis and the Holocaust," can be taken as a collective
charge sheet, as if compiled and filed by the entire spectrum of Ben-
Gurion critics. It is a full catalog of all the sins and crimes of which
the Orthodox, the academics, and various political circles left, right,
and center have ever accused Ben-Gurion, plus extensions and supple-
ments by the author. No stone ever flung at Ben-Gurion was too small
for Segev to pick up and throw at him again. Because of the book's
length it is possible here to examine only some of the most typical
accusations, moving from the trivial to the serious.

Two misrepresentations that recur in the academic studies of the
Yishuv during the Holocaust years also characterize the wider public
debate and Segev's volume. The first is the "condemnation of the
Diaspora" accusation, which asserts that a state of division and even
polarization existed between the Jewish community in Palestine and
the Jewish people in the Diaspora, and between the rescue of Jews and
the establishment of a Jewish state. Although this assertion is widely
made by anti-Zionist camps on both the Orthodox right and the political left, and its truth is taken as self-evident, to this day no serious
attempt has ever been made to document it.

The other misrepresentation is the result of looking at the
Holocaust situation from the perspective of today. As we have seen,
it became quite popular among all critics of Ben-Gurion to attribute

to the Yishuv and its leadership the capabilities and powers of the state of Israel. In consequence it is easy, even logical, to argue that the Yishuv had the capacity to rescue but did not use it.

Segev goes one important step further. He positions his point of historic observation in the Arab-Jewish conflict in Palestine, and from there looks critically at the Holocaust years. His reader is led to conclude that in Segev's mind Zionism has visited catastrophe—he uses indiscriminately the Hebrew word *shoah,* which today mainly denotes "Holocaust"—on both Europe's Jews and Palestine's Arabs. It was originally the Yishuv's Zionism—and its nefarious "condemnation of the Diaspora"—that prevented it from using the means at its disposal to rescue Europe's Jews. It was later that same Zionism—and its obsession with a Jewish state—that led the same Yishuv (and subsequently Israel) to expel the Arabs from Palestine and repress their remnants. Clearly, Segev's own attitude can be appropriately defined as "condemnation of Zionism." In his view, Israel, built on the ruins of Europe's Jews and Palestine's Arabs, has no right to exist as a Jewish state.

Characteristic of this viewpoint is his description of "the museum and the luxurious center [of Holocaust studies]" adjacent to Kibbutz Lohamei HaGetaot (Ghetto Fighters) that "cast their shadows over the kibbutz." He adds apologetically: "It is hard to avoid the cliché; it's a geographical fact." The kibbutz's "charter of foundation" describes it as a "settlement on the redeemed land of the Western Galilee—a living and productive monument to the ghetto uprising." He goes on to remind his reader that the kibbutz "was founded by survivors of the Warsaw Ghetto. . . . They settled on the land of the Arab village Samariah, which was destroyed during the War of Independence, its inhabitants deported." Then he quotes sardonically his museum guide, Tzvika Dror, a member of the kibbutz and an author and editor of Holocaust documentary publications, who refers to Samariah as "a village of terrorists."

In Segev's account of his visit to the kibbutz and its Holocaust museum, there is not a word about the astounding miracle that could happen only in Israel, new shoots of life sprouting from the dead. Instead he remarks, "There is no settlement in Israel that better illustrates the link between the Holocaust and the Palestinian [Arab] tragedy."[1]

Segev goes on to elaborate this link with an analogy: Ben-Gurion, the man responsible for the establishment of Israel, was equally indifferent to the tragedy of the Palestinian people and to the Holocaust and its Jewish victims. To drive home this point, Segev recounts both Ruth Aliav's highly imaginative oral memoir and Ben-Gurion's remark about Yiddish being (in Segev's translation) "discordant."[2]

For some reason, Segev treats his English readers to a brew of Aliav's fabrications far less rich than the one served up in his Hebrew version. But he compensates the English reader with a new episode, in which Aliav tells how "in the meantime [while she and Ben-Gurion were loading the books into her jeep] it began to rain. German women sat, dressed in black, on mounds of rubble and began to place stone on stone, brick on brick. And he said 'What's this?' I said: 'That's Germany's new future.' "[3] In Segev's retelling, the implication is that Ben-Gurion should have taken his cue from the German women, who built their new Germany on their own ruins, not on those of another people.

In April 1968, Segev and two of his colleagues on the editorial staff of the Hebrew University student newspaper *Nitsots* (Spark) interviewed Ben-Gurion in Sdeh Boker. Then eighty-two, "he was still sharp and radiated power." In this interview, part of which has already been quoted, Ben-Gurion was asked about efforts at rescue. "The greater part of the guilt for holding down immigration, and therefore for preventing the rescue of the Jews, fell on the Palestinian Arabs and the British, Ben-Gurion said. They could have saved many, but not all. They could, for instance, have bombed Auschwitz and Treblinka, he contended. Here he told us something that coming from him sounded like a historical anecdote. There had been this Jewish man, Ben-Gurion could not remember his name, who arrived with some Nazi proposal to free a million Jews in exchange for ten thousand trucks. 'Where could we find ten thousand trucks?' he asked dumbfounded as if hearing the idea for the first time. There was something almost surreal in the offhand tone in which he spoke of that attempt at rescue."[4]

Could there be a more convincing confirmation that Ben-Gurion's tone in discussing the Holocaust was "offhand" than the fact that he did not even bother to remember Joel Brand's name? But Segev conceals the fact that Ben-Gurion's fabulous memory had begun to wane well before he had the honor of being interviewed by Segev and his colleagues. Haim Israeli, Ben-Gurion's devoted personal secretary, tells a touching story of how, while driving northward on the old Tel Aviv–Haifa road in 1968, Ben-Gurion tormented himself for not being able to remember the name of Zichron Ya'akov, the settlement whose first almond trees he had planted as a young farmhand in 1909, trees that looked down on them majestically from the heights of Mount Carmel. Even before 1968 he had had difficulty, from time to time, in remembering names—even those of famous men involved with the Yishuv like Allenby and Wauchope.[5]

There is a method in Segev's writing: He is deliberately instilling in his reader prejudice and suspicion. Thus, although he clearly has available not only Rozka Korczak's own version of what happened during her speech at the Histadrut conference but also the conference minutes, he chooses to assert that she was offended by Ben-Gurion, ignoring the contradiction between his sources.

Segev knows well that Ben-Gurion did not mean to offend her—not only because she herself said and wrote so, but because on another page of his book he tells of another survivor, Halinka Goldblum (today Professor Yehudit Sinai), who met Ben-Gurion in Palestine in February 1943 and was impressed by his empathy. But Segev omits from his account much of what Ben-Gurion said and did at their meeting, as well as key elements of his reaction afterward.

The seventeen-year-old Halinka and several other young people had been brought to Haifa via Turkey through the efforts of the Yishuv's rescue mission in Istanbul. On February 13, 1943, Ben-Gurion went to Haifa to meet them. In a letter in English to Miriam Cohen, his close friend in New York, Ben-Gurion recounted: "I cannot get away from the nightmare brought over again by fifteen people [who] arrived last week from Poland. Among the arrivals there is a young girl [Halinka from Sosnowitz] . . . for three hours I heard a story [they talked in Yiddish] of horrors and misery, which no Dante or Poe could have ever invented, and you are completely helpless, and you cannot even go mad—and the sun shines in all her glory, and you too must go . . . on with your ordinary work . . . as if we—I mean we Jews—are living in a normal world, and there is only war and other normal troubles and worries—it is not easy, believe me, but we must; perhaps in continuing to do what we started *here* some sixty years ago we will save a remnant who wants to be saved; anyhow *this* is the only thing which I can do and it is my intention to do it, whatever I can and as long as I can do anything."

According to Halinka, Ben-Gurion "interrogated her in great detail, even the minutest ones . . . when I was done telling him . . . I could see tears in his eyes . . . Ben-Gurion sat down and wept."[6]

Given his objectives, it comes as no surprise that Segev also quotes in full Ben-Gurion's unfortunate utterance of December 1938, in a different translation: "If I knew that it was possible to save all the children in Germany by transporting them to England, but only half of them by transporting them to Palestine, I would choose the second—because we face not only the reckoning of those children, but the historical reckoning of the Jewish people." But Segev's analysis of this remark rests on a deliberate distortion of another statement by Ben-Gurion in order to show him in the most dehumanized light.

Referring to Ben-Gurion's speech at a Yishuv-wide rally in Jerusalem on December 12, 1938, he writes, "In the wake of the *Kristallnacht* pogroms, Ben-Gurion commented that 'the human conscience' might bring various countries to open their doors to Jewish refugees from Germany. He saw this as a threat [to Jewish Palestine], and warned: 'Zionism is in danger!' "[7]

The reader can draw only one conclusion: Zionism under Ben-Gurion had no soul. This kind of Zionism is ready to wantonly sacrifice human life for political gain. It sees human conscience as its mortal enemy. The Ben-Gurion who was ready to sacrifice half the children of Germany so that the other half could immigrate to strengthen the Yishuv so it would become a state also feared that the goodness of heart of "various countries" would undo Zionism by offering Jewish refugees another haven. However, Segev's version both misquotes and utterly distorts what Ben-Gurion said.

Segev took his quote from Ben-Gurion's five-volume *BaMaaraha* (Embattled). The speech begins with a review "of our political situation" against the "backdrop of the world situation and international circumstances bearing on our political struggle." Hence its published title: "The International Background of Our Problem." This background was darkened by the shadows of an imminent world war, by Britain's recent concession to Hitler with respect to the Munich Pact and the rape of Czechoslovakia, and by the "tightening of ties with the Axis powers by the Arab world, surrounding our little country from every corner." The resulting strengthening of the Arab countries evoked the dread that Britain, which had just turned its back on the Balfour Declaration,* would, out of "fear of the Arabs," abandon the Yishuv as it had abandoned Czechoslovakia. Against Britain's policy of liquidating the Jewish national home in Palestine, the Yishuv must mobilize "our entire potential" to defend "the aspiration of the Jewish people in its homeland, because the homeland is in danger." He did not say that Zionism was endangered by human conscience, and no exclamation point followed "the homeland is in danger."

Ben-Gurion went on to assert that "Germany's reign of violence and evil . . . aspires to rule the entire world, and one of its goals . . . is the total, physical destruction of the Jewish people, not in Germany alone, but all over the world." The sign of this was *Kristallnacht.* "Till now," he said, "even Satan dared not play such tricks. Now the leash is loosed, our blood, our honor, our possessions are at the mercy of wanton lawlessness, and there is no limit to the harm they plan for us." This situation had exposed to the whole world the urgent need to solve "a horrible, critical problem of hundreds of thousands of refugees—who can tell if their number will reach millions." Yet Britain, guided by "the human conscience"—Ben-Gurion intoned this phrase ironically—had shut Palestine's doors and at the same time "showers upon us territorial schemes." To those refugees Britain opened not its own doors but those of Tanganyika, Guiana, Angola "and a number of other lands."

---

* In the Woodhead Report, published Nov. 19, 1938, and adopted as British policy. It put an end to the Peel partition plan.

It was here that Ben-Gurion saw the danger. Those empty schemes "will evaporate, must evaporate—but in the meantime all those who wish, for one reason or another, to exclude Palestine from the framework of the solution of the Jewish problem will hang on to them." Thus the only true and radical solution to the Jewish problem—the immigration of the refugees to Palestine—would be nullified. It was for this reason that he concluded: "let us not be afraid to see things as they are: Zionism is in danger."[8]

Segev's misinterpretation of this quote could have been a bona fide mistake. But it is difficult to give him the benefit of a doubt when it is apparent he did not attempt to confirm his accusation against Ben-Gurion. Why else would he not identify for his reader those "various countries" whose " 'human conscience' might bring" them in 1938 "to open their doors to Jewish refugees" and thus, in Ben-Gurion's mind, endanger Zionism? Since Segev did not undertake this task, it must be done for him.

A glance into the intricacies of British diplomacy regarding the "Jewish question" in Romania will shed a broad light on the availability of "other countries" as havens for Jewish refugees. In this tale there is some evidence that might lead a student of diplomatic history to conclude that England was second to none in "human conscience." No government concerned itself with anti-Semitism in Central and Eastern Europe more than the British. It is indeed hard to believe the amount of energy, time, telegraphs, ink, and paper the Foreign Office expended in 1938 in protesting official and public anti-Semitism in Romania—to the point where King Carol II was told that a scheduled London visit hinged upon it.*

As Sir Reginald Hoare, British minister in Bucharest, put it in February in a telegram to the Foreign Office: "The King . . . enquired about London visit. I replied that during the late Government anxiety was felt lest anti-Semitic movement here have repercussions in London

---

* King Carol II did go in the summer of 1938 on a state visit to England and France, for the purpose of obtaining economic and military aid. He was turned down, and in despair approached Hitler. In return for a German guarantee of Romania's territorial integrity, he signed a treaty of alliance with Germany.

and render immediate visit inopportune." Hoare was referring to legislation barring academic education and certain professions—mainly medicine and law—to Jews, and revoking the citizenship of 500,000 of Romania's nearly 800,000 Jews. These were mostly Jews who in 1919, after the Great War, had fled Soviet Russia, Poland, Hungary, and Germany. "The King then said that replacement of Jews [that is, their intended expulsion from Romania] must and would continue. Would that be regarded as an anti-Semitic measure? I replied that I thought educated opinion would have regarded it as a perfectly reasonable one if taken nineteen years ago. Now it would be regarded as a submission to popular clamour which could yield no practical results. His Majesty did not demur." When Carol II said "no further measures had been or would be taken against the Jews I mentioned suppression [closure by government order] of Jewish papers."[9]

This is only one of the many instances in which the British government interfered in Romania's internal affairs on behalf of the Jews. But—without questioning its "human conscience" and good intentions, or those of its diplomats—it is hard to avoid a persistent suspicion that another, equally powerful motivation was at work here. The British were increasingly concerned lest the pressure of anti-Semitism in Romania cause an explosion that would lead its Jews, or at least those 500,000 robbed of their citizenship, to look for resettlement elsewhere—in Palestine, for example, where the Arabs and British least wanted them.

An indication that it was this concern that was closer to the British heart can be found in Sir Reginald's report to the foreign secretary, Sir Anthony Eden, on a previous interview that King Carol had granted him. "His Majesty appeared to me rather preoccupied by the Jewish and Iron Guard [the fascist party] problems. . . . With regard to the Jews, [said Carol] some measures must be taken to relieve the pressure and His Majesty mentioned various parts of the world where Jews might perhaps be admitted. The ideal thing would, of course, be an independent Jewish state and he [Carol] regretted that His [British] Majesty's Government had not originally tackled the Palestine problem from that aspect. . . . Before we left this subject I said that I was inclined to think that a small symbolical emigration of Jews from this country would very possibly constitute a satisfactory solution of the problem."

On January 25, 1938, A. D. M. Ross, a Foreign Office official, handwrote the following remark on Hoare's report: "The King's marked concern in the matter of the Jewish and the Iron Guard problems suggests that he would be particularly receptive of 'advice' from His Majesty's Minister."[10]

What this "advice" would be was not hard to guess. Sir Reginald had already outlined it very clearly in 1936, as is evident from a letter that he sent Counselor E. M. B. Ingram, head of the Foreign Office's Southern Department. This letter of January 11, 1938, attracted important minutes.

"I am inclined to think," Sir Reginald wrote Ingram, "that if we could arrange a 'symbolical' absorption of Jews from here [Romania] into some part of the Empire it would have a good effect both on nationalistic Roumanian opinion and on the Jews who, feeling that there was a possible way of escape, would be less panicky than they are now."

Sir Reginald went on to discuss "the regulations governing immigration into the principal Dominions," concluding "that they present almost insuperable difficulties to mass, or even group, immigration. But I remember reading the report of the Commission that went to have a look at British Guiana as a possible home for the Assyrians [sic!]. My recollection is that the Commission was quite favorably impressed by both the climatic and physical conditions, though I don't remember why the scheme broke down."

Here Sir Reginald quotes from his dispatch No. 267 of August 29, 1936, to the Foreign Office on the Jewish question in Romania: "There is in Roumania a collection of political rag-tag and bobtail who aspire to office largely on anti-Semitic platform. I cannot imagine them in office but it may well be that some of the Jews can. I think that these fears should be borne in mind because fear is the father of folly, and that if it be decided to restrict immigration into Palestine, authority should be reserved to relax those restrictive measures in the event of unexpected or dramatic developments in countries such as Roumania where there is an important Jewish minority."

This was Sir Reginald's position in August 1936, well before the appointment of the Peel Commission and its proposal to partition Palestine into a Jewish state and an Arab state. By 1938, in any case, the British government had reversed its policy and partition was no longer an option. The May 1939 White Paper was already in preparation. Thus Sir Reginald's 1938 letter goes on, "any relaxation of restrictive measures on [Jewish] immigration to Palestine has now become out of [the] question. I believe that in these circumstances it would be of very serious value to make a definite effort to find some other safety valve. The knowledge that we were looking would help to tide this over whereas if we all refuse to look for one there may be an unpleasant explosion." Sir Reginald then asks the Foreign Office "to work out a scheme for the settlement of the Jews who are assumedly about to be expelled from Roumania somewhere in the British Empire."[11]

Perhaps Segev could have found here a demonstration of "human conscience" working to resolve the Jewish problem—not exactly in the British Isles, but somewhere in the Empire, which was certainly preferable to the immediate neighborhood of Hitler's Germany; no doubt about it. But wait; we must be cautious in coming to such a conclusion. Sir Reginald himself demands caution, as he continues:

> But before approaching any other Department of His Majesty's Government or before considering whether we should or should not work only with the League [of Nations], we have to make up our minds as to whether we want to take any initiative. I am inclined to think if the nationalist element in Roumania got wind of any attempt by His Majesty's Government to find room for Jews in the British Empire they would only be the more encouraged to clamour for the ejection of more Jews. Moreover I don't think that those people in Roumania & elsewhere who have expressed disapproval of your [that is, our] "interference" so far would take a more sympathetic view of our action if we volunteered to take the Jews to our bosom. On the other hand if the result of the petitions by Jewish organisations to the League [of Nations] includes a request from the [League's] Council to examine

the possibility of finding a place for the Jews who have to leave Rou-
mania to settle, we shall obviously have to face our responsibilities.

In other words, Sir Reginald's "advice" is to allow only a "symbolical" number of Jews to emigrate from Romania, possibly even to
the United Kingdom, and look into finding a serious solution for the
bulk of these Jews only if the pressure from the League of Nations is
insuperable.

At this period the head of the Foreign Office's Eastern Department
was still the anti-Semitic, pro-Arab Sir George William Rendell, "our
sworn enemy" and "our greatest hater at the Foreign Office," as Ben-
Gurion described him.[12] Rendell, who was about to take up a post as
British minister in Sofia, Bulgaria, wrote a minute to Sir Reginald's
letter ruling out any absorption of Jews into the United Kingdom:

It would be admirable if we could find any room for Jews in either
the Dominion or the Colonial Empire. We have assumed a number of
obligations towards the Jews, which, though ill-defined and the subject
of much controversy, are nevertheless real. We have in fact obtained a
good deal of value for our money, but the genuineness of that money
has hitherto been open to question, since up till now, we have always
tried to fulfil our obligations towards the Jews at the expense of third
parties [the Arabs]. If we could now do something in the direction of
fulfilling those obligations at our own expense instead of at the expense
of others, it would go a very long way towards (a) giving real and
effective help to the persecuted Jews of Central Europe, *(b)* convincing
our critics at Geneva, and in the United States, of the sincerity of our
sympathy for the Jews and of our professed desire to help them, and
(c) providing a real solution of the Palestine problem *[emphasis added].*

Again, perhaps Segev could have found proof in Rendell's next
words of the existence of that "human conscience" which so scared
Ben-Gurion: "My own feeling is that we are under a strong moral
obligation to do something for the Jews within the Dominion or
Colonial Empire, and that it would be quite possible to do if the question were faced frankly and courageously." But, as usual, this mask

of human kindness slips when practical action is at hand, as opposed to expressions of lofty idealism. Rendell continues:

> It has, however, been difficult for the Eastern Department to raise the question hitherto, without drawing a red herring across the track of the far more immediate and dangerous problem of Palestine. There are obvious disadvantages in raising two controversial questions simultaneously. It will be difficult enough to get the Palestine problem considered objectively and solved rapidly and effectively on equitable and practical lines. Too many interests and prejudices are involved; and all those interests and prejudices would be likely to come into play if the question of doing something for the Jews within the Empire were raised at this stage. [Sir Reginald's letter] is mainly concerned with the situation inside Roumania. But this Roumanian situation corresponds so closely to that existing in Poland and in certain other countries that it is impossible to deal with it in isolation. Moreover, anything connected with the resettlement of Jews anywhere inevitably involves Palestine, and will continue to do so until the Palestine problem is disposed of.

Conclusion? "Query: Bring up in a year."[13] So the problem is not really so urgent that it cannot wait another year—that is (and Segev could not but be aware of the date), until after *Kristallnacht*, after the *Anschluss*. And we well know how humanely the British responded after those events: They offered shelter to 10,000 Jewish orphans from Germany and Austria, only so they could keep them out of Palestine.

Ever since January 1938, then, Sir Reginald had been pouring the same "advice" into the ears of King Carol and the various Romanian governments that came and went before the outbreak of the war. The "advice" was intended to ease the British difficulties more than those of the Romanians: In order to prevent pressure on Palestine's gates by masses of Romanian Jews, Britain was ready to absorb a "symbolical" number of them within the Dominions, the colonial Empire, and even the British Isles, to pacify both Jews and their haters in Romania, permit King Carol II to go on his scheduled state visit to Britain, and create a more favorable atmosphere for discussing Romania's political and economic needs.

On February 17, 1938, Sir Reginald called on the patriarch, Miron Cristea, then prime minister, and, as he reported to Eden, "was considerably disappointed to find that nothing would induce him to talk about anything but the Jewish problem. . . . [H]e unfortunately believes that the Jews have almost literally sucked the blood of the Roumanians and that a drastic remedy must be found. The rights of genuinely established Jews would be respected but after the revision of the papers of Jews had been completed the Roumanian Government would probably appeal to the League of Nations to find a solution, i.e., a home for those who had no right to be here [in Romania]."

Since just the previous day Sir Reginald had seen former prime minister G. Tataresco, who "said the same thing, . . . I imagine that the Roumanian Government is seriously contemplating something of the sort"—that is, an appeal to the League, a step that might put pressure on Britain to open Palestine's gates. The patriarch, Sir Reginald wrote Eden, "made one suggestion, which was that a detached and impartial Englishman should come out and conduct an unobtrusive but thorough investigation of the Jewish problem." Sir Reginald said he would report this home "but did not think the proposal would be received with favour, if only because a tour of inspection would almost inevitably give rise to hopes that His Majesty's Government were prepared to take an active part in solving the Jewish issue, and therefore to great disappointment if it proved they were unable to do so."

This letter, too, attracted comment. A. D. M. Ross minuted that "Sir R. Hoare rightly deprecates any attempt to constitute His Majesty's Government as the protector, official or unofficial, of Roumanian Jewry." On March 11 Sir Orme Sargent, the assistant undersecretary for foreign affairs, wrote the following icily precise prophecy: "Roumania is bound to go Nazi, and that will automatically settle the Jewish question."[14]

On April 14 Romanian foreign minister N. Comnen-Petrescu spoke to Sir Reginald, as the latter reported to Lord Halifax, lord president of the Council, "with passionate earnestness on the subject of the Jewish problem." Comnen-Petrescu said "that in the course of the next two or three months the Roumanian Government would know how many of the Jews resident in Roumania had no rights of citizenship." Although it would be impossible to induce Soviet Russia, Poland, Hungary, or Germany "to allow them to return to their original homes even if they were prepared to go," Romania certainly would be "unwilling to give them the rights of citizenship." Yet, said the foreign minister, "to keep them in the country as *staatslosen* [stateless persons] would be to create an element susceptible to any revolutionary propaganda. A home must be found for them and quite obviously Palestine was entirely inadequate for that purpose. A radical and at the same time humane and statesmanlike solution of the Jewish problem in Central Europe was a matter of urgency and of world wide importance." More telegrams and letters were exchanged, but that was all.

Is some "human conscience" manifesting here, bringing hope for the Jews to escape Romania and for Segev to prove his accusation against Ben-Gurion? Unfortunately, no; for Sir Reginald concluded only by reiterating his old "advice": "I still feel strongly," he wrote Lord Halifax, "that even if the number of Jews who eventually emigrated were only an infinitesimal percentage of the Jewish population of the country the psychological effect would be very valuable."

This time, however, he was thinking not only of the British government's Palestine policy, but also of its desire to prevent Romania from getting closer to Hitler's Germany. "I have nothing very substantial to go on," Sir Reginald told Lord Halifax, "but . . . I have an uncomfortable feeling that at a not very distant date serious trouble from the Iron Guard is to be expected. M. Comnen naturally did not give me any indication that such a thought was in his mind or in that of King Carol, but it would be natural if some such thought were present."

Sir Reginald now cited the opinion of a Mr. Short, a British expert sent by a royal research institute to examine anti-Semitism in Poland, who had also visited Romania. Short thought that "the Jewish problem is becoming desperately acute in Poland." Sir Reginald went on: "I am inclined to think that it is almost certain to become equally acute here. I would therefore urge that any proposals which the Roumanian Government may make with a view to a solution should not lightly be rejected because of obvious practical difficulties." In real terms, what this advice amounted to was that Britain should not create obstacles for Romania at the League of Nations[15]—not (God forbid) that Britain should come to the rescue of the Jews.

Sir Reginald took up this line repeatedly in many subsequent telegrams to the Foreign Office. They amounted, however, to no more than an exercise in futility, as they were meant to be: No action, beyond the exchange of telegrams and minutes, was ever taken.

So much for the dangers "human conscience" presented for Zionism. One difference between Segev and similar critics and Ben-Gurion is that Ben-Gurion saw in real time, in 1938, what Segev and company, despite history and the advantages of hindsight, could not see nearly sixty years later.

The danger Ben-Gurion envisaged was not, therefore, what Segev misrepresents him as fearing—that "various countries," responding to the call of their "human conscience" and out of the goodness of their hearts, might "open their doors to Jewish refugees from Germany" and thereby rescue them outside Palestine. In the aftermath of the Evian Conference of July 1938, Ben-Gurion knew well that no country on earth was prepared to admit "hundreds of thousands of degraded, ruined Jews," nor even hundreds. The danger he saw was that under Britain's Palestine policy they would not find haven anywhere and thus would fall into Hitler's hands.

Despite this fear, Ben-Gurion ended his December 12, 1938, speech in Jerusalem on a note of encouragement and hope:

> And despite all that, I wish to warn you against pessimism and despair. We have still friends in England, America and other countries; there is still a human conscience, and more important, there is a Jewish people and there is a Jewish community in Palestine, and their strength is not small and their capability not negligible—and if we know how to mobilize the Yishuv and the nation and how to help ourselves, we will find help from others as well.

Ironically, when the archbishop of Canterbury called on the House of Lords, in March 1943, "to move to resolve, That, in view of the massacres and starvation of Jews and others in enemy and enemy-occupied countries," the British government should take "immediate measures, on the largest and most generous scale . . . for providing help and temporary asylum to persons in danger of massacre," he had to back away in face of the government's opposition to his motion, apologizing that he never did "contemplate a flow of vast numbers" of refugees. "I have constantly reiterated my view that it would be, at best, but a trickle." Thus spoke one of England's noblest voices of human conscience.[16]

The historical evidence does not support Segev's interpretation; Ben-Gurion's meaning in the original Hebrew text is clear. It is apparent that Segev, an able, experienced writer, is willfully twisting Ben-Gurion's words. The question is: Why? He must have been moved to do so only by an aim so supreme in his mind as to justify such means. The answer is that Segev is connecting Ben-Gurion's 1934 campaign for the "Transfer Agreement" (Heskem HaAvara, the arrangement by which German Jews saved their possessions by selling them to the JAE Transfer company)—which to Segev amounts to "dealing with the devil"[17]—to Ben-Gurion's 1938 comment about "half the children of Germany" and his misquoted comment about the danger "the human conscience" posed to Zionism, in order to hint that Ben-Gurion was not above collaborating with Hitler.

Among the additional evidence Segev brings forth to strengthen this hint is the fact that Teddy Kollek, "later one of Ben-Gurion's chief assistants," met with Adolf Eichmann in the spring of 1939 in Vienna.[18] It is hard to tell whether Segev cites this out of ignorance or as malicious slander. Before the war and before the Final Solution, many a Jew, Zionist and non-Zionist, met with Eichmann (who in the course of his "Jewish studies" visited Jewish Palestine), for Eichmann was the official whom Jews had to deal with regarding any matters arising out of the implementation of Hitler's anti-Jewish policies. At the time, no one except perhaps Hitler knew of the 'final solution.' To single out Teddy Kollek's meeting with Eichmann at that time as proof of Ben-Gurion's collaboration with the Nazis is so ludicrous one cannot help but question Segev's motives for doing so.

Another piece of evidence—or perhaps a fresh accusation—is that "Ben-Gurion called for the rescue of German Jewry, 'a tribe of Israel,' and their transfer to Palestine, rather than action against Hitler." Here

Segev's English version is considerably softer on Ben-Gurion than his Hebrew original, where he accuses Ben-Gurion of calling for the rescue of Germany's Jews "instead of trying to bring Hitler down."[19] Why? Perhaps, as in the case of Aliav's book-hunting tale, where the English version is also kinder, Segev's patriotism prevents him from exposing Israel's shame to Gentile eyes, in the spirit of King David: "Tell it not in Gath, publish it not in the streets of Askelon; lest the daughters of the Philistines rejoice, lest the daughters of the uncircumcised triumph" (II Samuel 1:20).

Or did he put it this way in English only to avoid having to explain to the English reader how Ben-Gurion could have been able to bring Hitler down?

CHAPTER SEVEN

FIRST NEWS

SEGEV RESERVES THE most blistering lines in his *Rashomon* narrative for Ben-Gurion's part as Zionism's grave digger. His most serious accusation is, of course, that the JAE failed to rescue the Jews of Europe. He contends that it was possible to do more and blames Ben-Gurion for not having done more. What, and how? Segev's response is both theoretical and practical. This chapter is concerned with his theoretical argument; his practical one will be dealt with in Chapter 8.

Theory first: Segev believes that beginning in June 1942 the Yishuv press was able "to report [in real time, more or less]* that the Nazis were murdering Jews systematically and that gas chambers were among the methods in use." But, he goes on, "the first news of the extermination of the Jews . . . did not immediately arouse all who heard it." Why? A straightforward answer to this disquieting question is given right up front, as a guide to the perplexed reader: "the self-image of the [Zionist] political establishment in Palestine and its attitude to the Jews in the rest of the world." Here, too, the English edition is milder: The answer is "the Zionist establishment's view of the relative importance of the Jewish communities in Palestine and outside it."[1] In other words, the notorious "condemnation of the Diaspora" and the Yishuv's feeling of superiority to it were why the

---

* Phrase in brackets is omitted from the English edition.

first news was met with indifference, rather than eliciting an appropriate response.

In discussing "the first news"—some scholars define this as arriving in July, others in November 1942—Segev does not take into account the actions of the Mandatory Censorship Office. According to Haviv Knaan, an authority on this matter, that office "played havoc" with news about the Jews in Nazi-occupied Europe; until August 1942, it allowed only some of the news to be published. Thus, for example, when the *Struma*, a small boat with more than 750 Jewish passengers aboard, sank in February 1942 near Istanbul after the British had denied it entry to Palestine and Turkey, the Yishuv press was forbidden to present this *"Struma* tragedy" as a result of the Jewish plight in Europe.

On February 8, 1942, Ilya Ehrenburg's report on the atrocities perpetrated by the Nazis against the Jews in the Soviet Union—covered prominently in the Soviet press—was completely censored. On July 29, news about pogroms against Jews in Bukovina and Bessarabia met the same fate.[2] So in point of fact the Jews in Palestine were not initially aware of the full extent of Nazi actions against the European Jews. Consequently, they were quite unprepared for the news that came in November 1942, and like other Jewish communities, they did not know how to react to the so-called first news.

To make his argument convincing, Segev would have to show that other Jewish communities, free of the Zionist malady, reacted differently. This he does not do, leaving it a mystery whether he is withholding information or concealing the lack of it.

To take one example, the Jewish community in the United States reacted to the first news much like the Yishuv: with uncertainty, skepticism, and disbelief, and without taking any action. In this matter there was no difference between Zionists and non-Zionists.[3] The official announcement that systematic destruction was being carried out by the Germans in Europe was made in Palestine on November 22, 1942, and on November 23 in the United States. In Palestine it was made by the JAE and published the next day on the first page of all the Yishuv newspapers, while in the United States it was made by the Zionist Reform rabbi Stephen Wise, president of the World Jewish

Congress, a non-Zionist organization. The great majority of the American press buried it deep in the inside pages; in the *New York Times*, for example, it appeared on page 10.[4]

Segev also fails to explore the reaction of the Jews living in occupied Europe to the news that outlined their fate. Such an investigation has, however, been carried out by Gila Fatran, in an eye-opening study of Slovak Jewish leadership during the Holocaust. She describes two memorandums, one submitted to Jewish organizations in Switzerland on March 5, 1942, by the union of Jewish communities in Slovakia and the second on March 6 by the union of Orthodox rabbis there. Both memorandums emphasize "that under the prevailing circumstances expulsion amounts to the physical destruction of Slovakia's Jews."

Fatran remarks: "One should not attribute to the authors [of the memorandums] any knowledge of the 'final solution' being planned in Germany." In referring to physical destruction "they had in mind the severe war conditions prevailing in occupied Poland . . . and had also been hearing different rumors about what Jews were saying in sectors under Nazi conquest. Expulsion from Slovakia had begun at the end of March that year, and the first news of horrifying living conditions, death by starvation, and arbitrary killings reached Slovakia in May and June 1942. It caused many a Jew to escape to Hungary, acquire certificates of conversion to Christianity or of Aryan origin, and hide." But even after "the horrible news" that came at the end of August 1942, of the true function of Nazi labor camps, only "a negligible minority" among the young understood that the "labor camps" were a calculated deception. "The great majority reported for duty at the assembly spots, believing the official explanations, craftsmen making a point of bringing along their tools." They saw "in the hard work that supposedly awaited them a greater, improved chance to survive than the one offered by illegal rescue operations." Even after large-scale rail transports to Auschwitz began in September and October, the Slovak Jews did not know that the deported would meet their deaths in the gas chambers upon arrival. A letter sent by Rabbis Michael Dov-Ber Weissmandel and Abraham Abba Frieder on December 1, 1942, to Saly Mayer, the AJDC representative in Switzerland, "is the first documentary indication that information had been received in Slovakia that the organized destruction was the product of deliberate planning." Remarks by participants in a January 28, 1943, meeting of the Jewish Center *(Judenrat)* there show "that Slovakia's Jews possessed information regarding the bitter fate of the deported, even if they did not yet know about the systematic destruction."

This reaction is identical in nature to the Yishuv's reaction. Further, the transition in Slovakia from the phase of "first news" to that of certain knowledge is also parallel to that in Jewish Palestine. That is, even in the latter phase Slovakia's Jews found it hard to recognize the systematic destruction as reality. Fatran: "Awareness of total destruction had solidified in Slovakia's Jews through a process lasting long months. The steady, abundant flow of information about the harsh fate of the deported prepared their senses to absorb news items that appeared on first hearing to derive from the world of the absurd. The living testimonies supplied by the ones who managed to escape from the death camps, in the summer of 1943, brought to completion the process of the jelling of this awareness."[5]

In Fatran's view the obstacles to quicker, more complete absorption of the available information were: (1) "The intense confusion of emotions, which fed on deceitful promises ('Labor Camps mean labor'), wishful hopes ('temporary deportation'), and the genuine optimism of the young ('nothing to fear from hard work')." (2) The trust, inspired by the Germans, "that useful work means life." This was also the belief of ghetto leaders in Bialystok and Vilna and of the Jews of Holland. The majority of Jews under Hitler adhered to the belief "that labor camps could prevent deportation" to Auschwitz, while the Germans devised ploys and allotted considerable resources to kindle and strengthen such delusions. (3) The wishful hope that organizational and technical snags would occur and hinder the deportation of whole communities to the death camps, and that "severe setbacks in the war would put an end to the destruction." (4) Last but not least was "the innocent religious faith" that the Lord of Israel would not let his chosen people be destroyed.[6]

Even the Jews on the rail transports to Auschwitz mistrusted what they had heard about destruction, even as late as 1945. An example is the story of Dr. Lotte Salzberger. Early in 1945 she and her sister, both in their teens, were deported to Ravensbrück, where the rumor about the death camps reached them. For unknown reasons they were transferred to Theresienstadt. On arrival there they were held in solitary confinement for an entire month until Eichmann, who interrogated them—probably to discover whether the Germans' deception was effective—found out that they believed in the "rumors" about Auschwitz. He threatened them until he was convinced that they would never tell anyone about Auschwitz and the industry of death. "If you repeat these rumors you will go through the chimney," he warned them. On being released from confinement the two girls were quick to tell their fellow inmates all they knew about Auschwitz and its death machinery. "But no one believed us, the leadership in the camp . . . claimed we were two mentally sick girls."[7] Cleverly, Eichmann had let them live, for if they had been executed their story would have become credible to the other inmates.

Segev, however, in examining the Yishuv's reaction, does not discern any "confusion" of emotions or of hopes and beliefs. Consequently, he does not admit that the assimilation of such inconceivable information can be a complex process, not a one-time occurrence. He does not seek to identify and understand such a process because he already has a ready-made answer: Zionism, and the Yishuv's condescending attitude toward the Diaspora that was integral to it—and Zionism only—was responsible for the fact that the "first news" was not easily digested.

For supporting evidence he translates a comment published on the first page of *HaPoel HaTzair*, the Mapai weekly: "Had the [Nazi] enemy succeeded in striking us here [in Palestine], it would have been a blow to our souls. This devastation would no doubt have been much smaller quantitatively than devastation of Jews in Europe, but qualitatively, and in historical significance, it would have been the greater."[8]

This translation is faulty on two points. First, the Hebrew says that if the enemy succeeded in striking the Yishuv in Palestine, "it would have been a blow to the place where the soul lives." In other words: a lethal blow to the existence of the Jewish people in the future, or (in Zionist jargon) a death blow to their aspiration to renew their independent national life, which was feasible only in Palestine. Second, the Hebrew says that the devastation of the Jewish community in Palestine "would have been certainly smaller quantitatively than devastation of *Jewish centers in Europe* [italics added], but qualitatively, and in terms of historical significance, it would have been the greatest." In other words, the article does not consider the Jews of Palestine to be more important as individuals than the Jews of Europe, or superior in any way to them. The difference it emphasizes is in the location of the two communities. Palestine is seen as more important qualitatively and historically only because it was the Jewish people's first and only national cradle, and the place where foundations had been laid for its national rebirth and continued existence.

"It was against this background," Segev goes on, "that the *first news* [italics added] of the extermination of the Jews was received" by the Yishuv. But this is quite inaccurate. The reader who consults the Notes at the end of the book will discover that this comment, titled "Upon the Tolling of the Bells," appeared on May 20, 1943! That is, after the defeat at Stalingrad, after the Nazis (to quote that same comment again) "have been swept off the face of Africa," a moment "when the free world began to see the collapse of the wicked." The comment is mainly concerned with "the devastation of the House of Israel in the Diaspora," "the dread we lived through during the last two years, when the jackbooted enemy's legions pressed against the gates of this country," and the anxiety "about this lone corner in the world left to the Jewish people as a shelter from the destruction and annihilation visited upon it at this time." Here come the lines Segev quotes misleadingly and out of context, omitting their ending: "And who knows how many generations the surviving remnant would have had to wait again until the nation began to shake off the ashes of this devastation." This comment, therefore, was published quite some time after "the first news" and so is far from supporting Segev's contention.

On June 30, 1942, he continues, the influential Histadrut daily, *Davar*, reported that a million Jews had been murdered in Europe. The newspaper put the item on the front page but did not give it the main headline. This was because it "contained nothing new or startling—similar items had appeared in the paper before," as they had innumerable times in other papers as well. True, Segev admits, in a concession to historical truth, "from time to time, the papers accused one another of overstating the horrors" and inflating "every rumor about the spilling of Jewish blood, playing up the number of the victims and dead." Segev's source for this allegation is the religious daily *HaTzoffeh* of March 18, 1942.

He uses it, however, not to explain why these news items were relegated to second place, but rather to create the impression that the Yishuv knew "in real time" that the Nazis were murdering Jews systematically.

For support Segev calls on *Davar* again, this time from October 8, 1942: " 'We are printing this horrible report based on the above-mentioned source,' *Davar* wrote, distancing itself from an eyewitness report of the murder of Jews in mobile gas facilities near the Chelmno camp, in Poland. The article appeared on page 2. A story on trucks used to gas Jews appeared in the newspaper a few months earlier [June 28, 1942], without reservations but again without major play."[9]

Real time? According to the Holocaust Memorial Museum in Washington, "The first methodical gassings of Jews began on December 8, 1941, in the camp at Chelmno." *Davar* published this information twice, on June 28 and October 8, 1942. Is this real time?

Both dates are hidden in the thick mass of the Notes. What is more, Segev neglects to mention that *for its October 8 story Davar* relied— as it clearly notes—on a report by the Polish Bund published in the Yiddish-language New York daily *Forward* of July 31, "received at *Davar*'s editorial office yesterday."

Despite the *Forward*'s note that "this report has been checked and confirmed," *Davar* added a reservation: "we are printing this terrifying report on the responsibility of the above mentioned source." This, and only this, was the reason why the report was not given the main headline.[10]

Segev is a meticulous writer, and these fumblings cannot be taken for accidental omissions. They are too tightly knit with the book's main theme, to the degree that on a second reading they appear as its hidden underground foundation. This is more true of the English edition, simply because the Hebrew original is far more forthright. A whole paragraph that followed Segev's discussion of the Yishuv press's treatment of Holocaust news was omitted from the English edition. It is important for understanding Segev's turn of mind and worth repeating here:

> *The reports on the slaying of Jews did not come [to the Yishuv] as a surprise. . . . The tendency to always expect the worst is deeply rooted in Jewish tradition; paradoxically it serves as the basis for an equally deeply rooted optimism as well. Both tendencies derive from a long history of persecutions, expulsion and massacre, liquidation of whole Jewish communities, and millenniums of survival and revival. The reports from occupied Europe seemed therefore like a repetition of past persecutions and did not exceed that which was stored in the collective memory of the Jewish people. These reports confirmed what might be expected from Nazi Germany, and were compatible with the tenets of Zionist ideology.*[11]

Notable first is how Segev conveniently forgets here about the Yishuv's Zionist "condemnation of the Diaspora" and attributes to it two deeply rooted Jewish traditions, pessimism and optimism. Next, it is not quite clear which of the two had more influence over the Yishuv press. If the reports did not come at all as a surprise because they were déjà vu and expected, why did the papers, as I have already quoted Segev saying, "[accuse] one another of overstating the horrors," "inflating every rumor about the spilling of Jewish blood, playing up the number of the victims and dead"? Was it pessimism that relegated the horrifying reports to inside pages in the belief that worse was still to come (what could be worse?), or was it optimism discrediting them?

Besides, the editorial staffs of the Hebrew papers must have been incomparable imbeciles if reports of gassings and a million dead by June 1942 seemed to them only a "repetition" of past persecutions. If the Yishuv was unaffected by repetition, why was the entire Jewish people, the Yishuv included, so horrified by the Kishinev pogrom in 1903? Why was that atrocity not regarded as a repetition of the bloody riots of 1882—or of 1648–49?

But Segev would not be offended if his psychological and ethnic insights were not taken seriously, so long as his political view was respected, for his book's principal goal is political. Before examining his argument regarding the compatibility between Zionist ideology and what was expected from Nazi Germany, however, a simple question must be asked: Why does Segev refuse even to consider the hypothesis that the Yishuv behaved like all other Jewish communities—like all human societies—manifesting uncertainty, doubt, and disbelief when confronted with phenomena far beyond the reach of human imagination?

Bernard Levin, the perceptive essayist of *The Times* of London, must have had Segev and his like in mind when he wrote, on the fiftieth anniversary of Auschwitz's "liberation"—in an article subtitled "Still No Explanation of What They Found There":

> *My name is Levin, and Levin is almost always a Jewish name. I am a Jew. I am not at all a good Jew—I take no part in the religion of my forefathers, and indeed I am so* déraciné *that the only clue to my Jewishness (because the myth of Jewish noses was exploded long ago) is that I am circumcised. (No, come to think of it, there is one other indelible mark I carry—whenever I hear of a Jew having done wrong I feel a stab of pain.) And yet, exactly 50 years ago to the day, I discovered—what the world could not have believed until then—that had the Second World War been lost, I and all my family, together with every other Jewish family in Britain, would have been murdered, for no reason at all other than that we were Jews. And not long after that, I learnt that approximately six million Jews had indeed been murdered, again for no better reason. Surely, this is a phenomenon that requires from all of us the most searching examination? Of course; but you will find, to your great astonishment, that every attempt to understand what this truly incredible event means comes up against a wall of incomprehension . . . we cannot understand how it happened and a fortiori we cannot understand why it happened.*[12]

Here is a non-Jewish English Jew, utterly untainted by any debilitating Zionist affliction, still unable, fifty years after the event, to understand the Holocaust. Yet Segev blames Ben-Gurion and the Yishuv for not understanding it in "real time," that is, in the face of "the first news."

The question of why the Yishuv did not realize that a systematic, industrial mass extermination was taking place in occupied Europe until the latter part of 1942 was raised at the time. In May 1943 Zalman Shazar, a Mapai leader and later Israel's third president, gave the following answer: because "we did not understand the meaning of words. In simplicity, in all simplicity: We did not understand the true meaning of statements made to us, and statements we ourselves uttered."[13]

This was also true in occupied Europe, even in the Warsaw ghetto. In May 1942 Mordecai Anielewicz and other leaders of HaShomer HaTzair in the ghetto forbade their followers to be employed in any work that might aid the German war effort, "in order not to support the enemies of the Soviet Union."[14] Did they have less information about German intentions and actions? Had they not been driven into the ghetto, and had they not witnessed the "Aktions," the "transports" to the "labor camps" from which no one returned alive? Could they not distinguish the essential—their survival—from the trivial—protecting the Soviet Union? Even there, deep in the valley of death, people could not believe their eyes. A year later they were all dead.

Segev does not inform his readers of the huge resources, planning, cunning, deception, and diversion the Germans invested in camouflage and disinformation to cast a worldwide net of lies that would enable them to proceed uninterruptedly with the Final Solution.[15] The very difficulty people had in absorbing information, outside as well as inside occupied Europe, is in itself proof of their complete success.

It is inconceivable that Segev is not aware of this. His argument, therefore, that the reports reaching the Yishuv from Nazi Europe seemed a "repetition of past persecutions" and were consistent with both "the expectations from Nazi Germany" and the "Zionist ideology" must be aimed at the latter. Indeed, on another page he maintains, this time in the English edition as well, that the "founding fathers of the Zionist movement . . . assumed that, in the long run, Jews would not survive as Jews in the Diaspora; they would disappear, sooner or later, in one way or another." To freshen the validity of this statement Segev brings it up to date with a quote from Sharett of April 1943: "Zionism predicted the Holocaust decades ago."[16]

If one hears a tone of Zionist reproach, one is quite right. To establish that this was the Yishuv's attitude, Segev quotes a comment in *Davar* of November 27, 1942—the Notes tell us it was made by one Yitzhak Damiel-Schweiger, whose only claim to fame was his toy store on Allenby Street—that the extermination of the Jews was "punishment from heaven" for not having come to Palestine.[17]

The subtitle of Segev's book, "The Israelis and the Holocaust," intentionally ignores the radical transformation that took place in the meaning of the word *shoah*. There can be no doubt that in 1943 Sharett used it to mean "catastrophe." Whereas Segev's Hebrew original can be defended somewhat by the argument that in his quote he used Sharett's own word and it is not incumbent upon him to interpret Sharett, this argument is invalid with respect to the English edition. In April 1943, "Holocaust" had not yet acquired the meaning of "the mass murder of Jews in the war of 1939–45." Sharett's quote should have been translated as "Zionism predicted the catastrophe decades ago."[18]

Again, this is not a fortuitous oversight. The repeated, anachronistic use of "Holocaust" serves two of Segev's purposes. The first, as already noted, is to implant in the reader's mind the idea that Zionism's "condemnation of the Diaspora" (the English phrase he uses is "negation of the Exile"[19]) and its many ramifications (including, claims Segev, the Yishuv's "factionalism and infighting") reflected "not only the inability of the Yishuv to save European Jewry, but also the great spiritual distance between Palestine and the tragic events unfolding in Europe."[20]

Segev's second purpose is even more malicious: He deliberately creates the impression that the present meaning of "Holocaust" had been born in Zionist ideology long before the actual event took place. In other words, the Zionists had predicted the "Holocaust" and were therefore prepared well in advance to exploit it to achieve their goal. It is true that Zionism had been founded on the fear that permanent life in exile would doom the Jewish people to disappear, by degradation, assimilation, pogroms, etc., in generations to come. But Zionism had never envisaged industrial genocide, the extermination of 6 million Jews in the span of three or four years, and if only for this reason had never prepared in advance to make full use of such a catastrophe.

Yet this is exactly Segev's contention, and it is hard to avoid thinking that the imagination needed to invent such an accusation against Zionism is nothing less than the same imagination that planned the genocide that became the Holocaust. "Four weeks after the Nazi invasion of Poland," he writes in both editions, "the Mapai political committee discussed the question of what should be done 'after the Holocaust that has come upon Polish Jewry.' *This was not a slip of the tongue* [italics added]: even then, at the beginning of November 1939, the Holocaust was often spoken of in the past tense. . . . Instead of thinking of the Holocaust in terms that would require effective and immediate action, they exiled it from real time into history."[21]

Why? The answer is crystal clear: They did it to exploit the Holocaust for fund-raising campaigns and reparations from Germany, that is, money with which to build the state. In his guise as historian, Segev ponders: "It is uncertain who was the first to suggest that the Germans would have to pay reparations for the property they had expropriated from Jews and for the suffering they had caused. The idea seemed to have been in the air from the time the war started." Had his search been more thorough, Segev would have discovered that it was Dr. Chaim Weizmann, president of the World Zionist Organization, who insisted, as early as November 1939, that "it is a must to sue [the Germans] when the war is over . . . for damages to Germany's Jews."[22] But what has that to do with predicting the Holocaust and exploiting it for fund-raising? Is it not the most normal procedure to sue for damages from a vanquished enemy, and all the more so from Nazi Germany? Again, it is inconceivable that so able a writer would commit such lines to paper thoughtlessly.

Segev, however, charges on. How did the Yishuv "exile" the Holocaust "from real time into history"? He has another ready answer: by planning the memorial project for the Holocaust victims as early as 1942. He thus falsely turns a private idea submitted in September 1942 by Mordecai Shenhabi, a member of Kibbutz Mishmar HaEmek, to the curatorium of the Jewish National Fund, "to commemorate the *Shoah* [catastrophe] victims and the service of Jews in the Allied armed forces," into the actual erection of Yad VaShem in Jerusalem. Then Segev remarks, with barbed irony: "There was no clearer, more grotesque, even macabre expression of the tendency to think of the Holocaust in the past tense: while the Yishuv discussed the most appropriate way to memorialize them, most of the victims were still alive."

The truth is very different. The Yishuv never discussed ways to "memorialize" the Holocaust victims in 1942. Shenhabi's idea did not receive much attention either, according to Dr. Daliah Offer of the Hebrew University, who studied the subject. Shenhabi had to submit his idea again in May 1945; he also published it in the press, attracting reader letters. But by then other ideas were afloat, one of which was approved by the first postwar Zionist Conference in London, in August 1945. In 1946 the National Council discussed memorial schemes in minute detail, and it was David Remez, the council's chairman, who coined the title Yad VaShem, explaining that *Yad* (memorial monument) was intended to commemorate the Jewish soldier in World War II, and *Shem* (name) the Holocaust victims.

The public discussion did not end there. In July 1947 the poet Abba Kovner, leader of the uprising in the Vilna ghetto and the partisans, publicized his own plan, winning much response and support. In March 1948, at one of the worst hours in the War of Independence, a link was created between the Holocaust and the idea of Jewish revival. The war was conceived more as a life-and-death struggle than as just a battle for the political goal of creating the state. Whether accurately or not, it was widely believed that if the Arabs won the war, they would destroy the Jews in Palestine, individually and collectively, in a repeat of what had happened to Europe's Jews. According to some, this association with the Holocaust imbued the Jews of the Yishuv with exceptional courage, as if they were saying, "This time we will not be led to the slaughter." These ideas gave rise to the feeling, expressed in a slogan, that the war represented a movement from destruction to revival.

But not until five years after the establishment of Israel did Dr. Ben-Zion Dinur, the minister for education, draft the charter of

Yad VaShem, promulgated by the Knesset in August 1953 as "the law for the remembrance of the Holocaust and the heroism . . . a memorial authority is hereby established . . . for the commemoration of the six million members of the Jewish people" who were murdered by the Nazis and their collaborators, "and of the valor of the Jewish soldiers in the allied armies and the underground fighters" against the Nazis.[23]

As the foregoing demonstrates, Segev presents no proof for his allegations and only pretends to use the historian's tools to give them credibility. His is a political truth, the debunking of Zionism. He does not shrink from using against it any distortion or slander, and even uses his imagination, when necessary, to produce them. He is neither first nor original in his anti-Zionism. But in his excess he does achieve a distinction: Perhaps he is the first "Jewish revisionist," claiming that the Jews were endangered less by their enemies than by their own flesh and blood—the Zionists.

CHAPTER EIGHT

WHAT HAPPENED TO RESCUE?

SEGEV'S ACCUSATION THAT the JAE failed to offer rescue has a practical aspect as well. Its leaders, he asserts, "believed it was not their job to save the Jews of Europe." It will soon be clear how far from the truth this statement is. Yet to Segev it seems firm ground, sufficient to support the following poetic conclusion: "The story of the yishuv leaders during the Holocaust was essentially one of helplessness. They rescued a few thousand Jews from Europe. They could, perhaps, have saved more, but they could not save millions. 'This is one of the cases in which the historian feels that he wants to throw away all the rules he was taught—restrained language, precise examination of sources, cautious and supportable conclusions—and just sit down and cry,' wrote Israeli historian Dina Porat on the failure of an attempt to rescue close to thirty thousand children."[1]

Thus Segev opens his second chapter, leaving no doubt in the reader's mind that Porat wanted to put aside the tools of the historian and cry her heart out in protest against the leaders, who "could perhaps, have saved more"—perhaps even the children—but did not do so ("it was not their job," remember?). The "failure" was theirs alone.

While this conclusion is not much different from the scholarly consensus, in Segev's eyes the leaders' shortcomings were mental and ideological; he is therefore not merely pointing out the helplessness of Ben-Gurion and the JAE, as did other writers, but focusing on their unwillingness to mount meaningful rescue attempts. He also misses no opportunity to implant in his reader's mind that his "more" is far larger than the "few thousand" whom the JAE did rescue. At one point, when discussing the efforts to save Hungary's Jews, Segev's "more" becomes hundreds of thousands, even a million. To emphasize his point that the Zionist leaders' shortcomings prevented them from saving that many more, Segev makes it appear as if no other difficulties stood in their way.

But the truth is exactly the opposite. Porat, in fact, takes great pains to describe, in considerable detail, the rescue efforts by the Zionist leaders and the Yishuv's emissaries in Istanbul, with special emphasis on the case of the 29,000 children. "This is," she sums up, "perhaps the most heart-rending aspect of all the unsuccessful attempts to rescue the children. While Eichmann, his staff, and German Foreign Ministry officials exerted themselves lest a single Jewish child escape them, the British, self-righteous and seemingly passive, blocked all escape routes. In the middle were the handful of emissaries in Istanbul and [JAE] officials in Palestine, who tried to break through the walls with their bare fists, and the children, who never came." It was not against the leaders and the Yishuv's emissaries that she wished to cry out in protest; it was against the Germans and their collaborators, the British.[2]

Porat makes it clear that the Germans were primarily responsible for preventing the children's rescue; but she also sees through the ploys and deceptions the British used to shoot down the rescue plan. In this episode, she writes, Ben-Gurion made the children the top priority, although he was aware of the tremendous cost, way beyond the funds at the JAE's disposal. Yet "he told the Mapai Secretariat: 'There is only one matter that can brook no delay—bringing the children to Palestine.'" He appointed himself the director in charge of the children's rescue from Europe and their absorption in Palestine.[3] Indeed, the leaders of the Yishuv and its emissaries could not have done more for the children. The failure of this particular plan proved to them, too, that given both the Nazi presence in Europe and the British restrictions on immigration to Palestine, they did not have the capability for rescue on a grand scale.

Segev, however, seeking to prove that the leaders did not exert themselves to save the European Jews, supports his contention by interweaving his quotation from Porat, which refers to the end of 1942, with a September 1939 meeting of Mapai's central committee. In the second week of the war, he writes, that meeting "heard Ben-Gurion say that, since members of the party had no control over what was happening in Europe, there was no point wasting words on [Hebrew: philosophizing over] the moral aspects of recent developments. These, he said, should be treated as 'natural disasters.'" (The Hebrew phrase Ben-Gurion actually used was "nature's events," equivalent to the English phrase "acts of God.") Segev goes on paraphrasing Ben-Gurion's comments: "The First World War had taken Palestine from the Turks, and placed it under British rule. The British then gave the Zionists the Balfour Declaration—the recognition of the right of the Jews to establish a 'national home' in Palestine. The second war should end by giving them their own state. That, according to Ben-Gurion, was the 'political compass' that would guide the Zionist movement during the war."

Were these indeed Ben-Gurion's words? The stenographic record of that meeting has Ben-Gurion counting "four unknowns . . . over which we have no control: Italy, Russia, Turkey, America . . . their joining the war—all, some, or none—will affect its course and its prospects." It was the prospective actions of these "four unknowns" that he regarded as "nature's events," not "recent developments" that had already occurred.

As for Ben-Gurion's hope that the Second World War, like the previous one, would also produce benefits for Zionism, the record shows that he spoke in an entirely different vein: "Of one thing we must beware: drawing analogies with the war of 1914." For it was clear "that the present war will not resemble in any way the war of 1914." Furthermore, the Yishuv must prepare for the hard times in store—"for the millions of Jews in Poland, every day brings with it new devastations"—and in this struggle "we need a political compass . . . to guide our course," which was "the striving for a Jewish state in Palestine." And he added: "The Balfour Declaration was given to us. The state—if it comes to be this time—we shall have to establish ourselves."

His "political compass," then, was not meant to guide Zionism to ensure that the second war should end "by giving" the Zionists (who

Gurion, who all his life adhered to his "efficacy rule" and paid little or no attention to "symbolic acts." The conclusion is clear: It was not the striving for a Jewish state that interfered with rescue; rather, the prospects for rescue were simply nil.

Segev does not mention that the question of using JAE budgets for rescue had been discussed previously on numerous occasions and that at this central committee meeting Ben-Gurion's comments represented a broad consensus. Nor does he note that Ben-Gurion favored the establishment of an all-Jewish world organization to raise a rescue fund. Whether it would have been at all possible, under wartime conditions, to set up a body in which all other Jewish organizations, Zionist and non-Zionist, religious and nonreligious, took part, is an open question. It seems, sadly, that even total war and the Holocaust could not bridge the differences in the Jewish world, differences that kept it as fragmented and divided as ever. Had the Jews ever agreed among themselves on anything? Trying to establish such an organization would have been an exercise in futility, and it is quite easy to imagine Ben-Gurion—had he committed himself to such an undertaking—spending the war years in fruitless negotiations with intractable, not to say obstreperous, collaborators.

Segev should have asked himself honestly whether massive rescue might have become possible if Ben-Gurion and other Zionist leaders had proclaimed that, for the sake of rescuing Jews, they were completely renouncing Zionism. Can anyone prove, even theoretically, that renunciation of the Jewish state would have improved the prospects for rescue? Would this have led the Allied powers to agree to make massive rescue of Jews one of their war aims? Would it have brought the British and the Arabs to open Palestine's doors to greater Jewish immigration?

But there is no need for such speculations. To refute Segev's assertion it suffices to cite one quotation—out of many—and one abortive attempt at rescue. Ben-Gurion's maxim that no country on earth was willing to take in Jewish refugees was rooted in reality. As early as April 1936, as already mentioned, Ben-Gurion told Palestine's high commissioner, Gen. Sir Arthur Wauchope, that had there been the possibility of bringing Poland's Jews to the United States or Argentina, "we would have done so regardless of our Zionist ideology. But the world was closed to us."[7]

In 1943 an opportunity arose to rescue several thousand Jewish families from Poland if a country could be found to offer them temporary asylum. The JAE, assuming all the costs, asked the Union of South Africa's Board of Deputies to request such asylum there. In vain. Prime Minister Field Marshal Jan Smuts, a member of Britain's war cabinet and a self-professed Zionist, refused to let even eighty refugee families enter. "It is impossible," he said. "You must bear in mind there is fear of anti-Semitism . . . and for the good of the country it is best to avoid entry of more Jews."

In September, Yitzhak Gruenbaum, head of the JAE's Labor Department and chairman of the rescue committee, went to South Africa, and was told by Smuts: "I agreed to the entry of Jewish children, but I was unable to overcome the transport difficulties and to this day have not been able to bring them over." Gruenbaum asked in astonishment: "I can't understand it, I know that [non-Jewish] Polish children were brought over here. Why is it so difficult to bring over Jewish children?" Smuts pretended not to know, or not to believe, what was really happening to European Jews: "There is a labor shortage in Germany—how come instead of using Jews for labor the Germans slay them?" Smuts also told Gruenbaum that Weizmann had written him "that he [Weizmann] had intervened with the American administration to do something real to rescue Europe's Jews, and came back with empty hands."[*]

On his return Gruenbaum inquired of PGE's minister in Palestine about the entry of Polish children into South Africa. He reported to the JAE that the Polish diplomat had told him that the government of South Africa had granted PGE's request for asylum for children from Poland, "on condition that Jewish children would not be brought over with the Polish children." Gruenbaum asked the minister: "How does

---

[*] This dialogue is taken from the Hebrew minutes of a JAE meeting; to my knowledge, no minutes exist in English. No such letter to Smuts has been found in Weizmann's correspondence.

that square with what Smuts told me?" The Polish diplomat "didn't know how to explain the contradiction, yet he reiterated that this was the condition the government of South Africa had made for consenting to the admission of children from Poland." Did Field Marshal Smuts lie? the JAE asked Gruenbaum. He ducked the question, responding: "I am sure that the Polish minister told the truth."[8]

Without his anti-Zionist bias, perhaps Segev, too, would have concluded that the rescue efforts were defeated first and foremost by the Germans. Second in culpability were Germany's satellites, followed by the British, who not only failed to lift a finger to rescue Jews but (as will be seen later) did their best to obstruct the JAE's rescue efforts in order to block immigration to Palestine. Last came the indifferent world, especially the United States. Throughout the war, at the head of the rescue operations, whatever they were, stood the Zionists, with or without support from the non-Zionists.

Segev, however, is interested only in his two aspects of Zionism, the theoretical and the practical—"condemnation of the Diaspora" and the striving for a Jewish state—in his opinion the real culprits responsible for the lack of adequate rescue. Utterly ignoring the monumental difficulties obstructing the JAE's efforts, he aims to create the false impression that if the JAE had exerted all its powers and invested the major part of its budget in rescue efforts, many more would have been saved, and neutral countries, with the encouragement of the British, would have received the rescued with open arms. But this picture he paints had no basis in reality.

CHAPTER NINE

WEISSMANDEL'S CRY FROM THE HEART

SEGEV IMPLIES, BOASTFULLY, that he knows how two of the ransom plans, "Europa" and "Goods for Blood," could have saved 1 or 2 million more. First, deception, fraud, and "clandestine activities" should have been employed. Second, the Yishuv's leadership should have been removed, because Ben-Gurion and his JAE colleagues were not equal to the job, being either overaged ("elected to their posts years before the Holocaust") or unimaginative, or both.[1] However, he does not share with us the names of the more capable leaders who could have taken their place and successfully carried out the ransom plans.

There were four such plans: the Transnistria Plan (70,000 Jews), the Slovakia Plan (25,000),* the Europa Plan (all the Jews in occupied Europe), and a plan that evolved from it: the Nazi offer to swap the lives of Hungarian Jewry for goods—10,000 trucks, hundreds of tons of coffee, cocoa, tea, soap, etc.—known either as "Goods for Blood" or "Trucks for Blood."

It is in their attitude toward these plans that Michael Dov-Ber Weissmandel, the ultra-Orthodox rabbi, and Tom Segev, the ultra-leftist writer, meet. Both are fervent anti-Zionists—Segev would perhaps rather be called post-Zionist. However, their anti-Zionism emanates from entirely different grounds. Weissmandel's is rooted in

---

* Some versions put the number at 30,000.

the holy scriptures and a millennium-long tradition. His attitude derives from two verses of Genesis—"Give me the people and keep the goods for yourself" and "a gift sent [by Jacob] to my lord Esau"[2]—as well as the halakhah* that Esau, whose name became a synonym for all Gentiles, forever hates Jacob, whose name was changed to Israel following his all-night tussle with God.[3] That is, by nature Gentiles hate Jews, and to save themselves Jews bribe Gentiles with gifts, cost what it may, because people's lives are more important than money or its equivalent.

"Innumerable times," Weissmandel told his disciples, "was God's own people under threat of annihilation by their haters." Their hatred "attends us, with blood and tears, from generation to generation." But the merciful Lord has always shown compassion to his "wretched people" and "supported them with true leaders, pleaders par excellence." Thanks to them, "the children of our father Abraham go on living, and will live for eternal eternity."

The Jews had always lived, Weissmandel wrote in a letter, "in acquiescence, as God willed them to live, and could have gone on so living forever." But lately, "because of our many sins, a good many of our people have deserted the old way bequeathed to us by our fathers" and become infatuated with the false new way, "which ridiculed, mocked and sneered at the submissiveness of previous, older [and wiser] generations." This new trend had won over "almost the majority" of the Jewish people, who took to the "politics of nationalism" and "aggressive claims" just when this same majority came under threat of tyranny and extinction. At this very time, when the Jewish people in Europe were "under the heel of that villain [Hitler] and his cronies, the rulers of the countries bordering the cursed Germany, these foolish Jews, from the safety of the free world, from the United States and other countries [Palestine], made fun of him, hounded him and [finally] provoked him, in acts of endless ridicule and foolery, in the press and in [public] meetings, by denunciation and

---

* The entire body of Jewish law and tradition, comprising the laws of the Bible, the oral law as transcribed in the legal portion of the Talmud, and subsequent legal codes amending or modifying traditional precepts to conform to contemporary conditions.

by blowing the Shofar in front of a German consulate." Even at a time when the entire world was at "peace and calm with" the villain Hitler, the Jewish "nationalists" called upon all Jews to boycott German goods.* This they did despite the fact "that there was no other way than to try [again] submissiveness and inducement. [But] the self-appointed [nationalist] leaders have done the opposite—the opposite of wisdom and of the oath of God—and thus, to a large extent, by their own actions have maddened a mad dog to its greatest rage."[4]

Notwithstanding his fine intellect, Weissmandel was a man of great innocence and naïveté, living in a pre-Enlightenment, pre-Emancipation, pre-twentieth-century, closed world. That he was wrong in believing that he could save Jewish lives by bribing Hitler, like any other anti-Semite of old, as his forefathers and their forefathers had done time and again, cannot be held against him. Other ways and means failed just as badly.

Segev, on the other hand, comes from an entirely different world, the ultimate in political progressivism: secular, anticlerical, antiracist, antisexist, and antinationalist. It is not so much the loss of Jewish life that fuels his anti-Zionism as the stealing of the land of Palestine from the Palestinian Arabs and the exile Israel forced on many of them in 1948.

However their worlds differ, both see Israel, the Jewish state, as their mortal spiritual enemy. For Weissmandel, it was established and it exists flouting God's will. For Segev, it was established and it exists flouting justice, truth, and peace. Weissmandel would have liked it to disappear, so its Jews, and those who supported them in other countries, might be free to repent and revert to the good old ways of the Lord, as revealed for centuries past by the sages and the great rabbis. Segev would like Israel, the Jewish state, to make way for a post-Zionist, secular, radically supranational state that would undo the injustice done to the Palestinian Arabs. In his state, Arab and Jew would enjoy equal rights—that is, a law of return applying to Arabs as well as Jews. If all or nearly all Palestinian refugees and their offspring

---

* Meaning Jabotinsky's Revisionists and the World Jewish Congress.

returned, and the current demographic imbalance of twice as many Arab births continued, all that would remain of the Jewish sovereign state would be a Jewish community, like any other of the past or today.

This was also precisely Weissmandel's wish when he was alive. He would have accepted only a Jewish state established by an act of God, or (as is commonly said) with the advent of the Messiah. This meeting of minds is strange: not so much because the one believes absolutely in God and the other preaches absolute political justice; nor because Segev embraces as a model Weissmandel's rescue strategy—deception, fraud, and "clandestine activities"—in order to disparage Ben-Gurion and his JAE colleagues and to hint at nameless betters. It is strange because of the disparity in how they approach the Holocaust. To write his book, Weissmandel used for ink the blood of his heart. Therefore, despite its great unreadability, inaccuracies, and accusations quite counter to the facts, his book stands out in the Holocaust library. No other book brings home the horror of the Holocaust as does his. The author's pain, purity of soul, and love for his God and his people transcend all its literary and historical faults. The same could not be said for Segev's book. It is highly readable, and it has wit, color, and even some good points. But the pain, the torment, and the inner truth that make Weissmandel's volume singular are wholly missing.

Be that as it may, Segev recycles Weissmandel's accusations in order to find fault with the Yishuv's leaders. Had they been more capable, the ransom plans would have had a far better chance. "One thing can be said with certainty," he writes; "each of the [plans] . . . demanded capability and imagination beyond those possessed by Ben-Gurion and the other leaders of the yishuv." In a final sizing-up, he dismisses them as "small people, whose self-image as respected statesmen hampered their ability and willingness to get involved in fraud and clandestine activities." The Hebrew original is even more biting.[5]

In other words, other leaders—more ingenious, unhampered by their self-image, unfettered by Zionist shackles, and willing and able to undertake "fraud and clandestine activities"—could have saved tens of thousands more with the Slovakia Plan and a million or two more with the Europa Plan and Goods for Blood.

Although the notable Holocaust historian Professor Yehuda Bauer of the Hebrew University, Jerusalem, dismisses Segev's argument as "sheer nonsense,"[6] it is worth examining, if only better to understand Ben-Gurion's and his colleagues' predicament. It is well to bear in mind that whereas they had only three, or at maximum four years— years of war and Holocaust, each averaging at least 1 million murdered Jews—to explore ways and means of rescue, draw up plans and carry them out, Holocaust scholars have been at work for half a century, checking whether avenues of rescue existed and how any possibility for massive rescue operations might have been overlooked. Even so, none of the scholars has come up with anything. On the contrary, prominent Holocaust historians and scholars who have studied the Yishuv's reaction to the Holocaust and its rescue efforts in particular agree that none of the ransom plans had a real chance. They also agree that massive rescue was impossible and that the Yishuv could not have done significantly more than it did.

Professor Bauer suggests "that the possibility of saving Jews by negotiations existed—no one can tell how many . . . [but] in order to save a great many, a different order of priorities on the part of the Western powers was needed, a radical change in their way of thinking and in their [war] aims, as well as in the public opinion which supported their governments. This kind of rescue, on a larger order of magnitude, did not exist."

Professor Leni Yahil, of the Hebrew University, writes, in commenting on the Europa Plan, that "in point of fact there was no ground for negotiations, and the prospect for agreement and rescue was nil, even without the reservations and the restraints imposed on the Jews of the West, who saw no chance whatever of getting the Allies' consent to a deal of this kind. By April 1943 the Bermuda Conference was over, and in August Himmler ordered that negotiations on the Europa Plan be broken off. But the people in Slovakia [Weissmandel and his colleagues in the working group] were bitterly disappointed, because their entreaties [for the ransom money] did not receive a positive response."

Professor Friedlander told the newspaper *Lamerchav*: "I do not argue that from an operational-technical point of view more could have been done to rescue. . . . I argue that the leaders and the Yishuv as a whole did not pay adequate attention to rescue." Professor Gutman admits that the Yishuv and its leaders were powerless as far as massive rescue was concerned, and doubts the value of the ransom plans. His main complaint is what he sees as the "attitude" of Ben-Gurion toward Diaspora Jews, the Holocaust, and the survivors. Professor Yeshayahu Jelinek, of Ben-Gurion University in Beersheba, Dr. Dina Porat of Tel Aviv University, Dr. Yechiam Weitz of Haifa University, Dr. Hava Eshkoli (Wagman) of Bar-Ilan University, Dr. Gila Fatran of Tel Aviv University, and Dr. Hannah Yablonka of Ben-Gurion University in Beersheba, all agree that the Yishuv and its leaders could have done very little more than they did. The Europa Plan, says Dr. Yablonka, was not workable; her only reservation is that she lacks positive historical proof that it had no chance of success. Professor Avishai Margalit of the Hebrew University's department of philosophy, a member of the Israeli left, reviewing Segev's English edition for the *New York Review of Books*, wrote: "In my view there was little the Yishuv could have done to save the Jews of Europe."[7]

Nevertheless, Segev is convinced that Goods for Blood could have saved a great many. He is aware that the JAE was unable to procure 10,000 trucks and deliver them to the Nazis for use in the war, in return for a million Jews, without Allied approval, and this approval was expressly denied. "On the other hand," he writes, "it would seem that the agency did not do all it could to lead on the Germans behind the backs of the British." What for? Segev himself is clearly quite unlike Ben-Gurion and his colleagues in possessing cunning, and he treats us to a bagful of clever advice: "The Zionists already knew that the British were not interested in saving Jews and that no help could be expected from them. It was time for a great bluff. The yishuv leadership could have disobeyed British orders and negotiated secretly with the Nazis; they could have sent someone from a neutral country to represent them. They could have offered the Germans money instead of trucks, or at least an advance—anything to gain time, since the Russians were not far from Hungary" and would shortly bring deliverance.

Is it not amazing that fifty years after the event, and despite all the evidence that Goods for Blood was intended by the Nazis to open an avenue to direct peace negotiations with the Western Allies, Segev still believes that Himmler and his SS lieutenants were really only after trucks or money? It has apparently never occurred to him that if Himmler and the SS's main interest was pecuniary, they could have started to amass gold, jewelry, and billions and billions of dollars—or any other currency—by selling Jewish blood, long before Auschwitz's crematoria had been designed and ordered.

In contrast to the dim-witted "small people" at the JAE, Segev sets up Saly Mayer as an example of ingenuity and sophistication, to teach them and everybody else what could really have been done: "The negotiations with the Germans continued on another track [that is, a supposedly non-JAE track], beginning with a meeting between Saly Mayer, a Swiss representative of the AJDC, and several SS officers. They spoke while standing on the Sankt Margarethen Bridge, which connects Austria with Switzerland. There were further meetings as well. Mayer tried, and succeeded in, buying time. At one point he even obtained a few tractors for the Germans as a goodwill gesture. Himmler directed that no more Jews be deported from Budapest. Mayer deserves history's praise. Eliahu Dobkin later claimed that the Jewish Agency had set up these negotiations, but Mayer was not acting in its name—in fact, he was not a Zionist."[8]

In note 32, Segev cites his authorities: "Dobkin remarks in the secretariat of the Histadrut on October 11, 1944, and an essay on the subject by Yehuda Bauer."[9] But even a casual reader of this essay would see that Segev has distorted Bauer, who cannot therefore serve as his authority on this point.

Segev, taking it upon himself to bestow the accolade that Mayer "deserves history's praise," emphasizes that Mayer's venture, a model of "deception and clandestine activities," was not initiated by the JAE. Indeed, Mayer merits even a higher compliment: "he was not a Zionist." Bauer's version is quite different. "Trucks for Blood," Bauer writes, "was bound up with the SS's intention to pave the way for separate peace negotiations with the Western Allies, and the Jewish interest served as a suitable starting point as well as a secondary issue at the negotiating table." Since the Germans had a vital interest in this scheme, it had a prima facie good chance. But the Allies, well aware of Himmler's intention, prohibited any negotiations in which the Jews would "promise the Germans either goods or money." To buy time, however, the Americans agreed to allow a Jewish group in a neutral country to enter into negotiations on Goods for Blood, but gave this group nothing to negotiate with.

Bauer maintains that although the JAE's demand to conduct these negotiations had been rejected by the Allies, the JAE nevertheless kept "examining ways to resume the negotiations with the Nazis." Menahem Bader, one of the rescue emissaries in Istanbul, "was ready to represent the Jews in such negotiations, and was invited for that purpose" to Hungary. But the British and the Americans, knowing that he was in the employ of the JAE, saw through the trick and refused him permission to leave for occupied Europe. Dr. Joseph Schwartz, AJDC representative in Europe, being an American citizen representing an American organization, met with a similar refusal. "Only then, at the beginning of August 1944, did the name of Saly Mayer, AJDC representative in Switzerland, come up." But the Americans would not allow him "to appear as representing AJDC. He could appear only as a notable Swiss national and leader of the Jewish community there."

So we find that it was not because the JAE and its agents were "small, unimaginative people" that they were unable to attempt "deception and clandestine activities"; and, moreover, that Mayer got the job not because of his ingenuity but simply because the Americans did not identify him with the JAE. He could therefore represent it, and the AJDC, in their joint effort for rescue, without endangering the Allies' allegiance to their common resolution with the Soviet Union to fight the war until the Nazis surrendered unconditionally. As will be evident shortly, Dobkin told the truth.

Further, the negotiations Mayer was entrusted with were in fact meant to gain time—in Bauer's words, "to serve as a source of hope that in the meantime many lives of the putative Nazi victims would be saved." Bauer adds emphatically: "This approach dovetailed with that of the JAE, which proposed resumption of negotiations to gain time."

According to Bauer, the Nazis approved Mayer as their interlocutor "probably on the initiative of Dr. Kastner," head of the rescue committee in Budapest and a Zionist leader. Mayer's Sankt Margarethen Bridge negotiations with SS representatives, led by SS *Obersturmbahnführer* Kurt Becher, went on for five months, from August 21, 1944, to February 5, 1945, and, indeed, the Zionist Kastner took a very active part in most of them. He left Budapest on October 27 for Switzerland. He never returned to Hungary. Instead, to expedite the negotiations still further, he proceeded a few days later to Germany. Dressed in an SS uniform he traveled with Becher—by then in charge of all concentration camps—and other SS officers from camp to camp, using Schwalb's name to reassure camp inmates and allay their suspicions. He arrived in Bergen-Belsen on April 10, 1945, and prevented their last-minute execution. At the end of April, on the eve of VE-Day, he returned from Germany to Switzerland.[10] Segev, however, unimpressed by Kastner's outstanding bravery, omits his name.

Bauer notes that "the order to stop the deportation of Budapest's Jews on August 25 ensued from the negotiations on the Swiss border. The continuation of this line . . . cannot be imagined without Mayer's delaying tactics, although no lesser credit is due Kastner and [Andreas] Biss." Furthermore: "the passage to Switzerland of Kastner's rescue train [with 1685 Jews on board] is undoubtedly an additional direct result of the negotiations." And finally: "It is hard to tell if the negotiations also aided the survival of 17,000 Hungarian Jews [21,000, according to *The Encyclopedia of the Holocaust* (Hebrew)] deported to Strasshof [concentration camps near Vienna]. Indeed, it appears to be so." To demonstrate the uncertainty of the ransom negotiations, and emphasize how important it was to gain time, Bauer notes that "at the height of the negotiations, under Eichmann's orders between 30,000 and 50,000 Jews were forced to march on foot from Budapest toward the Austrian border, and many perished," giving this horrible event its name, "the death march."[11]

True—and it is clear why—Mayer "was not," to borrow Segev's words, "acting in [the JAE's] name." He was also not a member of the World Zionist Organization. He was, however, as Bauer says, "pro-Zionist"—and more. As president of the Jewish community of Switzerland, "he was actively involved in the JAE's deliberations in 1936–1937 over the future of Palestine." His good friend Joseph Schwartz was in constant, close contact with the JAE, and later with the government of Israel. In 1941 Mayer was "most impressed"[12] with the personality of Nathan Schwalb, a kibbutz member in charge of all HeHalutz activities in Europe, who had become the center of a widespread network of contacts in the occupied areas. They became fast friends, and, writes Bauer, "Schwalb soon converted Mayer to a fervent and effusive Zionism."[13]

Schwalb stood at Mayer's right hand throughout the negotiations with Himmler's SS representatives, and it was Schwalb who acted as liaison—through the good offices of Dr. Richard Lichtheim, the JAE's representative in Geneva—between Mayer and the JAE in Jerusalem. The cables Mayer exchanged in 1943 with Sharett, head of the JAE's political department, provide evidence of the close contact he maintained with the JAE. Could it be that Mayer's close contact with the JAE is why Weissmandel flung accusations against him in the same breath with those he makes against the JAE's rescue emissaries in Istanbul? If Mayer did not publicly proclaim his close contacts with the JAE, it is reasonable to assume that he kept quiet in order not to hinder the ongoing negotiations. Once the Americans identified him with the JAE, his position as a neutral negotiator from a neutral country would be destroyed.

Without questioning Mayer's right to praise, it seems clear that Segev would have better understood both Mayer's place in history and the negotiations on the Sankt Margarethen Bridge if he had bothered to interview Schwalb, or at least learn more about his role in the rescue efforts. For Schwalb was the linchpin of all rescue efforts in Nazi Europe, as well as their engine and rudder. If Segev was looking for a real hero worthy of "history's praise"—who not only understood that "it was time for a great bluff" but could also bring one off—Schwalb was his man. Had Segev extended his research to include Schwalb, he might even have found it in his heart to forgive him for his ardent Zionism.

Born in 1908 to a Hebrew school teacher in Stanislawow, a district capital in eastern Galicia, Poland,* and an important Jewish community, Nathan Schwalb† became a cofounder of Gordonia, a Labor Zionist youth movement, and a member of the Galician central committee of HeHalutz (The Pioneer, a world organization of young Zionists preparing themselves to settle collectively in Palestine as farmers and laborers). In 1930 he and his wife immigrated to Palestine with Gordonia's first pioneer group, which in 1931 founded their kibbutz in Hulda on the ruins of a former Jewish settlement, destroyed by the Arabs in the riots of 1929. A prominent figure in Gordonia and Mapai, which he joined, and in his kibbutz, Schwalb was sent in 1938 as the JAE representative to the World HeHalutz Center in Warsaw and to Vienna, to keep the movement alive in the aftermath of the *Anschluss* (Hitler's annexation of Austria).

Eichmann closed down HeHalutz, among other Zionist institutions, only to reopen it three months later so it could help get the greatest possible number of Jews out of Austria. It was in this context that Schwalb first met Eichmann; he remembers the map of Austria and the calendar on Eichmann's office wall, on which he made daily notations of the number of Jews leaving Austria, by locality. Later, after the rape of Czechoslovakia in 1939, and in the same context, they met again in Prague.

Along with other HeHalutz representatives from Central and Eastern Europe, Schwalb was summoned to the World Zionist Congress of August 1939 in Geneva to report to its committees concerned with the Jewish situation in Europe. There he met Saly Mayer, who had come primarily to attend the council of the Jewish Agency, which elected the JAE after the congress ended. On the congress's last day, Weizmann—a veteran admirer of Kibbutz Hulda's olives and of Schwalb—introduced him to Uncle Saly, as Mayer was affectionately known, remarking: "If this little fellow pays you a visit, one of these days, remember: he speaks for me."

---

* Today Ivano-Frankovsk, Ukraine.
† Dror (swallow) in Hebrew, which also means liberty, was foisted on him by Sharett in 1948 as his Hebrew name. He sticks, however, to Schwalb.

The German invasion of Poland on September 1 and the ensuing war found Schwalb and other representatives in the midst of their postcongress conference. They all believed, according to Schwalb, that Poland would hold out for ten months at least, "but it went down in twenty days."[14] He and the others could not return to their posts, and the JAE ordered Schwalb to carry on his HeHalutz job from Geneva. Worldwide there were 100,000 members, of whom 25,000 were then living either in camps or organized formations in occupied Europe.[15] All these "riches"—to use Schwalb's phrase—were now on his hands, and they were soon to expand beyond his, or anybody else's, imagination.

With the fall of Poland, and the ensuing chaos, he made it his duty to obtain real-time knowledge of and maintain contact with all Jews under Nazi domination—or, more specifically, those who could read and write, to extend through them aid, rescue, and hope to the rest. His "constituency"—again to use his term—encompassed all Jews from sixteen to sixty. But it soon expanded beyond Poland, Austria, and Czechoslovakia; as the war progressed, Schwalb's jurisdiction, by his own choice, spread over nearly all of continental Europe.

His first task, as he understood it, was to reestablish communication with areas under Nazi rule. "We"—Schwalb rarely used "I" in describing his exploits—"had to begin from scratch." This meant initiating a search for addresses. "For communication was everything. 'No addresses, no communication; no communication, no help, no rescue.' " This, however, was easier said than done. Destruction by fire of the HeHalutz World Center and of all its files, records, and archives; rapid disappearance of all Jewish centers and institutions and their replacement by Judenrats; and the mass "relocation" and "resettlement" of Jews all over Nazi Europe, made this task appear impossible. Getting a simple valid mailing address turned out to be a superhuman endeavor.

Yet this is exactly what Schwalb set out to achieve, and this is exactly what he did. Only a fully detailed account can do justice to this slightly built, nearly incorporeal, almost transparent thirty-one-year-old man, who, far away from home, family, and friends, leading the life of a church mouse—or a saint, if you will—attained the unattainable. Here I can provide only a brief sketch and an assertion that credit for his feat should go to his unequaled will and devotion, inborn street-smartness, irresistible personal charm, and prodigious memory. It should also be noted that Schwalb's rescue enterprise— like nearly all other such ventures at the time—could not have been carried out without the foundation previously laid down by the Zionist movement.

Luckily, Schwalb explained many years later, he retained "scores of Gordonia and HeHalutz" addresses in his memory, and he used these for starters. From his twelve-by-nine-foot room at 13 rue des Philosophes he started a handwritten correspondence, asking for information and current addresses. Each letter received he answered promptly, and to each new address he wrote asking for more information and addresses. Schwalb's addresses passed from mouth to mouth on the Geneva grapevine, swelling the volume of his incoming mail. His correspondence steadily broadened, despite the fact that his correspondents were constantly dwindling. He moved twice to more spacious lodgings—two rooms, one private, one for an office, with a typewriter and a telephone—in 1941 and then, at the end of 1943, to a building in the same street as the Zionist office. Since the end of 1942 he had the help of a Swiss Jewish secretary, Ruth Fleischacker, whom he married in 1946, three years after the death of his wife in Hulda, Palestine.

He worked day and night. By 1941 he was receiving and answering 150 missives a day, mostly letters but a few telegrams as well, from and to individuals and groups, Zionists, non-Zionists, and Judenrats, all to or from his private address. To avoid suspicion due to the volume of this correspondence, Schwalb used an alias (such as Yaskolski, Polish for swallow). By mid-1942 he weighed only ninety-three pounds, but his reward was immense: He was the only one able to keep in contact with the majority of Jewish communities in Nazi Europe.

To evade the Swiss* and German censorship, he and his correspon-

---

* A state of emergency was declared in Switzerland on Sept. 2, 1939, the day after the war broke out, and internal and external censorship was imposed.

dents used Hebrew codes: "Uncle Gershon," for example, meant "deportation" after the Hebrew *gerush;* thus "Uncle Gershon is visiting with us" meant "deportations have begun."

In May 1941, when his contacts were fully reestablished, and feeling that the time had come to act on Weizmann's introduction, Schwalb turned to Mayer and asked him for JDC subventions for agricultural training communes in Poland, for orphans and homeless Jews in Romania, and for child care for Croatian orphans whose parents had been sent to Auschwitz.[16] A few of them arrived in Palestine after the war, owing their lives, to a large extent, to Schwalb. Schwalb later did the same for orphans in Belgium. Subsequently, Mayer became a regular subscriber to Schwalb's information on suffering Europe.

By 1941 Schwalb became the preeminent one-man agency—"the center of a widespread net of contacts," in Bauer's phrase[17]—working on the Jewish situation in Nazi Europe; he reported to seven departments of the JAE and Histadrut in Palestine. His position, as well as his need for consultation, exchange of ideas, and social intercourse, cemented his ties with Abraham (Adolf) Silberschein and Benjamin Segalovitch. The three became a closely knit "troika" (in Schwalb's phrase), sharing information and devising strategies. In retrospect they appear as the supreme behind-the-scenes strategists of all rescue operations originating in Switzerland. There is no question that Schwalb was the moving spirit of this troika.

Silberschein was a thinker. A lawyer specializing in oil and fuel, world-famous as an arbitrator, a three-time member of the *Sejm,* Poland's parliament, and a fervent Zionist, he, too, had attended the 1939 World Zionist Congress. "Tied body and soul to Poland's three million Jews," as Schwalb put it, Silberschein helped improve their economic situation before the war by founding productive cooperatives all over Galicia. His profound knowledge of Jewish life in Poland gained him a prominent position in the World Jewish Congress, and he became its senior representative in Switzerland once the war started and he was stranded in Geneva.

Segalovitch, born and reared in Germany but a longtime Swiss citizen, was an official of the SIG* (Federation of the Swiss Jewish Communities), in charge of information and editor of its weekly, *Judische Nachrichten.* It was Segalovitch who first learned, from the German industrialist Eduard Schulte in July 1942, of the Wannsee Conference held in January of that year and the Final Solution it discussed. He was therefore the source of the two historic telegrams— one from Gerhardt Riegner of the Geneva office of the World Jewish Congress to its president, Rabbi Stephen Wise in New York, the other from Richard Lichtheim, head of the Zionist office in Geneva, to the JAE in Jerusalem—indicating that Hitler was conducting a planned, systematic genocide of Europe's Jews.

Schwalb's contacts with occupied Europe and his talent for human bonding led to the formation of yet another troika, with Saly Mayer and the Joint's Dr. Joseph Schwartz. This trio played a role more central to the subject under investigation here.

Saly Mayer, a lace manufacturer and former president of SIG for eight years, had been a member of the Jewish Agency council since 1937, when he was elected as a deputy non-Zionist member of the Jewish Agency's administrative board.[18] As already mentioned, he and Schwalb, twenty-six years younger, became fast friends.[19] Into this friendship Mayer brought his sidekick, the wealthy Pierre Bigar, owner of the famed Geneva Hotel Cornavin, at the Place de la Gare, and Uncle Saly's deputy when he was president of SIG.[20] Bigar played a pivotal role both in forging the new troika and in preparing for the negotiations with the Nazis over Goods for Blood, for Bigar, experienced in negotiations over prices, had a head for figures and finances and could think fast on his feet. The Swiss federal government appointed him head of the food-rationing department in Bern, and it is partly due to his efforts that there was no black market in Switzerland during the war.

Late in 1941, Schwalb met Schwartz at the Hotel Cornavin, in Mayer's company. Then forty-two, with a doctorate from Yale in

---

* Schweizerischer Israelitischer Gemeindebund.

Semitic studies and experience in academic teaching and social work, Schwartz was in charge of the Joint's European operations. During the war years he commuted between his head office in New York and his European office, which after the fall of France in 1940 had been moved to Lisbon.

Schwartz, too, was impressed by Schwalb's information and contacts, which was why Mayer set up the meeting. Schwalb, for his part, was astonished by Schwartz's mastery of Hebrew, old and modern, and taken by "his personality; he had a heart, not only brains." Soon they were calling each other by their first names: Yossel (Schwartz) and Nathan (Schwalb).

In later years Schwalb would refer to the Cornavin meeting as fateful. For it was here that Schwartz—representing, so to speak, the world's mightiest power and Jewry's largest and wealthiest community—was first presented with a complete, detailed picture of Jewish life in Nazi Europe. And it was here that Schwartz found, through Schwalb's contacts and addresses, a way to channel help, and later rescue, to Europe's Jews using JAE and Joint funds—and thereby a formula for raising more money in America. This occasion can therefore be seen as this trio's initial strategy meeting. Bigar provided them with facilities at his hotel, which became, in a way, their HQ. As with his first troika, Schwalb remained lifelong friends with his other partners too.

For sending food parcels and medicine there was no alternative to the postal service. But for purposes of rescue—as in the case of the ransom plans—the post and telegraph were totally inadequate. A quicker, safer channel of communication had to be found, and Schwalb set out to establish a network of couriers. Since he swore himself to complete secrecy, his lips still remain sealed. But the little known about his work in this area is quite incredible.

As a socialist and trade unionist, and helped by his charm and talent for human relations, Schwalb found his way into the innermost circles of Switzerland's labor, socialist, and liberal circles, which were preparing Switzerland's resistance in case of a Nazi invasion. He became especially close to those whose task it was to expose Fifth Column agents. Working his way up to the top level of the clandestine movement, he made the acquaintance of the top echelon: the very well known conservative aristocrats, Hans Hausamann and Franz Guebelin, and Hans Oprecht, president of Switzerland's socialist party and member of the Federal Council (the Swiss parliament). With Oprecht he became good friends.[21] These and other contacts helped Schwalb in his search for couriers—he was looking for "clever gentiles, Protestant or Catholic, idealist, Socialist, Swiss citizens with a heart"—which was amply rewarded.

For example, at Oprecht's home Schwalb met an official courier of the Swiss Foreign Ministry, who for three years was part of Schwalb's courier service. Schwalb's resistance associations also brought him into contact with foreign correspondents. Two were Protestants who worked for the famed *Neue Zuricher Zeitung*. One, stationed in Bucharest, traveled between Geneva, Vienna, and Bucharest by train. The other was posted in Budapest and visited Berlin and other capitals. The third, a Catholic, was a roving correspondent for *Thurgau Tagblatt*. With these and other couriers, Schwalb established three regular routes: Geneva–Prague–Bratislava–Budapest; Geneva–Bratislava–Budapest–Bucharest; and Geneva–Vienna–Berlin, with occasional stops at Bratislava or Budapest. For the sake of security he would alternate his couriers, never sending them on the same route more than two or three times in a row.

All his couriers were dependable and none asked for money, says Schwalb, and during the first two years of the war he did not use them to transfer money. This, however, is contested by Bauer, who notes that Schwalb "smuggled cash via couriers, many of whom were less than trustworthy—but he had no choice."[22]

Only in 1942, says Schwalb, in order to meet a payment due to Wisliceny "within forty-eight hours," as part of the Slovakia Plan, did a courier of his carry money for Gisi Fleischmann in Bratislava. But how would Fleischmann know how, when, and where to pick up the money on such short notice?

Schwalb solved this problem through another association—perhaps the most remarkable—which had brought him, the penniless kibbutz-

nik, together with the general director of the Geneva branch of UBS,*
one of the world's most prominent banks. This director, at an agreed-
upon hour, would telephone his counterpart at the National Bank of
Slovakia in Bratislava, where Gisi Fleischmann of the working group
would be waiting. She and Schwalb, under assumed names, could then
discuss freely and directly, in code, the down payments for the Slovakia plan.[23]

In a similar manner Schwalb talked once or twice a week with
Kastner in Budapest. In particular, these calls were used to give directions for the Sankt Margarethen Bridge talks[24] and to discuss what
later became known as the "Kastner Train"—the rescue train which
under Eichmann's orders brought to Bergen-Belsen, instead of
Auschwitz, and from there to Switzerland, 1685 Jews. It seems
Schwalb was not boasting when he said he "held all the strings" in
his hand.

One last example: It was one of Schwalb's couriers who on May
18, 1944, brought to Switzerland from Slovakia Weissmandel's letter
of May 16, with copies of the Vrba Report.[25] In Geneva Schwalb
handed a copy to Rosewell D. McClelland, the American War Refugee
Board representative in Switzerland, with whom Schwalb had developed close working relations—"we were in touch day and night"†—
as well as to other representatives of the free world and the Vatican.

Schwalb puts the number of Jewish lives he was involved in saving
at 250,000. It was he, the dedicated Zionist, who displayed the "cunning" and ability to engage in "the big bluff" called for by Segev,
using all the tricks in the book when it came to clandestine operations:
false Latin and Central American passports to enable refugees to exit
occupied Europe to neutral countries; and persuading an officer and
a sergeant of the border guard at the St. Gallen sector to turn a blind

---

* Union des Banques Suisses.
† Thanks to Schwalb, McClelland was able to cable the State Department in Washington
with a summary of Kastner's letter about the brutal house-to-house roundup in Bratislava
on the night of September 28, 1944, in which the Nazis arrested nearly 4,000 Jews, including
Gisi Fleischmann and Rabi Weissmandel.

eye to his running refugees across the Swiss border.* Most notable of all, he took it upon himself to use Jewish National Fund accounts in Geneva and other unoccupied European capitals as collateral for loans that extended the rescue budget allotted to him. The JAE agreed to repay them after the war. Not a few of the 25,000 Jews (out of a total of 100,000 refugees of all European nationalities) who found shelter in Switzerland during the war owe their lives to him.

Schwalb, therefore, emerges as the mastermind and behind-the-scenes director of nearly all rescue initiatives emanating from Switzerland, and as the mentor and guide of Saly Mayer in his negotiations with the Nazis over Goods for Blood. Schwalb himself took part in these negotiations three times.[26] A thick volume would be required to do justice to his exploits for the sake of rescue.

---

* These two were soccer fans, and Schwalb's first success was smuggling in members of *Hakoach Vien*, a well-known Austrian Jewish football club, and a host of other Jewish athletes.

CHAPTER TEN

"GOVERNMENTS AND ORGANIZATIONS"

T O PROVE HIS contention that the rescue plans failed because the JAE did not do the best it could, Segev must explain why two other plans, into which it put everything it had, did not work either. These were the plan involving the 5000 children from Bulgaria and the larger framework of which it was part, the plan of the 29,000 children (often referred to as 30,000) from the Balkans and Hungary.*

The British government's position, intimated behind the scenes late in 1942 to the JAE after much public pressure in Britain, that it would regard the admission of children into Palestine as an exception accorded high priority, briefly inspired the JAE, as has been seen, with the hope that the "5000 Plan" would materialize. "If we bring over the entire 5000, it would be fantastic," Ben-Gurion said. "It doesn't solve the problem of the 5 million. But not to bring over the 5000 doesn't solve the problem of the 5 million either."

In discussing the children's rescue plans within Mapai and the Histadrut, Haganah chief Eliahu Golomb pointed out three major problems: exit permits, transit permits, and means of transport, all of which lay outside the control of the JAE. "Transport," said Golomb,

---

* In a statement made by the British secretary of state for the colonies, on Feb. 3, 1943, it was announced "that the Government of Palestine had agreed to admit from Bulgaria 4,000 Jewish children, with 500 adults accompanying them, as well as 500 children from Hungary and Rumania," (Hansard [Lords]), (German Atrocities: Aid for Refugees) Mar. 23, 1943, p. 851).

"is a very serious problem." Ben-Gurion, believing that sea transport was preferable to land transfer, urged that the JAE acquire ships, expecting that the JAE would be able to run them faster and better than anyone else. "I say," he went on, "let us acquire all we can, and fast. We must organize all our people with shipping experience and order them to go to wherever boats are available and buy them." Because, he explained, transporting 5000 children by rail "will take, at best, a few months," and he was apprehensive lest the Nazis overrun Bulgaria, on the one hand, or Churchill persuade Turkey to join the Allies and open a new front against Germany, on the other. In either case the theater of war would change and confound the entire rescue plan. Then, "if we don't bring over those we could have brought, we shall have no excuse."[1] Time, therefore, was of the essence.

JAE pleas to governments and international organizations for help in rescuing the children were unavailing—Churchill turned down Ben-Gurion's request for an interview—but what hurt the plan most of all was the obstacles put in its way by the Turks (Ben-Gurion called them "heartless idiots"). Zvi Yehieli, a senior rescue emissary in Istanbul, detailed some of the difficulties. First, the negotiation over the transit of *each* group of children from Bulgaria through Turkey to its Syrian border lasted two months. Second, the Turkish train "Taurus Express" reached the Syrian border only twice a week, and because of the small number of passenger cars, the Turks limited each group of children to seventy-five, accompanying personnel included. Then, only after the Syrian border post reported to Ankara that one group had left Turkey for Palestine was permission for transit issued to the next group, which could set out only after the Turkish consulate in Sofia had received the permit. This meant a six-week interval between groups. A simple calculation, said Yehieli, showed that at this rate bringing 2500 children from Bulgaria to Palestine "will take at least a year." And this estimate did not take into account the time needed to bring the children from Romania, and later from Hungary, to Bulgaria.

At the end of February 1943, the JAE discussed ways to accelerate the children's immigration. Fearing that all the certificates would not be used, Ben-Gurion proposed asking the governments of Britain and the United States for a ship, "otherwise rescue in theory is of no value, if there is no way to rescue in practice." He reiterated this concern at the JAE meeting on March 7: "No one will deny that it is our duty to save every Jew who can be saved from the Nazi inferno, but to our great sorrow the authorization [by the British] of certificates [to Palestine] is only theoretical, for there is no assurance that we can use the certificates and bring out of occupied Europe such a number of Jews."[2]

This problem in effect put into question any sizable rescue by immigration to Palestine. In the same month, as already recounted in the Introduction, Whitehall had withdrawn the hope that children would be excepted from the White Paper quota. On February 3 Colonial Secretary Oliver Stanley reiterated the government's position publicly, but gave it a twist.[3] He made it clear that the White Paper remained in force as British Palestine policy, thereby snuffing out the quivering hope that the children's rescue immigration would break through the White Paper barrier, bringing in its wake massive rescue immigration of all, young and old.

Given the proportions and pace of the systematic extermination, Stanley's announcement was a cruel joke. Yet hope died hard, especially since there was suddenly good news and a new flicker of possibility. Returning in March from Istanbul, Eliezer Kaplan, the JAE's watchful treasurer, reported to the JAE that a deterioration of faith in Germany's victory had been noticed among its satellites, whose policies regarding Jews had become less rigid. Romania's government was ready to allow the exit of 5000 Jewish orphans if the JAE committed itself to bear all the costs. Kaplan had committed the JAE to allocate 2000 immigration certificates to the Romanian children, and to add to them as many more as required.[4]

Securing transportation was mainly the responsibility of Sharett and Weizmann. They met in Washington with Ambassador Lord Halifax and members of the British embassy, with Jewish members of Congress, and even with the president. Roosevelt promised a group of congressmen that he was ready to demand that Hitler let all children out and to inform him that if the Germans were butchering people to save food, he would take it upon himself to feed them. Roosevelt also promised to help the JAE get the shipping it needed. The argument that no ships were available for passengers was nonsense, he said, for American ships sailed to Europe loaded and came back empty. But after all their fine words were said, the Americans conditioned their support on British consent; and it was soon clear how very unlikely such consent was.

Meanwhile, Turkey was still "one big traffic jam," as Kaplan remarked,[5] with its government putting every possible form of red tape in the way of the children's transit. It rejected the JAE's request to allow the passage of 300–350 children a week, as well as a reduced request for 200. The only fast way—the sea route—was nearly impossible to implement: shipowners showed interest, the International Red Cross agreed to let the refugee ships sail under its aegis, and the Soviets promised them safe passage in the Black Sea. But the Turks, like the Americans, conditioned the ships' passage from Turkish to Palestinian ports on British consent.[6] Such consent was never given.

It now became clear beyond any doubt that the British were derailing rescue immigration, both on sea and on land. In behind-the-scenes diplomacy they encouraged the Turks to slow the children's transit. They also controlled the cumbersome procedure for issuing immigration certificates to Palestine, without which the Turks would not issue transit permits. This procedure was as follows: The application for an immigration certificate had to be sent to Bern, the capital of neutral Switzerland, which represented British interests with the Axis powers. There, each application was individually and minutely scrutinized—in order, the British claimed, to prevent Nazi secret agents from entering Palestine (disguised as children?). Once the applications were approved, the certificates were dispatched to the capitals of Bulgaria, Romania, and Hungary by a diplomatic courier, who made his round once a month. At this period the Nazis were exterminating 2800 Jews a day; a year later, Eichmann would send 12,000 a day from Hungary by rail to Auschwitz. The blood clock was ticking nonstop.

The British government was the major roadblock to the rescue of children, and to any other rescue as well. Only the Germans constituted a greater one, a fact that did not come to light until after the war. When Eichmann learned of the passage of the first groups of children through Turkey to Palestine, he conditioned the exit of the 5000 on an exchange of 20,000 young, able-bodied Germans detained as enemy aliens in Allied countries. This condition—unknown then to Ben-Gurion and his JAE colleagues—completely paralyzed the plan: The Allies refused the exchange, the negotiations lingered on, and no one knew better than Eichmann how fast the number of Jewish children was dwindling in Europe.[7]

In May there seemed to be a change, in all probability the result of public opinion. Kaplan was invited to Cairo to discuss sea transport for the children with the minister of state resident in the Middle East, Richard Casey. He told Kaplan that his government could only ask the Turkish government to expedite the children's passage, and was completely unable to procure them a quicker exit from the Balkans. Also, the government could not undertake to make British and American ships available to the JAE, but he himself was ready "to take upon himself the responsibility for transferring the immigrants from Alexandretta [port city in Turkey] to Palestine." Finally, he told Kaplan, the British embassy in Ankara had received authority to simplify the administrative procedures and had appointed one of its members to specially assist the children in getting to Palestine.

On his return to Jerusalem, Kaplan told the JAE that in his opinion "we have been assured support by the British. Whether this moves the Turks to extend us help, time will tell." Nevertheless, "we, on our part, are doing all we can to save the refugees. We are knocking on all doors, open and shut. However, it's not in our hands."

As Porat tells it, this news of an apparent breakthrough heartened the rescue emissaries in Istanbul. Within days, the Turkish government instructed its diplomats in the Balkans that any refugee who arrived in Turkey, by sea or land, would be issued a visa to Palestine by the British. On the strength of this assurance, the Turkish consul in Sofia began issuing transit permits to Jewish refugees. Permits were also given to individuals who had managed to make it to Turkey, by their wits and by all imaginable and mostly unimaginable circumstances. In Istanbul, the British consulate issued them entry permits to Palestine as members of the contingent of 500 adults who were to accompany the children. However, when some of them arrived in Palestine the mandatory government sent an envoy to Turkey to remind the embassy, and through it Whitehall, that adults were supposed to enter Palestine only as escorts of children. Since the transfer of children had not yet started, it was not legal to send adults ahead of them.

Whitehall stopped issuing visas, but the refugees kept coming to Bulgaria, and the Turkish consul there went on issuing them transit permits, on the ground that the mandatory government was authorized to deport them "to Mauritius or somewhere else." Finally, the British government officially requested that the Turkish government in Ankara instruct its consul in Sofia to stop issuing transit permits to Jewish refugees without consulting Ankara first. The Turks complied.[8]

On his return from the United States, Sharett joined the struggle against British authorities in Palestine, shuttling between Egypt, the seat of the British high command and the minister of state resident in the Middle East, and Turkey, the only link with occupied Europe. Briefly he, too, believed optimistically that the 5000 Children Plan was off to a good start. The British promised to grant any Jewish refugee who made it to Turkey an immigration certificate to Palestine, and Bulgaria announced it would allow the exit of 1000 Jews.

But then the British authorities in Palestine prevailed at Whitehall over Casey's policy, so that the government would not agree that Turkey allow into Istanbul ships from Balkan ports with Jewish children aboard. Meanwhile, Bulgaria, caving in to Nazi pressure, closed its borders. Casey's assurances evaporated, and with them the 5000 Children Plan. Till July 1943, only 184 Jewish refugees from Bulgaria arrived in Turkey, and in 1943 and 1944 only 3600 refugees, adults and children, immigrated via Turkey into Palestine.

Dr. Leo Kohn, a senior adviser in the JAE's Political Department, remarked in July 1943 in a note to Sharett: "It is an absurdity that for half a year it was not possible to get even one ship for refugees. It is an absurdity that out of 30,000 children certified for immigration, it was not possible to bring into Palestine even one."[9] It is an even greater absurdity that all the JAE could possibly do was to call it an absurdity.

These seeming fluctuations in British policy or, better still, the intramural struggle the JAE had perceived between the Palestine administration, Minister Casey, and Whitehall, made sense only many years later, when British government records of 1943 were made public. They laid bare a cynical attitude hard to believe.

In his announcement to the House of Commons on February 3, 1943, Stanley said the British government would be prepared—"provided the necessary transport facilities could be made available"—to admit them into Palestine as well as "to continue to admit into Palestine Jewish children with a proportion of adults up to the limits permissible" by the 1939 White Paper. These limits, which then stood at 29,000 souls, spelled also the scope of the government's rescue intentions. Ironically, Stanley himself had agreed to this simile at an interview he granted to representatives of the JAE in London on March 30, 1944, saying "that the problem of immigration [to Palestine] was now synonymous with that of rescue." For this, the so-called 5000 plan, was the one and only rescue scheme it ever undertook.

As Stanley premised his statement on "the conclusion reached by the War Cabinet in December 1942,"[10] it is plain to see that hardly anything was done in the month—January 1943—between that war cabinet's session and Stanley's statement to Parliament. However, on June 26 Stanley was able to report progress. Since his February 3 statement, he told the war cabinet, "negotiations" had begun and "have been in progress on the question of transport and on the method which should be adopted in Bulgaria for the nomination of" the 4500 would-be immigrants to Palestine.

Minister of State Casey was a member of the war cabinet and thus privy both to its "conclusion" and to the "negotiations" led by the Colonial Office. It stands to reason, therefore, that when he discussed transport with Kaplan in May he was acting in accordance with official policy.

On May 27, however, it was learned, as Stanley put it, "that the Bulgarian government, clearly under German pressure, had closed the Bulgarian-Turkish frontier to all Jews." In reaction "the Swiss Government has been asked to leave the Bulgarian Government in no doubt that if they persist in refusing to allow 4,000 Jewish children and the 500 adults to leave it would be regarded as a flagrant breach of an undertaking." But at the same time the Swiss government had been instructed to ask the Bulgarian government "whether it is their intention to deny passage to all Jews whatsoever or only to those not covered by an approved scheme." The Bulgarians said "that they will compile lists themselves and that when complete they will inform the Swiss Government." This answer was considered "not satisfactory" and Stanley opined that he "can only regard it as doubtful whether they will keep their promise." Consequently, the Bulgarian government was asked "to state categorically how many [Jewish] women and children they will be prepared to allow to leave and when." As will be seen, both the doubt whether Bulgaria's government meant to keep its word and the insistence on precise numbers did not reflect the British government's concern with the rescue of Jewish refugees so much as its fear that masses of those refugees might storm Palestine's gates.

But British fears were quickly put to rest by the Swiss chargé d'affaires in Sofia. One could almost hear in Whitehall a collective sigh of relief when the Swiss diplomat reported that the Germans meant "to turn back all Jews who attempt to cross Bulgarian frontiers into Turkey." This applied to Romania as well. It was clear—in Stanley's words—"that the German policy is to refuse to allow any Jews to leave countries under their control except for *quid pro quo* by way of exchange of their nationals," to which the British government could not agree.

This, Stanley averred, would mean in effect "there could now be no legal immigration to Palestine direct from Bulgaria or other enemy-occupied countries."

Stanley then proposed a change of policy. Was this change aimed at rescuing Jewish refugees who found their way to the Balkans by other strategies? Far from it. The proposed change was aimed only at putting the British government in a better light. Especially in America; the relationship with the United States at this stage of the war was of paramount importance to the British government. As there was no danger of Jewish refugees sweeping out of the Balkans or, for that matter, from anywhere else toward Palestine, Stanley thought the government could afford a more liberal immigration policy, one that would win favor with the public yet not conflict with White Paper restrictions.

Before laying out his proposals, Stanley reviewed some sore points that had tarnished the government's reputation. The "existing policy," he laid forth, required "(a) that all practical steps shall be taken to discourage illegal immigration into Palestine and no steps whatever shall be taken to facilitate the arrival of Jewish refugees in Palestine." This meant that "(b) future shiploads of illegal immigrants who nevertheless succeed in reaching Palestine shall be landed, placed in detainment camps, and those who pass security and economic absorption checks shall gradually be released against the current half-yearly immigration quotas."

In practice, though, "any Jewish refugees escaping over the frontier into Turkey and who do not attempt to go to Palestine by sea have been sent to Cyprus." While this policy, said Stanley, "is unsatisfactory" from the practical point of view—because of transport difficulties "and the fact there is only accommodation for 400 refugees there"—and a source of public criticism, it was also quite unnecessary.

"As under present conditions it seems likely that there can now be no legal immigration from Balkan countries," Stanley went on, "I think that a change of policy to meet the new situation is essential." Now Stanley could come forth and suggest to the war cabinet proposals that would put a human face on the British government's restrictive policy without changing it:

(A) In future all Jews, whether adults or children, who may succeed in escaping to Turkey will be eligible (after a preliminary security check in Turkey, which I hope can be arranged) for onward transport to Palestine where they will be placed in camps, go through a further security check, and if found satisfactory will be gradually released as legal immigrants against the [White Paper] current half-yearly immigration quotas.

(B) This policy will also apply to Jews who manage to escape to other neutral countries; but where they have escaped to countries in which they are safe they will normally remain there. Thus, the Jews at present in Mauritius, Cyprus and Spain would remain there (unless, as

is hoped, arrangement can be made in the case of Spain to remove them for the duration of hostilities to Allied territory in North Africa) and only in very special cases and for very special reasons would authority be given for any onward transport to Palestine.

(C) The numbers to be admitted under these new proposals will not entail any increase in the total number of immigrants permissible [by the White Paper] for the period ending the 31st March, 1944.

(D) No public announcement of this policy will be made as secrecy is essential in the interests of the refugees themselves; but I should tell the Agency in confidence of these proposals.

(E) These new arrangements are necessitated by the new situation which has arisen in the Balkans and must be regarded as subject to reconsideration at once if any serious change takes place, such as, for example, any collapse of the Balkan States.

To preclude any fear that his proposals would increase rescue in Palestine beyond the limits set by the White Paper, Stanley took his potential critics head-on: "It may be argued that by adoption of these proposals, we should be encouraging illegal immigration, but, when all possibilities of legal immigration have been destroyed by the Nazi ukase [edict], this must be accepted—if we are not to refuse all refuge to those escaping from Nazi cruelties."

And Stanley went on to further allay his cabinet colleagues' fears: "Certainly immigration being uncontrolled will be on less orderly lines, but I doubt whether the number of refugees, who manage to escape, will be large enough to make this a serious problem."

On July 2, 1943, the war cabinet approved Stanley's "proposed change of policy," with the stipulation that "there would be no public announcement of this change of policy, which would be subject to reconsideration in the event of any material change in the situation in the Balkans."[11]

The new policy was communicated on July 12 to representatives of the JAE in London, to Sir Harold MacMichael, the high commissioner in Palestine, to Casey, the minister of state in Cairo, and to the British embassy in Ankara.[12] On July 27 the Foreign Office communicated it to Ambassador Sir Hugh Knatchbull-Hugessen in Ankara, to

Ambassador Sir Samuel Hoare in Madrid, to Ambassador Sir Ronald Campbell in Lisbon, and to Ambassador Viscount Halifax in Washington.[13]

In theory, therefore, 29,000 Jews—"whether adults or children"—were allowed by the British government to save themselves in Palestine if they were able to "succeed in escaping from enemy controlled territory to Turkey." There they would be provided with "sea or rail" transport to Palestine, arranged by Britain and its diplomatic missions.

This policy also applied to Jews who were able "to manage to escape to other neutral countries." But the attendant proviso that if "they have escaped to countries in which they are safe they will normally remain there" made it as meaningless as the policy toward the Jews who could escape to Turkey. First, how were they to know "onward transport" to Palestine awaited them if the new policy was a well-guarded secret? Second, once those Jews escaped on their own to Turkey and other safe neutral countries, they were no longer in need of rescue by the British government.

Indeed, Stanley's new policy lasted from July 12, 1943, to October 5, 1944, nearly a month after the day Bulgaria was taken by the Red Army, when it was revoked. In all only 766 Jews, adults and youths, were able to benefit from Stanley's show of British largesse, and make their way to Palestine through Bulgaria and Turkey.[14] In effect the face-lift performed by Stanley and the war cabinet on British rescue policy left this policy unchanged. It was best defined by Deputy Prime Minister Clement Attlee on January 19, 1943. When asked in Parliament "what action has been taken . . . in regard to the massacre of Jews," Attlee answered: "The only real remedy for the consistent Nazi policy of racial and religious persecution lies in an Allied victory; every resource must be bent towards this supreme object."[15] How very true; but in the race between VE-Day and Auschwitz, the latter prevailed. When victory had finally come, Europe's Jewry had turned into ashes.

Such were the roadblocks to rescue, described here only scantily, to give just a hint of what they were like, but not mentioned by Segev at all. Either his findings revealed that they did not exist, or they were so minor, in his opinion, that they were not worth mentioning. He is not concerned with logistics, bureaucratic red tape, and war-related problems, or with difficulties deliberately created by British officials and policy that kept Palestine's doors shut, or with the indifference of the free world to Hitler's victims and its unwillingness to come to the rescue of Europe's Jews. For Segev, it suffices to assert that Ben-Gurion and his colleagues were not equal to their job. They did not understand that it was time for the big bluff. Had Saly Mayer, for example, been in their place, none of these minor difficulties would have been an obstacle, so why bother the reader with details?

But since Segev mentions Dina Porat's feelings (see Chapter 8), he should have made clear that it was because of these difficulties preventing the 5000 children from being saved—not the JAE's shortcomings—that she wanted to throw down the historian's tools and cry her heart out.

Instead, Segev is intent on proving that if all rescue had been done by non-Zionists, Europe's Jews would have fared better. This is the purpose of his unflattering comparison between Mayer, the non-Zionist worthy of History's praise, and Ben-Gurion and his JAE colleagues, "small, unimaginative people." Even if rescue had been their sole, burning desire, they could have done little, because of congenital limitations. Especially since, according to Segev, the Zionists were not really keen on rescue. Their leader, Ben-Gurion, was completely indifferent—to believe Segev, Ben-Gurion "spent most of his time on other matters" related to his obsession with the Jewish state—and his colleagues "spent significantly more on buying land and establishing new settlements" than they spent on rescue.[16]

Segev feels free to interpret Ben-Gurion's May 8, 1945, entry in his diary—"Victory Day, sad, very sad"[17]—to mean that he was sad not so much over the slaying of Jews as over the damage this did to Zionism. "Creation of the Jewish state," Segev writes, "that is the key to understanding Ben-Gurion's perspective on the extermination of the Jews. For him it was, above all else, a crime against Zionism."[18]

Again, Segev has not done his homework properly. Greeting a new session of the National Assembly in August 1944, Ben-Gurion spoke of the coming Victory Day: "From every front, east and west, north and south, tidings of new victories keep coming daily. The nations of

Europe are relieved: City after city, country after country is being liberated. Only at the House of Israel mourning does not cease: Liberation will not resuscitate the Jewish communities destroyed . . . and when millions of Jews were led to the slaughter . . . the world's rulers, staunch supporters of liberty and democracy, did not rescue our people, they did not even try to."[19]

Segev's purported interpretation of this quote from Ben-Gurion's diary is yet another example of him distorting documents from which he quotes. In a letter to his wife, Paula, written in London on May 11, 1945, Ben-Gurion clearly explains what makes him sad: the loss of so many Jewish lives. "Prophet Hosea's words 'Rejoice not, O Israel, for joy, like *other* people,'[20] come to mind again," he wrote. The same sadness had overcome him in 1905, when Russia was all joy at its "first revolution."*

This was not the first time, Segev may be interested to know, that Ben-Gurion had seen things this way. In September 1943, he said that the Allies' invasion of Europe could bring a triple salvation: "first of all, and foremost, the saving of Jews," then the saving of the Yishuv, "and finally and thirdly the saving of Zionism."[21]

Segev, one is moved to conclude, can be, when he wishes, selective in recognizing facts—as, for example, the fact that the major question that dogged Ben-Gurion throughout the Holocaust years was, as Ben-Gurion put it, "How to save the Jewish people?" It was his habit to say that "this comes before anything else, for no Jews, no Jewry." Along the same lines it can be said, "No Jewry, no Zionism." To him the two were inseparable. In summer 1944 Ben-Gurion told Chief Rabbi Herzog: "I am willing to give everything to save the Jewish people, even if they all become [Orthodox] like Rabbi Herzog wishes them to be, let there be only Jewish people—this is the main thing."[22]

Segev does his utmost to minimize the JAE's share in the rescue effort. He writes: "There had been about nine million Jews in Europe on the eve of the war; about six million were killed, leaving three

---

* Ben-Gurion witnessed the suppression of the 1905 revolution in Warsaw, and noted, in a letter to a friend, that the majority of the victims of the Cossack cavalry were Jews. See Shabtai Teveth, *Ben-Gurion: The Burning Ground* (Boston: Houghton Mifflin, 1987), p. 25.

million alive: the great majority of these were saved by Germany's defeat.* Some were spared thanks to the help they received from various governments and organizations such as the Joint Distribution Committee and from thousands of good-hearted people in almost every country—the 'righteous gentiles.' . . . Only a few survivors owed their lives to the efforts of the Zionist movement."[23]

Surely he is entitled to his opinion, but as a responsible writer—and it seems he takes himself as such—it is also his duty not to present his adversaries in a false light, as well as to make at least an attempt to prove his contentions. He is thus obliged to document that more Jews were saved "thanks to the help they received from various governments and organizations" than by the Zionist movement, and to clarify his definition of "saved." Furthermore, a quantitative comparison using such terms as "majority," "some," and "few" must give actual numbers.

Thus we must ask: Were the 400,000 Jews expelled by the Red Army in 1939 from the Soviet zone of occupation in Poland to the heartland of the Soviet Union among the saved? Were the 20,000 Jewish refugees who found shelter in Britain also saved? The implication of Segev's reference to "dramatic rescue operations such as the flight across the Pyrenees from France to Spain and the convoys of Jews that sailed from Denmark to Sweden" is that he would say yes. But if so, he should have added that the Soviet Union was not thinking so much of saving Polish Jews as of de-Judaizing and Sovietizing them, with a view toward annexing the eastern provinces of Poland. What was more, the Soviet Union did not allow them to leave, either during the war or afterward, and often obstructed true rescue operations.

And can Vichy France honestly be called a savior of Jews, given that hundreds had to fly "dramatically" to Spain? Did not this France prove itself a willing collaborator in dispatching more than 70,000 Jews to Auschwitz? Then, can Britain, which blocked every rescue operation, either to its own shores or Palestine's, be redeemed by the 20,000 refugees it did save? The same can be said of other govern-

---

* This qualification was omitted from the English edition.

ments, with the outstanding exception of Denmark, whose selfless heroism saved about 7200 Jews and their 700 non-Jewish relatives.

Furthermore, by comparing the JAE's actions with those of "various
governments," Segev deliberately fosters the impression that the JAE
was a sovereign administration that had at its disposal armed forces,
enforcement agencies, and rich resources, which, for its own deplorable reasons, it was slow to use. As if Segev does not know how poor
and impotent it was in relation to those governments—of Great
Britain, France, the Soviet Union, the United States, etc.—which could,
if only they would, have radically changed the balance of bereavement
of the Jewish people.

Finally, by placing side by side the 6 million killed and the 3 million
left alive, is he not insinuating—at least in his English edition—that
the latter were saved by, or thanks to, those "governments and organizations"? But about 3 million Jews, mostly in the Soviet Union
and to a lesser extent in Britain, had never been in Nazi hands. Segev
might as well have added, for good measure, the 5 million in the
United States and some hundreds of thousands in Latin America,
Australia, and South Africa.

There is something of the conjurer in Segev's presentation: He
makes the mouse he holds in one hand look as big as the elephant he
holds in the other. Thus one hand presents to us "Germany's defeat,"
the "governments and organizations"—notably the AJDC, despite the
fact that it cooperated closely with the JAE—and the "righteous gentiles"; the other, "the Zionist movement." He certainly cannot make
his argument without sleight of hand, for there are no reliable data
on which to base such assertions, and in fact Segev is the only one to
have made them, undeterred by their vagueness. No authorities other
than Schwalb (who claims he himself could have saved 250,000 more
lives if he had had more funds available) offer hard cold numbers.
They say only that "more" could have been saved—or, as Bauer puts
it without quantification, more money "might have made a real difference" (Bauer's and Schwalb's estimates are described in Chapter 11).

If among Jews who were "saved" Segev counts those who were
outside the Nazis' reach, it is possible to draw a much truer picture,

one that is also favorable to Zionism and the Yishuv. Two examples amply demonstrate this.

From the beginning of 1938 until mid-1941—when immigration nearly came to a complete halt—only 150,000 Jewish refugees entered the United States, as compared to 55,000 who entered Palestine.[24] The American Jewish community was then ten times larger than the Yishuv, and its financial resources infinitely greater. By this criterion at least—and assuming it had had the Yishuv's degree of determination to rescue—the American Jewish community should have admitted many more than 150,000 refugees. Each and every one would have been a veritable survivor.

The other example is the story of "Tuck's children." It began in mid-July 1942, with mass arrests of "foreign" and "stateless" Jews in Paris. In *The Abandonment of the Jews*, David Wyman writes that, in general, "The deportations from the camps in southern France and the round-ups in the Unoccupied Zone received widespread notice" in France, thanks to the "protests raised by the French archbishops and other members of the clergy," which drew repeated coverage. "Much of the French deportation story thus appeared in the American press. But it was almost never featured." Two reports did achieve front-page status, "apparently because these involved leaders of the Catholic church." As with all news about the Holocaust, American newspapers gave the roundups in unoccupied France "very little emphasis." The *New York Times*, however, ran the following report and analysis by its correspondent: "Foreign Jews and 'stateless' Jews who are being concentrated in unoccupied territory are those who entered France since 1938, it was said in authorized circles here [Vichy]. . . . Families are not being separated, but on the contrary all are being sent to their places of origin, whether Poland, Czechoslovakia, or Austria, it is asserted."

Despite the "fearful and chaotic conditions" under which the roundups in mid-July were carried out, writes Wyman, the American press generally ignored them. For example, although the United Press reported the "barbaric shoving of 4,000 children into box-cars for shipment across the Continent [to Auschwitz] without the necessities of life and without adult escort," only the *Los Angeles Times* ran the dispatch.

But the *New York Times* did report that "the 4th of July was celebrated in Vichy today by an open-air luncheon, given in the garden of the Ambassadors Hotel by chargé d'affaires and Mrs. S. Pinkney Tuck. . . . Contrary to the usual custom there were no ceremonies for the American war dead because of the special conditions prevailing at this time."[25]

Chargé d'Affaires Tuck was not, however, a man who would celebrate while turning a blind eye to Vichy's treatment of the Jews. Amid press reports that "it is likely that some 20,000 foreign Jews will have been deported from unoccupied France . . . and that all protests [of Protestants and Catholics] will have been proved unavailing," he interceded on their behalf. In the diplomatic phrasing of the *New York Times*'s Vichy correspondent, on September 10, 1942, Tuck, "in talking with Chief of Government Pierre Laval expressed sympathy with these Jewish refugees. Mr. Laval is said to have answered that he was ready to grant them visas to enter the United States instead of sending them to their homelands if the United States Government would agree to receive them."[26] Another *Times* report from Vichy hinted that this exchange exceeded diplomatic parlance: "Laval's conference today included talks with S. Pinkney Tuck [which] . . . were described as informative and are in contrast with recent negotiations that have dealt mainly with the internal labor problems [namely Vichy's excuse that the roundups were necessitated by a labor shortage in Germany] and relations with Germany."[27]

In fact, according to Wyman, "following an exchange of communications with the State Department, Tuck . . . saw Laval and registered an extremely sharp protest against the 'revolting' and 'inhuman' treatment of the Jews." Middle-level policy makers in the State Department were moved by "his deeply felt vehemence" to complain to Undersecretary of State Sumner Welles that "Tuck had exceeded his instructions." Wyman remarks that Tuck was, in fact, "even in advance of the leadership of the main American Jewish organizations, which on August 27 submitted a joint letter to the State Department calling on the United States to protest to the Vichy government." To which Welles replied that the American embassy in Vichy, "in compliance with instructions sent by the Department," had already made "the most vigorous representations possible."[28]

Tuck must have taken Laval's retort that he was ready to grant Jews visas for the United States if the U.S. government would agree to receive them as something of a challenge, and he rose to it. With Joseph Schwartz of the JDC and others, he prepared a plan for the emigration of 7000 Jewish orphans, certain candidates for Auschwitz. In September he cabled Secretary of State Cordell Hull that he was "greatly disturbed as to the fate of foreign Jewish children in the unoccupied zone who have been and are still separated from their parents. I am convinced that it is useless to expect any moderation from the French." Yet there was a chance Laval might agree to allow as many children to emigrate to the United States as the United States would be willing to admit, in order to allay the criticism of his anti-Jewish policies. Tuck suggested therefore that he be authorized to approach Laval to elicit his consent. His cable conveys his sense of urgency: It was obvious, he wrote, that the Nazis did not intend the children's parents to survive, and therefore those whose parents had been deported "may already be considered as orphans." Indeed, that September the JDC's representative in France sounded the alarm that Jewish children were being sent to Poland.

On October 9 Laval gave his consent, although on the express condition, which the State Department accepted, that the arrival of the children in the United States should not serve anti-German propaganda.

The State Department initially agreed to issue visas to 1000 children. Because of the high cost—transport and their support in America for the first year were estimated at $950,000, about half the annual rescue budget of the AJDC—partners were solicited: The Quakers Organization, some American relief agencies, and, most notably, the U.S. Committee for the Care of Children, under Eleanor Roosevelt's chairmanship, joined in after the JDC agreed to subscribe $800,000 for the program. Eleanor Roosevelt's committee, on its part, in response to the increasingly dire reports from France, increased the number to 5000. This led Canada to agree to accept 500 of the children. Britain, under much pressure, announced it would be ready to accept only those of the children who had relatives in the British Isles. Next Argentina joined in, ready to issue 1000 visas. Other countries in Latin America pledged smaller numbers, and the Union of South Africa declared itself ready to accept 200–300 children.* The JAE announced it would accept the entire 5000 into the Yishuv, but Britain would agree to issue only 1000 immigration certificates.[29] All this shows what a huge effort was required to save 5000 little Jews.

And were they, indeed, saved by the "various governments and organizations"?

Tuck's plan considerably reinforced the JAE's belief that the chances of rescuing children were a great deal better than those of any other type of rescue, and Ben-Gurion directed that "emphasis must be put especially on children's rescue." Nor did he mean their rescue only in Palestine. In his direct appeal to Churchill, Roosevelt, and Stalin, from the National Assembly in Jerusalem on November 30, 1942, he said: "Bring out first of all and most of all the Jewish children, and take them to neutral countries, to your countries! Send them over here, to our homeland!" This line was the main feature of the manifesto published by the National Assembly.[30]

But throughout October, the Vichy government stalled on releasing the children. "Vichy officials," writes Wyman, "hypocritically spoke of their government's great concern about separating families and its belief that eventual reunion was more likely if the children remained on the same continent as the parents." Nevertheless, Tuck's relentless pressure finally extracted from Laval a promise of 500 exit permits.[31]

At long last, at least the "first" 500 of Tuck's children seemed about to be delivered. As the children were being "processed" before boarding a train to Lisbon, twenty-eight Quakers, selected to accompany the first group to the United States, sailed on November 7 from New York to Lisbon to meet them. The fortunes of war, however, willed it otherwise. On November 8, the Allied invasion force landed in North

---

* This readiness was probably what Field Marshal Smuts was alluding to in his talk with the JAE's Gruenbaum; see Chapter 8.

Africa, and the next day the Wehrmacht took over unoccupied France. Relations between Vichy France and the United States were severed. All American Foreign Service personnel in France and North Africa, as well as newspaper correspondents and Red Cross workers, were recalled. On November 11, 1942, at 4:15 in the afternoon, Tuck and his embassy party boarded a train that took them from Vichy to Lourdes, from where they made their way to Switzerland.[32]

Still there remained a shimmer of hope that the Allies, the neutral states, and even collaborating France would pity the children whose exit had been already authorized. In an about-turn on its previous policy, Switzerland responded to the call of conscience and consented to receive the children—although not without a condition: Another state must pledge to receive them when they grew up. The United States, which had so kindly been willing to admit them as children, adamantly refused to guarantee to admit them as adults. The British likewise refused to make a commitment to Switzerland that children it agreed to shelter would be later admitted to Palestine as adults. In short, all of Tuck's children were doomed.

On February 3, 1943, Foreign Secretary Anthony Eden was asked in the House of Commons "whether he can make a statement on the 2,000 Jewish children in France who were refused visas for this country [the UK] and were, in consequence, deported to Germany?" Eden responded: "I have no knowledge of any Jewish children in France having been refused visas for this country, and having in consequence been deported to Germany. . . . I would emphasise that at the time at which application was made to His Majesty's Government for visas for refugee children to come to the United Kingdom from France there were in fact more visas available for other countries than there were children who were permitted to leave."

Miss Rathbone: "Is it not probable that the rather loosely worded statement refers to the refusal of His Majesty's Government at that period when there was still an Unoccupied France to grant visas for children who had near relatives in this country able individually to guarantee their maintenance?"

Eden: "I am dealing with the report concerning these children, and

I have pointed out that far more visas were available for several countries than there were children able to come out."[33]

On December 8, 1942, Ben-Gurion wrote Felix Frankfurter, the Jewish Supreme Court justice, that the Yishuv was "ready to adopt 50,000 children, and more, if possible [that is, if the British permitted it] . . . and we are already making all necessary arrangements." This is equivalent to an offer by the Jewish community in America to adopt 500,000 children. But as we have seen, the "arrangements" Ben-Gurion refers to were rendered unnecessary by the "governments" praised by Segev—above all, Great Britain.

CHAPTER ELEVEN

"More Money, More Rescue"?

Segev's chapter on the Yishuv's failure to rescue ends with a sigh: "It is difficult to compute how much money the yishuv actually spent on saving Jews; the total comes to several million dollars, according to one reckoning—about a quarter of the entire Jewish Agency budget."[1] His authority for this assertion is Porat's Hebrew original of *The Blue and Yellow Stars of David*. As usual, he is not very faithful to his source.

This sigh deserves analysis. Hard to compute? Yes, indeed. The financial aspect of rescue, as will be seen, was complex and still awaits thorough, expert study. But surely this is not the complaint that produces Segev's lament. For him the difficulty is the absence of a handy, simple, conclusive figure that can support his false and misleading conclusion that "significantly more was spent on buying land and establishing new settlements," providing absolute proof that the JAE allocated only an insignificant sum—as opposed to "significantly more"—to rescue. So his "difficult to compute" is more an apology to the reader than an admission of inadequate knowledge. That is, he would have liked to be able to state explicitly that while Europe's Jews were being slaughtered in the hundreds of thousands, the heartless, indifferent leaders of the Yishuv were buying land and building up new settlements—not to mention dispossessing Palestinian Arabs of their land—all to further their sick obsession with laying the foundations for a Jewish state. Unfortunately, however, the computing difficulty permits him only to hint at it.

Certainly Porat does not present a coherent, comprehensive picture of rescue finances. But she does write that "from February 1, 1943, to June 1, 1944, rescue allocation was equivalent to 25 percent of the Jewish Agency's total expenditures." An impartial reader would tend to think that a fourth of the budget of an impoverished organization is a very significant share, by any criterion. All the more since Porat adds—and this Segev omits—that "rescue was in fact the single largest item for the MRF [the Yishuv's Mobilization and Rescue Fund] and one of the major expenditures in the Yishuv, together with settlement, labor, housing, and preparations for future financial and industrial development." She goes on to say that from February 1, 1943, when the JAE's rescue committee was established, to June 1, 1945, when the war ended, "the Yishuv spent 1,325,000 Palestinian pounds on rescue: 645,000 from the Mobilization and Rescue Fund, 510,000 from the JDC, and 170,000 from Jewish communities in the free world." In other words, the Yishuv, one-tenth the size of the American Jewish community, raised more money for rescue. This was also more, Porat notes in her Hebrew original, than the entire JAE budget in 1943.

These figures, obviously, do not serve Segev's purpose of belittling the Yishuv's financial efforts toward rescue. He therefore draws from Porat's "a quarter of the entire Jewish Agency budget" the conclusion that "the total comes to several million dollars." But he does not quote her when she notes that in the early 1940s one Palestinian pound was equivalent to $4, as compared to $27.60 in 1989 (and, we may add, $32 in 1994). Thus she writes, for example, that "in 1944 the Yishuv spent 858,000 pounds (equivalent to $23,690,000 in 1989 [$27,500,000 in 1994])." Accordingly, the "quarter of the entire Jewish Agency's budget" that was allocated to rescue in the period from February 1, 1943, to June 1, 1944, amounted, in today's dollars, to a great deal more than "several million dollars." Segev does not make use of Porat's conversion or offer his own. He quotes from Porat only the bits that suit his purpose of underlining the paucity of the sum devoted by the JAE to rescue.

In anticipation of readers who might pause to wonder whether "several million dollars" might not represent a greater effort than meets the eye—after all, the Yishuv was small and not very well off, even poor in comparison with the American Jewish community— Segev is quick to offer a sound comparison: "significantly more was spent on buying land and establishing new settlements." Not a hint of the context from which his quote is lifted: that "rescue was in fact . . . one of the major expenditures in the Yishuv, together with settlement, labor, housing, and preparations for future financial and industrial development."[2]

Porat is fully aware of the obligations incumbent upon the JAE, but Segev conceals the fact that immigration and its absorption, for which the land and new settlements were intended, were the principal purpose and function for which the JAE had been created. Thus he deliberately chose his wording—"significantly more was spent on buying land and establishing new settlements"—to mislead the reader into thinking that instead of dedicatedly doing rescue work, the JAE was busy putting up new settlements to improve its standard of living— more spacious living rooms, swimming pools, perhaps—instead of spending more on saving lives from the gas chambers.

The truth is that only part of the Jewish National Fund's budget was spent on buying new land: It had old debts to pay and other expenditures, as Porat takes pains to explain. And only part of the JAE Settlement Department's budget went to establishing new settlements; a great deal was swallowed by old settlements that were not yet able to support themselves—all settlements whose members were new immigrants. For after all, who were the members of the Yishuv in the 1940s, if not mostly immigrants who had escaped Europe in the 1930s? Remember: At the end of December 1932, the Yishuv was only just under 200,000 strong. Ten years later, by the end of 1942, it had more than doubled, to 517,200. This, then, was the size of the Yishuv at the time when the fact of systematic extermination in Europe was confirmed and it began its rescue effort, early in 1943. In other words, nearly 317,200 members of the Yishuv had belonged to it for ten years or less. Had these settlements not been available to take them in, they, too, would have been standing in line for the gas chambers and crematoria.

By the end of 1945 the Yishuv had nearly trebled, to 592,000.

According to JAE statistics, nearly 400,000 new immigrants entered Palestine between 1919 and 1945. Of these 70 percent—nearly 300,000—entered between 1932 and 1945, most from Europe.

This is odd: According to Segev, there was hardly any rescue, and there could hardly have been any immigration, because of the war and the White Paper. So an obvious question arises: Who were these new lands and new settlements intended for? And why spend on them "significantly more" than on rescue?

Segev probably likes these questions, which appear to buttress his argument against the Yishuv leaders' fitness for their jobs—such small, unimaginative people could have been dully building just for building's sake—as if he knew nothing of the Yishuv's growth and the JAE's responsibility for looking after new immigrants, 40,000 of whom arrived in Palestine in the five-year war period.[3]

At the same time, it must be said that these questions arise largely due to the absence of a thorough, comprehensive study of rescue's financial side, which could answer them best. The need for such research is perhaps the main finding of Akiva Nir's study of the budget of the Yishuv's rescue mission in Istanbul.[4] Nir asserts that the mission spent 188,210 Palestinian pounds in 1943, 247,854 in 1944, and 285,403 in 1945—727,000 in all (equivalent by Porat's calculation to more than $20 million in 1989, or to $23.26 million in 1994). If these sums were expended by the Istanbul rescue mission alone, the implication is that the grand total of all rescue spending must have been considerably larger. But according to the official JAE statistical yearbook, the MRF (Mobilization and Rescue Fund) receipts for the five-year period 1940/41–1944/45* were 827,000 Palestinian pounds, out of which only 234,000 were spent on rescue. The balance, 593,000 pounds, went mostly to mobilization needs, support for soldiers' families, and the defense of the Yishuv (106,000 pounds), which means to the Haganah (the Yishuv's underground militia).

These figures, however, are at odds with Porat's "analysis of the Rescue Committee's monthly balance sheets." According to her, these

---

* This break corresponds to the Jewish calendar years 5741–45.

sheets "show that February 1, 1943, to June 1, 1945, the Yishuv spent 1,325,000 Palestinian pounds on rescue: 645,000 from the Mobilization and Rescue Fund, 510,000 from the JDC, and 170,000 from Jewish communities in the free world. The money was spent on two major efforts: 523,500 pounds on Aliya Bet [illegal organized immigration] in 1943 and 1944 . . . and the remainder to save Jews in Nazi occupied Europe."[5]

It is clear, therefore, either that the numbers under examination do not add up, or that not all the money earmarked for rescue was in fact spent on rescue. And there exists a third possibility, the most likely one, that the rescue budget was a mixture, put together in part from JAE budgets and in part from the MRF's fund drives. These scrambled eggs await an able scholar to unscramble them.

Yet this much is known: The financial confusion is part and parcel of the rescue debate that raged in the Yishuv in the years 1943–45. The debate centered on the way the JAE financed its activities. Traditionally, this had been done by the two main Zionist funds, the Foundation Fund and the Jewish National Fund (JNF), whose function was the purchase of land and its improvement—drainage, afforestation, etc. Following the outbreak of the war, a new, third fund was added, the Mobilization Fund. It was charged with encouraging voluntary recruitment to two armies: the British army, to fight Hitler, and the Haganah, to defend Jewish Palestine. The fund carried out these tasks by looking after the welfare of the Yishuv's soldiers in the British army and their families, and by beefing up the Haganah budget.[6]

In 1943, following the formation of the JAE's rescue committee, a Rescue Fund was instituted as well, but after a short while it was amalgamated with the Mobilization Fund, to become the Mobilization and Rescue Fund (MRF).

As Porat says (referring to the 5000 Children Plan), however, the JAE "decided not to initiate a significant fundraising campaign or to announce the allocation of a large sum" for rescuing children by bringing them into Palestine. First, the JAE was not yet convinced that large-scale rescue was possible; its members "were waiting for concrete ideas from the emissaries in Geneva and Istanbul." Second, there were strict mandatory regulations, in accordance with Allied resolutions, banning all transfers of money and material aid to enemy territory.

But, Porat adds, even if it were possible to get money out of Palestine in defiance of the regulations, "it would still be hard to transfer it to neutral countries (especially Turkey, where foreign currency regulations were very strict), and even harder to get it from there to Jews" in Nazi-occupied Europe: Jews there no longer had permanent addresses, and they faced mortal risks by making contact with the outside world. "If the money were entrusted to free-lance, non-Jewish couriers, the Agency could never be sure it would reach its destination."[7]

Thus the raising of funds and their allocation for rescue were contingent first of all on the feasibility of the rescue plans—not, as Segev would have his readers think, on "condemnation of the Diaspora" or the JAE's obsession with more land and new settlements. Segev oversimplifies the issue with the phrase "more money, more rescue": that is, he says, there could have been more rescue, but the heartless JAE leaders blocked larger allocations, because land and settlements were more important to them than Jewish lives in the Diaspora.

Certainly "more money, more rescue" was the premise on which public opinion at the time based its criticism of the JAE as well as its demand for large-scale rescue. But those responsible for the allocation of funds faced an entirely pragmatic dilemma: Which came first, achievable rescue plans or allocation of the funds required to achieve them? Porat is well aware of this question, and to illustrate it she cites demands made in mid-January 1943 by the Histadrut and by the National Council for swifter and more effective rescue action by the JAE. The Histadrut's executive committee passed a unanimous resolution calling for "special concerted efforts to discover means of rescue," however speculative. The National Council demanded that the JAE immediately allocate 250,000 pounds to investigate rescue possibilities.

Before this resolution was passed, mention was made in the National Council "of a bitter discussion with Kaplan, who had refused to allocate 'one penny' for the time being—saying that if and when money was needed, the Yishuv would be willing to collect it."

When the Histadrut offered the JAE 50,000 pounds to get started and asked it to match this figure, "the JAE rejected the offer; before any money was allocated, it had to be proved that rescue was somehow possible."[8] This, therefore, was the JAE's stance at the beginning of the rescue debate: Once practical plans were in hand, money would not be an object.

As the news reports of systematic extermination became more widely believed, and public criticism intensified accordingly, the JAE's position evolved into a guarantee of funds to all ongoing ventures, in the sense of "do and we will pay." In Porat's words, it "refused to allocate money for rescue from its budget, but it promised to honor any financial obligation incurred by others in such enterprises." The immigration and rescue activists "were frequently told, 'Do what you can—the Agency is behind you. If you find a way or a boat, money will not be a problem.' "[9]

To obtain an on-the-spot perspective of the rescue situation, the JAE sent Kaplan to Istanbul. When he returned to Jerusalem, at the end of March 1943, his attitude had changed; direct contact with the rescue work and firsthand reports of the atrocities in Europe had had their effect. He now supported, as Porat puts it, "the claim by the emissaries in Istanbul that, with systematic action and appropriate financial support, results were possible even though the rescue of thousands could not be assured." Thus softened, Kaplan approved the expenditure of 80,000 pounds for special programs in Istanbul and in Geneva, in addition to the regular budget of 10,000 pounds a month for the emissaries.[10]

As time went on, Kaplan's grants to rescue efforts increased. But he, Ben-Gurion, and the entire JAE refused to institute an outright formal JAE rescue budget as long as the feasibility of large-scale rescue activities and their cost had not been established. This is understandable for several reasons. First, without cost estimates no budget can be drawn up. The JAE simply could not take the public outcry "something more must be done for rescue"—a conflict typical of the relation between front-line operatives and the high brass at GHQ—as a guide to action. Had the JAE responded to this cry, it would have quickly run out of cash and credit, simply by pouring millions as bribes into

Nazi pockets without a chance that the Europa Plan or any of the other "ransom plans" would ever work.

Second, as early as January 1943 Kaplan said that he did not see much possibility of using large sums of money to help Europe's Jews, for aid routes were narrowing daily.[11]

It is easy to say, as Segev does: Turn the entire Zionist budget over to rescue. But this would be like demanding, in the midst of the Battle of Britain, that the British Department of Health close all hospitals and use the money to train more RAF pilots. And suppose the JAE had used, not a quarter of its budget for rescue, but its entire expenditures for the five years 1940/41–1944/45, namely, 32.3 million Palestinian pounds (then equivalent to $129.4 million), instead of only 1.3 million pounds ($5.3 million): Would that have been enough to buy Hitler off—assuming that a way had been found to transfer this sum to Germany? Hitler, as is well known, spent billions of dollars—not to mention uncounted thousands of German lives—to see his Final Solution through. Even when his routed armed forces needed rail transport desperately, the rail service to Auschwitz ran uninterrupted.

There was a final reason for the JAE's stance, perhaps the decisive one, which makes it important to sort out the rescue finances: It involved the broader definition of rescue. When, during discussion of the recently approved JAE budget for 1944, some claimed that from the 2.1 million pounds allocated for defense, land reclamation, and settlement a substantial sum for rescue could be spared, Haganah chief Eliahu Golomb came to Kaplan's support. The latter used to say, "It is essential to keep every penny" for "a rainy day," meaning right after the war, when many new immigrants "would be in need of employment and housing." Now, Golomb warned, tens of thousands of Jews who survived the Holocaust would come to Palestine empty-handed, needing everything, from a shirt to a roof over their heads.[12]

Had Segev paid more attention to Kaplan's and Golomb's arguments, as presented by Porat, he would have understood that rescue was not confined to bribe money and transport fares. The immigration budget—3.2 million Palestinian pounds in the five-year war period, including a direct expenditure of 1.3 million pounds on "rescue and help to refugees"—formed a pot of 4.5 million pounds ($18 million in 1945, $144 million in 1994).[13] But rescue in the broader sense did not stop there. The minute the survivors left Europe and arrived in Palestine, they were in immediate need of rehabilitation, for which land, housing, medical services, jobs, and schools were urgently required. A good part of the JNF's and the Foundation Fund's budget was allocated to meet such needs. This hidden part of the real rescue budget, as well as the part that enabled Kaplan to take on financial obligations in the name of the JAE—as when he lent the Istanbul emissaries 100,000 Palestinian pounds to purchase or rent ships[14]—awaits comprehensive study.

IN ANY EVENT, Ben-Gurion took an active part in the MRF's fundraising drives, during which he usually enumerated the JAE's overt rescue activities. One of these was the demand that the Western Allies drop leaflets from airplanes to warn the German people and the German armed forces that "they will be held responsible for the blood shed" and the "massacres of Jews." In January 1943 he also said:

> We have also appealed to neutral countries to let Jews pass through and afford them temporary asylum. We have demanded that the Polish Government in Exile guarantee the neutral countries that all Polish Jews given such asylum will be permitted to return to Poland. We have demanded that [neutral] Turkey, Sweden, Portugal and Switzerland temporarily receive the [Jewish] refugees. For the time being our demands have been met only minimally. . . . After all the shock, the blood of millions crying out, the screams of butchered children—we have been given only a few thousand [immigration certificates], and long and painful is the road until we get them out through the neutral countries, and until we bring them over here.
>
> We have been trying to find ways into the Jewish ghettos . . . in Poland [Ben-Gurion is referring to his talks with Kot] and into the rest of occupied Europe. Volunteers, in defiance of the danger to their lives, have stood up to be counted, and we are hoping to find a way to send them [the paratroopers] on their mission.[15]

It is quite obvious that if Ben-Gurion was unable to save tens and hundreds of thousands, it was not because he had been "busy with other matters," or because he was a fervent Zionist or a mediocre leader with an inflated self-image. He did not save a great many simply because any large-scale rescue was impossible. The "various governments" who saved so many exist only in the fertile imagination, or rather in the distorted perspective, of Segev and his like. The Yishuv leaders did not overlook any rescue plan. The children-rescue plans and the ransom plans were not thwarted by the JAE. They were defeated by the British government, which refused to respond to any of the JAE rescue requests.

Other rescue plans never came up—and not for lack of ingenuity. The most brilliant scholars, after decades of study, have failed to point out even one workable plan that was overlooked. Segev's claim that the "Zionist movement" saved fewer than "various governments and organizations" because the JAE spent more on land and settlements is without foundation in reality. Against the background of Hitler's obsession with his Final Solution, on one hand, and the Allies' indifference, on the other, his argument that more JAE money would have meant more rescue is equally unfounded.

After much defamation of Ben-Gurion and his JAE colleagues, however, in retrospect and out of his concern for their good name, Segev does offer them this generous advice: "There is no way of knowing if the Europa Plan ever really had a chance. Perhaps not. The only thing we may be sure of is that, had the leaders of the Jewish Agency been quicker about sending the money to Bratislava, they could at least have bought themselves the right to look the following generations in the eye and say without hesitation: We did what we could, we did not miss any opportunity."[16]

Contradictions like this are not scarce in Segev's book, but this one reflects on his sincerity. Would he really have wanted the JAE leaders to send Himmler and Eichmann hundreds of thousands, maybe millions of dollars, in the course of trying a plan whose chances he himself doubts, just to be thought of kindly by future generations? Would this really have made Segev, who belongs to one of these generations, alter his low opinion of Ben-Gurion and his colleagues? The truth is that he should take his hat off to them in humility and respect for having spent this money on land and new settlements, and not on the protection of their future reputations.

Indeed, the Jewish people as a whole should be grateful to Ben-Gurion and his colleagues for not having taken such advice, and instead having weighed very carefully how to spend the little money the JAE had. As already mentioned, the JAE did send to Bratislava the down payment (either $135,000 or $150,000) for the Europa Plan, even though they doubted that the SS would stop the extermination process in return for $2 million. Indeed, Porat is astonished that they sent even that much.[17] There can hardly be a doubt that if the Europa Plan had had a chance, Ben-Gurion and the JAE would have devoted themselves body and soul to assure its success.

But suppose the JAE had done as requested by Segev, and halted all activities other than rescue so that it had an abundance of money (relatively speaking) at its disposal. How many more lives could have been saved?

Although Segev does not know it, he could have called upon Schwalb to support his argument. For Schwalb claims that his troikas and the various rescue committees with which he was connected could have saved 250,000 more lives if America had raised and allocated more money earlier—for "surely, the big money could have come only from America, the U.S. government permitting." The novelist Amos Oz, a friend of Schwalb's, recalls having heard him say repeatedly: "To do a great deal more than we did was quite impossible."[18] Schwalb's, therefore, is an authoritative, Zionist calculation of an actual number of the "few" more who could have been saved.

In his estimate, Schwalb includes 30,000 Slovak and 200,000 Hungarian Jews. It seems he is assuming that the Slovak Jews would have been saved by the Slovakia Plan, while a large part of the Hungarian Jews would have been saved by time-gaining negotiations over Goods for Blood and gifts of money to SS officers. The remaining 20,000 could have been saved in all sorts of other ways. Schwalb has letters from survivors attesting to the fact that, although many Jews in occupied Europe who received the parcels of rice and medicine sent to them died in the death camps, a few who were not shipped to these camps escaped death from typhus (which had taken the lives of many before the shipments to the camps began) thanks to these parcels. Others could be saved by valid or false passports, by buying hiding places, and so on.

Thus Schwalb, too, seems to vindicate Weissmandel's strategy of rescue-by-bribe, the ransom plans: arguably the only plans that worked, although only partly. Otherwise Schwalb would not have said that more money would have saved 250,000 more Jews.

Surely, Weissmandel was aware that his imperfect plans were nevertheless the only plans that did work. This perhaps explains why he felt such hatred for Schwalb. For initially Schwalb, like his colleagues in Geneva and in the JAE, did not believe that rescue-by-bribe would work.

In time, however, Schwalb changed his mind, and was honest enough to admit it. In a letter to Dobkin of December 4, 1942, he wrote: "I did have, in relation to Slovakia [Plan], doubts, both moral and practical, whether to negotiate with them [the Nazis] at all, whether to believe their promises at all, etc. [However] the Slovak arrangement proves that despite all they make good on their word." Abraham Fuchs prints a photocopy of this letter in his biography of Weissmandel,[19] which faithfully echoes his hero's woes and grievances. Weissmandel died before Fuchs's labor of love was published, but he did have firsthand knowledge of Schwalb's and Mayer's misgivings about his strategy. It could be that in his unforgivingness he turned them—especially Schwalb, Mayer's mentor—into symbolic monsters, the first representing Zionism and the second America's complacence (since Mayer represented the American JDC).

In evaluating Schwalb's claim, it is important to bear in mind the near consensus among Holocaust scholars that the cessation of the deportations in Slovakia—which spared 30,000 lives there—had nothing to do with the $200,000 down payment to Wisliceny. This means that the Europa Plan, as a practicable possibility, existed only in the minds of Weissmandel and some of his colleagues in the working group.

In *American Jewry and the Holocaust,* his exhaustive study of the

JDC during the war period, Bauer notes that American Jewry gave the JDC very little money until 1944 ($37.9 million in 1939–43) and somewhat more in 1944 and 1945 ($35.6 million). The $194.3 million raised in 1945–48 showed, he writes, how late the reaction to the disaster of the Holocaust came.[20] Some of the expenditures of scarce JDC dollars, he adds, were, to judge with the benefit of hindsight, less than judicious. Over a million dollars were poured uselessly into a resettlement project in the Dominican Republic known as the Sousa venture.[21] Hundreds of thousands more were given to the Russians for other resettlement projects that never got off the ground, in addition to the millions given by the American people as a whole. Had these funds "been allocated to Gisi Fleischmann or Rezoe Kastner," says Bauer, "they might have made a real difference."[22]

Bauer never quantifies this "real difference," but, as we saw, Schwalb—who plays a major role in Bauer's books—sets it at 250,000. Bauer, however, disagrees on nearly all major points of Schwalb's argument, thus casting doubt on Schwalb's figure without clarifying what his own "real difference" would have amounted to.

In Schwalb's assertion that he and his colleagues could have saved more lives if America had "raised and allocated *more* money *earlier*" [italics added], "more" and "earlier" refer to the sums the JDC put at Mayer's disposal, which were indeed very small. In 1940 he received $6,370 and in 1941 $8,930 to support Jewish refugees who made it to Switzerland and to assist HeHalutz and Schwalb's communications network ($5,900). Following the meeting between Schwartz, Schwalb, and Mayer at the Hotel Cornavin late in 1941 (see Chapter 9), JDC dramatically increased Mayer's total for 1942 to $235,000. As described in Chapter 1, $105,295 of this amount was intended for supporting Jewish refugees (the youths in HeHalutz camps) in Switzerland, leaving Mayer with only $129,705 for his main responsibilities—France, Slovakia, Hungary, Croatia, and Bulgaria—and hardly any money to meet the demand of the Bratislava working group for the down payment of $200,000 to Wisleceny.[23]

Mayer faced yet another problem, which he could hardly expect Bratislava to understand: Since April 1942, Bauer points out, the Swiss had refused to allow charitable dollars to be brought into Switzerland and converted into Swiss francs in order to send them to an enemy country. Thus for the payment to Wisliceny, as well as for assistance to Jews in occupied countries, Mayer could use only money raised within the Swiss Jewish community. But most of those funds had to be used to support the 25,000 Jewish refugees then in Switzerland. On top of this, the JDC faithfully complied with the State Department's restrictions on spending American money in enemy territory.

So when the demand came from Bratislava to pay Wisliceny, Mayer not only did not have the money; he had no way to transfer it.[24] What he could do, and did, was promise Wisliceny, through the working group, that he could collect the money in U.S. currency *after* the war. Clearly this proposal had no appeal for SS murderers facing a strong possibility of being tried after the war as war criminals, which the Allies had repeatedly promised would happen. Mayer's response was therefore unsatisfactory, and infuriated Weissmandel and the working group. And—so it seems—Schwalb as well.

It is understandable that Weissmandel refused to understand these fine points, when thousands of Jews were being shipped daily to their deaths. This, it seems, was the basis for his charge that "Zionists" and "nonobservant" Jews like Schwalb and Mayer had abandoned the Jews under Nazi rule and written letters denigrating the sufferers and indicating that Zionism in Palestine was more important than rescue of the Jewish masses.

Weissmandel claims that when Wisliceny was not paid the second installment on time, a transport was sent to Auschwitz on Yom Kippur (September 21, 1942), the holiest day in the Jewish calendar.[25] Immediately afterward, Weissmandel claims, he himself managed to pay the money, which he got from his own Orthodox contacts in Hungary, and the deportations ceased for two years.

But Bauer's study utterly refutes Weissmandel's claims. The problems with Weissmandel's account begin, he writes, "when we remember that *after* Yom Kippur two transports went to Auschwitz, September 23 and October 20—that is *after* the second payment had been paid to" Wisliceny.[26]

Bauer then proceeds to destroy the rest of Weissmandel's case by presenting contradictory, more reliable evidence, as well as Wisliceny's own admission in his testimony of May 6, 1946, prior to his execution as a war criminal, that in August 1943 he "was ordered by Himmler through Eichmann to stop the negotiations [with the working group] and not have any further contact with his Jewish partners or else he himself would land in a concentration camp."[27] Bauer makes it clear that the discontinuance in November 1942 of the transports, which had begun on March 26, had nothing to do with the bribes paid Wisliceny and his cronies. Jelinek, too, believes that the failure to pay the full $200,000 by August 1943 did not bring about the renewal of the transports, nor did the first bribes result in their being discontinued. "These changes," writes Jelinek, "were due in large part to internal power struggles within the Slovakian polity."[28] Surely, the failure to meet the down payment by August 1, 1943, did not lead the Nazis to shelve the Europa Plan.[29] "More and earlier" money to Wisliceny would not have influenced Himmler's decision to stop the Europa Plan negotiations.

As for Goods for Blood (which will be described in detail in the next chapter), this plan had nothing in common with the previous ransom plans. It was not the working group's idea, or Kastner's, but entirely an SS initiative, meant to use Jewish lives as an avenue to a separate peace agreement between Nazi Germany and the Western Allies. By 1944 the situation had completely changed. The Nazis were losing the war, and Himmler and others were trying to save their own skins, as well as Germany's. In 1944 money could indeed buy lives— although as an alibi for the Nazis, not as ransom per se—and in 1944 the JDC did allocate more money for this purpose, as noted above, though still not enough from Schwalb's point of view. Goods for Blood, however, unlike the Europa Plan, was a plan only the Allies could have implemented, for it involved, in part, delivering 10,000 heavy-duty trucks for action in the Soviet theater—something the JAE and the JDC had no way of doing. All they could do was, by appearing to carry out businesslike negotiations, to gain time and delay deportations, and this they did as best they could, thanks to Schwalb, Mayer, and their colleagues in Geneva and Budapest.

Finally, these negotiations must indeed have helped save many lives. Of the 825,000 Jews living in Hungary, between 550,000 and 570,000 were murdered by the Nazis.[30] Of the 275–300,000 survivors, a good many—perhaps as many as 200,000—owed their lives to the JAE–JDC tactics. But the claim that 250,000 more lives could have been saved, had there been "more and earlier" money, must still be proven.

CHAPTER TWELVE

THE BRAND MISSION

T HE MAIN SOURCE of criticism of Ben-Gurion and his JAE among
people who—unlike the critics already described—have no set
personal, political, or religious prejudice toward them is the distorting
filter through which the Holocaust years are commonly perceived. The
tendency to attribute to the Yishuv and its leadership the status and
capabilities of the State of Israel and its government can be characterized as either the "1948 War of Independence syndrome" or the
"Entebbe syndrome."

In retrospect, it seems that as early as the 1950s the misperception
of the Yishuv as the equivalent of the state became widespread among
the younger Israeli generations. With respect to the Holocaust,
perhaps the logic went as follows. Given that in the 1948 War of
Independence the Yishuv and its leadership, under Ben-Gurion, defeated an enemy twenty times stronger in numbers and resources—
seven Arab states* fielding five regular armies and one semiregular
army, plus the Palestinian militia and a wide variety of Arab volunteers, all with the backing of a considerable part of the Moslem
world—it surely could have done more than it did against Hitler and
Germany. After the sensational July 1976 rescue of Israeli hostages at
Entebbe airport by an airborne Israeli force, still younger generations

---

* Lebanon, Syria, Jordan, Iraq, Egypt, Yemen, and Saudi Arabia.

found it hard to understand why similar forces were not used to rescue Jews from Auschwitz and other Nazi death camps.

Prime Minister and Minister of Defense Ben-Gurion and Minister for Foreign Affairs Sharett—seen coming and going around the world's capitals, meeting with heads of state, cabinet ministers, and diplomats, attending international conferences, appearing on radio and TV, and holding press conferences—somehow were assumed to have possessed the same status and power in the 1940s as well. And if so, the logic continued, why did they fail to use these resources as best they could to save more Jews during the Holocaust years?

The young seemingly have difficulty imagining a world without private telephones, private cars, running hot water, social welfare, and personal computers. Thus it must be hard for young people in general, and Israelis in particular, to realize how infinitesimally weak, poor, and helpless vis-à-vis the great powers—especially Nazi Germany—the JAE and the Yishuv were in the Holocaust years.

In terms of political status and military strength, the JAE and the Yishuv were basically a nonentity, possessing no real status or power in world affairs. The only status the JAE had was that accorded it by the mandate's articles IV and VI, in which the Administration of Palestine "is charged with the task of cooperating with the Jewish Agency in the development of the country. The primary duty imposed upon the Administration of Palestine is to facilitate Jewish immigration and encourage close settlement by Jews on the land."[1] But this left the JAE completely dependent on the mandatory government's interpretation of such cooperation, not to mention on its will to cooperate. And by the late 1930s, Palestine's British administration no longer considered its duty to lie in facilitating either immigration or settlement by Jews.

The truth of the matter is that the JAE had nothing in hand to negotiate with—no cards to play with, let alone a royal flush. It did not represent a large population, and whatever natural resources of commercial or military value Palestine possessed—even its important strategic location, as well as the port of Haifa and the Iraqi oil pipeline—were entirely under British control.

One cannot even say that the Yishuv's liabilities far exceeded its assets, because in terms of international politics it had no assets—none whatever. It had liabilities only, the worst of which was its inability to fight Hitler under its own name. It is hard to believe now, but the Yishuv was not allowed to fight Hitler. On one hand, Palestine had neither an army nor conscription, and the British would not conscript Palestinians—Jews or Arabs—into the British army. On the other hand, the Yishuv was forbidden to raise its own army, either to fight Hitler or to defend itself. The only defense force, other than the police, in which Jews could enroll was the Jewish settlement police, where the highest rank they could achieve was sergeant major.

The only way to fight Hitler was to volunteer for the British army. But in the early war years the British allowed Yishuv volunteers only in noncombat support units: transportation, fortifications, and construction. And even these roles were permitted only bit by bit. Combat units were strictly out of bounds for Yishuv volunteers. Yet even this form of recruitment, however humiliating, had to be seen as a British gesture of goodwill.

It took the JAE more than four years of tremendous efforts, led by Weizmann, Ben-Gurion, and Sharett (who walked his feet off in Whitehall's long corridors), to expand this goodwill to include combat units in a Yishuv formation. Finally the British government acquiesced, and the Jewish Brigade Group—meaningfully named in Hebrew "Jewish Fighting Force"—was created in July 1944, in time to take part in the last stages of the war in Europe.

Gaining British consent to establish this one combat unit was considered at the time an extraordinary political achievement of the JAE and celebrated as such. Another achievement, nearly of the same magnitude, was obtaining Whitehall's consent to utilize the Yishuv's technical know-how and fledgling industrial capacity in the Allied war effort. This, too, required an extended day-to-day effort in London, Cairo, and Jerusalem.

The Jewish Brigade Group and the Yishuv's participation in the war effort were seen then as successes in the JAE's campaign to thwart the May 1939 White Paper's restrictions on the Yishuv's growth and development. It was in reference to this campaign that in May 1940

Ben-Gurion coined his famous double formula, which, like a light in a coal miner's helmet, guided the JAE's policy during the years of war and Holocaust: "War against the Nazis as though there were no White Paper; war against the White Paper as though there were no war against the Nazis."[2]

However great these successes were considered at the time, they highlight, then and now, the JAE's total lack of real power, its help-lessness, and its reduction to the role of pleader, the Jew's traditional defense. The saddest expression of the JAE's position, which only un-derlined its impotence, was its efforts at rescue.

A case in point is the JAE's intention of sending to Poland 1000 "commandos"—the original number contemplated was greater—to encourage the Jews in the ghettos and prepare them to escape and to fight for their lives. For the Yishuv, for Poland's Jews, for Jewish his-tory, this would have been an endeavor of heroic proportions. But to the British, without whom such an enterprise could not have gotten off the ground, it meant very little. In a war involving many millions, 1000 armed men were not considered a fighting force worth reckon-ing. At best, such a force would benefit an underground, and in this case a Jewish one, whose contribution to the Allied campaigns was not readily apparent. The negotiations over the commandos lingered on and on, with the JAE pleading more and more, until finally the British trained 110 Yishuv volunteers (out of 250 who had signed up) as parachutists. Of these, thirty-five—"too few, too late," as the critics rightly remarked—were dropped behind the lines between October 1943 and September 1944, in Yugoslavia, Romania, Slovakia, and Hungary. Nine were captured and put to death by the Germans. For the Yishuv the parachutists became a heroic myth; but in the totality of the war and the Holocaust, they hardly shifted the balance. Nor, it seems, would 100 or 200 more have made a difference.

There was no possibility for mutual give and take between the JAE and the British government. The British could give immigration cer-tificates for Palestine—which they did slowly, very slowly—and the JAE could do nothing but wait, while the refugees also waited, on the slaughtering line. What could the JAE offer to expedite the certificate processing? Sympathy for the Allies? This was, rightly enough, taken for granted, because the Allies were fighting Hitler, the Jews' worst enemy ever.

The great need was not immigrant certificates, which at most could not amount to more than 29,000, the remainder of the quota set by the White Paper. What was needed was rescue of millions. Could it be done? To save a million from the gas chambers, the JAE had to persuade the Allies to include such large-scale rescue among their war aims. In the normal political-diplomatic discourse between the JAE and the Allies, there was hardly a chance for this. But suddenly, two developments placed the saving of a million on the Allied agenda.

In April 1944 two Slovak Jews—Alfred Wetzler and Walter Rosenberg (better known under his assumed name Rudolf Vrba)—did the impossible and escaped Auschwitz. Arriving in Zilina, inside Slovakia's northern, Polish border, on April 25, they met with local Jewish rescue activists. On hearing their report, the local group sent for an activist from the Bratislava working group, who debriefed them for two entire days. Their testimony in German, later known as the Vrba-Wetzler report, was typed in Bratislava on twenty-six single-spaced pages, with a sketch of Birkenau's death installations and railway junctions and sidings. Until then the Bratislava working group members had believed Birkenau to be a top-secret slave-labor camp, confusing it with the nearby Monowitz camp. Now it became known that Birkenau, about a mile from Auschwitz, was the hard core—the gas chambers and crematoria—of the Auschwitz complex's death machinery.

The Vrba-Wetzler report was astounding in every respect. Its authors' positions as administrative clerks in Auschwitz's registration office, along with their prodigious capacity for detail and figures, enabled them to note names, dates, and points of departure of all arriving rail shipments. This report made it absolutely clear that "deportations" and "transports" meant death. It was clear as well that the Jewish community of Hungary—the only one still intact—would be next on the deportation schedule. Three copies of the report were sent out: to Kastner's rescue committee in Budapest, to the Yishuv's rescue mission in Istanbul (the courier failed to deliver this copy), and to Rabbi Weissmandel and Fleischmann in Bratislava, who, together, passed its contents on (via Schwalb's courier) to Jewish organizations in Switzerland and to Orthodox rabbis in Budapest.[3]

The earliest mention of a copy of the report and sketch being sent to Switzerland occurs in a letter of May 16 that Weissmandel and Fleischmann sent to the Jewish organizations there, pleading for immediate action to save Hungary's Jews. Weissmandel listed the following urgently needed rescue actions:

> 1. *To demand that all countries issue a strong warning to Germany and Hungary against continuation of the murder of Jews.*
>
> 2. *To demand that the pope warn Hungary.*
>
> 3. *To publicize widely in the media the horrific extermination in Auschwitz.*
>
> 4. *To mobilize the International Red Cross to demand an urgent visit to Auschwitz.*[4]

Weissmandel himself met with the Vatican nuncio in Bratislava,[5] and a copy of the report was delivered to the Vatican on May 22, 1944. In three additional suggestions, he proposed the bombing of Auschwitz, a second plan for rescuing a million Jews,* which the Allies considered but rejected; it will be described in the next chapter.

Gila Fatran evaluates the report thus: "It was not the two Auschwitz escapees who revealed to Slovakia's Jews the fact of the ongoing extermination. [Yet] their testimony certainly removed any shred of doubt from skeptical minds or those who needed still more proof to believe in what was incredible to the human mind." The report was not circulated in Slovakia, she adds, because it contained nothing about the extermination that the working group or Slovakia's Jews did not already know. By that time, the Jews' resistance to being shipped to Auschwitz was at its strongest, and the report could not have intensified it.

However, the report was not circulated in Hungary either. Why

---

* The word "million" was used figuratively here. The actual number depended on the number of Jews in Hungary. By some estimates there were 750,000 Jews there; others put the figure at 800,000. There were also Jews who had come to Hungary from Slovakia, Poland, and elsewhere. There is no authoritative source for their number.

was this so, and why did Kastner's rescue committee not wake up to take belated action in reaction to it until the second week of June? "This remains an unexplained puzzle," remarks Fatran.[6] In 1953, testifying in Jerusalem's district court, Kastner intimated that Hungarian Jewry was just as aware of the extermination as the Jews of Slovakia. His associate, Joel Brand, said the same. Perhaps Kastner's delay in taking action was due to the fact that he trusted that Hungarian Jewry would be better served by the Goods for Blood Plan.

On April 24, 1944, a day before Alfred Wetzler and Rudolf Vrba submitted their Auschwitz report, Joel Brand—thirty-seven, a textile mechanic, married, a father of two and member of Kastner's rescue committee in Budapest—had been summoned to Eichmann's office. Eichmann, with 5 million Jewish lives to his name, arrived in Budapest on March 21, two days after Germany's occupation of Hungary, to head his "Kommando Eichmann." He entrusted Brand with the following "proposal": the SS's highest authority was prepared to "sell" 1 million Jews to world Jewry in return for 10,000 heavy-duty trucks—100 Jews a truck—800 tons of coffee, 800 tons of tea, 200 tons of cocoa, 2 million bars of soap, and a million dollars, in "dollars, Swiss francs, and some South American money." The said Jews would be free to go to Portugal, or any other country of their choice, except Palestine—the Nazis being bound by a pledge to Hajj Amin al-Hussaini, the Grand Mufti of Jerusalem, to ban Jewish immigration to Palestine. Brand was to return to Budapest within a fortnight of his arrival in Turkey, to report "world Jewry's reaction."*

Eichmann then facilitated Brand's going abroad to contact representatives of world Jewry in furtherance of this dubious project, which was to put the rescue of a million Jews on the Allied agenda. On May 15 Brand left Budapest for Vienna, where he was issued a German travel permit. He was also allowed to notify the Yishuv's rescue mis-

---

* Sharett told the British High Commissioner in Palestine that Brand "must return to Budapest with a reply within a fortnight from May 19." Sharett cabled Goldmann in New York that Brand must return "with reply within two or three weeks" beginning May 19, 1944.

sion in Istanbul by cable of his impending arrival and his wish to meet
JAE leaders. On the 19th he boarded a German courier plane that
took him to Istanbul. When it landed, the sand in the hourglass of his
mission began to run out.

Unknown to him—as he later claimed—another Hungarian Jew
boarded the same plane. This was Andor (Bandi) Grosz,* who was
being sent by *Hauptsturmführer* Otto Klages, head of the Gestapo
secret police in Hungary, to sound out Allied intelligence officers on
the prospects for a separate peace between Germany and the Western
Allies. Goods for Blood was meant therefore to drive a wedge between
the Allies and prepare the ground for a separate peace. To lure the
Western Allies into agreeing to such a peace, Eichmann pledged to
Brand that the 10,000 trucks "would be deployed solely on the
Russian front."

Brand was met on arrival by Chaim Barlas and Venia Pommerantz
of the JAE's rescue mission in Istanbul, and taken to the Pera Palas
Hotel. After debriefing Brand, the rescue mission reported to
Jerusalem, asking that a JAE representative be sent to meet Brand. It
also informed the American embassy in Ankara of these developments.

At the time it was a mystery why the Nazis chose Brand of all
people to be their emissary. In time an answer was found. The editors
of the *Encyclopedia of the Holocaust* are inclined to think that Brand
had been recommended by Grosz. This shady double-dealer worked
for Klages, and it was he, the editors believe, who assigned Grosz the
mission of traveling on Brand's plane and establishing contact with
Allied intelligence officers in Istanbul. If so, Brand and the Goods for
Blood proposal served to camouflage Grosz's more important
mission.[7]

Indeed, Grosz, who checked into the same hotel, found his way to
Ehud Avriel of the rescue mission and warned him: "Don't believe a
word of what this fool is going to tell you. I am the one who did it
all. . . . To save myself from certain death, I invented the greatest stunt

* Actually, Grosz had converted to Catholicism and married a Catholic wife in 1937.

of my career. This fool, Brand, is only the tool of my own salvation. Pay no attention to the fairy tales he will feed you—as if he were some envoy with supreme power over life and death."[8]

The American embassy in Ankara reported on the development in a dispatch to the Department of State in Washington:

> On May 19, 1944, the German courier plane from Vienna arrived in Istanbul with . . . Andre Gross [sic], alias Andre Anatol Gyorgy, a Hungarian Jew with a long record as a double agent [or, as Venia Pommerantz later commented, "even a treble and quadruple agent"]; and Joel Brand, a Hungarian Jew, by vocation a small manufacturer, but by choice an active Zionist and an agent in the Jewish underground. Gyorgy arrived on a Hungarian special passport, Brand used a German travel document [on which he was identified as "Eugene Brand"[9]], issued a few days previously in Vienna. Brand did not have a Turkish visa. Gyorgy's credentials in this connection are uncertain. Both, however, entered Turkey without difficulty, and remained free until May 25, 1944. On that day they were picked up by the Turkish secret police for questioning, Gyorgy on a smuggling charge, Brand for entering Turkey without a visa. Within the next few hours Gyorgy was released from custody, announced that the Gestapo had ordered his return to Germany, pleaded on bended knee before Allied intelligence officers for assistance in "escaping" to Syria, was documented for entrance into Allied territory, and departed on a southbound Taurus express.

Brand, on the other hand, "remained under the nominal supervision of the Turkish secret police, but returned to the Pera Palas Hotel each evening under guard." The cable described "the Brand proposals" as "allegedly an official German program to free the Jews in occupied Europe in exchange for nominal shipments of food supplies, soap and 10,000 trucks 'to be used only on the Russian front.' "[10]

A May 24 telegram from the British ambassador at Ankara to the Foreign Office in London describes how this information reached the JAE in Jerusalem. "Jewish Agency representatives in Istanbul apparently regard the [Brand] proposal as serious, as they sent a certain [Venia] Pomeranetz [sic] to Palestine to report to Zionist Executive."

Indeed, Pommerantz arrived in Jerusalem on the evening of the 24th and met with Ben-Gurion and Sharett. On the 25th he reported Brand's proposals to the JAE.[11]

At the May 25 JAE meeting, Ben-Gurion opined "that the whole business is quite likely to be a trick."[12] "The entire matter is fantastic," he said, "yet we should not underestimate its importance. This is also not the time to speak of 'Satanic' schemes. The Nazis have one only scheme: to wipe out the Jews. If there is even a hope of one in a million—we should cling to it." Sharett, he added, must go to Turkey at once, and the JAE so resolved unanimously.[13] In referring to "Satanic schemes," Ben-Gurion meant that the proposal should not be so described in public, lest the Nazis call it off, claiming to be offended. To intimates he acknowledged that in the "central issue" of rescue "we are conducting negotiations with Satan himself."[14]

On May 26 Ben-Gurion and Sharett reported the JAE's decisions to Sir Harold MacMichael, the British high commissioner, requesting him to cable the British government the content of Goods for Blood and the JAE's positive attitude toward it, and send the cable as well to Weizmann in London and Goldmann in New York.* MacMichael promised to help Sharett secure quickly an entry visa to Turkey.[15] Thus within less than a week Washington and London became aware of the entire Goods for Blood proposal through three sources: the JAE's rescue mission in Istanbul, the Turkish secret police, and the JAE in Jerusalem. From the start, Brand's mission was never a secret.

Kastner's rescue committee expected that the Nazis would not start the deportations from Hungary before receiving a reaction to the Goods for Blood proposal. Yet Eichmann did not wait even until Brand and Grosz's arrival in Istanbul. On May 15, the same day that Brand left for Vienna, the mass shipment of Hungary's Jews to the gas chambers began. It must be remembered that, throughout the Brand

---

* Goldmann saw Undersecretary of State Stettinius on the morning of June 7, 1944, after which he wrote him, that "it would be advisable to inform the Soviet Government" of Brand's proposals. Goldmann added: "I am glad you do not take the line that the offer should be flatly refused, but that the impression should be given that it is being considered. I have been told by Mr. Russell of the British Embassy that the Foreign Office is inclined to take the same line."

episode, the Jews in Budapest, Istanbul, Jerusalem, and London all expected they could gain time, delaying the shipments of 12,000 Jews a day to Auschwitz, which continued for five consecutive weeks, even if there was no real chance of getting the Allies' consent to trade trucks for lives.

Although MacMichael had promised to help Sharett get to Istanbul to meet Brand, the British refused him an exit permit,[16] under a variety of pretexts. Most likely, they had not yet made up their minds about Brand's proposals.

The British refusal to allow Sharett to go to Turkey came up before the JAE on May 29, when some doubts about its previous decision were expressed. But Ben-Gurion was adamant: "We mustn't miss any opportunity [of rescue] . . . if there is a way for Sharett to get to Turkey without a visa [meaning by defying the British and Turkish authorities] he advises that this be done."[17]

On May 31, the day Sharett planned to fly to Istanbul to meet Brand, the British decided against accepting Goods for Blood. In a meeting that day the War Cabinet Committee on the Reception and Accommodation of Refugees, which included Foreign Secretary Anthony Eden, Colonial Secretary Oliver Stanley, Foreign Undersecretary George Hall, and senior officials of the Foreign and Colonial offices, it was agreed to cable Washington the following:

> 1. *That it was not possible to consider any scheme which involved an evacuation of the order of magnitude envisaged in the [Brand's] proposal, since the necessary operations could not be undertaken without altering the course of the war.*
>
> 2. *That no dealing with the Gestapo or bargaining on the basis of the exchange of refugees against stores [goods] particularly of war-like material, could be permitted.*[18]

But from here on, to mislead the JAE and public opinion alike, the British maintained the posture of still considering the proposals. Under this guise they did their best to undermine Brand's mission.

Grosz's mission ended on June 1, when, shortly after crossing the Syrian border, he was picked up by British intelligence officers and incarcerated. Brand, however, was given a British visa to Palestine. This is confirmed in the American embassy dispatch: "He was released from custody on May 31, and departed for Syria and Palestine on June 5, 1944."[19] He was accompanied by Avriel, who before boarding the train had exchanged cables with the JAE in Jerusalem about this development. On June 6, the British allowed Sharett to go to Aleppo, Syria, where he would be permitted to speak to Brand. It was thus plain that the Palestine visa given Brand was but a ploy. The British had no intention of allowing him either a tête-à-tête with Sharett or entry to Palestine.

Indeed, on June 7, when the train stopped at Aleppo and Avriel got off to look for the JAE's contact man in order to arrange the meeting with Sharett, Brand was whisked away from the train by two German-speaking British agents to a nearby secret British installation.[20]

Using a rich variety of excuses—Brand was exhausted and in need of complete rest, etc.—the British postponed his meeting with Sharett for four full days. The meeting finally took place on June 11, at the place where Brand was being held. There Brand, Sharett, and an aide were allowed to sit and talk for six hours in German, in the presence of a British agent who took notes.[21]

Sharett's report of the conversation has Brand telling him of events in Hungary, the establishment of the rescue committee, its contacts with the Germans, and, in greater detail, of his own summons to Eichmann's office and the Goods for Blood proposal.

Sharett returned to Palestine to report to an extraordinary meeting of the JAE held at Ben-Gurion's Tel Aviv home on Wednesday, June 14. To Sharett in Aleppo, and to his British captors, Brand had pleaded to be sent back to Budapest—at great risk to his life—"with a message that we are continuing this fantastic scheme." If he was not sent back, he said, "the direst consequences [would] ensue for him and the Jews of Europe." On June 15, a day after his return from Aleppo, Sharett, with Ben-Gurion, called on Sir Harold MacMichael, the High Commissioner, to ask the British government: "(a) to enable emissary Mr. Joel Brand [who had been removed to Cairo] to return to Budapest; (b) to enable Sharett to fly to England; and (c) talk the [British] government into arranging a meeting with a representative of the enemy to discuss real possibilities for rescue [Goods for Blood]." MacMichael told them of Weizmann's June 7 interview with Eden. Weizmann, said MacMichael, thought the terms of Goods for Blood truly "fantastic," yet "by avoiding a negative response it perhaps was possible to win time [for Hungary's Jews]." To this Eden "responded positively." MacMichael, however, sternly warned his interlocutors "against any contact with the enemy." Sharett rejoined that "the non-return" of emissary Brand "will be interpreted [by the Germans] as closing the door" on Goods for Blood, especially since the "British authorities" in Turkey had "guaranteed" Brand's return. To which MacMichael responded that "one mustn't forget, not even for a moment, that England is at war" and that "matters are decided elsewhere [London], not in Jerusalem." Nevertheless he promised to inform London of Sharett's request for air travel priority and an entry permit to England.[22]

On June 17 the Zionist leaders in Budapest sent a telegram to the Yishuv rescue mission at Istanbul, demanding Brand's immediate return to Hungary. "If *not,*" it declared, "all will be in vain"—that is, the Jews' delaying tactic would be exposed and the rail transports would continue. Two days later, on June 19, Kastner and Moshe Krausz, the two leading Zionists in Budapest, managed to telephone a message to Geneva, which was relayed to Jerusalem, containing two demands: a warning to the Germans that "reprisals" would be taken if Hungarian Jewry were massacred, and an immediate decision by the Allies "to grant foreign citizenship to Hungarian Jews."[23] That is, they would be granted British, American, Canadian, or another nationality, thereby giving the Allies the necessary legal grounds to be concerned about their fate and adopt the appropriate measures to ensure their safety under international law.

Sharett received the telegram of June 17 on the 18th. He at once telegraphed to Weizmann in London and to Nahum Goldmann in New York, urging both to use their influence to persuade the British and American governments to allow Brand to return to Hungary at once.[24] At that time Brand was being held by the British in Cairo, ostensibly to resume his interrogation under closer scrutiny. But in fact the reason, soon to be manifest, was political.

In his telegram to Weizmann, Sharett explained that Brand had accepted his mission from the enemy on the "clear understanding" that he would return with a reply. He was "desperately anxious," as Sharett put it, to return with a report of his discussions so far, in the hope that telling the SS that its proposals were at least being considered "in high quarters" would help gain time and "prevent precipitation of calamity." Sharett added: "We consider his return is imperative if the slightest chance rescue is to be preserved. We regard this as the first indispensable step towards giving effect to the line agreed by Mr. Eden of gaining time and not closing door. For the same reason, we consider it equally essential that some immediate indication be given to the other side of readiness negotiate regarding rescue of Jews, urging, same time, discontinuation of deportation and slaughter pending meeting."[25]

In his telegram to Goldmann, Sharett noted that after hearing about his talk with Brand, the JAE had concluded that although the "exchange proposition may be a mere eyewash and possibility ulterior motives must be assumed, it is not improbable that even preliminary negotiations might result in salvation substantial number." Sharett then described a proposal by the JAE to explore the possibility of a meeting with "German representatives" in Lisbon or Madrid, whose goal would be "to discuss rescue Jews, urging same time discontinuation deportations and slaughter pending meeting." The groups that negotiated on behalf of the Allies, Sharett added, might be the Inter-Governmental Refugee Committee, the American War Refugee Board, the Red Cross, "or any other suitable agency."[26]

However, both High Commissioner for Palestine Sir Harold MacMichael and cabinet member and Minister Resident in the Middle East Lord Moyne were opposed to Brand's return, and the power was in their hands—to the degree that (through the censor's office or by other means) nearly all communications of the JAE were also in their hands. In this case, however, Sharett was able to make good use of the mandatory government's willingness to transmit the JAE's open telegrams to London enclosed in their own messages. His telegram to Weizmann wound up being enclosed in a telegram sent by Sir Harold to the colonial secretary.[27] On June 20 Lord Moyne telegraphed the

British government that he was opposed to Brand's return "until the situation is clearer."[28]

The next day Moyne refused to allow Sharett to send "through secret channels" a message to rescue emissary Barlas in Istanbul. Moyne claimed that the message gave "an indication of the British Government's policy as conceived by Sharett which may not in fact prove accurate." This could be a reference to Sharett's statement in his telegram to Weizmann—which he would also have made to Barlas—that Brand's return to Budapest was the first step in the "line agreed by Mr. Eden of gaining time and not closing door." Moyne also pointed out the danger, as he saw it, that the details contained in the message "would almost certainly reach Budapest within a short time,"[29] where the Germans would have been sure to see it. Not too subtle a hint at a possible connection behind the Allies' back between the JAE and the enemy. However, following an order from London two days later, he authorized the telegram.

The action now shifted to Whitehall. On June 21 the Foreign Office received Sharett's telegram to Weizmann appealing for Brand's immediate return to Hungary. Ian Henderson, a German and a Jewish specialist at the Foreign Office who saw it, noted that the government's only reply could be "that we will not let him go until we have seen Mr. Sharett." For Sharett "must be interviewed in London, and it is in London and Washington that the chief decisions must be taken." He added that "the Soviet Government have rejected the idea of negotiation."[30] This reinforced a previous message from Soviet deputy foreign minister Andrei Vyshinsky stating categorically that the Soviet government "does not consider it expedient or permissible to carry on any negotiations whatsoever with the Government of Hitlerite Germany. . . ."[31] Commenting on this message on June 22, A. W. G. Randall, head of the Refugee Department, noted: "This strengthens us for the forthcoming talks with Mr. Sharett, who will almost certainly press for contact with the Germans."

Historian and Churchill biographer Martin Gilbert writes in his excellently researched, eye-opening *Auschwitz and the Allies* that "Foreign Office opinion had become decisively sceptical not only of the Brand proposals, but even of the motives of the JAE." In any case the Foreign Office was in a position either to pass Sharett's telegram on to Weizmann or withhold it. This also became a subject of deliberation. On June 22 Randall minuted: "I think the message to Dr. Weizmann should be sent on, but I feel we are (as we realised at the beginning we should be if, for political reasons, we refrained from turning the whole scheme down) on a slippery slope and we need expect little help I am afraid from the Jewish Agency to arrest our rapid progress to the bottom. We shall therefore have to apply the brake ourselves."

Charles William Baxter, head of the Eastern Department, was equally emphatic: "We must realize," he wrote, "that Mr. Sharett's interests in the matter are opposed to those of HMG, for *his main object is to fill Palestine with Jews*" (italics added). Sir Robert Maurice Hankey of the Eastern Department described Sharett's motive in even stronger language: "He, *poor fellow*, is, after all, *solely* concerned to extricate as many Jews as he can from the clutches of the Nazis (and incidentally, *to pile them into Palestine* . . . and possibly doesn't care very much what the effect is on the war effort" (italics added).[32]

Sir Hughe Knatchbull-Hugessen, the British ambassador at Ankara, joined in the deliberation with a June 22 telegram. Sir Hughe first reported the opinion of Ira Hirschmann, the American War Refugee Board representative, who appeared entirely unconvinced that the Brand proposals were realistic, but "feels strongly that in order to gain time he ought to be sent to Hungary with some kind of proposals to keep the pot boiling." However, in another telegram sent the same day, Sir Hughe said, "Mr. Hirschmann is a go-getter, somewhat tenacious of his own ideas, and impatient of official methods. He is looking at the whole Jewish refugee question mainly from the point of view of the coming Presidential election in the United States and is I think inclined to resent the fact that it is not being dealt with by the United States alone as a purely American concern."[33]

The Foreign Office formalized its position on June 23: to detain Brand in Cairo, but not to dismiss his proposals altogether. As Randall minuted: "It is a delicate piece of prising we have to do, as between the US Government and the Zionists, but for the sake of our relations with the former, I think we must try to carry out the balancing feat,

at least until we get the venue of the discussions moved to London."
And Randall added that "in view of the alleged life and death interests involved, I am of the opinion that the final decision should go higher."[34]

It was on that same day—June 23, 1944—that the Allies first learned
that a total of more than 435,000 Hungarian Jews had been shipped to
Auschwitz since May 15; more than 12,000 a day for five weeks running:
"a pace unprecedented hitherto in the annals of the Holocaust."[35] This
information came from a letter by Krausz smuggled from Budapest to
Geneva by courier.[36] Nevertheless, Brand remained under custody in
Cairo. The British would not allow him to return to Hungary, or let the
rescue mission in Istanbul send its emmissary, Menahem Bader, there instead, as requested. Only in October was Brand finally allowed to
leave Cairo for Palestine. He arrived there a broken man, for he truly
believed Goods for Blood could have saved a million Jews.

Years later Ben-Gurion summed up Brand's mission thus: "Six million [murdered] in full view of the world, and the world did not shake!
They [the Allies] could have saved. In my opinion America stands guilty,
England stands guilty, they both could have saved, especially England.
The hell they couldn't . . . give [the Germans] ten thousand trucks, this
would not have decided the war! They [however] said, 'we will not do
this. . . . The Russians will suspect us of making peace with the Germans
behind their backs.' But they [the Allies] stand responsible."[37]

It must be acknowledged that even if the British, to whom the JAE
always had to turn first, had been more receptive to its pleas, they
would still have had to consider any proposal's pros and cons, especially how agreeing to it could benefit them. What could the JAE
have offered in return for saving a million Jews? To bring them to
Palestine—since no other country would take in even 50,000 Jews?
But the last thing the British wanted was to incite all the Arabs in and
around Palestine to rise in protest. And the Arabs would have had
good reason to do so, for bringing in a million Jews would have been
tantamount to delivering Palestine into Jewish hands.

The Arabs, by contrast, had a great deal to offer the British, especially in time of war. Imperial interests dictated that the British retain
them as friends, not make them enemies. It is well to bear in mind
that the possibility of the Arabs becoming their enemies was very alive

in the British mind, for Hitler's treatment of the Jews had won him Arab sympathy and support. Hajj Amin al-Hussaini, the Grand Mufti of Jerusalem, and Rashid Ali al-Gailani, several times prime minister of Iraq, can serve as examples. The former, notoriously anti-Zionist and anti-British and a popular leader of Palestine's Arabs, escaped the British and found a warm reception in Berlin. The latter sought help from Germany in 1941 for an attempt to prevent the British from making military use of Iraqi land and oil and also found refuge in Berlin. Both assisted with Nazi propaganda directed at the Arab world.

In other words, if the JAE wanted to save Jews from Hitler, it had better support the Allies and refrain from bringing pressure to bear in the matter of opening Palestine to immigration of Jewish refugees and survivors.

And there was also a too-often-forgotten practical issue. At the first JAE meeting that discussed Goods for Blood, Sharett spoke for the British official he would have to deal with: All right, suppose we do that, save a million, how are we going to feed a million people and transport them across the fronts, with the war raging all over Europe? And is Portugal ready to receive hundreds of thousands of Jewish refugees, and at such short notice? No, the war will end soon, and victory is the Jew's best friend.[38] Certainly this response agrees with the official government statement in the House of Commons, on January 19, 1943, and its repetition by Eden on February 24: "The only truly effective means of succouring the tortured Jewish, and I may add, the other suffering peoples of Europe, lies in an Allied victory. In devoting all their energies and resources to this end, the Governments and peoples of the United Nations are, therefore, seeking to bring relief to all the oppressed."[39]

Invariably, the JAE's demand for rescue action by the Allies met this same response: Victory over Hitler is the surest and speediest rescue, so please let us do our job, which is also in your best interests. The JAE had to admit the logic of this argument, but still could not accept it, given the brisk pace of the extermination. The Korherr report on the Final Solution submitted to SS chief Heinrich Himmler put the number of Jews destroyed by March 31, 1943, at about 3.5 million.[40] A year later it grew to 5 million and more. Was there any other way than Goods for Blood to stop it there and save Hungary's Jews?

CHAPTER THIRTEEN

THE BOMBING OF AUSCHWITZ

O NE WAY of stopping the extermination—bombing Auschwitz from the air—came up in reaction to the Vrba-Wetzler report. It is interesting that the first to propose it was Rabbi Weissmandel. In April 1944 he informed Jewish leaders in Hungary and Switzerland that an agreement had been signed by the railway managements of Slovakia, Germany, and Hungary to carry out 120 rail transports to Auschwitz; this information was leaked to the working group by an anti-Nazi Slovak rail official. Accordingly, Weissmandel advised his correspondents in Switzerland to demand that the rail tunnel between Kosice and Presov in Czechoslovakia, through which Jews were transported from Hungary to Auschwitz, be bombed.[1]

Fleischmann and Weissmandel's letter of May 16 to the Jewish organizations in Switzerland, quoted in Chapter 12, included three additional rescue suggestions:

> 5. To bomb [from the air] the death installations in Auschwitz.
> 6. To bomb [from the air] the rail lines leading to Auschwitz.*
> 7. To bomb [from the air] bridges and tunnels serving the rail transports to Auschwitz.[2]

During June the information based on the Vrba-Wetzler report and the suggestions for bombing Auschwitz killing installations and

---

* Nine days later, on May 25, Yehoshua Radler-Feldman (Reb Binyamin), a well-known Hebrew editor and essayist in Tel Aviv, suggested the same thing in a note to Sharett.

the railroads leading to Auschwitz, based on the Fleischmann-Weissmandel letter, reached Allied governments as well as the JAE. On June 18 the BBC ran a short summary of it.[3]

However, when those suggestions were brought up before the JAE, the issue of bombing Auschwitz became inextricably tied up with that of Brand's mission. The May 21 meeting discussed Gruenbaum's suggestion to call "A Day of Appeal to the Entire World" to come to the rescue of Hungary's Jews: a day of fasting, stoppage of work, and public prayers. As chairman of JAE's rescue committee, he also pressed the meeting to apply, through the American consul general in Jerusalem, to the War Refugee Board (WRB) in Washington, for money and ships. Ben-Gurion commented that calling a "Day of Appeal" was the prerogative of the National Council, the Yishuv's governing body.* As for a direct appeal to Washington, one is tempted to second-guess Ben-Gurion and speculate that there was more to it than met the eye. The JAE was authorized only by the mandatory government of Palestine and through it by the government in London. Strictly speaking, the JAE was not supposed to address foreign governments except with London's consent or knowledge. Since the Allies considered rescue a political matter, going to Washington behind London's back could be interpreted as a breach of the rules. And doing so would bring more than just diplomatic embarrassment; for Washington would not only support London, an ally far more important than the JAE, it might regard the JAE's move as a subversive act.

Thus Ben-Gurion considered this a risk not worth taking. His acute political intuition must have warned him that it was dangerous, for he could not possibly have known of talks recently concluded in London whose intent was to tighten the united front between the U.S. and the United Kingdom vis-à-vis the Zionist organization.

On April 17, 1944, Wallace Murray of the State Department and Edmund E. Boyd, an undersecretary at the Colonial Office, drafted a joint declaration whose intent was "To keep in check Zionist agitation in America and to impress upon Jewish leaders there their duty to

---

* A "Day of Outcry" involving prayers, fasting, mass meetings, and "A Plea to the World" for rescue was held on June 5, 1944.

restrain their followers from doing anything to embarrass the Allied war effort." It was decided, however, "that we would keep the joint declaration on our files and subsequently, if necessary, we would consider the matter again."[4]

Furthermore, the JAE believed that Goods for Blood offered better rescue opportunities than bombing Auschwitz. Simple logic suggested that Hungary's Jews would more likely be saved by keeping them away from Auschwitz than by bombing it after they had already arrived there. But without British support Goods for Blood had no chance. Ben-Gurion therefore proposed a committee to study Gruenbaum's suggestion, and its was duly elected: Gruenbaum, Kaplan, Sharett, and Joseph.[5]

Feeling constrained by his colleagues on the committee,[6] and more mistrustful of the British than they, Gruenbaum chose to act on his own. On June 2, he met with Lowell C. Pinkerton, the American consul general in Jerusalem, to discuss, as he put it, "rescue in general." This framework was broad enough to enable him to suggest that the U.S. Army Air Force be ordered to bomb Auschwitz, Treblinka, and other death camps, as well as their connecting highways and railways.

To explain his unauthorized move, as well as gather support for it, on June 7 Gruenbaum sent a précis of his talk with Pinkerton to all JAE members. After reviewing rescue work by the JAE and WRB in Turkey and Romania and recounting the latest "Polish style" deportations out of Hungary, he suggested to Pinkerton the following measures: "(a) renewal of warning against Hungarian participation and persecution and inclusion of Bulgaria in warning (the consul noted this down, to pass on to Washington). (b) Instructing American aviation to bomb the death camps in Poland. Here Pinkerton demurred: might not such bombing cause the death of many Jews, and might not German propaganda use it to broadcast to the world, lo and behold, that American too take part in destroying Jews?"

To this Gruenbaum replied that "Despite this possibility he stood by his suggestion, because the Jews in the death camps were doomed anyway, but in the confusion wrought by the bombing, some of them perhaps would be able to escape." Furthermore, Gruenbaum went on, death camps cost money and labor, and their destruction "might perhaps interrupt the mass killing and prevent the Germans from putting up similiar ones in the future. And, Germans guarding the camps may suffer loss of life as well."

A brief argument ensued, after which the unconvinced Pinkerton set a condition: he would pass Gruenbaum's suggestion to Washington only if it was made in writing. This was too far outside the official JAE line, so Gruenbaum reduced his request to merely "if railways between Hungary and Poland could be bombed." In this form Pinkerton agreed to send it on. That same day, June 2, at 6 P.M., he sent a cable "for War Refugee Board from Gruenbaum Chairman of Jewish Agency Joint Rescue Committee." According to reliable information, it said, "there has been a definite German decision to proceed as rapidly as possible with systematic deportation of Hungarian Jews to Poland . . . suggest deportation would be much impaired if railways between Hungary and Poland should be bombed."[*7]

Pinkerton's condition "forced" Gruenbaum—as Gruenbaum himself put it—to raise the case for bombing Auschwitz at the next JAE weekly meeting on June 11, 1944, at which he came under harsh criticism. Dr. Emil Schmorak of the General Zionists remarked that it had been reported that Auschwitz also contained a large labor camp, "and we must not take upon ourselves responsibility for a bombing that might cause the death of even one Jew."

Dr. Dov Joseph, of the Political Department, also objected "to demanding that the Americans bomb the camps and thus murder Jews." Gruenbaum, he said, did not speak as a private individual, but as a representative of a body, "and the body associated with us [JAE] must not bring up such a suggestion." Dr. Werner Senator, the American non-Zionist representative on the JAE board, objected too. "It is regrettable that Mr. Gruenbaum talked about it with the American consul in the first place." Chairman Ben-Gurion summarized for the record the meeting's spirit: "The Executive is of the opinion that it should not suggest to the Allies the bombing of locations where there are Jews."[8]

---

* On June 24 a similar demand was cabled to WRB by Rosewell McClelland, its representative in Geneva.

Sharett then saw Pinkerton over the weekend "and updated him on [Brand's] situation." Pinkerton, on his part, "promised to cable Washington." He kept his word, but did not let it disturb his weekend repose. Despite the ghastly contents of the cable—which stated that 350,000 Hungarian Jews had either already been gassed or were about to be gassed, and that 400,000 more were waiting their turn—he did not send it until Monday, June 19, when the consulate resumed its weekday routine.

Sharett reported on his meeting with Pinkerton to the JAE on June 18, in a meeting whose main agenda was how to win time for Hungary's Jews by leading the Germans to believe that Goods for Blood was negotiable. Ben-Gurion opened by explaining that the British in the Middle East tended to see everything through the prism of war, and its successful conduct was their only concern. In London, on the other hand, the British appreciated the political aspect as well. He believed that in London Sharett would be able, by personal persuasion, "to get [Goods for Blood] moving." Therefore, he said, Sharett's immediate departure was critical.

Others were less hopeful. Gruenbaum had already doubted whether any good could come of letting the British government in on Brand's mission. He now asserted that it had been clear to him from the start "that the government would use the information for its own good and do nothing for Jewish rescue." However, in arguing his position he contradicted himself, saying, "We must do all we can to bring about a meeting with the enemy" in which "a representative of the [British] government will take part."

Schmorak was just as skeptical of the British and equally incoherent in seeking a way to exert leverage that would induce them to release Brand as a green light for Goods for Blood. He advised the JAE "to use the American consulate to pass the [rescue] matter [to Washington and] also to friends in the U.S." To secure support for Goods for Blood, Schmorak was ready to drive a wedge between Britain and America. It seems that Sharett's report of MacMichael's assertion that Eden had responded "positively" to Weizmann's argument—that Goods for Blood was good for winning time—had already become in

Schmorak's mind a firm British commitment.* American pressure was needed, according to Schmorak, "to prevent Eden's declaration from becoming worth only the paper it's written on, and to ascertain that we will not end up as the ones morally responsible for Jewish massacre."

Thereupon Ben-Gurion commented, "We should not use the American consulate channels for rescue business. We use these channels for Zionist matters [that is, communicating with the American Zionist Emergency Committee and pressuring Washington through it.]—and this isn't quite the same."

The meeting endorsed Ben-Gurion's summation: "(a) the Executive will cable to [its branches in] London and America, requesting our colleagues to do their very best to bring about an act that would prove to the enemy that there is readiness [in London and Washington] for negotiating rescue of Jews; (b) the Executive will try hard to expedite Mr. Sharett's journey to England."[9]

On June 21 Sharett flew to Cairo to meet with Ira Hirschmann, who was about to interview Brand. When Brand arrived in Istanbul, Hirschmann was in the United States, but because "of some alarm at the Department of State" over the Brand proposals—regarding which the British ambassador, Lord Halifax, had called in person on Undersecretary of State Edward R. Stettinius Jr.—he was ordered to fly at once back to Turkey, to see Brand. However, by that time Brand had been moved by British security to Cairo, where Hirschmann interviewed him at great length on June 22. Subsequently Hirschmann and Sharett met. But the British did not allow Sharett to meet with Brand.[10]

Sharett also saw Lord Moyne on June 23, then flew to Jerusalem to report late in the evening of the 24th to a special meeting of the JAE. The next day, Sharett flew back to Cairo, and the following morning, thanks to Moyne's intervention, he was given a seat on a flight to England. Mrs. Blanche (Baffy) Dugdale, Lord Balfour's niece

---

* He was not alone in thinking this. Sharett cabled Goldmann in New York: "We are informed Eden in conversation with Weizmann agreed policy should be gain time avoid other side getting impression Allies are slamming door refusing even consider matter."

and Weizmann's admiring aide, wrote in her diary for the 26th: "The Foreign Office is expediting Sharett's arrival so as to hear more about the Istanbul story. . . . Meanwhile the massacres of Jews still go on." The next day she told her diary: "Sharett had just arrived. . . . [In a meeting at the Zionist office he] unfolded his most amazing story. . . . It was arranged he should go tomorrow to the Foreign Office and report all. These are probably deep waters, nothing can or should be done or said without knowledge and approval of [the British government]. All the Yeshiva [meeting] strongly feels this."[11]

At the time of its June 11, 1944, meeting, the JAE was well aware of the desperate situation of Hungary's Jews. Already on May 8 Gruenbaum had cabled Rabbi Stephen Wise in New York that a fate "like Poland" awaited Hungary's Jews, urging him to "take all steps [in] our power" to prevent it. On May 25 Dobkin cabled Wise and Nahum Goldmann that there was "clear evidence mass extermination being prepared according methods Poland" and that "over 300,000" of Hungary's 800,000 Jews already awaited deportation. On May 30 Gruenbaum cabled Anselm Reiss, envoy of the JAE's rescue committee in London, asking for information—since "We are anxious fate Hungarian Jews . . . deported Poland"—and instructing him to "approach all allied governments [and] suggest Polish government that partisans [the so-called Polish Home Army] be instructed to destroy the death camps for Jews, perhaps this would slow up the mass slaughter which is still going on." On June 19 Gruenbaum cabled Reiss and Ignacy Schwarzbart, a member of the National Polish Council in London, that he was still awaiting the Polish government's response, repeating the "Polish underground movement must begin destroy death camps." The answer of the Polish government-in-exile in London—"appropriate orders were issued by the Commander in Chief"—was sent on September 8 to Leon Kubowitzki of the World Jewish Congress in New York, who relayed it to Gruenbaum, adding, "It seems, however, that the Polish Home Army is in no position to carry out the instructions it has been given."[12]

In the meantime uncertainty still prevailed at the JAE, as reflected in its correspondence. On June 6, 1944, Gruenbaum cabled Chaim

Barlas, his emissary to Istanbul, asking "whether true that 150,000 Hungarian Jews already deported eastward" and "whether possible dispatch of [food and medicine] parcels from Turkey to Hungary." On June 11 he cabled Kubowitzki that he had "just received information 12,000 Hungarian Jews daily deported unknown destination" during the first ten days of May, adding, however, that there were "rumors deportation stopped subsequently." Only on June 24 was Schwarzbart advised by the Polish Ministry of the Interior in London that, according to information radioed from Poland on June 14, 100,000 Jews from Hungary had been gassed at Auschwitz.[13]

Obviously, on June 11 the JAE had no way of knowing that the Nazis were murdering on arrival the 12,000 Jews transported daily from Hungary to Auschwitz-Birkenau*—an unprecedented number, which indicated that the capacity of the gas chambers and crematoria had been considerably augmented. This information reached the JAE piecemeal, accumulating gradually. On June 17 Gruenbaum received Barlas's answers: "Unfortunately rumors regarding deportation true," and "dispatch [of parcels] possible but unnecessary." Then, on June 18, came the answers from Reiss in a cable signed by Schwarzbart: "According Polish government's last reports sixty-two railway carriages loaded with Jewish children between two and eight reached Poland from Hungary 13th May. Between 15th and 27th May six trains daily with adult Jews Hungary passed station Plaszow near Cracow probably for Oswiecim [Auschwitz]." This prompted Gruenbaum to cable back "Schwarzbart/Reiss" next day, June 19: "It seems that time has come Polish underground movement must begin destroy death camps"—adding, nevertheless, the following question: "Is it true deportation Birkenau has begun?"

Between June 23 and 27, it seems, the JAE realized† that the

---

* Birkenau was then believed to be a labor camp.

† A letter from Schwarzbart of June 24, 1944, confirming the gassing of 100,000 Hungarian Jews at Auschwitz, did not reach Gruenbaum until July 18, 1944. In Washington, a "most forceful and courageous plea for allied military concentration through air raids came in a memorandum" submitted on June 29 to John Pehle, director of the WRB, by a member of its staff, Benjamin Akzin, later a professor of law at the Hebrew University in Jerusalem and member of Israel's Knesset.

Hungarian Jews deported to Auschwitz-Birkenau were gassed on arrival. It then changed its mind, on the ground that bombing would save far more Jews than it would kill. Reporting on this change to the JAE's rescue committee, Gruenbaum said: "First of all we demanded the bombing of Auschwitz, of the death camps, because these death factories are capable of putting to death great numbers of Jews every hour, every day ... therefore the destruction of the death factories would have saved many Jews."[14]

Clearly, however, the dread of ever being charged with moral responsibility for massacre of Jews, which motivated the initial rejection of bombing on June 11, continued to guide the JAE. It maintained the position then expressed by Joseph ("the body associated with us [JAE] must not make ... a suggestion" to bomb Auschwitz), and by Ben-Gurion's summation ("the Executive. ... should not suggest to the Allies the bombing of locations where there are Jews"). This perhaps explains why there is no mention of this change of mind in the JAE's record. Later Gruenbaum successfully urged the Actions Committee to endorse this line saying: "First thing is to stop the massacre, and for that extraordinary measures must be taken, bombing of Auschwitz, destroying Auschwitz and its connecting railway lines. But in no way can the Actions Committee, in making such resolution say so openly and explicitly."

Instead, as attested by its correspondence, the JAE chose to give full support of bombing requests coming from Nazi-occupied Europe.[15] To do this it mobilized its offices in Jerusalem, London, New York, and Geneva. On June 23 Gruenbaum cabled Reiss, suggesting that "if possible ask Jewish National Committees [in Nazi-occupied Europe] opinion about bombing death camps in order slow down annihilation Hungarian and other countries' Jews."

On the same day, June 23, Pinkerton delivered Washington's reply to the requests he made on June 2: "the Department of State asking me to inform you that efforts to safeguard the position of Jews in Hungary have been made through various foreign channels and through the International Red Cross. Warnings regarding the treatment of Jews are being constantly transmitted by short wave radio and otherwise to Hungary."*

On June 27 two cables from the rescue committee in Budapest arrived at the JAE. In the first, sent on the 22nd, Kastner complained that the "delay" in responding to Goods for Blood had "brought about enormous losses." The second, sent by Moshe Krausz on the 19th, reported the deportation to Poland of 400,000 of Hungary's Jews and the impending deportation, within a week, of 350,000 more "from Buda[pest] and environs."

On the basis of Krausz's cable, in which he demanded the bombing of Auschwitz and the railway lines linking it with Budapest, Dr. Richard Lichtheim, the JAE representative in Geneva, sent on June 26 a telegram to Douglas MacKillop at the British Legation in Bern. Its first part included an up-to-date estimate of what was left of Hungary's Jewry: "In Budapest and the surroundings there are still between 300,000 and 400,000 Jews left including those incorporated in labour service but no Jews are left in eastern and northern provinces . . . the remaining Jews in and around Budapest have no hope to be spared."

The second part was a revised, more detailed version of Weissmandel's last three demands: "bombing of railway lines leading from Hungary to Birkenau," "precision bombing of death camp installations," and finally, bombing of "all Government buildings" in Budapest. The telegram reached the Foreign Office in London on June 27 and was copied for immediate distribution to the war cabinet. Gilbert notes that "it was at this moment" that the Hungarian deportations became known to Churchill. He at once minuted to Eden: "What can be done? What can be said?"[16]

On June 27 Gruenbaum cabled Sharett in London, repeating again Krausz's information—"over 450,000 Hungarian Jews mostly youth deported Silesia [Auschwitz's district]"—and voicing his conviction

---

* Pinkerton was paraphrasing Secretary of State Cordell Hull's telegram of June 22, 1944: "Warnings regarding treatment of Jews are constantly being shortwaved and otherwise transmitted to Hungary, also . . . efforts to safeguard position of Jews in Hungary have been made through International Red Cross and various foreign channels."

that "nothing but unprecedently [*sic*] drastic measures can halt whole-sale slaughter Hungarian Jewry," namely, the bombardment of Auschwitz. It reached Sharett the day after.

On June 29 Gruenbaum sent Sharett another cable to the same effect* and asked Pinkerton to transmit another cable to Rabbi Wise, knowing full well that the Department of State would scrutinize it closely. The cable repeated Krausz's information and urged again "the adoption extraordinary measures repeatedly suggested view interfering deportation including retaliatory measures."

In launching his campaign for "extraordinary measures" Gruenbaum induced the Hebrew Writers Association to appeal to for-eign newspapers and intellectuals, George Bernard Shaw among them, to "persuade Government destroy by bombing all routes leading death camps Poland" and thus "stop . . . the barbarous massacre" of Hungary's Jews. Shaw sent back this insensitive, though frank, rejoin-der: "I can do nothing to help Hungarian Jewry. Do you suppose that I am Emperor of Europe? Of course my sympathies are with the Jews but the connection of my name with their cause would create as much hostile prejudice as friendly support."[17]

Weizmann and Sharett wore their hearts out in in the effort to save the remainder of Hungary's Jews either by Goods for Blood or by Allied bombing of Auschwitz and the railway lines. As it turned out, they could have saved themselves the trouble. Foreign Secretary Eden had already made up his mind. On May 31 the War Cabinet Committee on the Reception and Accommodation of Refugees (Eden, Stanley, Hall, and senior officials of the Foreign and Colonial offices, see Chapter 12) rejected Goods for Blood out of hand.[18] From then on, in their talks with Weizmann and Sharett, the Foreign Office put on a performance that can best be described as *un ballo in maschera*.

To meet with Sharett, the Foreign Office designated three medium-level officials, of whom Randall, head of the Refugee Department, was senior. On reading the record of the meeting, Eden objected to

* Gruenbaum corrected this number to 400,000 in his second cable to Sharett, sent on June 29, this time citing Krausz as the source of the information.

Sharett's wish for British and American government representatives to meet representatives of the German government: "This is out of the question."[19]

On June 28 Sharett asked, at Weizmann's initiative for a meeting with Eden. Gilbert continues: "Eden was reluctant to agree to a meeting, minuting that same day to his Private Secretary: 'What do you say? Must I? Which of my colleagues looks after this? Minister of State or [Undersecretary of State for Foreign Affairs] Mr [George] Hall? At least the one of them responsible should be there to see these two Jews. Weizmann doesn't usually take much time.' "[20]

It was Hall who graciously consented to see Weizmann and Sharett on the 30th. Again Sharett pleaded for Goods for Blood in order to gain time, as well as for all sorts of warnings to Germans and Hungarians. Eventually, only his request to warn Hungarian railway workers by radio not to carry Jews to the death camps was acted on.[21]

When Churchill learned about the Brand proposals, he agreed with Eden. On July 2 he minuted to Eden: "Surely we cannot negotiate with the Germans on this matter, certainly not without the Cabinet being consulted. This is not the time to have negotiations with the enemy."[22]

But Goods for Blood was dead long before. The British treatment of Grosz and Brand, the emissaries sent by the SS to propose a separate peace and Goods for Blood, had killed both proposals nearly immediately. Had the Allies been willing to pretend to seriously consider these proposals, they might have duped the SS into believing that the proposals were negotiable, and saved Jewish lives simply by halting the transports from Hungary and gaining time. The emissaries' imprisonment, however, told the SS that their proposals had been rejected out of hand; thus the shipment of Hungarian Jews to the gas chambers ran on according to schedule. There remained therefore only one other way to rescue Hungary's Jews.

In the meeting with Hall on June 30 Sharett also requested the bombing of the death camps, a suggestion, he said, that had originated with Krausz (he did not know it was Rabbi Weissmandel's).[23]

The demand to bomb the death camps was taken up for consideration and further discussion—though ultimately without result. On

July 5, after the Vrba-Wetzler report had reached the Foreign Office, Eden was asked in the House of Commons whether he had "any information as to the mass deportation of Jews now proceeding from Hungary to Poland for the purpose of massacre" and whether "there are any steps which the United Nations can take to prevent . . . the total annihilation of European Jewry by Hitlerite Germany?"

Eden replied that he had "no definite information though there are . . . strong indications . . . that the German and Hungarian authorities have already begun these barbarous deportations and that in the course of them many persons have been killed." As to steps the United Nations could take, he said, "there are unfortunately no signs that the repeated declarations made by HMG in association with the other United Nations of their intention to punish the instigators and perpetrators of these frightful crimes have moved the German Government and their Hungarian accomplices. . . . The principal hope of terminating this tragic state of affairs must remain the speedy victory of the Allied nations."

Mr. Sydney Silverman: Does the information the Foreign Secretary has tend "in any way to confirm . . . that in recent days the number of the deported amounted to 400,000, of whom the number killed amounts already to 100,000?"

Eden: "In this terrible business I would really rather not give figures unless one is absolutely sure. . . . We have done all we can and we shall do all we can."[24]

With this statement in mind, it seems, he deigned to receive Weizmann and Sharett the next day, July 6, 1944. Their principal aim was to expedite Brand's return to Budapest—they had not yet given up on striking a deal or gaining time—but they also brought up again the JAE's request "that the railway line leading from Budapest to Birkenau, and the death camps at Birkenau and other places, should be bombed." Toward the end of their discussion, Eden told his visitors that "as regards bombing," he had "already got into touch with the Air Ministry about the bombing of the death camps. He would now add the suggestion about bombing the railway." So impressed were Weizmann and Sharett that the latter was quick to impart the good news to Ben-Gurion, who told the JAE that Sharett "informed us that

London agreed to the suggestion to bomb the railway lines between Hungary and Poland." Gruenbaum repeated the news to Barlas.[25]

Eden reported on this interview that same day to Churchill, claiming that Weizmann "recognized that there was little HMG could do." Weizmann had suggested, though, that something might be done "to stop the operation of this death camp [Auschwitz]" by bombing the railway lines to it and to "similar camps," and also by bombing the camps themselves "so as to destroy the plant used for gassing and cremation."

In his minute to Churchill, Eden added that he had told Weizmann "that I would now re-examine it and the further suggestions of bombing the camps themselves." To Churchill he avowed: "I am in favour of acting on both suggestions." Churchill replied on July 7, giving Eden his all-out support for the bombing proposals: "You and I are in entire agreement. Get anything out of the Air Force you can, and invoke me if necessary."[26]

It must be noted here that the JAE had asked for Allied bombing. The impression that it particularly requested Royal Air Force bombing was created, perhaps, by Eden reporting that Weizmann "recognized that there was little HMG could do," and by Churchill's urging Eden to "get anything out of the Air Force you can." However, there can be no doubt that the JAE left the choice of air force to the Allies themselves. In a cable to Wise and Goldmann in New York, and to Sharett in London, Gruenbaum called on the "United Nations"* to bomb and destroy "railway lines leading [to] Oswiecim" and "Oswiecim [the death camp] itself." This was also the understanding of the War Department in Washington, in referring to the request for "Anglo-American action in the matter of the death camps."[27]

Indeed, what good reason could the JAE have to insist on a Royal Air Force bombing or reject one by the U.S. Army Air Force?

Churchill's intercession, if genuine, could have meant that he was

---

* Gruenbaum told the Actions Committee in August that the Russians had rejected out of hand the JAE's demand that they bomb the death camps from their nearby air bases. The Russians' answer was that "they are not engaged in the rescue of Jews or Tartars, but in the rescue of human beings as such."

World War II
European Theater 1944

Combat Range[a] of some American and British War Planes
versus distance to Auschwitz-Birkenau (in miles)

DISTANCE FROM BASE TO TARGET AND BACK

Foggia[b] (Italy)–Auschwitz–Foggia	(617)	1,234
Foggia–Ostrava[c]—Foggia	(592)	1,184
Foggia–Blechhammer[d]–Foggia	(625)	1,250
Foggia–Warsaw–Foggia	(787)	1,574
Lincoln[e] (England)–Auschwitz–Lincoln	(875)	1,750
Lincoln–Ostrava–Lincoln	(841)	1,682
Lincoln–Blechhammer–Lincoln	(826)	1,652
Lincoln–Warsaw–Lincoln	(903)	1,806

COMBAT RANGES

Bombers

British made Lancaster III[f]	2,250
American made B-17G (Flying Fortress)[g]	2,000
American made B-24J (Liberator)	2,290

Fighters and Attack Aircraft

British made Mosquito XVI (bomber)	1,370
British made Mosquito 2[h] (fighter-bomber)	1,860
British made Mosquito VI (fighter-bomber)	1,860
American made P51-D (Mustang)[i]	2,300

Distances to Auschwitz

From Blechhammer	(50 20 N 18 13 E)	48
From Ostrava	(49 50 N 18 15 E)	45
From Bohumin (Odenburg)	(49 55 N by 18 20 E)	39
From Most (Bruex)[j]	(51 31 N 13 39 E)	248

---

[a] Distances by Israel's Institute of Geodesy, Mapping & Geographic Information, Feb. 5, 1996.
[b] Base of U.S. 15th Air Force.
[c] Formerly Moravská Ostrava, an industrial center in north Moravia heavily bombed by the Allies in 1944.
[d] German name of Blachownia Slaska, near Kozle (Cosel), also known as Auschwitz IV, site of the often bombed Oberschlesische Hydriewerke (Upper Silesian Hydrogenation Works), a chemical complex producing synthetic fuel.
[e] Base of British Royal Air Force and U.S. 8th Air Force.
[f] With 14,000-lb bomb load only 1,660 miles.
[g] There were several versions of the B-17 Flying Fortress used by U.S. air forces and the Royal Air Force, some with shorter, some with operational range.
[h] The major Mosquito variant.
[i] The P-51D was the most common version of the P-51. It saw service in the Royal Air Force as well.
[j] Site of an oil refinery in the Sudeten region, one of the targets bombed by US 8th Air Force in the May 12, 1944, oil offensive, and thereafter.

Map sources appear on page 285.

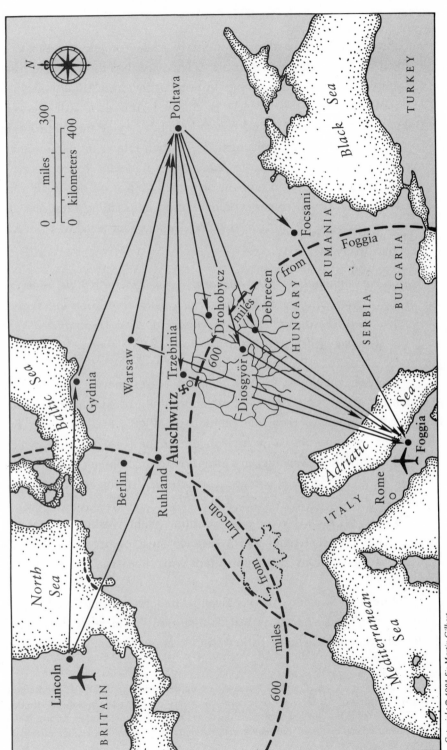

unequivocally for according the military rescue of Jews, in this case Hungary's Jews, a far higher priority. This, needless to say, could have represented an important change in both British and Allied policy. In late January 1944 the recently established American War Refugee Board (WRB)* had requested British help in carrying out its program of rescue. The British government, as Wyman relates in his illuminating *The Abandonment of the Jews*, "was reluctant to cooperate," partly because the presence of the Secretary of War on the WRB "implied that the armed forces would be used in rescuing refugees." In trying to reassure the British, the War Department set down the following policy:

> *It is not contemplated that units of the armed forces will be employed for the purpose of rescuing victims of enemy oppression unless such rescues are the direct results of military operations conducted with the objective of defeating the armed forces of the enemy.*[28]

This policy rule—a closely guarded secret, never given as the grounds for rejecting all pleas for the bombing of Auschwitz and the railroads—failed to reconcile London to WRB's establishment. For there was yet another cause for concern at the Foreign Office, which was quick to draw Washington's attention to the "danger if impression would be given that [the] two governments are drifting apart in refugee policy."

To head off such development London sought Washington's assurance "that [WRB's] relief and assistance must of necessity be comprised of such actions as are consistent with successful prosecution of the war."

Before long Washington was given to understand that London saw this consistency menaced by WRB's intention "to increase the flow of [Jewish] refugees through Turkey from occupied areas." This, clearly,

---

* On January 22, 1944, President Roosevelt set up, by executive order, "a War Refugee Board consisting of the Secretary of State, the Secretary of the Treasury and the Secretary of War, to take action for the immediate rescue from the Nazis of as many as possible of the persecuted minorities of Europe—racial, religious or political—all civilian victims of enemy savagery."

put London's Palestine policy and its White Paper in grave danger. Washington lost no time in allaying these new British fears. It was planned, the State Department told the Foreign Office, to evacuate Jewish refugees, if possible, to Hungary [at that time still unoccupied], Switzerland, Sweden, Spain, and North Africa—as a matter of fact anywhere except Palestine. Furthermore, Washington agreed to a joint refugee policy—aptly disguised as Middle East policy—which was eventually hammered out by the two governments in London in April 1944.[29]

For if London dreaded an influx of Jewish refugees to Palestine and, for different reasons, to the United Kingdom, Washington was equally inhospitable. When John W. Pehle, the executive director of WRB, advised Roosevelt, on March 29, to bring in Jewish refugees to the United States by presidential executive order as a measure for their rescue—because he thought it would be impossible to get the consent of Congress—Secretary of War Henry L. Stimson put up, before the secretary of state, the following squashing objection:

Our present immigration laws were the result of a very deeply held feeling of our people that the future immigration of racial stocks should be so limited as to coincide with the existing ratio of such stocks already within the country. Furthermore these laws were adopted at the close of the last war by overwhelming majorities of our Congress for the purpose of preventing the entrance into this country of large blocks of immigrants who were likely to come from the very countries in which most of the present refugees with whom we are concerned now originate. Our people then showed that they strongly feared that an uncontrolled immigration from such countries would modify the proportion of the racial stocks already existing in our own populations and would with difficulty be assimilated into our own population and brought into conformity with our own institutions and traditions. . . . [This] proposal would meet with a similiar reaction from our people today who would feel that it was merely the beginning of a permanent immigration.[30]

Either way, priority for saving Jewish lives by bombing the death camp and deportation railroads remained low. Given that the

Auschwitz death machinery stopped operating on November 29, 1944, and assuming a positive response to Churchill's instruction of July 7, there were left only 145 days to save the camp's victims by bombing. Since Auschwitz's output fluctuated between 2,000 to 10,000 lives a day, every minute was precious.

Indeed, Eden took action at once, or so it seemed. On the day he received Churchill's instruction, July 7, he wrote to Secretary of State for Air Sir Archibald Sinclair describing the "further information" Weizmann had brought him, according to which 400,000 Hungarian Jews had already been deported to "what he called 'death camps'" at Birkenau. Eden's letter continued: "Dr Weizmann . . . suggested, *and both the prime minister and I are in agreement with his suggestion* [italics added], that something might be done to stop the operation of the death camps by (1) bombing the railways lines leading to Birkenau (and to any other similar camps if we get to hear of them*);[31] and (2) bombing the camps themselves with the object of destroying the plant used for gassing and burning. I should add that I told Weizmann that, as you may know, we had already considered suggestion (1) above, that I would reexamine it and also the further suggestion of bombing the camps themselves."

According to Gilbert, Eden's letter was drafted for him by A. E. Walker of his staff. Before signing the draft, Eden deleted the phrase in italics. In the original draft, too, the account of Weizmann's suggestions was followed by "Could you let me know some time soon how the Air Ministry view the feasibility of these proposals?" Eden deleted the words "some time soon." Then he added: "I very much hope that it will be possible to do something. I have the authority of

---

* As a matter of fact, Auschwitz-Birkenau was the only active death camp among the six concentration camps in July 1944. Belzec operated between March and December 1942, and Chelmo from December 1941 until April 1943 (and again, very briefly, in summer 1944). Since October 1941, 60 percent of Majdenek's inmates had died of vile conditions, and the rest by gassing and shooting; it was shut down in July 1944. Sobibor operated between April 1942 and October 1943; and Treblinka from July 1942 to August 1943. Having broken German ciphers, British intelligence had known for certain since February 1943 of the existence of Auschwitz and of all other Nazi concentration camps—except Belsen—where "unexplained" deaths took place.

the Prime Minister to say that he agrees."[32] It seems, then, that Eden's support for this action was not quite wholehearted.

It is well to note that neither Eden nor Churchill commented on Auschwitz being inside or outside the Royal Air Force's range. This seems all the stranger since Eden told both Weizmann and Churchill that he had "already got into touch with the Air Ministry about the bombing of the death camps." If so, something about the range must have been said to him. Yet neither at the outset of the negotiation with the JAE nor at its close did the Foreign Office ever bring up this issue, destined to fuel a hot and lasting controversy among historians, analysts, and survivors.

At that stage of the war it was common knowledge among the Allied air high command that "Oswiecim" in Upper Silesia—as the U.S. Fifteenth Air Force* identified the I.G. Farben synthetic oil and rubber plants (known also as Buna Werke) at Monowitz, 2.5 miles west of the death camp (Auschwitz)—was well within range of Allied bombers. This large industrial complex had drawn its workforce from the death camp and was designated by the Germans as Auschwitz III.

Already on April 4, 1944, an American aerial reconnaissance plane had taken twenty exposures of "Oswiecim."[33] On three of these the death camp itself appeared for the first time. The intelligence report interpreting these photographs identified the industrial installations at Monowitz but took Auschwitz to be another labor camp. On May 31 Birkenau (Auschwitz II) itself was photographed. But this time too aerial intelligence failed to identify it for what it was. On June 26 a third series of photographs was made. Again only the industrial installations at Monowitz were identified and recognized. The same thing occurred on July 8.

Thus since April 1944 "Oswiecim" the plant had been recognized as a potential Allied bombing target. Auschwitz-Birkenau the death camp was seen as just one more labor camp and of no particular interest.

---

* The U.S. Fifteenth Air Force, which had operated since December 1943 from southern Italy, reached full strength in the spring of 1944 and started pounding industrial complexes in Central and East Central Europe.

On June 2 "Oswiecim" was marked for bombing by U.S. heavy bombers and fighter-bombers, and Operation Frantic was launched. This was a United Kingdom-Italy-USSR-Italy-United Kingdom shuttle system that enabled U.S. and Royal Air Force bombers and fighters, flying either from Britain or Italy, to extend their range by using Soviet air bases at Poltava, Mirgorod, and Piryatin in the Ukraine, then fly to Italy and from there to Britain.

Operation Frantic ended on September 22, having lasted nearly four months. It had begun with the Fifteenth's bombers taking off from Foggia on June 2 and bombing the marshaling yards at Debrecen, in Hungary, on their way to Poltava. Thus Weissmandel's suggestion of bombing the rail lines from Hungary to Auschwitz was already possible early in June.[34]

On July 8 "Oswiecim"—the Monowitz plant—was photographed from the air by the Allies for the fifth time.[35] On July 18 it was designated as a bombing target for the first time.

On August 6, the U.S. Eighth Air Force's seventy-six Flying Fortresses and sixty-four fighters, flying from bases around Lincoln, England, struck the Focke-Wulf aircraft factory in Gdynia, in the north of Poland, then landed in Poltava. On the 7th, from their bases in the USSR, these war planes raided oil refineries at Trzebinia, thirteen miles northeast of Auschwitz. That same day, flying from Foggia, the U.S. Fifteenth Air Force raided Blechhammer, forty-seven miles northwest of Auschwitz. On other dates the Fifteenth's heavy bombers raided oil, iron, and chemical plants as well as marshaling yards at Ostrava and Bohumin, in Czechoslovakia—forty-five and thirty-nine miles, respectively, west of Auschwitz.

The death camp became the virtual center of a close ring of repeatedly hit targets.[36] By the end of 1944, Blechhammer, for example, had been bombed at least nineteen times, on two occasions twice a day. Blechhammer (Blachownia Slaska in Polish) was the site of a Jewish forced labor camp, established in April 1942 by the Nazis as a manpower reservoir for a work force of 5,500 men who were to build, repair, and operate the Oberschlesische Hydricwerkc (Upper Silesian Hydrogenation Works), a large petrochemical plant whose main product was synthetic fuel. On April 1, 1944, it was placed under the Auschwitz Command as Auschwitz IV.

Lieut. Victor Perlstein of Chicago, a B-17 navigator with the Fifteenth, took part in four of the Blechhammer raids. Looking back as a veteran of fifty combat missions, he wrote that secondary targets were always given in mission briefings but Auschwitz was never one of them.

Another factor must be noted: by the spring of 1944, according to official U.S. Air Force historians cited by Wyman, "the German Air Force was a defeated [and 'wrecked'] force." After April 1, "U.S. bombers were never deterred from bombing a target because of probable losses." By September, added Air Marshal Sir Arthur Harris, commander of the Royal Air Force's Bomber Command, "the air defence of Germany crumbled to pieces; the German army was driven out of France and the enemy's early warning system was lost; at the same time the ground stations for navigational aids could be moved on to the Continent and the range of [Royal Air Force bombers] greatly extended. . . . Extremely complicated operations were planned. . . . The accuracy of the attacks was far beyond all reasonable expectation."[37]

Finally, the free world's press and radio reported Allied bombings as front page news and as headlines in radio newscasts. "Shuttle to Russia Links 3 Air Forces," ran the six-column main headline of the *New York Times* on June 3, 1944, with a fine map under it. A two-column headline—"All Areas in Eastern Europe Now in Range of Bombers"—capped Drew Middleton's June 2 cable from London. "The objectives brought within the range of Russian-based heavy bombers can be divided into two groups," he wrote. "The first group comprises strategic targets such as aircraft factories, oil refineries, armament plants in Eastern Germany, Poland and Czechoslovakia. Some of these have been attacked in the past but not with great tonnage of bombs. . . . The second group includes those railroad centers and supply dumps on which Germany depends in operations on the Eastern front."

The next day, Sunday, an even larger and more detailed map

opened the paper's "Week in Review" section.[38] Like the previous day's map, it showed that the British and American war planes taking part in the shuttle bombing had to fly most of the time over German and German-held territory on their routes to and from the Ukraine— thus demonstrating that the German air force was no longer the important factor it once had been.

So well informed was the public of the shuttle operation that it was the subject of suggestions sent by private citizens to the JAE's rescue committee. One of these, dated June 2, the day the operation started, called on the JAE "to appeal to Combined Chiefs of Staff committee . . . to systematically bomb the railway lines connecting Hungary and Poland, to where Jews are transported to for massacre."[39]

It was also probably the shuttle bombing that emboldened Gruenbaum to take another unusual step. On June 30 he initiated a long interview with the New York Times Jerusalem correspondent, in which he "asserted that death factories . . . like . . . Oswiecim [and] Treblinka must be demolished" by "Allied Strategic Air Forces."

A severly truncated version (eighty-nine words) of this interview appeared on a remote inside page of the Times's July 2 issue. Although it referred to "death camps in Poland" it did not name them, nor did it mention Gruenbaum's plea to bomb them. It did state that "by June 17, 400,000 [Hungarian Jews] had been sent to Poland: the remaining 350,000 are expected to be put to death by July 24."

Quite likely Gruenbaum, chairman of the JAE's Rescue Committee, was not considered the kind of objective source that the Times respected. For four days later, on page 6, under the headline "Two Death Camps Places of Horror," the paper ran a long (842 words) summary of a 9,000-word report "by the Very Rev. Paul Vogt, head of the internationally known refugee organization, the Fluchtllingshilfe of Zurich."

This organization, the Times pointed out, "has gathered, checked and finally permitted the publication of its information." Vogt said that it was German "carelessness," engendered by more than two years of successful concealment of the existence of two "model extermination camps for Jews" at Auschwitz and Birkenau, in upper Silesia, that had finally led to the revelation of many startling facts and figures concerning their operation for the two years ended April 15, 1944, during which the execution and "disposal" of 1,715,000 Jews had been effected "without a hitch."

The *Times*'s Bern correspondent, who telephoned the summary to New York, added: "Incontrovertible confirmation of these facts and figures, Mr. Vogt admits, has been forthcoming simultaneously with the launching of a new campaign, this time directed against Hungarian Jews, some 400,000 of whom have already been deported with 'losses' of some 30 per cent en route to their 'internment' at these camps."[40] It was the prestige of the Reverend Vogt and the Bern dateline, one suspects, that enabled the *Times* to put his report at center stage, call the death camps by name, and describe their horrors at length, three privileges Gruenbaum was denied.

In August Gruenbaum was able to tell the Actions Committee that "two or three times" the Allies had bombarded targets in Silesia, "but not [nearby] Auschwitz."[41]

It is against this informational and operational background that the rest of Churchill's "intercession" must now be told.

On July 15 Sinclair replied to Eden's letter of the 7th. He had examined the possibility of bombing for the purposes of "(a) interrupting the railways (b) destroying the plant (c) other interference with the camps" and had been advised by his staff "that (a) is out of our power . . . the distance of Silesia from our bases entirely rules out our doing anything of the kind." He added, however, that bombing "might be carried out by the Americans by daylight but it would be a costly and harardous operation. It might be ineffective . . . and I am not clear that it would really help the victims." He therefore saw "just one possibility, and that is bombing the camps, and possibly dropping weapons at the sane time, in the hope that some of the victims may be able to escape." He ended by "proposing to have the proposition put out to the Americans, with all the facts, to see if they are prepared to try it. . . . I will let you know the result when the Americans have considered it."

Calling on the Americans is arguably the best proof that the JAE had been understood to request Allied bombing. But Sinclair must have been aware of the already cited Anglo-American policy banning employment of "units of the armed forces . . . for the purpose of rescuing victims of enemy oppression." In all probability he could have anticipated the American reaction—if he did not already know it.

Eleven days before,[42] on July 4, John J. McCloy, Assistant Secretary of War, who played a major role in opposing the bombing pleas, wrote to John W. Pehle, the executive director of the War Refugee Board, that the proposal to bomb "certain sections of railway lines between Hungary and Poland . . . to interrupt the transportation of Jews from Hungary" was, in the opinion of the War Department, "impracticable. It could be executed only by the diversion of considerable air support essential to the success of our forces now engaged in decisive operations and would in any case be of such very doubtful efficacy that it would not amount to a practical project." As late as November 10, 1944, McCloy kept insisting that Birkenau could be attacked only from distant British bases, and that this "would necessitate a round trip flight of approximately 2,000 miles over enemy territory"—as if he had never heard of the Fifteenth at Foggia, Italy, and its raids on "Oswiecim." Nearly forty years later McClelland would comment that "the abysmal lack of understanding of what was happening at Auschwitz [where between mid-May and mid-July of 1944 over 400,000 Hungarian Jews were gassed] on the part of the American military authorities is embodied in the letter McCloy sent Leon Kubowitzki on August 14, 1944, when he observes: 'There has been considerable opinion to the effect that such an effort [i.e., the bombing], even if practicable, might provoke even more vindictive action by the Germans.' "[43]

Or was Sinclair simply hitting the ball back into Eden's court, to invite Churchill's intercession at America's highest political and military level? Hadn't Churchill urged Eden to "invoke me if necessary"?[44] Great war leader that Churchill was, it would make sense to expect him to have taken on the challenge—perhaps even to turn the military rescue of death camp internees into one of the Allied war aims. Alas, the records show that July 7 was the last time he was involved in the matter.

Was the Royal Air Force, then, truly unable to reach Auschwitz and the Hungarian railroads from its bases in England as Sinclair had indicated to Eden?

In examining the question it must be borne in mind that Prime Minister Churchill was also Minister of Defence, and must have well known the capabilities of the Royal Air Forces when instructing Eden. As prime minister he must certainly have been party to the ongoing Operation Frantic and perhaps also to the Royal Air Force's plans for its part in the operation. He may have not known the fine points, but he had no equal in his taste for grand strategy and far-reaching initiatives, especially those dependent on Stalin's consent. It is therefore inconceivable that Churchill did not know, if he wanted to, that Auschwitz was within the reach of the Royal Air Force and the U.S. Eighth and Fifteenth Air Forces. And there is no better proof of this than the aid these forces had given to the Warsaw uprising.

During August and September, in twenty-two nights of operations, two full Royal Air Force Liberator squadrons plus smaller units—181 heavy aircraft in all—took off from Mediterranean bases, appeared over Warsaw, and dropped arms and supplies to Polish resistance fighters. On September 18 the last Operation Frantic mission, a large-scale operation from England escorted by the Eighth, used the shuttle bases in Russia. One hundred ten B-17s and 150 Mustangs dropped more arms and supplies on Warsaw; sixty-four of the Mustangs landed in Poltava, the rest in Foggia.[45] Auschwitz, located in the southwestern corner of Poland, was more accessible than Warsaw and just as worthy.

In the light of these operations Sinclair's statement that the distance of Silesia from Royal Air Force bases "entirely rules out our doing anything" to bomb Auschwitz completely contradicted the facts.

True, the Royal Air Force was confined to "night" and "area" bombing and unable to carry out precision daylight bombing. It therefore could not, as Sinclair pointed out, pinpoint destruction of Auschwitz's railway lines, gas chambers, and crematoria. But this was true of nearly all other Royal Air Force bombardments.

What is more, Sinclair's assertion is contradicted by a statement by "Bomber" Harris, the legendary British air marshal, who wrote that by the middle of 1944 his planes could make "precision attacks . . . against targets as distant as . . . Brux in Czechoslovakia."[46] During the shuttle bombing they could have made such attacks against Auschwitz just as easily.

Precision was not even the JAE's primary consideration.* In its memorandum of July 11 to the Foreign Office—drafted by Sharett— the JAE made it clear that bombing the death camps was "hardly likely to achieve the salvation of the victims to any appreciable extent" and that it might "possibly [bring] the hastening of the end of those already doomed." The "main purpose" of the bombing of Auschwitz, the JAE's note went on, "should be its many-sided and far-reaching moral effect." Namely, to inform the Nazis and their collaborators, as well as their victims, that there was no tacit agreement by the Allies and the free world to the massacre of Europe's Jews, and that the murderers would not go unpunished. This moral effect, the JAE said,

would mean, in the first instance, that the Allies waged direct war on the extermination of the victims of Nazi oppression—today Jews, tomorrow Poles, Czechs, or whatever race may become the victim of mass murder during the German retreat and collapse. Secondly, it would give the lie to the oft-repeated assertions of Nazi spokesmen that the Allies are not really so displeased with the work of the Nazis in ridding Europe of Jews. Thirdly, it would go far toward dissipating the incredulity which still persists in Allied quarters with regard to the reports of mass extermination perpetrated by the Nazis. Fourthly, it would give weight to the threats of reprisals against the murderers by showing that the Allies are taking the extermination of Jews so seriously as to warrant the allocation of aircraft resources to this particular

---

* This is the answer to arguments such as that of Richard Foregger, in the *Journal of Military History* 59 (October 1995); 687–96. He asserts that "claims" that the map of Auschwitz-Birkenau from the Vrba-Wetzler report and the "Topographical Sketch of the Concentration Camp at Oswiecim drawn according to the description of a former prisoner of the camp would have enabled Allied bombers to locate and destroy the killing installations are not valid" because the maps were inaccurate and therefore were useless. However, the JAE never asked for precision bombing, or for absolute destruction of the death machinery.

operation, and thus have a deterrent effect. Lastly, it would convince the German circles still hopeful of Allied mercy of the genuineness of Allied condemnation of the murder of the Jews, and possibly result in some internal pressure against a continuation of the massacres. The first report that the RAF or the American Air Force had bombed the death camps in upper Silesia is bound to have a demonstrative value in all these directions.[47]

What happened then to Churchill's intercession? Eden wrote that Sinclair's reply to his July 7 letter was "a characteristically unhelpful letter. I think that we should pass the buck to the ardent Zionists, in due course, i.e. tell Weizmann that we have approached Sir A. Sinclair & suggest he may like to see him." This suggestion must be viewed in the light of Eden's earlier remark that at least one of his colleagues "should be there to see these two Jews." Nevertheless, he noted that Sinclair "wasn't asked his opinion of this. He was asked to act."

It seems that Eden was pleased by this failure. Otherwise he would have clashed with the Foreign Office over the episode known as Horthy's Offer.

Earlier that month, newspapers and diplomatic sources had reported that Admiral Miklos Horthy, regent of Hungary, had ordered that, effective July 7, 1944, all deportations of Jews be stopped. The Red Cross was authorized "to direct the evacuation of Jewish children to countries willing to receive them," even to Palestine. A fortnight later Horthy broadcast his order to his nation.* Randall of the Foreign Office Refugee Department noted on July 19: "This raises big issues, i.e. we may have a flood of applications to enter Palestine etc. We shall have to be careful."[48] On August 17, however, the British and U.S. governments announced that they had both decided to accept Horthy's offer to release Hungary's Jews and would "make arrangements for

---

* Believing that the American air force bombardment of the Budapest railway terminal on July 2, 1944 was the result of Jewish pressure exerted in Washington, Horthy informed the Germans on July 3 of his decision to stop all deportations (Dina Porat, *Hanhagah beMilkud* [Tel Aviv: Am Oved, 1986], p. 379).

the care of such Jews leaving Hungary who reach their frontiers from Hungary." This caused grave concern at the Foreign Office.*

On August 25 Ian Henderson minuted that the government would "undoubtedly be subjected to severe pressure in the US and elsewhere to allow such people to enter Palestine." Such a proposal, he emphasized, "could not be entertained for one moment."[49]

The deportations from Hungary to Auschwitz stopped on July 9, but only briefly. Schwalb claims that Horthy's offer resulted in the cancellation of only one rail transport. In mid-August Gruenbaum told the Actions Committee, "I know of no changes." By the end of August he was better informed, having received "uncomfirmed reports" of "recommenced deportations," and "one reliable report" of a transport of 15,000 "just been [sic] sent to Germany." He cabled to Sharett and others in the free world that the new Hungarian government had ordered resumption of the transports.[50]

Indeed, Horthy's regime was overthrown by the Nazi-like Hungarian Cross Arrow, and the transports were renewed with a shipment of Budapest Jews on October 15. Besides, Eichmann found other means of deportation: On November 8 thousands of Budapest Jews were forced, by his order, to walk toward labor camps in Austria, and many died on the way.[51] Thus whatever effect Horthy's offer had in Hungary, in Auschwitz the gas chambers weren't idle for a moment. They fed on transports from Corfu, Athens, Rhodes; from northern Italy; from Transylvania; from Paris, Belgium, Berlin, Slovakia; from other concentration camps that had outlived their usefulness, and from the Lodz ghetto in Poland. Tens of thousands more Jews went up in smoke before the gas chambers were finally turned off.[52]

At the Foreign Office, however, Horthy's offer engendered what might be called a welcome confusion. Some officials thought Auschwitz was no longer a bombing priority. Roger Allen, of the Foreign Office intelligence liaison, noted that he knew of no information "sug-

---

* The Foreign Office also warned Washington that "the Representatives of the Jewish Agency appear to be about to exert heavy pressure in favour of greatly increased Jewish immigration to Palestine as a corollary to the offer of the Hungarian Government."

gesting that Jews are being gassed and burnt at Birkenau. It may well be so but I cannot recall having seen any recent information."[53]

These remarks were telling signals of a Foreign Office retreat, what Gilbert calls "the final deception." At least the Air Ministry suspected as much, and there ensured a dispute as to which ministry was to blame for dropping the bombing of Auschwitz-Birkenau. It seemed at times like a wrestling bout between two oiled adversaries; the Foreign Office, being better oiled, was far more slippery.

Outwardly it did pretend to be seriously considering the bombing requests. Weizmann and Sharett in London, and Gruenbaum in Jerusalem, all exerted their utmost efforts in pleading for the bombing. What more could they have done? Yet the more they pleaded, the more they exposed their helplessness.

Since the July 7 letter to Sinclair, the Foreign Office had failed to provide the Air Ministry with the ground photographic intelligence on Auschwitz it needed to plan a pinpoint air raid, although such intelligence was available. Air Commodore Grant protested in a letter to William Cavendish-Bentinck, chairman of the Joint Intelligence Committee of the Chief of Staff: "I am perturbed at having heard nothing from the Foreign Office about the problem of Birkenau since [Roger] Allen telephoned me on the 5th of this Month [August]." Grant went on to explain, "The information at present in our [the Air Ministry's] possession is insufficient for a reconnaissance aircraft to have a reasonable chance of obtaining the cover [intelligence] required" for photographing "the camps and installations in the Birkenau area." And "only the Foreign Office can obtain [through the secret intelligence services] the information which I need."

Moreover, Grant felt the Foreign Office was having second thoughts about the priority of bombing Auschwitz: "In his conversation Allen hinted that the Foreign Office were tending to reconsider the importance that they had placed upon the liberation of the captives at Birkenau." But if it was fresh information, Grant went on, that had led Eden "to revise his opinion it will be necessary for him to inform the Secretary of State for Air who will, no doubt, then modify or rescind the instructions which he has issued to the Air Staff." Grant must, therefore, have taken Allen's hints and Eden's prolonged silence to mean that the Foreign Office was attempting to back off from its urgent request for the bombing of Auschwitz-Birkenau without admitting as much—or, better still, to place the responsibility for not doing so on the Air Ministry. But Grant did not fall for this maneuver: "Only if and until" the Foreign Office requested it officially and clearly would the priority—"Which is now of the very highest"—of bombing Auschwitz-Birkenau be lowered.⁵⁴

How right Grant was in his suspicions of the Foreign Office's tactics is demonstrated by irrefutable evidence. The Foreign Office had obtained plans and descriptions of both Auschwitz and Treblinka from the Polish government in exile in London. The necessary ground photographic intelligence, writes Gilbert, "had in fact existed since May 31, with further aerial photographs of Birkenau having been taken on June 26." These photographs had hitherto been submitted to intelligence scrutiny only for the purpose of planning the bombing of Monowitz. But they were readily available for further study, if required, near London—meaning that there was no need for any further, risky effort to acquire such information. However, no search was made for these existing photographs, so they were never sent to the Air Ministry to enable it to plan an Auschwitz-Birkenau air raid, at any point during the JAE's inquiries of August, September, and October 1944. "Indeed," adds Gilbert, "the first analysis of the Birkenau photographs, pinpointing on them the gas chambers, crematoria, railway sidings, trains in the sidings, huts etc., was not made until February 1979, with the publication in Washington of Dino A. Brugioni and Robert G. Poirier, *The Holocaust Revisited: A Retrospective Analysis of the Auschwitz-Birkenau Extermination Complex*."

The wrestling bout continued, with neither side willing to assume responsibility for the shelving of the raid on the death camp. On August 15 Sinclair noted: "The ball is in the F.O. court."⁵⁵ Indeed, in view of the alleged termination of the Hungarian deportation, the Foreign Office suggested that the JAE in London withdraw its request for bombing. But the JAE refused and emphasized that the bombing was urgent. When Joseph Linton, the JAE political secretary in London, was told in an August 18 letter that "technical difficulties" (lack of topographical information) were causing the delay in bombing, and asked whether the JAE still "wish[ed] it [the bombing] pursued," he sent the Foreign Office plans and descriptions of both Auschwitz and Treblinka, which he had obtained from the Polish government in exile in London, Sharett, for his part, "replied affirmatively."[56]

All that remained now for the Foreign Office was to find the least disgraceful way out. On August 18 Henderson suggested putting the blame on Grant—"if the Air Ministry have strong objections [i.e., that the bombing of Birkenau would cost Allied lives and aircraft] they should say so and we can return a negative reply to the Jewish Agency"; while Allen, more manfully, suggested "(a) we put them [the Air Ministry*] in touch with the source of topographical information or (b) we tell them the whole scheme is now dead."[57]

Since it is inconceivable that the Foreign Office, even though it had traditionally done its best to diminish Jewish pressure on Palestine's doors, could have been acting according to this policy in preventing the bombing of the camps, another reason must be found. Was it callousness, the idea that this was war and Jews were its victims like any others; or the prejudicial notion that Jews were a wailing lot, always complaining; or sheer disbelief in their tales of horror? It is really hard to tell.

In any case, following very effective Allied air raids on German oil targets, the first bombing of the Monowitz industrial complex ("Oswiecim") took place on August 20. One hundred twenty-seven Flying Fortresses of the Fifteenth dropped a total of 1,336 bombs each containing 500 pounds of high explosives. The raid began at 10:32 in the evening and lasted twenty-eight minutes. Only one bomber was shot down. Considerable to heavy damage to buildings and installations was reported.

One Auschwitz inmate, who watched the raid, later recalled: "We thought, they know all about us, they are making preparations to free

---

* It is interesting that both the Foreign Office and the Air Ministry said nothing about Auschwitz being out of range nor raised Foregger's argument that the Auschwitz maps drawn from the Vrba-Wetzler report and other reports were too inaccurate to allow Allied bombers to locate and destroy the killing installations.

us, we might escape, some of us might get out, some of us might survive." But this was not to be: The bombs were targeted accurately at the industrial plant nearby. Auschwitz-Birkenau and their gas chambers, outside the targeted area, remained intact.

It would not have taken much to order the Fifteenth[58] to drop some of of those 1,336 bombs on the Birkenau gas chambers.

On September 1 a letter signed by Minister of State at the Foreign Office Richard Law was sent to Weizmann. Originally the letter was to be signed by Eden himself, but the foreign secretary perhaps wanted to avoid the interview the letter was likely to provoke Weizmann to request. "I am sorry to have to tell you," Law wrote, "that in view of the very great technical difficulties involved, we have no option but to refrain from pursuing the proposal in present circumstances."[59]

On July 25 Gruenbaum cabled Wise and Goldmann in New York urging them to press the United States to apply "measures according our previous proposals," and on August 31 he cabled Sharett in London, asking this time that Auschwitz itself be bombed."[60] On September 20, the JAE again asked the Foreign Office that Auschwitz be bombed. "We were informed some time ago," wrote Linton, "that there were technical difficulties [in the way of bombing Auschwitz] ... Since then however, we understand that the fuel depots in that [Monowitz] area have been bombed on two occasions. If the position has changed, it might perhaps be possible to reconsider the question of bombing the Camp."[61]

Linton could not have known that the reply to his request had already been given indirectly two weeks earlier, on September 6, by Deputy Chief of the Air Staff N. H. Bottomley. On that day he wrote to Lieut. Gen. Carl Spaatz, commander of the U.S. strategic air forces in Europe: "The Foreign Office have now stated that Jews are no longer being deported from Hungary and that in view of this fact and because of the serious technical difficulties of carrying out bombing they do not propose to pursue the matter further. This being so we are taking no further action at the Air Ministry and I suggest that you do not consider the project any further."[62]

On August 25 American reconnaissance planes took more aerial pictures of "Oswiecim." Again, the cameras recorded the industrial plant and nearby Auschwitz-Birkenau with its main camp, the railway sidings, the gas chambers, and the crematoria. One of the photographs showed people on the way to a gas chamber.

On September 13 the U.S. Fifteenth Air Force attacked "Oswiecim" for the second time. Despite effective antiaircraft fire the target was hit, though slightly. Nevertheless, this time a few bombs were dropped on Auschwitz-Birkenau by mistake, destroying SS barracks, killing fifteen SS men and wounding twenty-two, and damaging the railway embankment and sidings leading to the crematoria. The bombs also killed twenty-three Jews and wounded sixty-five.

Fearing exposure of the truth and retribution, since Allied victory was no longer in doubt, Himmler ordered on November 29 that the crematoria at Auschwitz be destroyed. Only then did the industrial extermination at Auschwitz come to an end, and the Auschwitz evacuees were marched westward in enormous columns.

The Fifteenth continued to attack its "Oswiecim" on December 18 and 26. On January 14, 1945, it made its twelfth photographic reconnaissance flight over the plant, and once more Auschwitz-Birkenau appeared in the photos. On January 18 the SS evacuated Auschwitz's inmates; only those who were too sick were left behind to be shot later. On the 20th the SS blew up the already largely dismantled remaining crematoria; and on that same day "Oswiecim" was bombarded by the Fifteenth for fifth and last time.[63]

On January 25 the SS shot 350 Jews remaining in the sick bay at Auschwitz. On the 26th they blew up the last remnants of the gas chambers and crematoria. On the 27th, at three in the afternoon, Soviet troops entered Auschwitz-Birkenau and Monowitz. As the saying goes, they "liberated" Auschwitz.

Why did Allied bombers on missions to Blechhammer, Ostrava, Bohumin, Trzebinia, and "Oswiecim" not train their sights on Auschwitz-Birkenau as well?

Years later, Avriel wrote: "Brand could not understand that we [the JAE's rescue mission] were here on sufferance; that we led a thinly disguised existence between enemy camps, trying to make use of the Allies, whose war we supported with all our all too meagre resources . . . the reward thrown at us was out of pity, not gratitude or deservedness."[64] Did Avriel think that this pity was not entirely innocent of mockery, but could not find the heart to say it in so many words? Or perhaps he refrained because, after all, Great Britain and the United States have done more for the Jews than any other nations.

In 1930 Ben-Gurion had written: "Our only sin is our weakness. Woe to the weak!"[65] Never in history, it seems, was this adage of his ever so fully proven. Had the inmates of Auschwitz been American, French, Swedish, Arab, or any other people with a country and a government of their own, would the Foreign Office have behaved the same way?

CHAPTER FOURTEEN

WHO WAS WHO IN PUBLIC OPINION

W HERE WAS BEN-GURION throughout Gruenbaum's "bomb Auschwitz" campaign? Not one "bomb Auschwitz" cable from him has ever been found. Formally, Gruenbaum was the chairman of the JAE's Rescue Committee and its official spokesman. In this capacity he acted and spoke for Ben-Gurion as well. As chairman of the JAE, Ben-Gurion bore the same responsibility for Gruenbaum's campaign as for any other JAE activity. Formality, however, never stood in Ben-Gurion's way; more than once, when he thought it necessary, he superseded a colleague's authority and took control himself, as he did in the case of the children's rescue project in December 1942 (see Introduction p. lxi).

The questions therefore are why did he not take the bombing campaign into his own hands, and would he have made a difference? Would the JAE's cables to London and Washington, with Ben-Gurion's name on them instead of Gruenbaum's, have tilted the Allies toward a decision to bomb the death camps and their railroad connections?

Ben-Gurion apparently did not think so. He must have thought it hardly mattered who signed the JAE's appeals; they were bound to fail to awaken world sympathy. On July 2, 1944, Gruenbaum told a JAE meeting that he intended to inform the foreign press "of our demand to stop the massacre [of Hungary's Jews] at all costs."

Ben-Gurion: "At what cost and by what means does he [Gruenbaum]* suggest the massacre be stopped?"

Gruenbaum: "Only a reporter who wishes to trip him [Gruenbaum] up would raise such a question. There is talk of the Allies destroying lines of communication in Yugoslavia. Why not destroy also the lines of communication between Hungary and Poland?"

Ben-Gurion (as if he had read Gruenbaum's mutilated interview in the *New York Times* of that same day): "There is no call for a foreign press conference. Western journalists have a completely different mentality; nothing good would come out of such a conference."[1]

Even among those Holocaust scholars who acknowledge that Ben-Gurion and the JAE did not have the means to persuade the Allies to include the mass rescue of Europe's Jews among their war aims, there are some who ask why Ben-Gurion did not rouse public opinion among Jews worldwide—and especially in the United States—to support this demand.

Here, today's distorted perception of the Yishuv in the Holocaust years creates two misperceptions. Not only are Ben-Gurion and his JAE seen as equivalent to the prime minister and government of the State of Israel, but it is assumed that today's American Jewish community and today's methods of influencing public opinion also existed in 1940–45. Another syndrome, quite the opposite of the aforementioned 1948 war and Entebbe syndromes, seems to be at work in this case: the intifada syndrome. If the Palestinians could attract worldwide attention starting in December 1987 by throwing stones at Israeli soldiers, why could not the Jews—of Palestine, the United States, and Great Britain—have done the same in the 1940s? After all, no matter how hard-pressed the Palestinians were under Israeli occupation, their situation could hardly be compared to the systematic annihilation of Europe's Jews. Why, asked the deputy editor of a mass circulation Israeli paper in 1987, did Ben-Gurion and the JAE not organize in 1942 or 1943 a 400,000-strong protest meeting in the City Hall

---

* The JAE adopted the British cabinet's practice of using the third person in its minutes, to avoid direct quotation.

Square of Tel Aviv, as their party did in 1983, opposing Israel's involvement in Lebanon?[2]

It can just as easily be asked: Why did the Palestinians not begin the intifada in 1968 or 1978? While people readily understand technological anachronism—why electricity was not used in nineteenth-century coal mines or submachine guns in the American Civil War—they lack this perception regarding the development of techniques for manipulating public opinion.

Explaining why Ben-Gurion did not mobilize public opinion in the free world for the mass rescue of Europe's Jews requires going back to his earliest days as an apprentice Zionist statesman. In a speech in Berlin on September 29, 1930, he asserted that the "recognition and sympathy" of "world public opinion," not "power politics, even if we wanted to rely on it," was "what we need for the sake of our [Zionist] endeavor."[3] From the start, then, he saw in public opinion a powerful force he should strive to win over. When he first joined the JAE in 1933, he told Weizmann—whose strong suit was his high-level personal connections in Whitehall—"that we must now address ourselves especially to public opinion, to the press."[4] In January 1936, in reaction to signs that the British government was going to restrict Jewish immigration to Palestine, he noted in his diary that "the German disaster must serve as a lever . . . British public opinion is affected . . . and showing interest and sympathy in the fate of Germany's Jews. On this basis we must approach HMG." He told a JAE meeting, "there are chances for success only by influencing British opinion."[5] That year he referred frequently to the important role of British opinion: "in terms of our [political] action, the English people is the big newspapers, Parliament members and ministers"; and "we are facing a bitter political struggle; our referee is the British people and its public opinion."[6] In August 1936 he wrote to his party: "English public opinion is our principal and crucial support besides the Jewish people."[7] Tirelessly he repeated this refrain.

As the war developed and his trust in the Allied victory grew stronger, he broadened his view of public opinion to include all "the English-speaking" nations. In 1941 he wrote guidelines for Zionist strategy—which the British censors photographed while examining his luggage before he boarded a ship to America—in which he asserted that with Hitler's defeat the English-speaking nations would have the decisive voice in the postwar world order. Zionism, therefore, must address itself to American-British opinion.[8]

In July 1943 he told the Zionist Actions Committee that "the primary task of our Zionist policy is to bring to the attention of the world—to the attention of the English-speaking world—these two facts: The harrowing disaster of agonized Jewry and the [absorptive] capability of Jewish Palestine. These two facts must be brought to the attention of the English and the American peoples."[9]

Ben-Gurion's failure to awaken public opinion in Britain and America to the need to rescue Europe's Jews cannot therefore be attributed to either political myopia or lack of trying. The reasons lie elsewhere, and the two major ones are intertwined. The first is the complete overshadowing of Ben-Gurion by Weizmann; the other, what Justice Brandeis and Robert Szold (Brandeis's right-hand man in dealing with Zionist affairs) referred to as the "timidity" of America's Jews and their leaders. This second reason will be dealt with in the next chapter.

It is hard today to realize that before and during the years 1940–45, Ben-Gurion was completely dwarfed by Chaim Weizmann. Weizmann, as already noted, was the undisputed world leader of the Jews, Zionists and non-Zionists alike—especially in the English-speaking countries. Feeling equally at home in Great Britain and America, Weizmann was well aware of the weakness of the Jewish communities in both countries, a weakness Ben-Gurion himself referred to in Hebrew as "cowardliness." For this reason, Weizmann chose to convey their demands for rescue through secret diplomatic channels—a strategy he felt very comfortable with, and which perfectly suited his personality and talents. Since American Jewish leaders welcomed this strategy, it is clear that if Ben-Gurion had set out to contravene it he would have been roundly defeated. Jewish leaders, both lay and religious, saw in Weizmann the only leader qualified to speak in the name of the Jewish people. This opinion reflected his status in both Whitehall and the White House. By the same token, the attitude of these leaders toward Ben-Gurion reflected his inferior status. To be precise, he was a near nonentity.

It can be assumed that the political leadership at the time—Jewish and non-Jewish—looked for information and orientation to the leading print media, *The Times* in Great Britain and the *New York Times* in America. If this assumption is correct, it is also reasonable to assume that exposure in their pages can serve as a guide as to who was who in world and national politics. By this criterion, Ben-Gurion could not compete with American Jewish leaders, and even less with Weizmann.

Between 1919, the year they began their postwar Zionist leadership (Weizmann as head of the World Zionist Organization and Ben-Gurion as head of United Labor in Palestine), and December 1946 (when Weizmann lost his presidency and Ben-Gurion gained the defense portfolio, in addition to his chairmanship of the Zionist Executive), Weizmann had far more visibility in both *The Times* and the *New York Times*. Whereas Weizmann was mentioned in 673 news items, editorials, articles, and letters to the editor, Ben-Gurion was mentioned in only 53. Leaving out 1946, a year when Weizmann had 76 mentions and Ben-Gurion 22, the totals are 597 for Weizmann against Ben-Gurion's 31.*

Weizmann, laureate of the Balfour Declaration, the foundation on which the Zionist Yishuv was built, gets notices in both papers not only as head of the Zionists and their president, or as the only identifiable Zionist Jewish voice, or for his diplomatic dexterity and public speaking. He is newsworthy in more than one category. Both papers run profiles and interviews, showing him meeting nobles and heads of state. He is received at the White House in 1919 by President Woodrow Wilson, and later by Presidents Warren Harding, Calvin Coolidge (twice), Franklin Roosevelt (twice), and Harry Truman (twice). In 1923 the papers report audiences with Victor Emmanuel III, king of Italy, Pope Pius XI, and Italian statesman Alcide de Gasperi. In 1939 they cover Weizmann's two interviews with British prime minister

---

* These comparisons are based on the annual indexes of *The Times* and the *New York Times,* and therefore represent close estimates more than definitive figures.

Neville Chamberlain and his testimony before the Tory Committee for Imperial Affairs. His contacts with Winston Churchill are noted, as are his ties with other British statesmen and generals. In 1931 Weizmann is reported to turn down a Tory offer to run for Parliament. In 1941 the *New York Times* notes his meetings with the British ambassador in Washington, Lord Halifax.

His achievements in chemistry are also covered. Weizmann, a professor at Manchester University, had made a major contribution to the British war effort by inventing a process that yielded acetone, a solvent needed to produce munitions. On his seventieth birthday in 1944, the papers report the congratulations of South Africa's prime minister Field Marshal Jan Smuts and scores of others, among them Henry Wallace, Lord Halifax, Henry Morgenthau Jr., Senator Robert Wagner, and the president of Harvard University. In 1936 Weizmann is elected one of the ten great Jews of his generation.

Both papers report his changing moods, the state of his health, his travels, dinners, and speeches. As early as 1923 they highlight his close ties with American Jewry; in 1936 he is guest of honor at a dinner given him by their leaders. In 1942 his name is registered in the Jewish National Fund's golden book, and his conversations with Jewish leaders in Great Britain and America receive repeated coverage. He is also the subject of human interest stories, as when his younger son, Michael Weizmann, an RAF pilot, is reported missing and presumed killed in action.

Needless to say, in those years Ben-Gurion never came close to this status. Except for one meeting in 1931 with Ramsay MacDonald, the first Labour prime minister, in his capacity as secretary general of the Histadrut, the Yishuv's labor federation, in his twenty-seven years as the Histadrut's secretary and the JAE's chairman, Ben-Gurion never met a sitting British prime minister. His efforts in 1941 and 1942 to see Roosevelt resulted in a meeting with Benjamin (Ben) Cohen, a member of Roosevelt's circle of advisers, and Judge Samuel I. Rosenman, Roosevelt's personal counsel and chief speechwriter; this was the highest he ever got in the White House until he met John F. Kennedy on May 30, 1961, in New York, two years before he retired from Israel's government.

As late as 1947 Ben-Gurion appeared in the news columns only in his role as a Zionist. Between 1935, when Ben-Gurion was elected chairman of the JAE, and September 1939, when the war broke out in Europe, he had eight mentions in *The Times* and eleven in the *New York Times*. On November 26, 1938, a letter to the editor he had written the day before was published in *The Times*. So surprised was he that he noted it in his diary as a landmark.[10]

The *New York Times* gave him a three-column story for the first time in May 1939.[11] It appeared on page 30, with Ben-Gurion's name in the subhead: "Britain Is Warned By Zionist Leader; Ben Gurion [*sic;* for a while Ben was taken for his first name[12]] Says the Proposed Plan for Palestine Creates Sort of Ghetto for Jews." In the story he is quoted as saying, in reaction to the May 1939 White Paper: "Jews who must choose between utter extinction and immigration to Palestine under conditions called illegal naturally will not waver for a moment in their choice" even though "the British have both the physical and political power to combat these unfortunate homeless people."

In 1940 and 1941 he was mentioned in six news items by the *New York Times* and not once by *The Times*. In 1942 he was mentioned only once by *The Times,* in connection with the Balfour Declaration's twenty-fifth anniversary, an event always celebrated with a reference to it as Weizmann's singular achievement. That year, thanks to the Biltmore Conference in May, Ben-Gurion was mentioned in the *New York Times* twice. Again he scored a first: on the 11th his name appeared in a three-column headline—"Ben-Gurion Outlines Program For Solving Palestine Problem"—and the story was on page 6. Here, also for the first time, Weizmann took second place. Still, although Ben-Gurion was identified by his full title, "chairman of the World Zionist Executive," the degree of his anonymity is evident in the further description of him as "Mr. Ben-Gurion, a Palestinian."[13]

On May 12, the Biltmore Conference was reported on page 5 of the *New York Times,* which mentioned Ben-Gurion and Weizmann in the same breath. It was also the nearest he had gotten thus far to the front page. On May 26, the paper gave all the credit for the conference to Weizmann.[14] It is clear that Ben-Gurion's two mentions in the *New York Times* in 1942 occurred because he appeared on the American

Jewish scene. Once he was back in Palestine, he receded into the shadows.

In retrospect, it is noteworthy that the New York paper recognized Ben-Gurion as the author of two of the Biltmore Program's most important, far-reaching articles: article 7, calling for the formation of "a Jewish military force fighting under their own flag and under the high command of the United Nations" against Hitler; and article 8, demanding "that the gates of Palestine be opened; that the Jewish Agency be vested with control of immigration into Palestine and with the necessary authority of upbuilding the country . . . and that Palestine be established as a Jewish Commonwealth. . . ." However, neither *Times* noted in later years that Ben-Gurion had been more faithful than Weizmann to the Biltmore Program.[15]

Part of the reason for his obscurity was British censorship. It took two forms. The first was the internal, tacit self-censorship of the BBC (British Broadcasting Corporation) in reporting the Jewish plight in Europe. This form of censorship primarily affected Britain itself. A 1993 British study, based on official documents of the Public Record Office and in the archives of the BBC, shows that "anti-Semitism in the higher ranks of the Foreign Office and the BBC during the Second World War led to a policy which suppressed news about Germany's attempt to exterminate European Jews."

This research demonstrates "that both Foreign Office and BBC officials held a low opinion of Jews, and believed this was shared by the public. They deduced that saving millions of Jews would not be seen as a desirable war aim by the British." News reports "could only be carried if, in the view of the BBC and the Foreign Office, they were well sourced. If the sources were Jewish, the reports tended not to be believed." Thus only when the BBC could not doubt the source, as in the case of a speech by Anthony Eden on December 17, 1942, before the House of Commons, did it mention mass extermination of the Jews.

The study quotes a policy directive issued on November 17, 1943, by BBC director general Robert Foot: "We should not promote ourselves or accept any propaganda in the way of talks, discussion, features with the object of trying to correct the undoubted anti-Semitic feeling which is held very largely throughout the country."* The BBC should confine itself to reporting in news bulletins "the facts as they are reported from time to time of Jewish persecutions as well as any notable achievement by Jews, particularly in connection with the war effort (e.g., recent case of the Jewish soldier who won the VC)." Foot added "that in the interests of the Jews themselves, this is the right policy to adopt at the present time, and any other policy would tend to increase rather than decrease the anti-Jewish feeling in this country."

In hindsight, the Foreign Office appears astonishingly skeptical about atrocities, simply because they were reported by Jews, their victims. As late as August 27, 1944, Victor Cavendish Bentinck, assistant undersecretary, was still doubting the existence of gas chambers: "I think we weaken our case against the Germans by publicly giving credence to atrocity stories for which we have no evidence."[16]

Equally malignant, and perfectly consistent with the BBC's silent self-censorship, was the open, legal censorship reigning in Palestine. To avoid it, Sharett used, as early as 1936, to fly to Cairo in order to telephone or telegraph freely to the Zionist office in London.[17] Shutting down of newspapers that disobeyed the censor's rulings was common. Guidelines promulgated in 1936 to preserve law and order were progressively broadened, with the outbreak of the war, to cover not only military operations, the war effort, and civil unrest, but also (under the rubric of civil unrest) some aspects of the plight of Europe's Jewry and protests and demands for rescue. In effect, the British used the wartime censorship to suppress any expression of protest or bitterness against either the mass murder in Europe or the shutting of Palestine's doors to refugees.

On March 5, 1940, the censorship in Palestine got some attention on page 6 of the New York Times: "The editors of two leading Hebrew

---

* This basically was the government's policy. On March 23 Viscount Samuel said in the House of Lords: "The Government say . . . that public opinion in this country must be considered; they say that there is floating about in this country a certain amount of Anti-Semitic prejudice" that must not be stirred up "into formidable opposition." (Hansard [Lords] [German Atrocities: Aid for Refugees], Mar. 23, 1943, pp. 826, 827.)

daily newspapers in Palestine have been charged with publishing matter prohibited by the censor, according to a message received today by the London office of the Jewish Agency for Palestine. One of them, Berl Katznelson, is a laborite leader and editor of *Davar*, laborite newspaper, while the other is B. Krupnick, editor of *Haaretz*. Both were released after posting 50 sterling pound bail. It is understood, says the Jewish Agency, that the charges relate to the publication of a protest issued by the Jewish National Council in Palestine against the new land regulations."[18]

On December 4, 1940, the censor prohibited the publication of the debate in the House of Commons—published by the London press—regarding the illegal immigrants aboard the *Patria* and the *Atlantic* (see Chapter 15). On February 16, 1941, the JAE was told that Ben-Gurion, who had just returned from Britain and America, had not brought his papers with him, for fear of the censorship. Instead, he had left them back in the States with Arthur Lourie, secretary of the American Zionist Emergency Committee.[19]

Whole paragraphs of Ben-Gurion's speech to the Mapai conference of March 1941 were censored, including his report on the drowning of the passengers on the refugee ship *Salvador*. This was done to suppress any news story that might reveal that the ship had been on its way to Palestine and that only inhuman suffering could have driven these refugees onto a dilapidated ship like the *Salvador*.[20]

Two weeks later, Ben-Gurion told Mapai's central committee that the British censorship in Palestine "serves not only the war's needs, nor even the White Paper's needs, but [especially] the [British] need to repress the freedom of speech of the Jews among themselves and in matters pertaining only to Jews. . . . It is inconceivable that censorship can silence us when we want to tell the Jews in Palestine that philanthropic [work] is not the solution [to the Jewish problem]. The High Commissioner doesn't allow us to tell the Jews that our future doesn't lie in philanthropy. The sentence [in my speech in the conference] that we are a people, they allowed [for publication], but [its conclusion] that we are a people like any other people, this we can't say [for publication]."

On April 27, 1941, Sharett told a JAE meeting that he had sent

Eliahu Elath—the future first Israeli ambassador to Washington—to Istanbul, to cable from there an article to the *New York Times*.[21] In March 1942 the Histadrut's executive committee was told that Ben-Gurion had smuggled out of Palestine an article to be published in the *New Judea* in London, which he was unable to publish in Palestine for fear of the censor. The article began by acknowledging that censorship in wartime was vital for preventing the enemy from getting hold of useful information. "But," it went on,

in Palestine there is a peculiar kind of censorship. For a considerable time the people in Palestine never knew there was a war on. The censorship . . . was directed against the Jews; the Jews were not allowed to know what was happening to their people in Poland. On my return to Palestine, about a year ago, from England, filled as I was with the deepest admiration for the British people, I tried to express it; I wanted to remove some of the bitterness felt against the bureaucracy in Palestine by telling the Jews of the brave and heroic people in Great Britain—people so unlike some of those who were responsible for the cruelty inflicted on Jewish immigrants. I endeavoured to tell them of the great-hearted British people. I also wanted to inform them of the position of the Jews in Rumania [sic] and Poland. But the censor interfered. I was not even allowed to say that we Jews are a people. That apparently, was regarded as giving information to the enemy.[22]

Thus—a fact of particular importance to this chapter—the "Appeal to Human Conscience,"[23] which Ben-Gurion addressed to Churchill, Roosevelt, and Stalin from the rostrum of the National Assembly at its extraordinary session of November 30, 1942, to mark the day of mourning and fasting following the JAE's official announcement of the systematic destruction going on in Nazi Europe, was severely censored in Palestine, and thus hardly noticed by the world press. The *New York Times* gave it a one-column headline—"Palestine Assembly Appeals To Allies"—and a 227-word story on page 7, which began: "Appeals to the United Nations, especially the United States, Britain and Russia, to bend every effort to terminate the slaughter of Jewish communities in Nazi held Europe and to rescue those threatened with extinction, especially the children, were made at yesterday's special session of the Jewish National Assembly." Ben-Gurion's name was omitted, as were the fact that he was the key speaker and the sentences in which he warned that the responsibility for the destruction "should be also on all those who are able to rescue but do not do so, all those who are able to prevent the destruction and will not, and all those who are able to save and will not do so." Also omitted was his call to the three leaders to "First and foremost save the Jewish children, secure admission for them to neutral countries!! Admit them to your own countries! Admit them here, to our homeland! Give them all that is in your power to escape the dungeon and the scaffold, escape to any country not under Nazi rule." And of course his condemnation of the White Paper—"as long as the gates of our country are shut to Jewish refugees—your hands too are red with the Jewish blood that is shed in the Nazi inferno"—was omitted too.

This plea, meant to shake the free world and call its attention to the extermination of Europe's Jews, was, at least as regards American and British opinion, a complete failure. This was the opinion of Anselm Reiss of the Representation of Polish Jews. The Yishuv's outcry, he told the Histadrut executive committee, "except for the *Manchester Guardian,* hardly captured the world's press for more than a day or two. We well know how governments hesitate to introduce the Jewish question into their politics."[24]

The *Guardian* was an outstanding exception. Following Ben-Gurion's speech at the National Assembly session, this paper brought up "the extermination policy" of Nazi Germany in two editorials within four days. The first strongly urged the Allied governments to "issue a joint statement putting on record their knowledge [of Germany's crimes against the Jews] and the proofs of this annihilation policy and saying formally that its fruits are included within the scope of those war crimes for which retribution will most surely be exacted." It concluded, "The other thing to be done is to lend all aid to the rescue of such Jews as somehow get away. A small number do escape and we, and all the states whom we can influence, should spring to their aid. But we must set the example."

The second editorial went even further. It called for "active rescue" and asserted that it was up to the British government "to help any country that is protecting refugees." It concluded by asking the government what it was doing to tear away the veil of secrecy shrouding the extermination of the Jews: "What directions does the Government propose to give the BBC, what instructions to our agents in European and Asiatic countries, what suggestions to our Allies?"[25]

This was certainly the strongest, if not the only, friendly—pro-Jewish, pro-Zionist—voice in the English-language press worldwide. But the event that inspired the editorials—the National Assembly session and Ben-Gurion's speech—did not itself appear in the *Guardian,* or in any other daily. Instead, the *Guardian* carried under the one-column headline "SLAUGHTER OF JEWS—A Day of Fast" the following November 29 dispatch by Palcor, the JAE's News Agency: "Rarely have the walls of the ancient monumental Hurvah Synagogue [in old Jerusalem] . . . witnessed lamentations so heart-rending as to-day during the midday service when 700 rabbis . . . the greatest rabbinic conclave since . . . two thousand years ago—gathered to beseech the Almighty's intervention against the slaughter of European Jewry. . . . The Chief Rabbi, Dr. Herzog, opened the service and proclaimed December 2 as a Day of Fast. Later the Shofar was blown amid widespread weeping. . . . Representatives of the national institutions and other notables of the Jewish community attended the service."[26] But Palcor's dispatch of November 30, on the National Assembly and Ben-Gurion's speech, did not pass the censorship. Nothing more clearly epitomizes the British government's position: Religious expressions, prayers, lamentations, and the like over the extermination, even demands upon the Almighty, were permitted; but national and political protests or demands upon Britain and the Allies were not.

Only at the end of January 1943 did the censors drop their objection to the argument that Jews were "a people like any other people." They then passed an article by Ben-Gurion, an abridged and watered-down version of his "appeal to human conscience." It was published in Palestine and *The Middle East,* a Tel Aviv trade and industry monthly. *Davar* was quick to take advantage of this opening, blazoning the appeal under a bold two-column headline on its first page: "Allow Us To Fight [Hitler] as a People!"[27]

But there was another, and more important, reason that made it impossible for Ben-Gurion to rouse world opinion: He was completely eclipsed, until the war's end, by Weizmann.

In 1943 Ben-Gurion was mentioned five times in *The Times* (London): in reference to the Biltmore Program, to Jewish underground activity in Palestine, and to his resignation from the JAE, a tactic he employed in his power struggle with Weizmann.

That year the *New York Times* mentioned him three times, twice in connection with British seizure of illegal arms from the Yishuv, and once in reference to his resignation.[28] In 1944 the New York paper passed him over completely, while the London paper gave him five news items, regarding his dispute with Weizmann, the withdrawal of his resignation, his Arab policy, a planned visit to Italy (which did not materialize), and his reaction to the murder of Lord Moyne, minister resident in the Middle East, by Lehi men (the Stern gang). In 1945 *The Times* mentioned Ben-Gurion only once, in reference to his reaction to a statement of Foreign Secretary Ernest Bevin on the situation in Palestine.[29] In America his prominence grew that year: his name appeared eight times in the *New York Times*, though not yet on its front page. He did not receive this honor until January 8, 1947, as the Yishuv's leader in its struggle against the British government and army. The *Times* (London) first gave him front-page prominence eleven months later, on November 27, quoting his call for Jewish mobilization toward the establishment of the state.[30] After that, Ben-Gurion overshadowed Weizmann in both print and electronic media.

During the war years, then, the British and American press treated Weizmann as a world-renowned leader and scientist, whereas Ben-Gurion was regarded as a little-known leader in remote Jewish Palestine, of local fame and interest only. Little wonder that the *New York Times* gave preference not only to London-based Weizmann, but to local American Jewish leaders as well. Israel Goldstein, for forty-three years the rabbi of the prominent Conservative congregation B'nai Jeshurun in Manhattan, an outstanding orator, and an important Zionist, received during the war years 238 mentions in the *New York Times*.

Running not too close a second was Rabbi Stephen Wise, famous for his sermons to his Reform congregation at the Free Synagogue in Manhattan and arguably the individual who came closest to being *the* American Jewish leader. Wise, a very prominent and influential Zionist, had 168 mentions.

The Reform rabbi Abba Hillel Silver, of Tifereth Israel Congregation in Cleveland, perhaps the greatest of all American Jewish orators (in appreciation, his congregation built him one of the largest temples in the world, with two auditoriums that could be joined to contain the High Holidays public), appeared on the American national Zionist scene only in August 1943, when he was called to head the American Zionist Emergency Council. Accordingly, during the years 1940–42 he got only 21 mentions, as against 37 in 1943–45. On November 26, 1943, he was quoted as expressing an opinion in line with Ben-Gurion's view of the timid American. Addressing the Hadassah annual convention, reported the *New York Times* on page 17, "Dr. Abba Hillel Silver . . . co-chairman of the American Zionist Emergency council, told the delegates that 'opposition to Zionism among Jews is largely rationalization of fear and a product of wishful thinking.' "[31]

All three American Zionist leaders had the upper hand over Ben-Gurion, who was mentioned nineteen times altogether in the *New York Times* during the six war years.[32]

But Weizmann, at eighty-eight mentions, did better than Silver. Given that he spent the better part of the war years in London, and that Rabbi Goldstein and Rabbi Wise were both mentioned largely as New Yorkers, in the metropolitan pages, thanks to their sermons, he may have done better than them all.

There were indeed very good reasons for Weizmann's prominence. Not the least of these was his principal rule of never clashing in public with the government of the day, either in Britain or the United States, a rule tremendously popular with leaders of the English-speaking Jewish communities. An attempt to make the mass rescue of Europe's Jews one of the Western Allies' war aims would first of all have required constant public clamor and a relentless campaign against the White House and Capitol Hill. That Ben-Gurion was fit and willing to lead such a battle is certain. That there was no chance he would be allowed to do so is certain as well. The conditions under which his tactics could be accepted did not as yet prevail. Such is the way of history: More often than not the right voice is present, but not the platform from which it can speak. The conjunction of voice and platform would occur only after the war, after the Holocaust.

CHAPTER FIFTEEN

THE TIMID AMERICAN

B EN-GURION WAS well aware of the weak position he and the JAE held in world opinion. This is evident from his remarks and proposals regarding Europe's Jews. In December 1942 he told the JAE that "the fate of Poland's Jews threatens those of Europe and beyond," and "there has never been a time when destruction awaits all of us, as it does in the time in which we live now." Thus the JAE "must concentrate (a) on rescuing Jews," although "this does not depend on us"; he himself "cannot tell whether it is possible to save many Polish Jews, but it is still possible to save the Jews of other countries." How? Supporting a proposal of Dobkin's, he said, "It is vital to publish a book on the atrocities the Nazis have perpetrated against Polish Jews and translate it into many languages, so others will know what awaits them." Obviously, if he and the JAE had had a higher status in world opinion, especially in Britain and the United States, he would not have resorted to projects of this sort. He made it quite clear that he was aware of their weakness in this regard. At that same JAE meeting he said: "We are generally in a bad position, for we have to appeal to Roosevelt to do our job for us"—that is, to reprimand Hitler and the German brass—"and there is no way of knowing whether he will do it or not."[1]

Perhaps this was why, as he reported later, "We requested our friends in Britain to demand that the British government warn the German military, through diplomatic channels and by radio broadcasts, that they will be held responsible for the massacre if they do not put an end to it." Furthermore, "We asked our friends in Britain to demand that the [British] government drop leaflets from the air . . . addressed to the Jews of Poland, and to those in other countries in which they are massacred," to reassure them "that the Jews in Palestine, Britain and America are doing all they can to save them."[2]

Menahem Ussishkin, a senior Zionist leader, was offended by these feeble measures. "We shall not beg on our knees!" he thundered at a JAE meeting. Ben-Gurion was not perturbed. "No negotiation is shameful in and of itself," he responded. It depended on the context. He himself was "ready to go on all fours, if he knew that by doing so he could save the people." To make this position completely clear, Ben-Gurion repeated it in the Zionist Actions Committee: "I am ready to go down on my knees for rescue." But, he added, "We don't have to kneel, [simply] because getting down on our knees is not going to help."[3]

To attain a position from which he could influence American opinion, Ben-Gurion would have had to go to the United States for a longer stretch than the total of fourteen and a half months he spent there at various periods between 1940 and 1945. Certainly, had he done so he would have had more opportunities to speak his mind, more freely and loudly, than he ever did in Palestine. For one thing, he would not have been silenced by British censorship.

We have already seen how this censorship interfered with his November 30, 1942 appeal to the Allies at the special session of the National Assembly in Jerusalem. Two years later, on July 10, 1944, at a ceremony marking the fortieth anniversary of Herzl's death, held on Mount Scopus, Ben-Gurion made yet another appeal to human conscience. The moment was equally ominous. Hungary's Jews were being shipped to Auschwitz at the rate of 12,000 a day, a fact Ben-Gurion referred to at the opening of his keynote address: "Herzl came to us from Hungary's Jewish community—a community now agonizing on the Nazi gallows, being shipped daily to slaughter in death cars." He had left to the Zionists as legacy and testament the obligation "to raise in the world's ears a thunderous and grievous cry." This cry, addressed to the Allies, took up the better part of Ben-Gurion's speech. It was largely construed on the immortal lines Shakespeare put in Shylock's mouth: "Hath not a Jew eyes? Hath not a Jew hands . . . ? fed with the same food, hurt with the same weapons, subject to the same diseases, healed by the same means, warmed and cooled by the same winter and summer as a Christian is? If you prick us, do we not bleed? . . . If you poison us, do we not die?"*

Here is a part of Ben-Gurion's address:

It is in line with Herzl's spirit and commandment that we raise our voice in a loud and bitter scream: What have you done to us? Not they—cruel, bloodthirsty beasts that the Nazis are. With them we have no common language or rapport—they are outside the pale of humanity. But you, what have you done to us, you freedom-loving peoples, guardians of justice, defenders of high principles of democracy and of the brotherhood of man? What have you allowed to be perpetrated against a defenseless people while you stood aside and let them bleed to death, never lifting a finger to help, never offering succor, never calling on the fiends to stop, in the language of punishment which alone they would understand? Why do you profane our pain and wrath with empty expressions of sympathy which ring like mockery in the ears of millions who are being daily burnt and buried alive in the Nazi hell centers of Europe? Why have you not even supplied arms to our ghetto rebels, as you have done for the partisans and underground fighters of other nations? Why did you not help us to establish contacts with our ghetto rebels, as you have done in the case of the partisans in Greece and Yugoslavia and the underground movements elsewhere? If instead of Jews, thousands of English, American, or Russian women, children, and the aged had been tortured every day, burnt to death, asphyxiated in gas chambers—would you have acted in the same way? . . . Isn't our blood as red as yours, our honor as dear as yours? Aren't we scorched by insult as badly as you, and is our value any lesser than yours?[4]

This time the censor allowed these lines, and they were published in full in the Hebrew *Davar*.[5] But the American and British press

---

* *The Merchant of Venice*, 3.1:47–66.

passed them up completely, apparently finding both their author and their content of no interest whatever.

Certainly, if Ben-Gurion wanted to escape the censor he should have spent the Holocaust years in the United States. Suppose he had done exactly that, on the assumption that arousing American public opinion was more important than being chairman of the JAE, the Yishuv's leader, and the supreme commander, so to speak, of its struggle for independence. Would he have been allowed to speak freely by American Jewish leaders, Zionist or non-Zionist? And if he was, would he have converted them to his line? Or—what seems more likely—would he only have alienated them and made them his fierce opponents? And if this happened, would he have had the speaking opportunities and press exposure necessary to achieve his goal?

These questions amount, in effect, to asking whether Ben-Gurion aspired to, or was able to assume, leadership of American Jewry. The evidence shows that he was willing to give it a shot. This was most probably the main goal of his almost regular visits to the United States after 1938. But there was never more than a sliver of hope for even partial success.

It was during these visits, before the war and during its early stages, that he was struck with what he termed the "cowardice" of American Jews, "a cowardice the like of which I have seen nowhere."[6] Leaders and rank and file alike, fearful for their individual and collective status, shrank from any action that might single them out as an ethnic group and stir up an anti-Semitic reaction. But the very nature of Zionism, and consequently any rallying to its support, necessarily involved asserting a distinction that was open to interpretation—as interpreted it was—as double loyalty, or in Ben-Gurion's words, "lack of American loyalty."[7] Little wonder that Ben-Gurion's strong "activist" strategy —combating immigration restrictions, raising a Jewish army, fighting the White Paper, and campaigning for a Jewish state, all of which called for the support of American opinion in fighting the British government—alarmed American Jews and rendered them uncooperative. This was particularly so when he urged them to bring pressure to bear on the White House and the administration to include the rescue of Europe's Jews among the war aims; the more he pressed them to resort to open public action, the more reluctant they became.

On January 5, 1939, he quoted in his diary Supreme Court justice Louis Brandeis, who told him that the chances of rallying the wealthy Jews in America were poor because of their "timidity."[8] A week later he quoted his good friend Robert Szold's comment that "America's Jews live in great fear of growing anti-Semitism, and quite a few were apprehensive over Felix's [Frankfurter] nomination [to the Supreme Court, as Brandeis's successor], to the extent that some of them tried to talk the president [Roosevelt] into withdrawing it." Szold "admitted . . . that nearly all Jews in the West were fearful . . . due to a Jewish inferiority complex." In a letter to his wife, Paula, Ben-Gurion wrote that "American non-Zionists are as fearful as others . . . of the growing anti-Semitism."[9] He believed it was this "timidity" that thwarted his endeavors to mobilize American Jewry to take political action and support his initiatives. At a meeting of the Zionist Emergency Committee (founded by American Zionist groups late in 1939) that heard his proposal to raise a Jewish fighting force that would also "serve to unify American Jewry" during the war, he was not well received. The members resented Ben-Gurion because he was asking them to step out of line. Their greatest fear was of being accused of divided loyalty.

Ben-Gurion used to tell the story of how, when Jewish youths in Boston's Jewish neighborhoods of Dorchester, Mattapan, and Roxbury were beaten daily in October 1943 by anti-Semitic thugs, Jewish leaders were afraid to protest against the inaction of the Boston police; it was the New York paper *PM* that publicized the incidents and called for an investigation.[10] But above all, "Jewish timidity" was symbolized for him by a Hebrew Immigrant Aid Society man he saw dealing with immigration officials on a New York pier in September 1940. The sight of this Jew "trembling before some official" etched itself deep in his mind, surpassing everything he "remembered or imagined possible only in czarist Russia."[11]

This American fearfulness became so important to him that he made curing it his first task. But his attempts at therapy encountered great resentment and he was forced to desist.[12]

In the summer of 1939 he told Mapai's central committee: "It is almost definitely futile to expect American Jewry to support us in our struggle . . . the Jews are afraid to appear as a political [ethnic] factor in Jewish matters."[13] In November 1940, during his first visit to America after the war had broken out, he wrote Paula: "I am clear on one thing: the Jews in America are in a state of fear. They fear Hitler, they fear Hitler's allies, they fear war, and they fear peace. During the [presidential] election campaign they were afraid that [Wendell] Willkie would be elected, and they were also afraid to openly back Roosevelt. The Zionists fear the non-Zionists, and the non-Zionists fear the non-Jews."[14]

Yet Ben-Gurion was not one to give up easily. In 1940 and 1941, and even as late as summer 1942, he still believed he could overcome this "timidity" and win over American Jewry. This was his primary reason for his frequent, long visits as "a Zionist preacher" (as he referred to his mission): to attempt to come between the American Jewish leaders and Weizmann, and to convert the Americans to his cause. So sure was he of the rightness of his course and of his ability to carry it through that he invited Weizmann to a showdown. This encounter was held at his initiative in Rabbi Wise's home, on Saturday, June 27, 1942, with eight bigwigs of American Zionism sitting in judgment. So ferocious was Ben-Gurion's attack on Weizmann—he called him a traitor to his face—that Wise called it "an act of political assassination."[15] This event was perhaps the high point of Ben-Gurion's attempt to win over American Zionism and with it American Jewry as a whole. He failed, however, and in October 1942 returned to Jerusalem like a wet dog with his tail between his legs.[16]

It is generally agreed that American Jewry was in fact unable to act collectively for rescue. But some scholars reject Ben-Gurion's explanation of timidity, offering different reasons. Professor Henry Feingold of the City University of New York, for example, affirms as an incontrovertible fact that "American Jewry failed to adaquately respond to the crisis, failed to adequately use the power available to it and dissipated its considerable organizational and human resources in internal strife." However, he identifies the source of this failure as the "incredible disunity within the American Jewish community." And he goes on to explain that "the bitter communal strife actually increased as the crisis developed, until it seemed as if American Jewry was more anxious to tear itself apart than to save its brethren caught in the Nazi clutches." Feingold blames this "disunity" for the failure "to send decision makers [Washington] a coherent signal" regarding the need for rescue and "to mobilize those Jews who had achieved place and power in the Roosevelt administration." When one such Jew, "Henry Morgenthau Jr., the Secretary of the Treasury and Roosevelt's closest Jewish friend, was activated it led to the establishment of the War Refugee Board and to the circumvention of the immigration law, the zenith of the American rescue effort."

So the role Ben-Gurion attributed to cowardice Feingold assigns to disunity. Is it too far-fetched to argue that these two are related? That is, those who were afraid of being perceived as a single, close-knit, secret society would refuse to unite with those who condemned their fear and called for open Jewish political action. This question must have occurred to Feingold too, for he writes, "Only for the antisemite were Jews imagined to be a unified conspiracy to dominate the world."

It would be preferable if disunity were the product of cowardice in this case, for cowardice can be overcome. The worst possibility would be that the two have nothing to do with each other. If a deep hereditary disunity, reaching back to the origins of Jewish history, is a Jewish "national trait" (so to speak), all attempts to eradicate it are destined to failure. If Feingold's emphatic conclusion is correct—"Not only was there no one to order the Jews to unify, but in America there was not even a memory of unity which might be recouped"[17]—it is silly today, as it would have been fifty years ago, to expect Ben-Gurion to remedy this and unify American Jews.

Whether or not more could have been done, Ben-Gurion was unable to do it. There was little indeed he could do in America for rescue. Influential Jews like Morgenthau were outside his sphere. To a man, they were all either non-Zionist and/or Weizmannites.

In the wake of his galling experience at Wise's home, Ben-Gurion must have concluded that, even if he did stay in America during the war years, his activist policy made it unlikely that he could attain influence equal to Weizmann's. He must therefore have decided it was better, for all concerned, that he remain in Jerusalem. He did not return to the States until mid-June 1945, after the war in Europe had ended.

By contrast, Weizmann, prince of the Jews, was revered and loved there in equal measure. One demonstration of these feelings was a letter Rabbi Wise sent the delegates to the Biltmore Conference of May 1942 just before it opened. Although Ben-Gurion had done more than Weizmann to bring the conference about, the letter emphasized Weizmann's preeminence. "We are to welcome our beloved leader Dr. Chaim Weizmann. . . . We shall also have an opportunity to hear a full report by Mr. David Ben-Gurion." Wise opened the conference itself by addressing "Dr. Weizmann, ladies and gentlemen." He continued: "This conference could not more fittingly open its deliberations than by making record of its gratitude to him who is by right of uncancelable service, the great leader of the World Zionist Movement, Dr. Chaim Weizmann." Thereupon the delegates rose to their feet, applauded, and sang in Weizmann's honor the Zionist hymn "Ha-Tikvah." Yet this manifestation was nothing compared to the dramatic, emotional close of the conference. The minutes tell the story:

Wise:

Dr. Weizmann, beloved leader and friend. You it was who . . . won the Balfour Declaration from Great Britain. (Applause) You it was who pleaded with the Paris Peace Conference in 1919, that the British Government be given the Mandate for Palestine. I believe, Dr. Weizmann, it will be you, who will again from Britain, the U.S. and the U.N., at the Victory Peace Conference win a charter for the Jewish Commonwealth. (Applause and cheering) Some years ago, through the generosity of a group of friends, there was presented to me a ring, worn and held, up to the hour of his death, by the immortal founder of the Zionist Movement, Dr. Herzl. Dr. Weizmann, at the peace conference, when you present the claims of the Jewish people, I want you to have in your hand, on your finger, the ring of your predecessor in the leadership of the Zionist Movement, and as you wear the ring of Theodor Herzl, God give it that to you, and through you, to us, your people, there comes the charter of the Jewish People, of the Jewish Common-

wealth in Palestine, and God give it, that for years and years you wear
it in health and strength and triumph, this ring of Theodor Herzl, your
great predecessor. (Dr. Wise hands ring to Dr. Weizmann as they em-
brace. The audience arose, applauded and cheered as Dr. Weizmann
arose.)[18]

That there was genuine love and admiration for Weizmann the man
was unquestionable: in Jewish Palestine, in Jewish America, in Jewish
no-matter-where. But in America, on top of this, there was also much
agreement with Weizmann's secret, low-profile diplomacy, far removed from Ben-Gurion's public-opinion-rousing methods. Yet at the
same time Ben-Gurion recognized America as Zionism's best friend
precisely because public opinion played so important a role in both its
foreign and domestic policies. In London, where top-level connections
still counted the most, Weizmann was by far best suited to be Zionism's primus, and would never have agreed to become, as Ben-Gurion
demanded, only primus inter pares. But in America, public opinion
was the strongest political force, and events that could be brought to
bear on it counted more than connections. Ultimately, with Weizmann's removal in December 1946 from the Zionist presidency amid
the mounting struggle for Jewish independence in Palestine, Ben-
Gurion's argument would be fully substantiated. Indeed, on November 2, 1947, it was not Weizmann who received from the United
Nations "the charter" of the Jewish state, but Ben-Gurion—without
Herzl's ring on his finger.

During the war years, however, Weizmann's soft-pedal policy was
religiously embraced by most American Zionist and non-Zionist leaders. An earlier case in which Weizmann's and Ben-Gurion's strategies
had collided was the reaction to the *La Patria* episode. In November
1940 the Royal Navy intercepted at sea two refugee ships, the *Pacific*
and the *Milos,* and towed them to Haifa, where their 1771 passengers,
along with 130 refugees from the *Atlantic,* were transferred to the
Patria. This French vessel, which the British had requisitioned for expulsion duty, was to take them to Mauritius, an island in the Indian
Ocean. This incident unleashed a storm in the Jewish world.

Ben-Gurion, who was then in New York, prepared to move heaven and earth with the assistance of American public opinion. But on November 18, he received a cable from Weizmann, explaining that Colonial Secretary Lord Lloyd intended to turn all ships carrying illegals away from Palestine. Lloyd's argument was that the Nazis were using the ships to introduce "German *agents provocateurs*" into Palestine. Weizmann directed Ben-Gurion to "prevent rise of feeling which may complicate situation" and set back the Jewish army project. Ben-Gurion cabled in reply that although he recognized the "necessity avoiding any possible embarrassment [to] HMG," deporting the illegals was not the right way to make sure there were no German agents among them. He was, he added, "reliably informed" as to the *bona fides* of the refugees and "urge[d] therefore very strongly their immediate landing."[19] The JAE offices in Jerusalem and London joined in the fight to revoke the deportation decree, and New York was asked to do its part. Ben-Gurion began coaxing members of the Emergency Committee into action, which resulted in a cable of protest sent by William Green, president of the American Federation of Labor, to Minister of Labour Ernest Bevin in London.

Once the American press published the British government's decision to deport the illegals, Ben-Gurion's proposed response of staging protest rallies in major American cities was unanimously rejected by the Emergency Committee on November 22. The main thing the committee agreed to do was send a delegation to the British embassy, on condition that it behave with due restraint. Learning of this meeting, Justice Brandeis—the one who had initially opened Ben-Gurion's eyes to the timidity of the American Jewish leadership—himself expressed opposition to publishing any response to the deportation decision, in line with Weizmann's directive not to embarrass the British government. Only at the Histadrut fund-raising annual convention in New York, also on November 22, was Ben-Gurion allowed to speak uninterruptedly against the British policy, which the convention went on to condemn.[20]

In Palestine, meanwhile, developments reached the boiling point. On November 21 a special session of the National Assembly in Jerusalem declared a general strike in the Yishuv. With the JAE's approval, on November 25 the Haganah placed an explosive device on the hull of the *Patria,* which was anchored out in Haifa's harbor, with the intention of causing a leak that would prevent the ship from leaving. But the *Patria* sank within minutes of the explosion, and some 200 deportees drowned. This disaster had only a slight effect on the British. As a humane gesture they permitted the survivors to remain in Palestine, under custody, but the deportation policy, they declared, remained in force. On December 9, the *Atlantic,* with 1645 illegals aboard, set sail for Mauritius, which was their "home" for five years.

Once again Ben-Gurion found himself in isolation in New York. Not only were the members of the Emergency Committee opposed to any response that might upset or embarrass Britain, but Justices Brandeis and Frankfurter, among others, told the committee that they opposed any announcement liable to put stress on the United States' relations with Britain. This was Ben-Gurion's first disappointment in Frankfurter, indicating that he was not to be trusted. Later Frankfurter made it clear that he wanted a Jewish army to be recruited not in the United States but "in other countries," and he expressed his "reluctance to speak in America on this issue." Only then, Ben-Gurion told Mapai on his return to Palestine, "did his [true] position become clear to me." In other words, when it came to Jewish matters, this brave adjudicator was as timid as his brethren.

Ben-Gurion found himself in a quandary. On the one hand, his political instincts told him that a storm of public opinion intense enough to oblige the British government to take note would make it possible to prevent deportations, allow more European refugees to enter Palestine, and help raise a Jewish army. On the other hand, this option was blocked by American Jewish timidity. Any hope he may have had left was blasted at an Emergency Committee meeting on November 29, when a proposal he made to issue a press release about the Emergency Committee delegation's visit to the British embassy on November 26 was dropped from the agenda. Wise claimed that the talk with Lord Halifax had left him with the impression that secret talks had a chance of bringing about helpful cooperation with Britain, and this chance must not be spoiled by a statement to the press.

Ben-Gurion explained that it was not so much this particular instance of silence that worried him but the principle behind it. He could not come to terms with the idea that the American Zionists would refuse to act, solely out of fear that the British and U.S. governments might not approve a public protest. When the debate ended, the majority voted with Wise, rejecting Ben-Gurion's proposal.[21]

It might be objected that this timidity was confined to issues with Zionist overtones, and therefore cannot be used as a yardstick for judging the overall American Jewish reaction to the Nazi genocide. Unfortunately, however, this yardstick is accurate. In time American Jews and their leaders were ready to come down harshly on British restrictions on Jewish Palestine. But in no way were they willing to harshly criticize the Allies' conduct of the war or their war aims. Whatever protests American Jewry was ready to mount against the mass murder of the Jews in Europe, they were always very careful not to criticize their government for failing to include mass rescue among its war aims.

It was this timidity that governed the American Jewish rescue campaign. A perfect example, which was also the high-water mark of Jewish American protest, was the famous Madison Square Garden meeting of July 21, 1942, initiated by the Zionist Emergency Committee and sponsored by major American Jewish organizations.* To reassure Washington and Whitehall, Rabbi Wise, the Emergency Committee chairman, gave them advance notice, "to make it quite clear that the meeting would not be a Zionist meeting, and would not call for a Jewish Army. . . . It is to be a meeting of protest and sorrow at the fate of the Jews in Europe and a demand will be made that the Yishuv shall not be compelled to suffer the same fate."[22] Glaringly absent is a demand that the American administration, or the Allies, include prevention of mass murder of Jews among their war aims.

Prior to the meeting Wise cabled Churchill, asking him to cable a message to the meeting and also asking whether he could give an assurance regarding "the formation of a Jewish Army in Palestine." The prime minister's office consulted the Colonial Office and then referred the cable to the Foreign Office with the following directive: "We should

---

* The American Jewish Congress, B'nai Brith, and the Jewish Labor Committee.

like to reply" to Wise that "the PM considered the telegram and thinks he cannot do better than call attention to the Parliamentary Question and Answer in the House of Commons on July 7 on this subject" (in which Churchill had said there was no need for a special Jewish army). The Foreign Office was advised to refer Wise to the British embassy in Washington.

According to a cable sent by Sir Ronald Campbell of the embassy to the Foreign Office, Wise called at the embassy and gave assurances that the meeting would be "a mass demonstration against Hitler atrocities." He asked "if HMG could send message to effect that Jewish hostages of Hitler will be avenged and that role which Jews are playing in resistance to Nazi aggression will be recognized."[23] Given these assurances, Churchill was advised by the Foreign Office that he could send a cable to the meeting, and he did so.

Following this exchange Wise "made explicit" to the Emergency Committee that the meeting would restrict itself to expressing a strong protest against Nazi atrocities and demanding that the Yishuv not fall under Nazi occupation.[24]

The meeting was considered a great success. It was attended by a crowd of 20,000, gathered inside and outside the hall, and reported on page 1 of the *New York Times*. The double-column headline ran: "President Pledges Nazi Punishment After War." A letter from Roosevelt and Churchill's message to Wise won the meeting this distinction. Along with the headline, the subheadlines—"Nazi Punishment Seen by Roosevelt, Says Hitler Will Be Held to 'Strict Accountability'; Churchill Greets Rally"—encapsulated whatever political import the meeting had, making clear that it was in agreement with the Allies' conduct of the war and that no whisper about including the mass rescue of the Jews in the Allied war aims had been heard.

The meeting was best summarized by Professor David S. Wyman in *The Abandoment of the Jews*: "Nothing [in the *New York Times* article] indicated that hundreds of thousands of Jews had been murdered. In fact, Jews were barely mentioned, and the event came across as no more than a 'mass demonstration against Hitler atrocities.' "

Similar meetings were held in other U.S. cities. Wyman goes on: "The *Chicago Tribune* provided substantial publicity prior to the

Chicago mass meeting, but its report on the demonstration itself, while comprehensive, offered little understanding of what had caused the meeting. The *Los Angeles Times,* on the other hand, publicized the demonstration in Los Angeles for more than a week and made it clear throughout that the issue was 'the terrible mass murders of Jews in Nazi-controlled Europe.' "[25] It was practically alone in doing so, and produced, therefore, little effect.

Whatever awareness of the annihilation of Europe's Jews was stimulated by these mass meetings, it soon died out. Sharett, reporting to the JAE in April 1943 on his own American trip, said: "The whole affair was followed by silence, they [American Jews] felt they did the best they could, stood up to be counted, etc." Only in the wake of the horrific information the Yishuv obtained from the sixty-nine exchangees in November 1942 and the mourning and protests of the Yishuv did the American Jewish community renew its efforts to arouse American opinion. A second round of mass meetings in large cities, modeled on the first one in Madison Square Garden, was planned.[26]

But delay followed delay. Queries from the JAE were answered by cables from Goldmann claiming "technical difficulties" and "unavailability of notable key-note speakers." Joseph, who handled liaison with American Jewish leaders, reported to the JAE, as if with a sigh: "It all goes to show how undependable they are." He wired a strongly worded cable demanding, on behalf of the JAE, that the Americans "immediately stage the meetings."[27]

At last, on March 1, 1943, a second mass rally was held at Madison Square Garden under the slogan "Stop Hitler Now." Again it made the front page of the *New York Times,* though with only a single-column headline: "Save Doomed Jews, Huge Rally Pleads." This time there were no greetings from Roosevelt and Churchill. The notables who took part were of a lower order: the archbishop of Canterbury and New York governor Thomas Dewey sent messages; New York mayor Fiorello La Guardia and other dignitaries were present. The huge meeting—21,000, according to the *New York Times*—unanimously adopted an eleven-point program of action to "stop Hitler now," which, said the paper, "will be submitted to President Roosevelt and through him to the United Nations." But the demand to include the rescue of Jews among the Allies' war aims was not one of the points. These were devoted to urging countries partly under German domination, such as Romania and Hungary, to allow emigration of Jews and to requesting that the free world countries admit greater numbers of Jewish refugees, open Palestine's gates, and make the usual threats to the Germans and their collaborators regarding postwar justice for their crimes.[28]

Goldmann, excited by this rally, wrote Gruenbaum in Jerusalem describing the "carefully prepared" eleven-point resolution, which made "two main demands; namely, [that the United Nations] approach Germany with a request to let the Jews go, and an offer to feed European Jewry if Germany will halt the massacres."[29]

Sharett, who attended the New York rally, was impressed by the enormous crowd both inside and outside the Garden and by "the deep excitement that filled the hall, the Kaddish and the weeping by tens of thousands of people—a phenomenon I never witnessed in my life." But he was disappointed by the speakers, "who did not rise to the occasion . . . especially disappointing were the non-Jewish speakers. They spoke mainly of the war against Hitler, the need to triumph over him and to eradicate any mention of him from the face of the earth. Only a very small practical demand was made on the Administration—the gist of it was nothing but commiseration, sympathy etc." Again, the Allies were not asked to include the mass rescue of Jews in their war aims. As for the two demands in the rally's resolution, they were rejected out of hand by the British government.[30]

"Stop Hitler Now" was repeated in other cities, with lesser demands. Goldmann himself, summarizing the rallies and the activity they generated, admitted: "We are trying to do whatever is possible, but unfortunately, the results are less than meagre. . . . Only a very broad approach and very radical measures . . . would have a chance to stop the destruction of European Jewry. But I do not see any readiness for such broad and radical action on the part of the governments. Public opinion is aroused, but not sufficiently, either among Jews or non-Jews. As usual the masses are better than their leaders. . . . Men like [Judge Joseph M.] Proskauer and others will not agree to very radical action and every little step has to be discussed by 20 people, which makes speed and action very difficult."[31]

Sharett agreed. American Jewry seemed to him like a herd of sheep without a shepherd, unguided and unmotivated.[32] The leaders they did have—Weizmann, Wise, and others—valued maintaining good relations with Britain and the White House above all else, and would not risk this harmony by demanding that rescue be a war aim. Weizmann, who participated in both Madison Square Garden rallies, did not mention them in his letters and reports.[33] Unlike Ben-Gurion, he never thought it necessary to criticize or condemn American Jewry.

Ben-Gurion's reaction to the Americans' failure to act was swift. In April 1943 he told a Maccabee conference in Palestine:

> One cannot charge Roosevelt's Administration with anti-Semitism. Yet American Jews fear to appear as Jews. I never met a fear so throbbing in other Jews. . . . [T]hey are perennially concerned with what Americans might think of them if they take a stand on this or that American policy, all the more with respect to Jewish issues. . . . This would explain the saddest behavior during these months of horror, the like of which History has never known. . . . [T]here is now a mighty shock vibrating through this Jewish community, in regard to what goes on in Europe . . . all on account of the fear.[34]

However, he saw almost no possibility of relieving this fear and mobilizing American Jews to forceful public action toward making mass rescue a war aim. Major scholars like Professor Wyman and also Professor Deborah Lipstadt of Emory University—in her enlightening work *Beyond Belief*—appear, in retrospect, to agree with him.

CHAPTER SIXTEEN

FROM HOLOCAUST TO REVIVAL

B EN-GURION HAD to be a man of powerful will, clear vision, and singular courage not to be diverted from his course by the temptation to calculate his actions and behavior in such a manner as to answer future criticisms and ensure himself vindication. He could have satisfied many of his contemporaries and members of future generations by wearing his heart on his sleeve, daily lamenting the catastrophe, and accompanying his tears with heartrending sighs. Certainly both in the Yishuv and the Diaspora, Jews expected their leaders to personify their grief and mourning during the Holocaust years. Yet Ben-Gurion preferred to hide his feelings, keeping them very private, and to go on about his duty as he understood it: to make the Jewish people secure against another destruction. As he saw it then and afterward, the only way to do this was by establishing a Jewish state that could defend itself and ingather the exiles. Following this path, he was at peace with himself, betraying no signs of pangs of conscience.

Nevertheless, as we saw, within the academic "atmosphere" his struggle to carry out the Biltmore Program and his giving one day a week, when he could, to the planning committee were seen as indifference to the Holocaust and its victims. One example of how misplaced such criticism could be is the complaint by Dr. Deborah Hacohen of Bar-Ilan University in Ramat Gan that he did not attend the JAE meeting on November 22, 1942, that heard Dobkin's report on the traumatic experiences of the "sixty-nine exchangees." As she put it, "that meeting was scheduled to discuss the Holocaust. . . . Where was Ben-Gurion . . . ? What did he ever do for rescue?"[1]

The truth is that Ben-Gurion was always kept informed of major, and quite frequently of incidental, developments; in fact, Dobkin had already reported to him in person about the sixty-nine's testimony well before the meeting. Moreover, it is inconceivable that the meeting's resolution to issue a formal JAE announcement that Europe's Jews were subject to systematic destruction, and to call a general strike and a day of mourning and fast on November 30, was made without Ben-Gurion's prior knowledge and consent. Conclusive proof of his involvement is the telegrams he sent on November 24—in accordance with the November 22 meeting's resolutions—to Justice Frankfurter in Washington and others, alerting them to the ongoing destruction. As Dobkin reported that same day, the 24th, to Mapai's central committee: "Ben-Gurion wired today to some personages he is in contact with, Frankfurter" and others.[2]

In any case, Ben-Gurion was in the chair at the JAE meeting of November 29 that discussed strategy in light of the information brought by "the sixty-nine." He called for "saving every Jew possible," especially the children. On the 30th, as we saw, he delivered his appeal "To Human Conscience" at the extraordinary session of the National Assembly, with its sharp admonition to Great Britain and the United States.

Why, therefore, was he absent on the 22nd? In a letter of the 23rd to Miriam Cohen, his intimate friend in New York, he wrote: "I got a light cold and for the second day I am in bed—left alone to myself." Was a light cold, Ben-Gurion's critics wondered, enough reason to lie two days in bed when Europe's Jews were being brought hourly to be massacred? Accordingly, Dr. Hacohen complained that on November 23 Ben-Gurion went to a day-long colloquium held in Rehovot by the JAE's Institute for Economic Research (the planning committee's forerunner), in which he took an active part. "This conference begins at 9 a.m. and he sits there till evening, he lectures, he talks and he enthusiastically debates with scores of people, with a vehemence that can't be described. If he was so seriously ill the evening before, how come the following day he talked a whole day at Rehovot, without budging from there?" Upon checking further, she acknowledged that the colloquium was actually held on the 24th. But she still insisted that the proceedings "began in the morning and continued throughout the day. . . . Ben-Gurion listened to most of the lectures and debated with the other listeners."

Closer scrutiny of the colloquium's minutes shows that, in fact, Ben-Gurion attended only part of the morning session; he opened his speech by saying, "I regret not having heard the previous lectures." Nor did Hacohen notice that his remarks do reveal a concern with rescue. He did not want to start an argument, he said, on "whether Zionism means the Jewish plight . . . whether Zionism means redemption or rescue. . . . [O]ne thing concerns me, and it must concern every Jew . . . whether in the place called the Land of Israel [Palestine] something can be done for the great problem now facing us in a terrible way, that there will be large masses whose economic existence will be completely eradicated."[3] This comment expresses an understanding of the catastrophe Hitler was visiting on Europe's Jews that was very much in line with classical Zionism's predictions.

Both Hacohen's mistakes and her correction are the product of her suspicion that it was not his indisposition that prevented him from attending the JAE meeting on the 22nd but rather his disregard for its subject. This, it seems, is the price Ben-Gurion paid for the glorification, bordering on idolatry, of which he was the object in his lifetime. No one today can believe that he could either be simply sick, as any human being has a right to be, or overcome by exhaustion ensuing from the emotional stress caused by the sickening news "the sixty-nine" had brought. Neither he nor anyone else was thinking in November 1942 of the Holocaust, as Segev and to some extent Hacohen, too, try to make us believe.

It might be asked: Why was Ben-Gurion still talking about economic destruction? Wasn't it he who had predicted Hitler's destruction of the Jews long before anybody? Even more, he was fully informed of the horrifying tales of "the sixty-nine" and the JAE's decision to publish an official announcement. How then could he be talking in terms now suddenly made obsolete? Was he really obsessed by the Jewish state to the exclusion of everything else?

Such questions seem reasonable. But often reason has little to do with political and historical developments, especially in situations of immediacy such as the need to grasp the evolving Holocaust. The human mind and soul simply refused to digest and internalize the concept of a planned, systematic, production line of mass murder. In this Ben-Gurion was like all his fellows. As explained in Chapter 4, even in the latter part of 1943, and more remarkably in January 1944, he still found it hard to come to terms with the Holocaust: "I do not know how many millions have been destroyed," he said then. "Nobody knows." Only late that January did he finally internalize "six million," and make his famous statement: "The Jewish people is no more, there is something else now."[4]

It was during that same period—the latter part of 1943 and early 1944—that his planning committee moved into high gear with the goal of establishing a Jewish state as a bulwark against further destruction. Thus it is certain that until the news of the Final Solution was finally absorbed, Ben-Gurion's understanding of mass rescue was primarily economic.

This understanding had matured earlier in 1942, most of which he spent in the United States. There he reached the conclusion "that our most important task" was to persuade the American administration that Palestine, "seen in America as even smaller than it really is, will be capable of absorbing more millions than the million and a half people it already has." For that purpose "we primarily need a serious, faithful presentation of what we have already achieved in Palestine and of what can still be achieved if the country is developed under appropriate political rule." In other words, Palestine must be shown to be capable, under a suitable administration, of absorbing millions of Hitler's victims. This was the task he assigned the planning committee.

While still in the United States he tightened his ties with the JAE's Institute for Economic Research and its chief, Dr. Arthur Ruppin. At his request, "all the [Institute's] data and plans" were shipped to him in the United States. He immersed himself in statistics and analyses, writing to Ruppin, "Your work and the Institute's are of supreme political value," and "I have read it with great interest, greater than any detective story." If he had read the minutes of the JAE's meeting of August 9, 1942—and there is reason to believe he did, for the JAE's minutes were regularly sent to him—in which Schmorak said that "it is very desirable to restart the economic committee as an 'active committee,' " he must have thought there was a good chance the JAE would approve the planning committee he had made up his mind to propose.[5]

And indeed, even before the JAE's authorization he had begun setting it up. After careful screening with his aides, he selected as chief of staff David Horowitz, future first director general of Israel's Ministry of Finance and later first governor of the Bank of Israel. Horowitz would remember Ben-Gurion's explanation of his thinking: "to establish a committee for long-range planning, to prepare an innovative plan for the absorption of millions within a few years . . . as a directive for the plan Ben-Gurion made the assumption of complete political freedom of action, whose only meaning could have been national independence."[6]

Soon after his return to Palestine, in his first report on his American trip, on October 6, 1942, Ben-Gurion proposed to the JAE "to charge me, with the aid of the Institute for Economic Research . . . [to study] what is needed to bring over all at once two million Jews to Palestine" after the war ended. It seems that in contemplating this vision he decided that in order to make it a reality he had himself to assume the chairmanship of the committee that would plan and prepare such a massive enterprise of immigration and absorption.

On October 18 he "announced" to the JAE "that he was thinking of devoting himself to the planning issue" and that "this work will demand all his time, and he therefore would be unable to attend to any other business, except chairing JAE meetings." He added that "all actions will be taken with JAE's knowledge" and that "without doubt financing will be required." And indeed Kaplan allotted "to the item intended by Ben-Gurion" 25,000 Palestinian pounds, then equal to $100,000 ($3.4 million today), out of the "extraordinary budget" for 1942, as compared to 4000 pounds allotted in 1940 and 1942 to the Institute for Economic Research.[7] In December 1942 Ben-Gurion told the JAE that he meant to use part of his planning budget "to send active emissaries" to countries from which immigration was expected, as well as for preparing "the Yishuv, and its youth in particular . . . for a Jewish state." He was concerned with "the postwar situation of our economy," especially agriculture, and he advised the JAE "to start looking after the economy."[8]

This sudden, vigorous interest in economics must have made Ben-Gurion's JAE colleagues doubt the evidence of their eyes and ears. They were used to hearing him say he was "a man who knows nothing of economic theory, not even that such theory exists," or that he "was no economist and even less of a financier," which he said was his reason "for not taking part in budgetary debates." And now, as if out of the blue, the man who never stopped declaring that for him "there always exists the political aspect" suddenly assumed the chairmanship of an economic committee and swore to "devote" himself to this committee and to this committee alone. So extreme was his devotion to it that when, on October 26, 1943, during one of his struggles with Weizmann, he announced that he would resign from all his JAE functions, he made the chairmanship of the planning committee the only exception.[9]

As has been said, from 1934 to the end of 1942 Ben-Gurion envisaged Hitler's destruction of Europe's Jews occurring mostly through economic means: banning them from professions, state administration, commerce, trades, and any other employment, making them disappear through destitution, famine, disease, and degeneration. It was therefore economic salvation in Palestine that he had started to prepare for them. This is why he resolved to "devote" himself to the planning committee. But as it became evident that Hitler was carrying out a completely different, and much more rapid, type of destruction—the gas chambers—there was no longer any point to giving all his time and energy to economic salvation—that is, to the chairmanship of the planning committee.

In January 1944, when Ben-Gurion accepted the figure of 6 million dead, he informed Mapai's head office that "one day a week I am occupied with the planning committee in Jerusalem." In June, when victory over Hitler was within sight, and the JAE began preparing for the expected international discussion of the Jewish and Palestine questions at the peace conference and the UN, Ben-Gurion redefined the role of the planning committee. "This planning committee has a political goal," he asserted; its duty was "to serve as a clearing house for basic information . . . and prepare maximal development plans" from which the JAE would generate the "political propositions" it submitted to "world rulers," as well as "immigration and absorption schemes" the JAE would submit to "the Jewish world" in order "to enlist its resources." Most important of all was the "One Million Plan": detailed blueprints for solving all problems attending the transport, absorption, settlement, employment, and education of 1 million immigrants to Palestine right after the war, as well as for assuring the necessary financial means to implement the scheme.

Ben-Gurion told the committee members that their point of departure was the Biltmore Program, "in which we demand a Jewish state." He also told a constitutional subcommittee that its duty was to ensure that the One Million Plan's implementation "would be achieved without dispossessing Palestine Arabs, and without their transfer" elsewhere. In March 1945 he charged this subcommittee with defining "the legal and economic status of the Arab inhabitants of Palestine." One member of the committee, a prominent economist, interpreted Ben-Gurion's instructions as follows: "He requires a general [economic] plan, to show and to prove that if we were to be given the rule [of Palestine] . . . it would be possible to create the [necessary] conditions to create livelihoods for all the Arabs living in Palestine and for millions of Jews to boot."[10]

This new Zionist rationale, which bound rescue up with immigration, had been—as Ben-Gurion told the JAE in June 1944—his preoccupation "for all those four years." It motivated him to lead the planning committee, so as to oversee the transition from Holocaust to revival.[11] For the Holocaust neither he, the Yishuv, nor the Jewish people could have prevented, and he could not undo what had been done. But instead of drowning in a sea of tears, he chose, as was his wont, to turn a disadvantage into an advantage—to erect a Jewish state that would preclude another Holocaust.

All his life Ben-Gurion read in his bedside Bible, and Isaiah was his favorite prophet. There is no telling how many times he read Chapter

24 and pondered the prophet's vision of the earth's devastation. It is easy to imagine that when he read "The foundations of the earth will rock, The earth will split into fragments . . . be riven and rent,"[12] his immediate thought was "Hark, is it not the time to reach for a plow?" Certainly this is what he did. When the Nazis shook the earth and split it under the feet of the Jews, Ben-Gurion built a plow with which to make the graves into blooming fields, turning death into revival.

NOTES

PREFACE

1. Tom Segev, *HaMillion HaShviyi,* 2nd ed. (Jerusalem: Keter, 1991); Tom Segev, *The Seventh Million* (New York: Hill & Wang, 1993).

2. Dina Porat, *Hanhagah beMilkud* (An Entangled Leadership) (Tel Aviv: Am Oved, 1986); Dina Porat, *The Blue and Yellow Stars of David* (Cambridge: Harvard University Press, 1990).

3. Bernard Joseph, *British Rule in Palestine* (Washington, D.C.: Public Affairs Press, 1948), p. 91.

4. Sir John Hope Simpson, *Palestine: Report on Immigration, Land Settlement and Development,* Cmd. 3686 (London: HMSO, 1930); Palestine's *Official Gazette,* Oct. 24, 1930, quoted in *Davar,* Oct. 26, 1930.

5. *New York Times,* Nov. 26, 30, 1942.

6. Zionist Actions Committee, Mar. 22, 1934; Central Zionist Archives, Jerusalem, Z4/289/17; *Davar,* Apr. 3, 1934; David Ben-Gurion, *Zihronot* (Memoirs), 5 vols. (Tel Aviv: Am Oved, 1973), p. 2:38; Mapai Conference, Jan. 22–23, 1937; Histadrut Executive Committee, Mar. 8, 1937; Records of the JAE, Central Zionist Archives, Jerusalem, Aug. 21, 1938.

7. Segev, *Seventh Million,* pp. 97, 98.

INTRODUCTION

1. Zionist Actions Committee, June 26, 1939; Ben-Gurion at Labor's faction meeting, World Zionist Congress, Aug. 18, 1939; Hadassah National Board, Oct. 22, 1940.

2. Shabtai Teveth, *Ben-Gurion: The Burning Ground* (Boston: Houghton Mifflin, 1987), pp. 458, 587, 674.

3. Mapai, Conference, Mar. 5, 1944.

4. Ben-Gurion in National Council, Sept. 17, 1939, published in *Davar,*

Sept. 22, 1939, titled *Likrat HaBaot* (Facing the Future); Zionist Actions Committee, Dec. 7, 1932.

5. Tuvia Friling, "Ben-Gurion and European Catastrophe, 1939–1945," doctoral thesis, Hebrew University, February 1990, pp. 6–13; Moshe Kleinbaum's (Sneh) letter to Ben-Gurion, Nov. 20, 1939; A. Bialopolsky's letter to Ben-Gurion, Dec. 2, 1939.

6. Histadrut Executive Council, Nov. 25–26, 1942.

7. Shabtai Teveth, *Ben-Gurion VeArviyei Eretz-Israel* (Jerusalem–Tel Aviv: Hotsaat Schocken, 1985); pp. 133, 134; Shabtai Teveth, *Ben-Gurion and the Palestinian Arabs* (New York: Oxford University Press, 1985), p. 77.

8. Teveth, *Burning Ground,* p. 678.

9. Ben-Gurion's letter to Berl Locker, Apr. 22, 1933, Ben-Gurion Archives, Sdeh Boker.

10. Ibid, pp. 518, 519.

11. Ibid, p. 850; *Davar,* July 30, 1939.

12. Mapai council, Jan 19, 1933, Mar. 5, 1941, Mapai political committee, Mar. 9, May 4, 1936, Mapai, central committee, Dec. 7, 1938, Feb. 19, 1941; Ben-Gurion Diaries, Jan. 3, 1939; Records of the JAE, Central Zionist Archives, Jerusalem, Feb. 16, 1941.

13. Davar, July 30, 1939; Mapai convention, June 12, 1941, Mapai central committee, Mar. 19, 1941; Records of the JAE, Central Zionist Archives, Jerusalem, May 16, 28, 1941; Ben-Gurion's documents intercepted, Oct. 15, 1941, PRO FO371/27129; Berl Katznelson's Notebooks, Labor Party Archives, Zofit.

14. Zionist Actions Committee, Oct. 15, 1942; Mapai convention, Oct. 25, 1942, Mapai central committee, Dec. 8, 1943; Records of the JAE, Central Zionist Archives, Jerusalem, Dec. 6, 1942.

15. Teveth, *Burning Ground*, pp. 852–54.

16. Records of the JAE, Central Zionist Archives, Jerusalem, Apr. 8, 1940; Sir Leon Simon to Ben-Gurion, Nov. 9, 1941, Weizmann Archives, Rehovoth.

17. Ben-Gurion's speech at the Zionist Council in New York, Dec. 14, 1941; Mapai seminar at Kfar Yedidiah, Nov. 5, 1943; Ben-Gurion's remarks to Wauchope, Apr. 2, 1936, in Ben-Gurion, *Zihronot,* 3:105.

18. *Time,* Apr. 4, 1938, quoted in Deborah Lipstadt, *Beyond Belief* (New York: Free Press, 1993), pp. 90, 108, 109.

19. *Encyclopedia of the Holocaust,* Israel Gutman, ed. (Tel Aviv: Sifriat Poalim, 1990), p. 871; Records of the JAE, Central Zionist Archives, Jerusalem, June 13, July 3, 1939, June 20, 1944; Ben-Gurion in Zionist Actions Committee, Nov. 10, 1942; Ben-Gurion with Mapai activists, Dec. 8, 1942.

20. Minutes of Biltmore Conference, May 12, 1942, Central Zionist Archives, Jerusalem; Dr. G. Cyderovich's memorandum, July 1944, Israeli De-

fense Force Archives, Givaatiim, 3342; Records of the JAE, Central Zionist Archives, Jerusalem, Feb. 16, 1941, Oct. 6, 1942; Mapai central committee, Feb. 19, 1941; Zionist Actions Committee, Feb. 24, 1941.

21. HaKibbutz HaMeuhad Conference, Jan. 19, 1944; Ben-Gurion in Mapai's Political Committee, Jan. 26, 1944; Wasi, Cywia, and Icchak's letter from Warsaw to Tabenkin, Ya'ari, and Dobkin, Nov. 15, 1943, Yad VaShem 025/96.

22. Dina Porat, *The Blue and Yellow Stars of David* (Cambridge: Harvard University Press, 1990), pp. 7, 64, 65; Records of the JAE, Central Zionist Archives, Jerusalem, Nov. 22, Dec. 20, 1942; Friling, "European Catastrophe," pp. 33, 43, 46, 47.

23. Mapai's seminar at Kfar Yedidiah, Nov. 5, 1943; HaKibbutz Ha-Meuhad Conference, Jan. 19, 1944; Zionist Actions Committee, Jul. 5, 1943; Ben-Gurion in Haifa, Ha'aretz, Aug. 6, 1944.

24. Records of the JAE, Central Zionist Archives, Jerusalem, Mar. 7, 1943; Zionist Actions Committee, Dec. 7, 1939.

25. Ben-Gurion Heritage Institute Oral Documentation, Sdeh Boker, Anselm Reiss, cassette #147.

26. Ben-Gurion at Poalei Zion meeting at Winthrop Hotel in New York, Dec. 12, 1940; Records of the JAE, Central Zionist Archives, Jerusalem, Apr. 6, 1941, Dec. 6, 1942; Histadrut Conference, Apr. 9, 1941; Zionist Rally for Yishuv Unity in Tel Aviv, Apr. 13, 1941, Israeli Defense Force Archives, Givaatiim 1384; Ben-Gurion's letter to Justice Frankfurter, July 2, 1942, enclosing Ben-Gurion's Memorandum on Defense of Palestine and the Jews, addressed to FDR, Central Zionist Archives, Jerusalem A/264/36; Ben-Gurion's diary entries July 1, 2, 3, 1942, Ben-Gurion Archives, Sdeh Boker.

27. Histadrut Executive Committee, Dec. 31, 1942.

28. National Assembly, Nov. 30, 1942, Central Zionist Archives, Jerusalem; *Yediot Merkaz Mapai* #172, Dec. 4, 1942; Ben-Gurion, *BaMaaraha* (Embattled), 5 vols. (Tel Aviv: Am Oved, 1957), 3:114.

29. Ben-Gurion's letter-cable signed Avi Amos (Amos's father) to Justice Frankfurter, Dec. 8, 1942; Ben-Gurion's letters to Nahum Goldmann, Robert Szold, and Stephen Wise, Dec. 6, 1942; Ben-Gurion's letter to Berl Locker, Dec. 8, 1942; Ben-Gurion's letter to Goldmann for Records of the American Zionist Emergency Council, Central Zionist Archives, Jerusalem, Dec. 8, 1942; Ben-Gurion Archives, Sdeh Boker. Sharett's letter to American consul general Pinkerton in Jerusalem, Nov. 23, 1942; Friling, "European Catastrophe," p. 34.

30. Records of the JAE, Central Zionist Archives, Jerusalem, Dec. 6, 13, 1942.

31. Records of the JAE, Central Zionist Archives, Jerusalem, Dec. 20,

1942; Porat, *Blue and Yellow,* pp. 52, 53; *New York Times,* Dec. 11, 18, 1942.

32. Records of the JAE, Central Zionist Archives, Jerusalem, Nov. 29, Dec. 6, 13, 1942.

33. Records of the JAE, Central Zionist Archives, Jerusalem, Nov. 22, Dec. 13, 1942; Mapai secretariat, Nov. 24, 1942; Friling, "European Catastrophe," p. 49.

34. Ben-Gurion at Mapai Activists' meeting Dec. 8, 1942, Ben-Gurion Archives, Sdeh Boker; Avi Amos (BG) to Frankfurter, op. cit.; Records of the JAE, Central Zionist Archives, Jerusalem, Dec. 13, 14, 20, 1942; Mapai secretariat, Dec. 23, 1942; Friling, "European Catastrophe," p. 54.

35. Records of the JAEP Central Zionist Archives, Jerusalem, Aug. 23, Nov. 1, 1942; *Encyclopedia of the Holocaust,* p. 571.

36. Hansard, Feb. 3, 1943, 386 H.C. DEB. 5S(69); Avi Amos to Frankfurter, op. cit.; Ben-Gurion at Mapai Activists' meeting, op. cit.; Records of the JAE, Central Zionist Archives, Jerusalem Feb. 7, Mar. 7, Sept. 26, 1943; Ben-Gurion with elections Mapai activists, Apr. 25, 1943, Ben-Gurion Archives, Sdeh Boker; Ben-Gurion, *BaMaaraha,* 3:126; Friling, "European Catastrophe," pp. 56, 66, 67; *Davar,* Feb. 4, 1943; Bernard Wasserstein, *Britain and the Jews of Europe, 1939–1945* (New York: Oxford University Press, 1979), pp. 179, 180.

37. Yehuda Bauer, "Efshar Lehaashim VeEfshar Lehaashim VeGam Lisno," *Ha'aretz,* June 23, 1994; D. Porat, *Ha'aretz,* May 13, 1984; Gila Fatra, *Haim Maavak Al Hisardut Hanhagat Yehudei Slovakia BaShoah 1938–1944* (Struggle for Surviving? The Leadership of Slovakian Jews in the Holocaust 1938–1944) (Tel Aviv: Mosreshet, 1992).

CHAPTER ONE

1. Yeshayahu Jelinek, "HaRav Weissmandel, 'Tohnit HaRabanim'—Mezima Anti-Zionit?" *Yalkut Moreshet* no. 58 (September 1994): p. 83; Gila Fatran, *Haim Maavak Al Hisardut* (Struggle for Surviving?) (Tel Aviv: Moreshet, 1992); Dina Porat, "Parashat Weissmandel KeHahpasha," *Ha'aretz,* May 13, 1984; Yehuda Bauer, "Efshar Lehaashim VeEfshar Lehaashim VeGam Lisno," *Ha'aretz,* June 23, 1994; Yehuda Bauer, *American Jewry and the Holocaust* (Detroit: Wayne State University, 1981), p. 373.

2. Michael Dov-Ber Weissmandel, *Min Hametzar* (From the Straits) (New York: Congregation Beth Hamidrash Chemed, 1980).

3. Nathan Schwalb interviews, Jan. 4, 12, Feb. 2, 9, 16, 23, 1995; Dina Porat, " 'Amalek's Accomplices' Blaming Zionism for the Holocaust: Anti-Zionist Ultra-Orthodoxy in Israel During the 1980s," *Journal of Contemporary History* (London) 27 (1992): pp. 695–729.

4. Yehuda Bauer, *Jews for Sale?* (New Haven: Yale University Press, 1994).

5. Porat, " 'Amalek's Accomplices,' " pp. 699, 750.

6. Shalom Shalmon (Zoller), *Pishei HaZionut BeHashmadat HaGolah* (The Crimes of Zionism in the Destroying of the Diaspora), 4th ed. (Jerusalem: The author, 1988), quoted in Porat, " 'Amalek's Accomplices.' "

7. Schwalb's letters to Kaplan and Dobkin, Dec. 4, 1942 and Mar. 10, 1943; Schwalb's interviews. Israeli State Archives, Jerusalem, and Lavon Institute, Tel Aviv.

8. Schwalb's letter to the JAE's rescue committee in Jerusalem, Dec. 4, 1942, Central Zionist Archives, Jerusalem, S26/1444; Schwalb's letter to Kaplan, Mar. 10, 1943, Central Zionist Archives, Jerusalem, S/84.

9. Schwalb interviews; Bauer, *American Jewry,* pp. 374, 375; Porat, " 'Amalek's Accomplices,' " op. cit.

10. Akiva Nir, "Vaadat HaHatsalah BeKushta—HaKesher Im Slovakia (Haavarat Ksafim LeSlovakia 1943–1944)," Seminar Paper #33855 Dgamim LeMehkar BiTkufat HaShoah, Hebrew University; Dina Porat, *The Blue and Yellow Stars of David* (Cambridge: Harvard University Press, 1990); Bauer, *American Jewry;* Bauer, *Jews for Sale?*

11. Nir, "Vaadat"; Porat, *Blue and Yellow,* p. 183; Bauer, *Jews for Sale?,* p. 81; Bauer, "Efshar"; Bauer interview, July 8, 1994.

12. Bauer, *American Jewry,* p. 367.

13. Fatran, *Haim,* pp. 252–55; Abraham Fuchs, *Karati VeEin Oneh* (The Unheeded Cry) (Jerusalem: The author, 1985), pp. 27, 28; Weissmandel, *Min Hametzar;* Jelinek interview, Dec. 19, 1994.

14. Jelinek, "HaRav Weissmandel," p. 84.

15. Bauer, *American Jewry,* pp. 447, 448.

16. Fuchs, *Karati,* p. 26.

17. Weissmandel, *Min Hametzar,* last page (unnumbered) of the Publishers' Preface.

18. Porat, " 'Amalek's Accomplices,' " pp. 707, 708.

19. Records of the JAE, Central Zionist Archives, Jerusalem, Nov. 22, 1942; *Ha'aretz,* Nov. 23, 1942, and Hebrew daily press of same day; *HaShomer HaTzair Weekly,* Jan. 6, 1943; Histadrut Executive Committee, Feb. 11, 1943; David S. Wyman, *The Abandonment of the Jews* (New York: Pantheon, 1984), pp. 42, 43, 50, 58, 80, 167, 178, 179, 184, 236, 362.

20. *HaMashkif,* Aug. 6, 1944.

21. Yechiam Weitz, "HaShinui BeDimuio Shel Israel Kasztner," *Cathedra* no. 69 (September 1993): 140; Shalom Rosenfeld, *Tik Plili 124* (The Kastner Trial), (Tel Aviv: Karni, 1955); Porat, " 'Amalek's Accomplices' "; *Maariv,* Jan. 25, 1985 (Hanoh Bartov); *HaOlam HaZeh,* Sept. 14, 1955; Isser Harel, *HaEmet Al Retzah Kastner* (The Truth About the Kastner Murder),

(Jerusalem: Edanim, 1985), quoting from *HaOlam HaZeh* and Avneri in the Knesset, pp. 84, 88, 97, 149, 150, 299, 326 and passim.

22. *Davar,* Apr. 26, 1957.

23. Herut party's Manifesto, June 27, 1955, in *Cathedra* no. 69 (September 1993): 154.

24. Jim Allen, *Perdition* (London: Ithaca Press, 1986).

25. Moshe Scheinfeld, *Srufei Hakivshanim Maashimim: Teudot, Mismahim VeEduiot Al Poshei Shoah Yehudim* (Victims of the Ovens Accuse: Evidence, Documents, Testimonies on Jewish Holocaust Criminals), 4th ed. (Jerusalem: Hug Bnei Tora, affiliated to Young Agudath Israel in Eretz Israel, 1978).

26. Ibid., quoted in Porat, " 'Amalek's Accomplices' "; see also Yoram Kaniuk, "HaZionim—Poshei HaShoah" (The Holocaust Criminals Are the Zionists), *Maariv,* May 11, 1984.

27. See Ch. 2.

CHAPTER TWO

1. Meged's story can be found in Larry Collins and Dominique Lapierre, *O Jerusalem* (New York: Simon & Schuster, 1972), pp. 490, 492.

2. Anita Shapira, "Historiographia VeZikaron: Mikre Latrun Tashah" (Historiography and Memory: Latrun's Case, 1948), *Alpayim* no. 10 (1994): 11, 13, 14.

3. Haim Guri, letter to the editor, *Haaretz,* Jan. 16, 1985; Haim Guri, "The Naked and The Dead" in *Davar,* Aug. 12, 1986; Matti Meged interview with Tamar Meros, "The Sand and the Sandglass" in *Musaf Haaretz,* Jan. 9, 1987; Matti Meged interview with Tom Segev, "The National Bluff and the Private Fib," *Koteret Rashit,* Jan. 21, 1987; Gen. Shlomo Shamir, letter to the editor, *Haaretz,* 2 Feb 1987; Haim Guri, letter to the editor, *Davar,* Feb. 6, 1987; Yehuda Ben-Dror, letter to the editor, *Haaretz,* Feb. 8, 1987; and Matti Meged, letter to the editor, *Haaretz,* Apr. 2, 1987.

4. Gabi Daniel (Benjamin Harshav), "Peter HaGadol" (Peter the Great) in *Shirim Bamerhav, Igra* II (Almanac for Literature and Art), (Jerusalem: Keter Publishing, 1986), p. 199.

5. Idith Zertal, "The Poisoned Heart: The Jews of Palestine and the Holocaust," *Tikkun* 2:2 (1987): 47–50, 120–22.

6. Interview with Saul Friedlander, *LaMerhav,* Apr. 25, 1968.

7. Ben-Gurion's letter to A. S. Stein, member of *Davar* editorial board, Aug. 17, 1955 (in reference to Kastner's trial).

8. Gershom Schocken's minutes and lecture, Jan. 22, 1974, Institute for Zionist Research, Tel Aviv University; Schocken's letter to Professor Daniel Carpi, Jan. 23, 1974.

9. Dina Porat's interview, *Davar*, Oct. 3, 1986; Porat to author, Mar. 22, 1994.

10. Yechiam Weitz, *Mudaut VeHoser Onim* (Jerusalem: Yad Izhak Ben-Zvi, 1994), p. 5; Weitz's remarks at Yad VaShem ceremony, May 11, 1994; Weitz to author, May 24, 1994.

11. Hava Eshkoli, *Ha'aretz,* June 3, 1994.

12. Anita Shapira, *Berl* (Tel Aviv: Am Oved, 1980), p. 762, n. 173.

13. Joel Palgi, *Ruah Gdola Baa* (Tel Aviv: Am Oved, 1977), pp. 15, 17.

14. Shapira, *Berl,* p. 665.

15. Dina Porat, *The Blue and Yellow Stars of David* (Cambridge: Harvard University Press, 1990), p. 226.

16. Shapira, *Berl,* p. 665.

17. Exodus 19:5; Deuteronomy 26:18; Ben-Gurion, *The Ingathering of the Exiles and an Exemplary Nation* (New York: Macmillan, 1963).

18. Tom Segev, *The Seventh Million* (New York: Hill & Wang, 1993), pp. 467–69.

19. Ben-Gurion speaking to industrialists and businessmen in Jerusalem, Sept. 23, 1943.

20. Segev, *Seventh Million,* p. 294.

21. Ben-Gurion to Jerusalem students, Mar. 6, 1961.

CHAPTER THREE

1. Dina Porat, *Hanhagah beMilkud* (An Entangled Leadership) (Tel Aviv: Am Oved, 1986), p. 11; the entire Gutman episode is omitted from the English version.

2. Records of the JAE, Central Zionist Archives, Jerusalem, Aug. 16, 23, 1942; Dobkin's Teheran Report, Sept. 8, 1942, Israeli Defense Force Archives, Givaatiim 414.

3. Sharett's letter to Kot, Nov. 5, 1942; Kot's letter to Sharett, Nov. 7, 1942; Epstein's (Elath) report on meeting Kot, Nov. 10, 1942, Central Zionist Archives, Jerusalem Z4/14.752; Records of the JAE, Central Zionist Archives, Jerusalem, Nov. 22, 1942; Zionist Actions Committee, Feb. 2, 1943; Ben-Gurion at rally of Mapai activists, Dec. 8, 1942; David Engel, "The Polish Government-in-Exile and the Holocaust: Stanislaw Kot's Confrontation with Palestinian Jewry; Selected Documents November 1942–January 1943," *Polish Government-in-Exile II.*

4. The *Reprezentacja's* Report for 1940–1945, Central Zionist Archives, Jerusalem J/25/2 Nov. 27, 1942.

5. Records of the JAE, Central Zionist Archives, Jerusalem, Nov. 22, 1942; Mapai central committee, Nov. 24, 1942; Histadrut Executive Committee, Nov. 25, 1942.

6. *Reprezentacja*'s Report.

7. Anita Shapira, *Berl* (Tel Aviv: Am Oved, 1980), p. 665.

8. Avi Amos's letter/cable to Frankfurter, Dec. 8, 1942.

9. Minutes of Ben-Gurion–Kot meeting, Yad VaShem 055/2, quoted in Engel, "Polish Government-in-Exile."

10. Records of the JAE, Central Zionist Archives, Jerusalem, Nov. 29, Dec. 6, 1942.

11. David Engel, *In the Shadow of Auschwitz* (Chapel Hill: University of North Carolina Press, 1987), pp. 197, 198; David Engel, *Facing a Holocaust* (Chapel Hill: University of North Carolina Press, 1993), pp. 21, 22.

12. Engel, *Facing a Holocaust*, pp. 45, 216; Anselm Reiss, *BiSaarot HaTekufa* (Tel Aviv: Am Oved, 1982), p. 228; Records of the JAE, Central Zionist Archives, Jerusalem, Dec. 6, 1942.

13. Ben-Gurion at rally of Mapai activists, Dec. 8, 1942.

14. Zionist Actions Committee, Nov. 10, 1942; *Representacja*'s report, Dec. 5, 1942.

15. Porat, *Hanhagah beMilkud*, p. 11.

16. Engel, "Polish Government-in-Exile."

17. Engel, *Shadow of Auschwitz*, pp. 150–56; see also Engel, *Facing a Holocaust*.

18. Reiss, *BiSaarot*, pp. 213, 214; *Reprezentacja*'s Report, Jan. 19, 1943.

CHAPTER FOUR

1. Mapai central committee, Dec. 7, 1938.

2. Ibid.; Ben-Gurion at a Yishuv rally, Dec. 12, 1938; *Yediot Merkaz Mapai*, no. 142 (Dec. 28, 1938).

3. Deborah Lipstadt, *Beyond Belief* (New York: Free Press, 1993), pp. 114, 115; Records of the JAE, Central Zionist Archives, Jerusalem, Dec. 11, 1938, Jan. 1, 1939; Joseph's cable to Lourie, Dec. 12, 1938, Central Zionist Archives, Jerusalem S25/7627; see also Ben-Gurion's cables to Lourie, Dec. 13, 15, 1938, Central Zionist Archives, Jerusalem S25/7626; Public Record Office CAB 59 (38) 6; Hadassah National Board Jan. 11, 1939; *Encyclopedia of the Holocaust*, p. 221; Hansard [Lords], (German Atrocities: Aid for Refugees), Mar. 23, 1943, pp. 853, 854.

4. Korczak's letter to author, Nov. 19, 1980; *Rozka, Lehavot Baefer* (Flames in the Ash) (Tel Aviv: Moreshet & Sifriat Poalim, 1988), p. 213.

5. Official Record of Sixth Histadrut Conference (Jan. 28–Feb. 2, 1945), published by Histadrut Executive Committee, The Lavon Institute for Labor Research, Tel Aviv, July 1945, p. 302.

6. Korczak's letter, Nov. 19, 1980.

7. *Davar*, Feb. 2, 1945.

8. *Mishmar,* Feb. 2, 1945.

9. *Ha'aretz,* Feb. 2, 1945.

10. *Neuewelt* (Yiddish weekly, Tel Aviv), Feb. 9, 1945, p. 4.

11. Stenographer's minutes at the afternoon session of the Histadrut Conference, Jan. 2, 1945, Ben-Gurion Archives, Sdeh Boker; stenographer Ben-Zion Maimon interview, Apr. 20, 1995.

12. Korczak's letter, Nov. 19, 1980; Ben-Gurion's diary entries, July 9, 1945.

CHAPTER FIVE

1. Ruth Klueger and Peggy Mann, *The Last Escape* (New York: Doubleday, 1973).

2. Tom Segev, *The Seventh Million* (New York: Hill & Wang, 1993), p. 115; Tom Segev, *HaMillion HaShviyi,* 2nd ed. (Jerusalem: Keter, 1991), pp. 102–4; Aliav's deposition, Dec. 4, 1978, Ben-Gurion Heritage Institute Oral Documentation, Sdeh Boker, cassettes #458, 460.

3. Ben-Gurion's correspondence, by letter and cable, dealing with the acquisition of books is open to the public in the Ben-Gurion Archives in Sdeh Boker.

4. Judah Nadich, *Eisenhower and the Jews* (New York: Twayne Publishers, 1953), pp. 228 and passim.

5. Nadich interview, Oct. 15, 1981; Kollek interview, July 24, 1988; Avriel interview, Oct. 30, 1981.

6. *Unzer Weg,* Oct. 26, 1945; Mapai secretariat, Nov. 22, 1945; Ben-Gurion's letter to Goldmann, Sept. 27, 1945.

7. Mapai, Nov. 22, 1945.

8. Nadich, *Eisenhower,* p. 229.

9. Mapai, Nov. 22, 1945; Nadich, *Eisenhower,* pp. 230, 232; Ben-Gurion's diary entries, Oct. 19, 1945, and following days.

10. Levi Shalit, "David Ben-Gurion Visits Holocaust Survivors in Germany, a Chapter of Jewish History Before the Rise of Israel," essay in manuscript.

11. Nadich diary; Ben-Gurion Heritage Institute Oral Documentation, Sdeh Boker, Nadich's deposition Apr. 18, 1977, cassette #264; Nadich, *Eisenhower,* pp. 238, 239; Ben-Gurion's diary entries, Oct. 24, 1945.

12. Ben-Gurion's diary entries, Sept. 25, 1945.

13. Ben-Gurion's diary entries, Oct. 25, 28, 1945.

14. *Unzer Weg,* Oct. 26, 1945; Ben-Gurion Heritage Institute Oral Documentation, Sdeh Boker, ibid., Nadich's deposition; Ben-Gurion's diary entries, Oct. 21–23, 1945.

15. Nadich, *Eisenhower,* pp. 230–33; Ben-Gurion Heritage Institute Oral

Documentation, Sdeh Boker, Nadich's deposition, Apr. 18, 1977, cassette #263; Ben-Gurion's diary entries Oct. 29, 1945.

16. Ben-Gurion's diary entries, Oct. 29, 1945; Nadich diary.

17. Ben-Gurion Heritage Institute Oral Documentation, Sdeh Boker, Surkis's deposition, July 10, 1975.

18. Ben-Gurion Heritage Institute Oral Documentation, Sdeh Boker, Avriel's deposition, Nov. 29, 1978, Ben-Gurion Heritage Institute Oral Documentation, Sdeh Boker, cassette #452.

19. Ben-Gurion's letter to Nadich, May 1947.

CHAPTER SIX

1. Tom Segev, *The Seventh Million* (New York: Hill & Wang, 1993), pp. 450, 451.

2. Tom Segev, *HaMillion HaShviyi*, 2nd ed. (Jerusalem: Keter, 1991), p. 164, and *Seventh Million*, pp. 115, 180; see also chs. 9 and 10.

3. Segev, *Seventh Million*, p. 115.

4. Ibid., p. 469.

5. Haim Israeli interview, Apr. 28, 1994.

6. Segev, *Seventh Million*, p. 97; Avihu Ronen, "Shlihutah Shel Halinka," *Yalkut Moreshet*, no. 42 (December 1980); Ben-Gurion's letter to Miriam Cohen, Feb. 15, 1943.

7. Segev, *Seventh Million*, p. 28.

8. David Ben-Gurion, "Hareka HaBeinleumi Shel Baayatenu," *Ba-Maaraha*, 5 vols. (Tel Aviv: Am Oved, 1957), 2:80 and passim.

9. Sir R. Hoare's telegram to the FO # 58 (R 1756/9/37) from Bucharest, Feb. 23, 1938, Public Record Office, Kew, FO 371/22449; Bela Vago, *The Shadow of the Swastika: The Rise of Fascism and Anti-Semitism in the Danube Basin, 1936–1939* (Farnborough, England: Saxon House, 1975), p. 296.

10. Sir R. Hoare to A. Eden, #22 (Public Records Office, Kew, FO R 679/9/37) Bucharest, Jan. 19, 1938, in Vago, *Rise of Fascism*, p. 268.

11. Sir R. Hoare's letter to E. M. B. Ingram, Jan. 19, 1938 Public Records Office, Kew, FO/371 22453 (R 457/153/37), in Vago, *Rise of Fascism*, p. 262.

12. Ben-Gurion's diary entries, Jan. 31, Feb. 22, 1938; Mapai central committee, Apr. 4, 1938; Records of the JAE, Central Zionist Archives, Jerusalem, Apr. 6, 1941; see also Elie Kedouri, *In the Anglo-Arab Labyrinth* (Cambridge: Cambridge University Press, 1976), pp. 262–63.

13. Sir R. Hoare to E. M. B. Ingram, in Vago, *Rise of Fascism*, p. 262.

14. Sir R. Hoare's report to A. Eden #70 Feb. 24, 1938 (R 2058/153/37), in Vago, *Rise of Fascism*, pp. 298, 299.

15. Sir R. Hoare's letter to Lord Halifax, Apr. 14, 1938, #146 (4/101/38), in Vago, *Rise of Fascism*, pp. 310–11.

16. Ben-Gurion, *BaMaaraha,* 2:80; Hansard [Lords], (German Atrocities: Aid for Refugees), Mar. 23, 1943, pp. 811, 812, 859.

17. Segev, *Seventh Million,* p. 23.

18. Ibid., p. 31.

19. Ibid., p. 26; Segev, *HaMillion HaShviyi,* p. 21.

CHAPTER SEVEN

1. Tom Segev, *HaMillion HaShviyi,* 2nd ed. (Jerusalem: Keter, 1991), pp. 63, 64; Tom Segev, *The Seventh Million* (New York: Hill & Wang, 1993), pp. 72, 73.

2. Haviv Knaan, *Milhamtah Shel HaItonut* (The Press's Struggle) (Jerusalem: Hasifria HaZionit, 1969), pp. 141, 142.

3. See Deborah Lipstadt, *Beyond Belief* (New York: Free Press, 1993), and David S. Wyman, *Paper Walls* (Amherst: University of Massachusetts Press, 1969).

4. Lipstadt, *Beyond Belief,* p. 181.

5. Gila Fatran, *Haim Maavak Al Hisardut* (Struggle for Surviving?) (Tel Aviv: Moreshet, 1992), pp. 97, 118, 132, 203, 204, 206.

6. Ibid., pp. 102–4, 132.

7. Lotte Salzberger, *Mussaf Ha'aretz,* Oct. 22, 1993.

8. Segev, *HaMillion HaShviyi,* pp. 63, 64; Segev, *Seventh Million,* p. 72; "Im Tziltzul HaPaamonim," *HaPoel HaTzair,* May 20, 1943; *HaTzoffeh,* Mar. 18, 1942.

9. Segev, *Seventh Million,* p. 73; *HaTzoffeh,* Mar. 18, 1942.

10. Segev, *Seventh Million,* p. 73; *Davar,* June 28, 30, Oct. 8, 1942.

11. Segev, *HaMillion HaShviyi,* p. 65.

12. Bernard Levin, "The Final Question," *The Times* (London), Jan. 27, 1995, p. 15.

13. Segev, *HaMillion HaShviyi,* p. 65; Rally of Jewish Workers for Rescue, May 6, 1943, quoted in Yechiam Weitz, *Mudaut VeHoser Onim* (Jerusalem: Yad Izhak Ben-Zvi, 1994), p. 50.

14. Emmanuel Ringelblum, *Yoman Ureshimot MiTkufat HaMilhama* (Diary and Notes from the Warsaw Ghetto: September 1939–December 1942), 2 vols. (Jerusalem: Yad VaShem, 1992), 1:367.

15. *Encyclopedia of the Holocaust* has a two-page story on this camouflage entitled by the Germans *Aktion 1005,* pp. 664–65.

16. Segev, *HaMillion HaShviyi,* p. 85; Segev, *Seventh Million,* p. 98; Zionist Actions Committee, Apr. 18, 1943, Central Zionist Archives, Jerusalem S/25 1851.

17. Segev, *Seventh Million,* p. 98; *Davar,* Nov. 27, 1942.

18. Segev, *HaMillion HaShviyi,* pp. 90, 92.

19. Segev, *Seventh Million,* p. 109.

20. Segev, *HaMillion HaShviyi,* pp. 65, 96; Segev, *Seventh Million,* p. 108.

21. Segev, *Seventh Million,* p. 103.

22. Segev, *HaMillion HaShviyi,* pp. 90, 92; Records of the JAE, Central Zionist Archives, Jerusalem, Nov. 26, 1939; Mapai central committee, Nov. 27, 1939.

23. Segev, *HaMillion HaShviyi,* pp. 90, 92, 417; Segev, *Seventh Million,* p. 104; *Encyclopedia of the Holocaust* p. 541; Dalia Ofer, "HaShoah BeSiah Shel HaYeshuv VeHaMedinah 1942–1953" (The Holocaust in the Discourse of the Yishuv and the State), a seminar on the Holocaust, Hebrew University, June 15, 1994; World Zionist Conference, London, August 1945, Central Zionist Archives, Jerusalem Z4/10254; *Sefer HaHukim Shel Medinat Israel* (Israel's Book of Laws), p. 5499.

CHAPTER EIGHT

1. Tom Segev, *The Seventh Million* (New York: Hill & Wang, 1993), p. 82.

2. Dina Porat, *Hanhagah beMilkud* (An Entangled Leadership) (Tel Aviv: Am Oved, 1986), pp. 285, 308; Dina Porat, *The Blue and Yellow Stars of David* (Cambridge: Harvard University Press, 1990), p. 163.

3. Porat, *Hanhagah beMilkud,* pp. 149–51.

4. Tom Segev, *HaMillion HaShviyi,* 2nd ed. (Jerusalem: Keter, 1991), p. 72; Segev, *Seventh Million,* p. 82; Mapai central committee, Sept. 12, 1939.

5. Segev, *Seventh Million,* p. 83; Mapai central committee, Aug. 24, Sept. 23, 1943; Ben-Gurion speaking to industrialists and businessmen in Jerusalem, Sept. 23, 1943.

6. Mapai central committee, Aug. 24, 1943.

7. Ben-Gurion's talk with Wauchope, Apr. 2, 1936; Ben-Gurion, *Zihronot,* p. 3:105.

8. Records of the JAE, Central Zionist Archives, Jerusalem, Sept. 26, 1943.

CHAPTER NINE

1. Tom Segev, *HaMillion HaShviyi,* 2nd ed. (Jerusalem: Keter, 1991), p. 78; Tom Segev, *The Seventh Million* (New York: Hill & Wang, 1993), p. 90.

2. Genesis 14:21, 32:19.

3. Genesis 32:28.

4. Michael Dov-Ber Weissmandel, *Min Hametzar* (From the Straits) (New York: Congregation Beth Hamidrash Chemed, 1980).

5. Segev, *HaMillion HaShviyi,* p. 78; Segev, *Seventh Million,* p. 96.

6. Segev, *HaMillion HaShviyi,* p. 83; Segev, *Seventh Million,* p. 95; Yehuda

Bauer, "Efshar Lehaashim VeEfshar Lehaashim VeGam Lisno," *Ha'aretz,* June 23, 1994.

7. Yehuda Bauer, *HaShoah—Hebetim Historiyim* (Tel Aviv: Moreshet & Sifriath Poalim, 1982); Leny Yahil, *HaShoah* (The Holocaust: The Fate of European Jewry, 1932–1945), 2 vols. (Tel Aviv: Schocken, and Jerusalem: Yad VaShem, 1987), 2:792; Saul Friedlander's interview, *LaMerhav,* Apr. 25, 1968; Israel Gutman's interview, Jan. 20, 1994; Dina Porat, "Parashat Weissmandel KeHahpasha," *Ha'aretz,* May 13, 1984; see also Gila Fatran, *Haim Maavak Al Hisardut* (Struggle for Surviving?) (Tel Aviv: Moreshet, 1992), and Fatran's reaction, "Rabbi Weissmandel's Affair an Inappropriate Example," *Ha'aretz,* Apr. 22, 1994; Hannah Yablonka's M.A. thesis, "The Europa Plan," Hebrew University, August 1984; Hava Eshkoli (Wagman), *Elem: Mapai Nohah HaShoah 1939–1942* (Jerusalem: Yad Ben-Zvi, 1994); Yechiam Weitz, *Mudaut VeHoser Onim* (Jerusalem: Hotsaat Yad Ben-Zvi, 1994); Yechiam Weitz, "Sheelat HaPlitim HaYehudiim BaMediniut Ha-Zionit," *Cathedra* no. 55 (Nisan 1990); Avishai Margalit, "The Uses of the Holocaust," *New York Review of Books,* Feb. 17, 1994.

8. Segev, *HaMillion HaShviyi,* p. 83; Segev, *Seventh Million,* p. 95.

9. Segev, *Seventh Million,* p. 354; Yehudah Bauer, "Parashat HaMassa Umatan Bein Saly Mayer LeVein Netzigei HaS.S BaShanim 1944–1945," in Israel Gutman, ed., *Nisionot Ufeulot Hatsalah BiTkufat HaShoah* (Rescue Attempts and Actions During the Holocaust) (Jerusalem: Yad VaShem, 1976), pp. 11 and passim.

10. *Encyclopedia of the Holocaust,* p. 663; Yechiam Weitz, *HaIsh Shenirtzah Paamaiim, Hayav, Mishpato Umoto shel Dr. Israel Kastner* (The Life, Trial and Death of Dr. Israel Kastner), (Jerusalem: Keter, 1995), p. 41.

11. Bauer, "Parashat," p. 27.

12. Yehuda Bauer, *American Jewry and the Holocaust* (Detroit: Wayne State University Press, 1981), p. 272.

13. Ibid., pp. 219, 220, 221.

14. Schwalb interviews, Jan. 4, 12, Feb. 2, 9, 16, 23, 1995; Mayer's election to the Jewish Agency Council in *Sefer HaKongress* (World Zionist Congress's Report), 1937, pp. (in Hebrew characters) 14, 58, 74, 85.

15. Schwalb interviews, op. cit.; HeHalutz Reports in *Sefer HaKongress* (World Zionist Congress's Report), 1939, pp. 349, 354.

16. Bauer, *American Jewry,* pp. 283–85, 323, 349–50.

17. Schwalb interviews, op. cit; Bauer, *American Jewry,* pp. 200, 272, 284.

18. *Sefer HaKongress* (World Zionist Congress's Report), 1937.

19. Bauer, *American Jewry,* pp. 220, 221.

20. *Sefer HaKongress* (World Zionist Congress's Report), 1939, p. 12.

21. Werner Rings, *La Suisse et la Guerre* (Lausanne: Editions Ex Libris,

1975), pp. 175 ff.; E. Bonjour, H. S. Offler, G. R. Potter, *A Short History of Switzerland* (Oxford: Clarendon Press, 1963), pp. 367–70; Schwalb interviews, op. cit.

22. Schwalb interviews, op. cit.; Yehuda Bauer, *Jews for Sale?* (New Haven: Yale University Press, 1994).

23. Schwalb interviews, op. cit.; Bauer, *American Jewry,* pp. 374, 375.

24. See, for example, Bauer, *American Jewry,* p. 422.

25. Bauer, *Jews for Sale?,* p. 182.

26. McClelland's cable to Secretary of State, Oct. 13, 1944, National Archives, Washington, D.C., 840. 48 Refugees/10-1344; Schwalb interviews, op. cit.; Bauer, *American Jewry,* pp. 412–13, 426.

CHAPTER TEN

1. Mapai secretariat, Oct. 2, 1943; Histadrut Executive Committee, Feb. 11, 1943.

2. Yehieli's report in Mapai central committee, Feb. 24, 1943; Records of the JAE, Central Zionist Archives, Jerusalem, Feb. 28, Mar. 7, 1943.

3. Hansard, Feb. 3, 1943, 386 H.C. 5S.

4. Records of the JAE, Central Zionist Archives, Jerusalem, Mar. 28, 1943; Tuvia Friling, "Ben-Gurion and European Catastrophe 1939–1945," doctoral thesis, Hebrew University, February 1990, pp. 56–58, 61.

5. Records of the JAE, Central Zionist Archives, Jerusalem, Mar. 28, Apr. 27, 1943.

6. Records of the JAE, Central Zionist Archives, Jerusalem, Mar. 28, Apr. 27, May 2, 1943; Mapai secretariat, May 3, 1943; Friling, "European Catastrophe," pp. 64–66.

7. Mapai secreteriat Feb. 10, 1943; Histadrut Executive Committee, Feb. 11, 1943; Records of the JAE, Central Zionist Archives, Jerusalem, Apr. 4, 1943; Friling, "European Catastrophe," pp. 64–66; Histadrut Executive Committee, Jan. 27, 1944; Dina Porat, *The Blue and Yellow Stars of David* (Cambridge: Harvard University Press, 1990), pp. 154, 155; Menahem Bader, *Shlihuiot Atsuvot* (Sad Missions) (Tel Aviv: Sifiriat Poalim, 1978), pp. 51–53; Haim Barlas, *Hatzalah BiYemei Shoah* (Rescue During the Holocaust) (HaKibbutz Hamhuhad, 1975), pp. 240 and passim.

8. Records of the JAE, Central Zionist Archives, Jerusalem, June 6, 1943, July 23, 1944; Barlas, *Hatzalah BiYemei Shoah,* p. 247; J. S. Macpherson's letter to Sharett, July 16, 1943, Ben-Gurion Archives, Sdeh Boker; Porat, *Blue and Yellow,* p. 160.

9. Records of the JAE, Central Zionist Archives, Jerusalem, July 25, 1943; Porat, *Blue and Yellow,* p. 162; Friling, "European Catastrophe," p. 70; Leo Kohn's letter to Sharett, July 29, 1943.

10. Public Record Office, Kew, FO/371 36680, W9840, Secret, Memorandum by the Secretary of State for the Colonies, "Immigration into Palestine," Jun. 26, 1943, with reference to CAB (War Cabinet) W.M. (42), regarding the immigration into Palestine of Jews from the Balkans; letter by Sir George Gater, Permanent Under Secretary, Colonial Office, 75113/44/(S), Apr. 5, 1944, to Jewish Agency Executive, London.

11. CAB 65 W.M. 92 (43), Secret, Conclusions of a Meeting of the War Cabinet held at 10 Downing Street, on Friday, 2nd July, 1943.

12. FO 371/36680, W10240, Cypher Telegram 75113/43, No. 737, 11.45, From: S. of S. Colonies, To: Sir H. MacMichael (Repeated Minister of State, Cairo, Repeated to Ankara), 12th July, 1943.

13. FO 371/36680, W9840/225/G, Secret, From: A. W. G. Randall, To: Sir Hughe Knatchbull-Hugessen, Angora, Sir Samuel Hoare, Madrid, Sir Ronald Campbell, Lisbon, Viscount Halifax, Washington, 27th July, 1943.

14. Permanent Undersecretary Sir George Gater's confidential letter to JAE by direction of the Secretary of State for the Colonies, dated October 5, 1944, Central Zionist Archives, Jerusalem; Zeev Venia Hadari, *Tsomet Kushta,* Misrad HaBitahon (Tel Aviv: HaHotsaa LaOr, 1992), p. 325.

15. Parliamentary Debates, Fifth Series—Vol. 386, House of Commons Official Report, Second Volume of Session 1942–1943, 19 January 1943, Hansard, p. 32.

16. Tom Segev, *HaMillion HaShviyi,* 2nd ed. (Jerusalem: Keter, 1991), p. 90; Tom Segev, *The Seventh Million* (New York: Hill & Wang, 1993), p. 102.

17. Segev, *HaMillion HaShviyi,* p. 102; Segev, *Seventh Million,* p. 114.

18. Segev, *Seventh Million,* p. 97.

19. Ben-Gurion's greetings to the Presidium of the National Assembly, Aug. 12, 1944, Central Zionist Archives, Jerusalem S.44/560.

20. Hosea 9:1; Ben-Gurion's letter to Paula, May 11, 1945.

21. Ben-Gurion at Mobilization and Rescue Appeal fund-raising in Jerusalem Sept. 23, 1943.

22. Minutes of meeting between Ben-Gurion, Kaplan, Gruenbaum, and chief rabbis, June 24, 1943.

23. Segev, *HaMillion HaShviyi,* p. 83; Segev, *Seventh Million,* p. 96.

24. American Reaction section in the Holocaust Museum in Washington, D.C.; David S. Wyman, *The Abandonment of the Jews* (New York: Pantheon, 1984), pp. 3, 14, 22, 24, 209; see also Deborah Lipstadt, *Beyond Belief* (New York: Free Press, 1993), and Howard Sacher, *A History of the Jews in America* (New York: Knopf, 1992), p. 523.

25. Wyman, *Abandonment,* p. 38; *New York Times,* Sept. 11 (p. 3), Nov. 11 (p. 3), 1942.

26. *New York Times,* Sept. 11, 1942, p. 3.

27. *New York Times*, Sept. 22, 1942, p. 7.

28. Wyman, *Abandonment*, p. 36.

29. Zionist Actions Committee, Jan. 18, 1943 (Dobkin); Yehuda Bauer, *American Jewry and the Holocaust* (Detroit: Wayne State University Press, 1981), pp. 254–69; Michael R. Marrus and Robert O. Paxton, *Vichy France and the Jews* (New York: Basic Books, 1981), pp. 266–67; Records of the JAE, Central Zionist Archives, Jerusalem, Sept. 26, 1943.

30. Records of the JAE, Central Zionist Archives, Jerusalem, Nov. 29, 1942; National Assembly, Nov. 30, 1942.

31. Wyman, *Abandonment*, p. 37.

32. *New York Times*, Nov. 12, 1942, p. 3.

33. Hansard, Feb. 3, 1943, 386 H.C. 5S.

CHAPTER ELEVEN

1. Tom Segev, *The Seventh Million* (New York: Hill & Wang, 1993), p. 102.

2. Dina Porat, *The Blue and Yellow Stars of David* (Cambridge: Harvard University Press, 1990), p. 92.

3. A. Gertz, ed., *Statistical Handbook of Jewish Palestine* (Jerusalem: Jewish Agency for Palestine, 1947), p. 374.

4. Dina Porat, *Hanhagah beMilkud* (An Entangled Leadership) (Tel Aviv: Am Oved, 1986), pp. 117ff.; Akiva Nir, "Vaadat HaHatsalah BeKushta— HaKesher Im Slovakia (Haavarat Ksafim LeSlovakia 1943–1944)," Seminar Paper #33855, Dgamim LeMehkar BiTkufat HaShoah, Hebrew University.

5. Porat, *Blue and Yellow*, p. 92.

6. Ibid., p. 74.

7. Ibid., p. 75.

8. Ibid.

9. Ibid., p. 76.

10. Ibid., p. 81.

11. Ibid., p. 77.

12. Ibid., p. 87.

13. Gertz, *Statistical Handbook*, p. 364.

14. Porat, *Blue and Yellow*, p. 89.

15. Porat, *Hanhagah beMilkud*, p. 118; Ben-Gurion in Mobilization and Rescue Appeal rally, at Ohel Shem Hall in Tel Aviv, Jan. 11, 1943, Ben-Gurion Archives, Sdeh Boker.

16. Segev, *Seventh Million*, p. 92.

17. Porat, *Hanhagah beMilkud*, pp. 340, 345; Yehuda Bauer, "Efshar Lehaashim VeEfshar Lehaashim VeGam Lisno," *Ha'aretz*, June 23, 1994; Yehuda Bauer interview, July 8, 1994.

18. Amos Oz to author, Mar. 22, 1995.

19. Schwalb's letter to Dobkin, Dec. 4, 1942, Central Zionist Archives, Jerusalem S26/1444; Abraham Fuchs, *Karati VeEin Oneh* (The Unheeded Cry) (Jerusalem: the author, 1985), p. 203.

20. Yehuda Bauer, *American Jewry and the Holocaust* (Detroit: Wayne State University Press, 1981), pp. 366, 458.

21. Ibid., p. 200.

22. Ibid., p. 458.

23. Ibid., p. 297.

24. Ibid., p. 458; Yehuda Bauer, *Jews for Sale?* (New Haven: Yale University Press, 1994), p. 76.

25. Bauer, *Jews for Sale?*, p. 78.

26. Ibid.

27. Ibid., p. 95.

28. Yeshayahu Jelinek, "HaRav Weissmandel, 'Tohnit HaRabanim'— Mezima Anti-Zionit?," *Yalkut Moreshet* no. 58 (September 1994): 84.

29. Bauer, *Jews for Sale?*, ch. 6, "What Really Did Happen in Slovakia?"

30. *Encyclopedia of the Holocaust*, p. 1282.

CHAPTER TWELVE

1. Bernard Joseph, *British Rule in Palestine* (Washington, D.C.: Public Affairs Press, 1948), p. 91.

2. Shabtai Teveth, *Ben-Gurion: The Burning Ground* (Boston: Houghton Mifflin, 1987), p. 718.

3. Schwalb interviews, Jan. 4, 12, Feb. 2, 9, 16, 23, 1995; Yehuda Bauer, *Jews for Sale?* (New Haven: Yale University Press, 1994), p. 81.

4. Michael Dov-Ber Weissmandel, *Min Hametzar* (From the Straits) (New York: Congregation Beth Hamidrash Chemed, 1980), pp. 118, 119.

5. Yeshayahu Jelinek, *Ha'aretz*, May 13, 1994.

6. Gila Fatran, *Haim Maavak Al Hisardut* (Struggle for Surviving?) (Tel Aviv: Moreshet, 1992), pp. 232–38.

7. Report by Reuben B. Resnik, JDC's representative in Istanbul, June 4, 1944, National Archives, Washington D.C., 840.48 Refugees/6276: Memorandum by L. A. Squires, American vice consul in Istanbul, June 4, 1944, National Archives, Washington D.C., 840.48 Refugees/6312: MacMichael's telegram to Colonial secretary May 26, 1944, FO 371/42758; Sharett cable to Goldmann via the American General Consulate in Jerusalem, June 19, 1944, National Archives, Washington D.C., 840.48 Refugees/6344. Yechiam Weitz, *HaIsh Shenirtzah Paamaiim, Hayav, Mishpato Umoto shel Dr. Israel Kastner* (The Life, Trial and Death of Dr. Israel Kastner), (Jerusalem: Keter,

1995), p. 25; Yehuda Bauer, "Shlihuto Shel Yoel Brand," *Yalkut Moreshet* no. 26 (November 1978): 23.

8. Ehud Avriel, *Open the Gates* (New York: Atheneum, 1975), p. 176.

9. Squires's memorandum, Ibid. Zeev Hadari (Venia Pommerantz) in *Ha'aretz,* Jan. 29, 1995.

10. Squires's memorandum, Ibid.

11. Public Record Office, Kew QFO papers 371/42758 of May 24, 1944; Records of the JAE, Central Zionist Archives, Jerusalem, May 25, 1944.

12. G. H. Hall's letter to Weizmann, June 22, 1944, Public Record Office, Kew FO 371/42758.

13. Records of the JAE, Central Zionist Archives, Jerusalem, May 25, 1944.

14. Ben-Gurion with representatives of Sephardic Jewry, July 6, 1944, Ben-Gurion Archives, Sdeh Boker.

15. Sir Harold MacMichael to Secretary of State for the Colonies, May 26, 1944, FO 371/42758.

16. Zeev Hadari (Venia Pommerantz) in *Ha'aretz,* Jan. 29, 1995.

17. Records of the JAE, Central Zionist Archives, Jerusalem, May 29, 1944.

18. Public Record Office, Kew CAB 95/15, May 31, 1944.

19. Squires's memorandum, Ibid.

20. Avriel, *Open the Gates,* pp. 183ff.

21. Public Record Office, Kew FO 372/42759 minutes of June 12, 1944; Sharett's Report, in Records of the JAE, Central Zionist Archives, Jerusalem, June 14, 1944.

22. PRO FO 371/42759, W9944 quoted in Martin Gilbert, *Auschwitz and the Allies* (New York: Holt, Rinehart and Winston, 1981), p. 242; Weizmann's letter to Eden, Jun. 9, 1944; WL XXI 166; FO 371/42758, Jun. 15, 1944.

23. Martin Gilbert, *Auschwitz and the Allies,* p. 240.

24. Records of the JAE, Central Zionist Archives, Jerusalem, June 18, 1944.

25. Gilbert, *Auschwitz,* pp. 240, 241.

26. Ibid., p. 241.

27. Ibid., p. 240.

28. Ibid., p. 242.

29. Public Records Office, Kew Top Secret FO 371/42759. W. 9943 #1494.

30. Gilbert, *Auschwitz,* p. 241.

31. Ibid.

32. Ibid.

33. Ibid., p. 242.

34. Ibid.

35. Zeev Hadari (Venia Pommerantz) in *Ha'aretz*, Jan. 29, 1995.

36. Gilbert, *Auschwitz*, p. 244.

37. Ben-Gurion to Mapai students, Jerusalem, Mar. 6, 1961.

38. Records of the JAE, Central Zionist Archives, Jerusalem, May 25, 1944.

39. Hansard, Feb. 24, 1943, 387 H.C. DEB 5S.

40. The report of Mar. 2, 1943, by SS Inspector of Statistics Richard Korherr; *Encyclopedia of the Holocaust*, p. 1083; James Taylor and Warren Shaw, *A Dictionary of the Third Reich* (London: Grafton, 1987), p. 193; Yosef Algasi, "HaPitaron HaSofi VeHasifrut HaMakhisha Et HaShoah" (The Final Solution and the Denial of the Holocaust), M.A. thesis, Tel Aviv University, March 1979; *Zmanim* no. 8 (Spring 1982); Yosef Algasi to author, Dec. 22, 1993.

CHAPTER THIRTEEN

1. Gila Farran, *Haim Maavak Al Hisardut* (Struggle for Surviving?) (Tel Aviv: Moreshet, 1992), p. 234; Michael Dov-Ber Weissmandel, *Min Hametzar* (From the Straits) (New York: Congregation Beth Hamidrash Chemed, 1980), p. 122.

2. Weissmandel, *Min Hametzar*, pp. 118, 119; David S. Wyman, *The Abandonment of the Jews* (New York: Pantheon, 1984), p. 290.

3. Rosewell McClelland, the wartime representative of the War Refugee Board in Bern, Switzerland, writes in the *Washington Post*, Apr. 27, 1983, that Weissmandel's letter, based on the Vrba-Wetzler report, reached Isaac Sternbuch of the Union of Orthodox Rabbis in Switzerland in mid-May 1944. Sternbuch relayed the message—with its urgent plea to bomb the rail line from Hungary to Auschwitz—to Jacob Rosenheim, the president of Agudas Israel in New York, who received it in mid-June. Rosenheim in turn sent it on to the WRB in Washington, where it arrived around June 18, 1944.

McClelland says that he received a copy of Weissmandel's letter from Jaromir Kopecky, the representative of the Czech government-in-exile in Geneva, in the presence of Gerhardt Riegner, the representative in Switzerland of the World Jewish Congress (who transmitted a long telegraphed summary to Washington on June 24); Richard Lichtheim of the JAE in Geneva; and Walter Garett of the British Exchange Telegraph (both of whom had already sent its main elements to their principals). "The Foreign Office, as a matter of record, had it on June 27," containing "the recommendation for bombing" which "At that stage . . . was expanded from the rail line" to Birkenau's "gas chambers and crematoria."

Richard Foregger writes in the *Journal of Military History* no. 59 (October 1995): 687–96, that the Vrba-Wetzler report was translated into several languages and sent out by underground couriers to Budapest, Istanbul, Geneva, and the papal chargé d'affaires for transmission to the Vatican. A second report, based on the accounts of Czeslaw Mordowicz and Arnost Rosin, who escaped from Auschwitz on May 27, 1944, was also sent out from Bratislava. Both of these reports were delivered to Kopecky around June 19–20, 1944. A third account, by the Polish major Jerzy Tabeau, who had escaped on Nov. 19, 1943, rounded out the full report. McClelland received the complete version, including the map, sometime before June 24. See also Rudolf Vrba, "Footnote to the Auschwitz Report." *Jewish Currents* no. 218 (March 1966).

4. Records of the JAE, Central Zionist Archives, Jerusalem, May 21, 1944; Public Record Office, Kew, CO 733/461/PT4.

5. Records of the JAE, Central Zionist Archives, Jerusalem, May 21, 1944.

6. In his letter to Barlas, June 21, 1944, Gruenbaum writes he appealed to Pinkerton "before my hands were tied." Central Zionist Archives, Jerusalem, S26/1284.

7. Pinkerton's cable in Gruenbaum's name, June 2, 1944, National Archives, Washington, D.C., 840.48 Refugees/6193; McClelland's cable to WRB, June 24, 1944, National Archives, Washington, D.C., 840.48 Refugees/6387; Gruenbaum's report on talk with Pinkerton, June 7, 1944, Central Zionist Archives, Jerusalem, A127/544; Gruenbaum's letter to Barlas, June 21, 1944, Central Zionist Archives, Jerusalem, S26/1284; Wyman, *Abandonment*, p. 289.

8. Gruenbaum's letter to Barlas, June 21, 1944, Central Zionist Archives, Jerusalem, S26/1284; Records of the JAE, Central Zionist Archives, Jerusalem, June 11, 1944.

9. Records of the JAE, Central Zionist Archives, Jerusalem, June 18, 1944; Pinkerton's cable, June 19, 1944, requesting to transmit Sharett's cable to Goldmann, National Archives, Washington, D.C., 840.48 Refugees/6344.

10. Ambassador Steinhardt's letter to S. Pinkney Tuck, American minister in Cairo, June 20, 1944, Ben-Gurion Archives, Sdeh Boker; Hirschmann's memorandum to Ambassador Steinhardt, June 22, 1944. Strictly Confidential (relative to interview with Joel Brand), National Archives, Washington, D.C., 840.48 Refugees/7-644; Records of the JAE, Central Zionist Archives, Jerusalem, June 24, 1944.

11. *Baffy, The Diaries of Blanche Dugdale 1936–1947*, ed. N. A. Rose (London: Vallentine, Mitchell, 1973), p. 214.

12. Gruenbaum's cable to Wise, May 8, 1994, Central Zionist Archives, Jerusalem, S26/1251 A; Dobkin's cable to Wise and Goldmann, May 25, 1944, Central Zionist Archives, Jerusalem, S26/1251 A; Gruenbaum's cable to Reiss, May 30, 1944, Central Zionist Archives, Jerusalem, S26/1232; Gruenbaum's cable to Schwarzbart-Reiss, June 19, 1944, Central Zionist

Archives, Jerusalem, S26/1226; Kubowitzki's cable to Gruenbaum, Oct. 10, 1944, Central Zionist Archives, Jerusalem, A127/543.

13. Gruenhaum's cable to Barlas, June 6, 1944, Central Zionist Archives, Jerusalem, S26/1251 A; Gruenbaum's cable to Kubowitzky, June 11, 1944, Central Zionist Archives, Jerusalem, A127/544; Schwarzbart's airgram to Gruenbaum, Schmorak, Dobkin, and Shapira, June 24, 1944, Central Zionist Archives, Jerusalem, S26/1232.

14. Darlas's cable to Gruenbaum, June 14, 1944, Central Zionist Archives, Jerusalem, S26/1251 A; Schwarzbart's cable to JAE, June 19, 1944, Central Zionist Archives, Jerusalem, S26/1251 A; Gruenbaum's cable to Schwarzbort-Reiss, June 19, 1944, Central Zionist Archives, Jerusalem, A127/544; Mc-Clelland in the *Washington Post*, ibid.; meeting of the presidium of the rescue committee, Oct. 10, 1944, Central Zionist Archives, Jerusalem, S26/1238 R.

15. Records of the JAE, Central Zionist Archives, Jerusalem, June 11, Aug. 22, 1940; Zionist Actions Committee, Sept. 5, 1944; Krausz's cable to JAE, Jun. 19, 1944, Central Zionist Archives, Jerusalem, S26/1251. Telegram #2949, Urgent, War Cabinet Distribution, copy in Premier papers 4/51/10, quoted in Martin Gilbert, *Auschwitz and the Allies* (New York: Holt, Rinehart & Winston, 1981), p. 252.

16. Gruenbaum's cable to Reiss, June 23, 1944, Central Zionist Archives, Jerusalem, S26/1232; Hull's cable to Pinkerton, June 22, 1944, National Archives, Washington, D.C., 840.48/Refugees 6193; Pinkerton's letter to Gruenbaum, June 23, 1944, Central Zionist Archives, Jerusalem, S26/1251 A; cables from Hungary, June 19 and 22, 1944, Central Zionist Archives, Jerusalem, S26/1251 A; Lichtheim's cable to MacKillop, June 26, 1944, Central Zionist Archives, Jerusalem, L22/56; in his handwritten letter in Polish to Barlas, June 30, 1944, Central Zionist Archives, Jerusalem, A127/544, Gruenbaum writes: "We communicated to Moshe [Sharett] the propositions submitted by Krausz . . . namely to cause bombardment of the railways connecting Hungary and Poland and of the death camps in Poland;" Gilbert, *Auschwitz*, p. 251.

17. Gruenbaum's cable to Sharett, June 27, 1944, Central Zionist Archives, Jerusalem, A127/543; Gruenbaum's cable to Sharett, June 29, 1944, Central Zionist Archives, Jerusalem, z4/14870; Gruenbaum's letter to Pinkerton, June 29, 1944, and his cable to Wise of the same date, Central Zionist Archives, Jerusalem, S26/1251 A; Hebrew Writers Association's letter, July 4, 1944, and Shaw's reply, Central Zionist Archives, Jerusalem, S26/1251 A.

18. Public Record Office, Kew CAB 95/15 May 31, 1944.

19. Record of Interview with Mr. Sharett, June 28, 1944, FO 371/42759, W 10260, folio 146.

20. FO 371/42897, WR 49, folio 70, quoted in Gilbert, *Auschwitz*, p. 255.

21. Sharett's cable to JAE. June 30, 1944, quoted in Chaim Barlas,

Halsalah BiYemei Shoah (Rescue During the Holocaust) (HaKibbutz Hameu-had, 1975), p. 319; Public Record Office, Kew FO 371/42807, WR, folios 70–1, 73, quoted in Gilbert, *Auschwitz*, p. 255.

22. Martin Gilbert, "Bartering in Lives", *Jerusalem Post Magazine*, Feb. 8, 1980, and "The Final Deception," *Jerusalem Post Magazine*, Mar. 7, 1980; Public Record Office, Kew, Prime Minister's Personal Minute, M782/4, FO 371/42759; W 10025, folio 68, quoted in Gilbert, *Auschwitz*, p. 260.

23. FO 371/42807, WR 49, folio 73, quoted in Gilbert, *Auschwitz*, p. 255.

24. Hansard, July 5, 1944, Hungary (Mass Deportations of Jews). H.C., p. 265.

25. Records of the JAE, Central Zionist Archives, Jerusalem, July 16, 1944; Gruenbaum's letter to Barlas, Aug. 30, 1944, Central Zionist Archives, Jerusalem, S26/1284; Aide-Memoire by Weizmann and Sharett left with Eden, July 6, 1944, WL XXI p. 321; Gilbert, *Auschwitz*, p. 269.

26. Foreign Secretary's Minute, P.M. 44/501, Premier papers 4/51/10, folios 1365–7; Prime Minister's Personal Minute, M 800/, Premiers papers, 451/10—quoted in Gilbert, *Auschwitz*, p. 270.

27. Gruenbaum's cable to Sharett in London, June 29, 1944, Central Zionist Archives, Jerusalem, Z4/14870; Gruenbaum's cable to Wise, Goldmann, Sharett and Brodetzky, Aug. 31, 1944, Central Zionist Archives, Jerusalem, A127/544; Zionist Actions Committee, Aug. 22, 1944; Pinkerton's letter to Gruenbaum, Oct. 25, 1944, Central Zionist Archives, Jerusalem, A127/543.

28. Press Release by Stephen Early, secretary to the president, Jan. 22, 1944, National Archives, Washington, D.C., 840.48 Refugees/5070; Wymann, *Abandonment*, p. 291; John J. McCloy, assistant secretary of war at the time, reiterated this line in 1903; see Morton Mintz, "Why Didn't We Bomb Auschwitz," *Washington Post*, Apr. 17, 1983, p. D1.

29. Ambassador Winant's cable to secretary of state, Feb. 25, 1944, Stettinius to Winant, Feb. 29, 1944. Hull to Winant, Mar. 25, 1944, National Archives, Washington, D.C., 840.48 Refugees/5260; Conversations with Mr. Wallace Murray regarding the Middle East, first meeting, Apr. 11, 1944, Boyd's letter to the Foreign Office, and draft of joint declaration, Apr. 17, 1944, fifth meeting, with Murray, Kohler, Peterson, Daxter, and Hankey, Apr. 19, 1944, CO 733 461/47, 75782/14B.

30. Stimson to Cordel Hull, Mar. 31, 1944, National Archives, Washington, D.C., 840.48 Refugees/5499.

31. *Encyclopedia of the Holocaust*, 3:690, 700; I. C. B. Dear, ed., *The Oxford Companion to the Second World War* (New York: Oxford University Press, 1995), p. 839; F. H. Hinsley, ed., *British Intelligence in the Second World War* (London: HMSO, 1981), 2:673.

32. Air Ministry papers, 19/218, quoted in Gilbert, *Auschwitz*, p. 172.

33. USAAF's film negatives published in Israel Air Force's Album, 1995, *Auschwitz Mabat Al*, in commemoration of the 50th anniversary of Auschwitz's "liberation," pp. 39, 51; Gilbert, *Auschwitz*, p. 190.

34. Kit C. Carter and Robert Mueller, *The Army Air Forces in World War II: Combat Chronology 1941–1945* (Washington, D.C.: Office of Air Forces History, 1973), p. 359; *Auschwitz Mabat Al*, pp. 6, 15, 18; Gilbert, *Auschwitz*, pp. 216, 220, 249, 275, 282.

35. *Combat Chronology*, pp. 417–419; Gilbert, *Auschwitz*, p. 301.

36. *Encyclopedia of the Holocaust*, p. 194; Avigdor Perry (formerly Victor Perlstein), 'Halsh SheHikca LaPekudah Le-Haftzitz Et Auschwitz" (The Man Who Waited for the Order to Bomb Auschwitz), *La Isha*, no. 2295, Apr. 8, 1991.

37. David Horovitz, "Why The Allies Didn't Bomb Auschwitz," *Jerusalem Report*, Jan. 12, 1995; Arthur Harris, *Bomber Offensive* (London: Greenhill Books, 1951), p. 230.

38. *New York Times*, June 3 and 4, 1944.

39. Dr. S. Low's letter to JAE's Rescue Committee, June 2, 1944, Central Zionist Archives, Jerusalem, S26/1251 A. See also in the same file Reb Binyamin's note to Sharett, May 25, 1944.

40. Julian Meltzer's cable via Imperial Press to the London office of the *New York Times*, June 30, 1944, Central Zionist Archives, Jerusalem, S26/1251 A; *New York Times*, July 2, 1944, p. 12;7, July 6, 1944, p. 6;2.

41. Zionist Actions Committee, Aug. 22, 1944.

42. Wyman, *Abandonment*, p. 292; Public Records Office, Kew FO 371/42809, WR 277, folios 147–8, quoted in Gilbert, *Auschwitz*, p. 285. Public Records Office, Kew FO 371/42809, WR 285, folio 150, quoted in Gilbert, *Auschwitz*, p. 287.

43. J. J. McCloy to Pehle 4 July 1944, cited in Barlas, *Harsalah BiYamei Shoah*, p. 293; Mintz, "Why We Didn't Bomb Auschwitz"; Wyman, *Abandonment*, p. 294; McClelland in *Washington Post*, Ibid.

44. Prime Minister's Personal Minute, M 800/4, Premiers papers, 4/51/10 and Air Ministry Papers 19/218—quoted in Gilbert, *Auschwitz*, pp. 270, 271–272.

45. Hilary St. George Saunders, *Royal Air Force 1939–1945* (London: HMSO, 1954), 2:240–241; *Combat Chronology*, p. 454.

46. Harris. *Bomber Offensive*, p. 231.

47. Central Zionist Archives, Jerusalem, Z4/14870; Barlas. *Hatsalah BiYemei Shoah*, p. 293; Gilbert, *Auschwitz*, p. 279.

48. Telegram from the Foreign Office, London, dated July 22, 1944, transmitted on July 26, 1944, by K. I. Poate, of the British Embassy in Washington, to C. L. Warren of the State Department, National Archives, Washington,

D.C., 840.48 Refugees/7-2644; Gilbert, *Auschwitz*, pp. 285, 287, quoting FO 371/42009, WR 277, folios 147–148, and WR 285, folio 150.

49. Gilbert, *Auschwitz*, p. 300, quoting from Public Record Office, Kew, FO 371/42814 WR 705, folio 138, and WR 708, folio 156.

50. Schwalb interviews, Jan. 4, 12, Feb. 2, 9, 16, 23, 1995; Zionist Actions Committee, Aug. 22, 1944; Gruenbaum's cable to Chief Rabbi Ehrenpreiss in Sweden, Aug. 31, 1944, Central Zionist Archives, Jerusalem, A127/544; see also cables to Wise, Goldmann, Sharett, and Brodetzky of the same date; Martin Gilbert, "HaDiunim VeHaTguvot Nohah HaTviot LeHaftzatzat Auschwitz," in *Mahnot HaRikuz HaNaziim* (Jerusalem: Yad VaShem, 1984), p. 364.

51. Yehuda Bauer, *American Jewry and the Holocaust* (Detroit: Wayne State University Press, 1981), p. 424.

52. Horovitz, "Why The Allies Didn't Bomb Auschwitz."

53. Millard and Allen's minutes, Public Record Office, Kew FO 371/42809, WR 731, quoted in Gilbert, *Auschwitz*, p. 303.

54. Gilbert, "Final Deception"; Air Ministry papers 19/218/M.8565/S.2294, quoted in Gilbert, *Auschwitz*, p. 304.

55. Public Record Office, Kew FO 371/42814, WR 749, folio 190, quoted in Gilbert, *Auschwitz*, p. 304.

56. Sharett's cable to JAE in Jerusalem, Aug. 18, 1944, Central Zionist Archives, Jerusalem S25/1678; PRO 371/42814. WR 749, folio 191, quoted in Gilbert, *Auschwitz*, p. 305; PRO FO 371/42814, WR 749, folio 188, quoted in Gilbert, *Auschwitz*, p. 305.

57. Public Record Office, Kew, FO 371/42814, WR 749, folio 188, quoted in Gilbert, *Auschwitz*, p. 305.

58. Kenn C. Rust, *Fifteenth Air Force Story* (Temple City, Calif.: Historical Aviation Album, 1992), p. 32; Gilbert, *Auschwitz*, pp. 307–308.

59. PRO FO 371/42814, WR 749, folio 200, quoted in Gilbert, *Auschwitz*, p. 306.

60. Gruenbaum's cable to Wise and Goldmann, July 25, 1944, Central Zionist Archives, Jerusalem, S26/1236; Gruenbaum's cable to Sharett, Aug. 31, 1944, Central Zionist Archives, Jerusalem, A127/544.

61. PRO FO 371/42818, WR 1174, folio 30, quoted in Gilbert, *Auschwitz*, p. 318.

62. Air Ministry papers, 19/218, 12/22, quoted in Gilbert, *Auschwitz*, p. 319.

63. *Combat Chronology*, pp. 450, 524, 530; Wyman, *Abandonment*, p. 299; Gilbert, *Auschwitz*, pp. 190, 191, 249, 250, 279, 282, 283, 307–9, 331, 334, 335.

64. Ehud Avriel, *Open the Gates* (New York: Holt, Rinehart & Winston,

1981), p. 179; Ehud Avriel, *Pithu Shaarim* (Tel Aviv: Sifriat Maariv, 1976), p. 142.

65. The United Party's role, Jan. 6, 1930, Lavon Institute IV 1/405.

SOURCES (map, page 201)

Wesley F. Craven and James L. Cate, eds., *The Army Air Forces in World War II*, vol. III (Chicago: 1951).

I. C. B. Dear, ed. *The Oxford Companion to the Second World War* (Oxford and New York: Oxford University Press, 1995).

Robert Goralski, *World War II Almanac: 1931–1945* (New York: Putnam, 1981).

Jane's All The World's Aircraft, 36th ed. (London: Sampson Low, Marston & Company, Ltd., 1948).

John W. R. Taylor, ed. *Combat Aircraft of the World* (London: Ebury Press & Michael Joseph, 1969).

CHAPTER FOURTEEN

1. Records of the JAE, Central Zionist Archives, Jerusalem, Jul. 2, 1944.

2. Zeev Sternhell, *Binyan Umma O Tikkun Hevra* (Nation Building or a New Society) (Tel Aviv: Am Oved, 1995), p. 467, n. 5; Prof. Zvi Yavetz, lecture "Fifty Years after Goga-Cuza Government," Dec. 27, 1987, Institute for Zionist Research, Tel Aviv University. Levi Yitzhak Hayerushalmi, deputy editor of *Maariv*, in a symposium on Porat's *Hanhagah beMilkud* at Tel Aviv University, summer 1987.

3. Ben-Gurion, *Anakhnu Veshkhenenu* (We and Our Neighbors) (Tel Aviv: Hotsaat *Davar*, 1931), p. 258.

4. Ben-Gurion's letter to Sharett, Nov. 29, 1933.

5. Ben-Gurion's diary entries, Jan. 16, 1936; Records of the JAE, Central Zionist Archives, Jerusalem, Jan. 19, 1936.

6. Ben-Gurion's diary entries, Feb. 5, 1936; Records of the JAE, Central Zionist Archives, Jerusalem, May 15, 1936; see also Histadrut Executive Committee, May 11, 1936; Ben-Gurion, *Zihronot III*, p. 177.

7. Ben-Gurion's letter to Ihud (World Mapai Union) Conference, Aug. 18, 1936.

8. Records of the JAE, Central Zionist Archives, Jerusalem, Mar. 9, 23, 1941.

9. Zionist Actions Committee, July 5, 1943.

10. *The Times* (London), Nov. 26, 1938; Ben-Gurion's diary entries, Nov. 26, 1938.

11. *New York Times*, May 14, 1939.

12. Ibid., Jan. 16, 1939 (p. 6:2); Jan. 17, 1939 (p. 8:4); Apr. 4, 1939 (p. 6:5); June 20, 1939 (p. 9:1).

13. Ibid., May 11, 1942.

14. Ibid., May 26, 1942 (p. 13:4).

15. Shabtai Teveth, *Ben-Gurion: The Burning Ground* (Boston: Houghton Mifflin, 1987), p. 817.

16. *The Independent on Sunday,* Aug. 22, 1993; see also *Baffy, The Diaries of Blanche Dugdale 1936–1947,* ed. N. A. Rose (London: Vallentine, Mitchell, 1973), p. 198.

17. Ben-Gurion's diary entries, June 3, 1936; Ben-Gurion's letter to Paula, June 11, 1936.

18. *New York Times,* Mar. 5, 1940.

19. Ben-Gurion's letter to Arthur Lourie, Jan. 16, 1941; Records of the JAE, Central Zionist Archives, Jerusalem, Feb. 16, 1941.

20. Mapai central committee, Mar. 19, 1941.

21. Records of the JAE, Central Zionist Archives, Jerusalem, Apr. 17, 1941.

22. Histadrut Executive Committee, Mar. 19, 1942; *New Judea* (London), November/December 1941.

23. Ben-Gurion at the National Assembly, Nov. 30, 1942; *New York Times,* Dec. 2, 1942.

24. Histadrut Executive Committee, Dec. 31, 1942 (Anselm Reiss).

25. *Manchester Guardian,* Dec. 5, 1942 (p. 4); Dec. 8, 1942 (p. 4).

26. *Manchester Guardian,* Dec. 5, 1942 (p. 6).

27. *Palestine and Middle East* vol. 15 (January 1943); *Davar,* Feb. 5, 1943.

28. *The Times* (London), Sept. 3, 28, 1943; Oct. 7, 29, 30, 1943; *New York Times,* Aug. 15, 1943; Oct. 7, 28, 1943.

29. *The Times* (London), Nov. 15, 1945.

30. *New York Times Index; The Times* Annual Index.

31. *New York Times,* Nov. 26, 1943 (p. 17:4).

32. Ibid., 1940, 4; 1941, 2; 1942, 2; 1943, 3; 1944, 0; 1945, 8.

CHAPTER FIFTEEN

1. Records of the JAE, Central Zionist Archives, Jerusalem, Dec. 6, 1942.

2. Ben-Gurion to Mapai activists, Dec. 8, 1942.

3. Records of the JAE, Central Zionist Archives, Jerusalem, Apr. 6, 1941; Zionist Actions Committee, May 7, 1941.

4. Although Ben-Gurion was certainly aware of the desire for revenge expressed in Shylock's retort, he did not allude to it. But it is worth mentioning that he suggested the following reaction by the Yishuv to the Arab riots of 1929: "Not a lament, not a sigh, but a mighty resounding roar: We shall not

back off." He then called for the "recruitment and settlement of "50,000 young immigrants" and the launching of an appeal in the United States and in other countries to raise the necessary 5 million pounds ($20 million). He specified its goal thus: "The Jewish people will redeem the spilled blood of their children, by increasing the Yishuv by thousands and tens of thousands of new builders and defenders. This should be our one and only revenge." (David Ben-Gurion, *Anakhnu Veshkhenenu* [We and Our Neighbors] [Tel Aviv: Hotsaat *Davar*, 1931], p. 167; Shabtai Teveth, *Ben-Gurion and the Palestinian Arabs* [New York: Oxford University Press, 1985], p. 78).

5. Ben-Gurion's Herzl Day Address, Central Zionist Archives, Jerusalem, S4/4201; *Davar*, July 13, 1944.

6. Mapai central committee, Feb. 19, 1941.

7. Mapai centeral committe, Sept. 12, 1939.

8. Ben-Gurion's diary entries, Jan. 5, 1939.

9. Ben-Gurion's diary entries, Jan. 13, 1939; Ben-Gurion's letter to Paula, Jan. 8, 1939.

10. *PM*, Oct. 18, 1943; *Christian Science Monitor*, Oct. 18, 26, 1943, and subsequently; *Jewish Frontier*, November 1943; Mapai political committee, Jan. 26, 1944; Howard Sacher, *A History of the Jews in America* (New York: Knopf, 1992), p. 523.

11. Shabtai Teveth, *Ben-Gurion: The Burning Ground* (Boston: Houghton Mifflin, 1987), p. 768.

12. Ibid., p. 769.

13. Mapai central committee, July 5, 1939.

14. Ben-Gurion's letter to Paula, Nov. 9, 1940.

15. Teveth, *Burning Ground*, pp. 822ff.

16. Ibid., pp. 727ff.

17. Henry L. Feingold, "Did American Jewry Do Enough During the Holocaust?" The B. G. Rudolph Lectures in Judaic Studies, Syracuse University, April 1985.

18. Teveth, *Burning Ground*, p. 820.

19. Weizmann to Ben-Gurion, Nov. 18, 1940, Weizmann Letters XX/63; Ben-Gurion cable to Weizmann, Nov. 19, 1940; Ben-Gurion's diary entries, Nov. 20, 1940.

20. Teveth, *Burning Ground*, pp. 773, 774.

21. Ibid., pp. 774–76.

22. Minutes of the Office Committee, Records of the American Zionist Emergency Council, July 15, 1942, Central Zionist Archives, Jerusalem, Z5/354.

23. Public Records Office, Kew FO 371/31379.

24. Records of the American Zionist Emergency Council, July 15, 1942, Central Zionist Archives, Jerusalem, Z5/354.

25. David S. Wyman, *The Abandonment of the Jews* (New York: Pantheon, 1984), p. 26.

26. Records of the JAE, Central Zionist Archives, Jerusalem, Apr. 27, 1943; Mapai central committee, Apr. 27, 1943.

27. Hadassah National Board, Jan. 6, 1943; Records of the JAE, Central Zionist Archives, Jerusalem, Feb. 14, 1943.

28. *New York Times*, Mar. 2, 1943.

29. N. Goldmann's letter to Y. Gruenbaum, Apr. 5, 1943, Central Zionist Archives, Jerusalem, S26/1234.

30. Viscount Cranborne in the House of Lords, Hansard [Lords], (German Atrocities: Aid for Refugees), Mar. 23, 1943, pp. 845ff.; *Davar*, Mar. 26, 1943.

31. N. Goldmann's letter to Y. Gruenbaum Apr. 5, 1943.

32. M. Kaufmann, *Lo-zionim Bamaavak al Hamedinah* (Non-Zionists in the Campaign for the State) (Jerushalem: Hasifria Hazionist, 1984), p. 89.

33. For example, Weizmann's letter to Berl Locker, July 27, 1942, Weizmann Letters XX/317.

34. *Davar*, Apr. 4, 1943.

CHAPTER SIXTEEN

1. Dr. Deborah Hachohen at Holocaust symposium at Ben-Gurion House, Mar. 22, 1994.

2. Records of the JAE, Central Zionist Archives, Jerusalem, Nov. 22, 1942; Mapai central committee, Nov. 24, 1942.

3. Institute for Economic Research Colloquium at Rehovoth, Nov. 24, 1942, Ben-Gurion Archives, Sdeh Boker (note Mr. Hoffien's remarks in afternoon session); Ben-Gurion's letter to Miriam Cohen (later Mrs. Taub), Nov. 23, 1942; Dr. Deborah Hacohen's correction in her letter to author, Apr. 4, 1994.

4. Ben-Gurion to HaKibbutz HaMeuhad Conference, Jan. 19, 1944; Records of the JAE, Central Zionist Archives, Jerusalem, Jan. 26, 1944.

5. Dr. A. Ruppin's letters to Ben-Gurion, Jan. 20, June 3, 1942; Ben-Gurion's letter to Ruppin, Apr. 28, 1942; Ben-Gurion's cable to Sharett, May 9, 1942, asking for D. Horowitz's economic memorandum; Records of the JAE, Central Zionist Archives, Jerusalem, Feb. 15, Aug. 9, 1942.

6. Ben Gurion's diary entries, Oct. 18, 1942; David Horowitz, *HaEtmol Sheli* (My Yesterday) (Jerusalem–Tel Aviv: Shocken, 1970), p. 250.

7. Records of the JAE, Central Zionist Archives, Jerusalem, Oct. 18, 1942; Dec. 13, 1942.

8. Records of the JAE, Central Zionist Archives, Jerusalem, Dec. 27, 1942.

9. Ben-Gurion's talk with P. Rutenberg, June 27, 1937, in Ben-Gurion, *Zihronot* IV, p. 252; Ben-Gurion's speech at the National Assembly, Mar. 24, 1943; *Davar*, Mar. 30, 1943; Ben-Gurion's letter to Avraham Harzfeld, Nov. 26, 1942; Ben-Gurion's letter to Ruppin, Apr. 28, 1942; Ben-Gurion's letter to H. Margalit of Anglo-Palestine Bank, Apr. 5, 1943; Mapai secretariat, Mar. 25, 1947; Zionist Actions Committee, Oct. 26, 1943; Records of the JAE, Central Zionist Archives, Jerusalem, Oct. 31, 1943.

10. Mapai party's bureau, Jan. 13, 1944; minutes of planning committee, Jan. 13, June 4, 1944; Records of the JAE, Central Zionist Archives, Jerusalem, June 20, 1944; Zionist Actions Committee, Mar. 13, 1945.

11. Records of the JAE, Central Zionist Archives, Jerusalem, June 20, 1944.

12. Haim Israeli interview, July 29, 1994; Isaiah 24:19 (Jerusalem Bible version).

INDEX

politicization of, xix–xxi, xxx, 1–22
postwar Jewish soulsearching and, 21–22, 96–97
press accounts of, xxviii–xxix, l–li, lix, 27–28, 89, 90, 93–98, 146–147, 232–235
"real time" vs. historical concept of, 88, 94, 99–101
restriction of Jewish immigration to Palestine in, ix–xi, xiv, xxi, xxvi–xxvii, xxxiii, xxxviii
scholars and historians of, liii, lxiii, 5, 6, 14, 21, 23–34, 35–36, 72, 115, 116
survivors of, 9–11, 16, 21, 23–25, 33, 51, 61–70, 120, 167
systematic persecution and murder of Jews in, xiii–xvii, xviii, xxviii–xxx, l–li, 27–28, 35–41, 88, 94, 126
warnings and reports of, xv, xvi, xxviii–xxix, xl–xli, l–li, 27–28, 88–101, 126
Zionist reaction to, xv, xvi, xvii, xix–xxi, xxvii, xxix–xxx, l–li, 1–22, 26–34, 61–70, 99
see also concentration camps; *shoah*
Holocaust Memorial Museum, 94
Holocaust Revisited, The: A Retrospective Analysis of the Auschwitz–Birkenau Extermination Complex (Brugioni and Poirier), 216
Horowitz, David, 257
Horthy, Miklos, 213–214
Hosea, 143
Hrushovski, Benjamin, *see* Harshav, Benjamin
Hull, Cordell, 148, 195n
Hungarian Jews, xvi–xvii, xxiii, lviii, 6, 9, 11, 16–18, 78, 80, 103, 131, 172
death camp losses of, xvi–xvii, 6, 16–18, 167, 184, 190
rescue efforts for, 103, 162, 167, 172–204
survival of, 120, 167
Hungary, 2, 42, 90, 117, 120, 131, 134, 171
Allied bombing raids on, xvii
Nazi invasion and occupation of, xvi
Hussaini, Hajj Amin al-, Grand Mufti of Jerusalem, xxxvii, xxxviii, lv, 174, 185

I. A. Topf & Sons, xv–xvi
Ichud movement, 16
I. G. Farben, xvii, 205
Ingram, E.M.B., 79

Inter-Governmental Refugee Committee, 181
International Red Cross, 134, 150, 181, 194, 195n, 213
intifada, 222, 223
Iran, lxi
Iraq, lv, 37, 41, 168n, 185
massacre of minorities in, lvi
Irgun Zvi Leumi, 18, 19
Iron Guard, 78–79, 84
Islam, lv–lvi
Israel, li, 4, 6, 17, 21–22, 72
Arabs in, 115, 222, 223
Gaza and West Bank occupied by, 22
immigration and economic development in, 21
military forces of, 168–169
1948 Arab invasion of, 24–25
1948 establishment of, viii, xxii, xxxiv, 14, 24, 73, 105, 114
1949 elections in, 17
1955 elections in, 19
political parties in, 17
Six-Day War of, 21
see also War of Independence; *specific Israeli leaders*
Israeli Army:
Holocaust survivors in, 23–25
Israeli-born soldiers in, 24, 25
Six-Day War and, 21
see also War of Independence
Istanbul, xvi, 89, 156
JAE rescue mission in, 8, 15, 103, 105–106, 108, 119, 121, 132–133, 155, 158, 172, 175
Italy, xvii, xviii, xiv, 9, 104, 206
reunification of, xxxi

JA, *see* Jewish Agency
Jabotinsky, Ze'ev, x, xxv, xxxiv, 114n
Jacob and Esau story, 113
JAE, *see* Jewish Agency Executive
Jarblum, Marc, 52
JDC, *see* American Joint Distribution Committee
Jelinek, Yeshayahu, 10–11, 117, 166
Jerusalem, ix, xlii, lix, 7, 43–44, 45, 60
JAE offices in, xv, xvi, xvii, 15
Jewish population of, 24
Jordan's siege of, 24
Yad VaShem memorial in, 40, 100–101
Jerusalem Program, xv
Jewish Agency (JA), xl, 5, 8, 20, 118, 122, 126, 157–158, 183, 230